The Iceman, the Arsonist, and the Troubled Agent

TRAGEDY AND MELODRAMA ON THE MODERN STAGE

BOOKS BY ROBERT BECHTOLD HEILMAN

America in English Fiction 1760–1800 (1937)

This Great Stage: Image and Structure in King Lear (1948)

Magic in the Web: Action and Language in Othello (1956)

Tragedy and Melodrama: Versions of Experience (1968)

The Iceman, the Arsonist, and the Troubled Agent: Tragedy and Melodrama on the Modern Stage (1973)

The Iceman, the Arsonist, and the Troubled Agent

Tragedy and Melodrama on the Modern Stage

BY ROBERT BECHTOLD HEILMAN

Seattle: UNIVERSITY OF WASHINGTON PRESS

This edition is not for sale in the British Commonwealth (excluding Canada) or Europe. Exclusive rights for these territories have
been granted to George Allen & Unwin Ltd., London.

Library of Congress Cataloging in Publication Data

Heilman, Robert Bechtold, 1906–
    The iceman, the arsonist, and the troubled agent.

    Includes bibliographical references.
    1. Tragedy—History and criticism.   2. Melodrama—
History and criticism.   3. Drama—20th century—
History and criticism.   I.   Title.
PN1897.H4   809.2'51   72–10391
ISBN 0–295–95253–9

To
Champlin B. Heilman

Preface

THE initial work on this volume was done when I was a Guggenheim Fellow in 1964–65, and the final work when I was a Senior Fellow of the National Endowment for the Humanities in 1971–72. I am very grateful for these grants, which provided temporary respite from a mode of professional life not always conducive to the steady application needed by the book-length project. In both years I was on professional leave from the University of Washington, and I am glad to acknowledge this generous support. I spent most of each year of leave in the Reading Room of the British Museum, a happy place to work. I am grateful to several journals that have published earlier and shorter versions of different chapters in this volume—*The Southern Review* (Tennessee Williams), *The Denver Quarterly* (Max Frisch), *Modern Drama* (Friedrich Duerrenmatt), and *Shenandoah Review* (dramas on the money theme).

Sherry Laing's amiable assistance was largely responsible for getting the manuscript into readable condition. Edith Baras, my annalist, detected all slips in dates and quotations, had a genius for ferreting out essential evidence buried outside the bounds of memory, and never let a first printing pass for a first night. Dorothee Bowie was invaluable in helping make study-time available. My wife's essential role, which she has sturdily held for an unusually long run, was described by J. M. Barrie in a play of 1908.

Our son, to whom I dedicate this volume, was the first of us to get beneath the more obvious surfaces of modern drama; now an experienced teacher, he continues to be a shrewd and engaging critic of the theater.

ROBERT B. HEILMAN

London
June 1972

Contents

[ix]

Part III. Place and Persons: Three Europeans

Part IV. Time and Theme

Introduction

ᴛʜᴏᴜɢʜ birth ordinarily precedes baptism, I want to comment on them in the reverse order, since a note on genesis leads naturally into an account of growth, shape, and other such vital statistics. The title represents an effort to find a compressed statement of rather variegated contents. My central business is modern versions of classical genres, and this means the different ways in which dramatists look at character. These are not really few or simple; an ideal title would contain a half-dozen elements, including some subordination. Impossible, clearly. So my three-headed caption is selective, and I hope it implies ramifications rather than restrictions.

"The Iceman" is clearly an allusion to Eugene O'Neill's *The Iceman Cometh*. I intend it as a metaphor for a wide range of characters who find it difficult to face the world or themselves and opt out, or who lack the endurance and perceptiveness to cope with the way things are. They are the material of what I call the "melodrama of the victim." They appear frequently in O'Neill and in Tennessee Williams, and they are related to the large family of "little men" such as Mr. Zero and Willy Loman. "The Arsonist" is an allusion to Max Frisch's *The Firebugs* (the American title; the English title is *The Fire Raisers*). I intend it as a metaphor for a wide range of strong and aggressive people, fierce competitors, seekers of victory, revengers, destroyers—Frisch's dangerous pair, Brecht's Pierpont Mauler, Duerrenmatt's Claire Zachanassian, the factional leaders in Galsworthy's *Strife* and Büchner's *Danton's Death*, Miller's Eddie Carbone, Camus's Caligula, and Pirandello's "Henry IV." Such men of energy can develop in either of two ways. If they are essentially single-minded, their histories become what I call "melodramas of triumph." If they are divided, that is, caught between conflicting courses, impulses, or imperatives, they are the materials of tragedy. My third element, "the Troubled Agent," represents a primarily tragic conception of character: the vigorous man with enough moral sensitivity to be troubled by what he does, to inquire into it, and sometimes to judge himself. Arthur Miller is increasingly interested in this kind of man—in *The Crucible*, *After the Fall*, and *The Price*; the troubled man is represented strikingly by Nikita in Tolstoi's *The Power of Darkness*, General Harras in Carl Zuckmayer's *The Devil's General*, the Mother in Camus's *The Misunderstanding*, Alfred Ill in Duerrenmatt's *The Visit*, and Garcin in Sartre's *No Exit*. "Agent," too, has a useful double sense. Primarily it means a man of action, a doer, but it can also mean an auxiliary participant. In the latter sense it would apply to such highly significant supporting characters as the schoolteachers in both Duerrenmatt's *The Visit* and Frisch's *Andorra*.

The interpretative shorthand which I have used here must seem to beg many questions of type and nomenclature. But these remarks only anticipate the full exploration of these issues in the following chapters.

Now back from baptism to birth. I once thought of saying that *The Iceman, the Arsonist, and the Troubled Agent* was born like Athena from the head of Zeus or like Eve from a lesser part of Adam. Triple difficulties arose. One is that this genealogy would seem to overpraise the pages that follow—to snatch for them the wisdom of mountain and garden, of mind and earth, of Olympus and Eden. Again, since both creatures invoked are female, one could think of quarters in which the sex itself would seem traduced by the comparison. In different quarters, however, one might appear to have classed criticism, not among the great hardheaded activities of the large world, but among the intuitive shortcuts of life and the wily household arts.

So I must leave out Athena and Eve. I bid them adieu regretfully, for in one detail their stories figure admirably the birth of this volume: it first existed as part of another body. Several of my present chapters belonged to the first manuscript of my *Tragedy and Melodrama: Versions of Experience* (1968). The publishers found that manuscript too bulky for their comfort and that of the reader; they proposed, as a remedy, that the chapters devoted to modern drama as such be put into a separate volume. I accepted the proposal, which looked sound in theory and manageable in execution.

The apparently manageable usually has a secret ingredient, if not of the unmanageable, at least of the unforeseen. Here, the unforeseen was that the chapters on the modern, when taken out and told to make it alone, looked surprisingly naked. They had been conceived in a certain context, were now thrust out in harsh rebirth, and needed support. Their old life was not transferable, and they had to be supplied with a new life. In literal terms, one could not attempt to write critically about a set of plays without providing the critical foundations. One might, of course, direct readers to the theoretical sections of *Tragedy and Melodrama*, and declare these chapters a prerequisite to *The Iceman, the Arsonist, and the Troubled Agent*. But books are not like university courses, and to have to do one to get into another would be an uninviting labor. Whatever the relationship between a first and a second, the second has to be readable as an independent entity. The first two chapters are meant, then, to give the present volume its independent life. Chapter 1 could belong only to this book, for its subject is specifically modern: those habits of our thought and feeling apparently favorable or unfavorable to the writing of tragedy. Chapter 2 makes the fundamental distinctions between tragic and melodramatic form: it outlines briefly the theory that is developed at length in *Tragedy and Melodrama*, but with a new ordering, a somewhat altered perspective, and variations in emphasis that should make this statement different from its predecessor without superseding it. One change is that my understanding of melodramatic excellence has, I think, become clearer, and this is reflected in the theoretical discussion. Chapters 4 to 11 then deal with individual plays, some grouped by authorship, some by chronology, and some by theme.

Another aspect of "nakedness": the modern plays that added excessive bulk to a study of many periods did not provide enough bulk for a study of only their own period. I found it desirable to add more of them—I beg the question of "enough"—to have what would look like a convincing representation of the period. Besides, playwrights characterized as individuals wrote new plays and changed the picture, and more plays by European playwrights were translated and thus changed another picture. These two situations led to the addition of other materials to the original manuscript.

What is "modern"? The term is a loose one. To scholars it means the four centuries since the Renaissance, to most other grownups the four decades of adult life, to university students the four years since high school, to other kinds of people the events since 1918, or since 1945, or since 1958 (Sputnik), or since 1969 (the first moon landing), or since youth were first spotted as heretical or age as archaic. I use *modern* arbitrarily to include a period of about a century, enough to afford at least a working perspective. Originally I planned to include a larger number of nineteenth-century plays, some because they seem to anticipate more recent theatrical practices, but many because they are intrinsically interesting: plays in older idioms are not dead, nor is their way of engaging us dead. But here again there arose the problem of bulk, this time on the side of excess rather than deficiency.

Out of the hundreds of plays widely known in the period, and the thousands that might be garnered in by the latent encyclopedism of even a critical surveyor, which should be included? If only because no one can read analyses ad infinitum, there has to be a relatively limited sampling. The critic must hope that it is adequate—not too sketchy, not wholly chancy and irrational, not simply a reflection of his own prejudices, neither too dependent on nor too independent of whatever consensus lurks among those who editorialize and anthologize in the field. If it has been done right, it will give the reader a sense of reviewing a representative selection. The sampling extends into a number of countries but is restricted to translated plays. I have wanted to deal, as far as possible, with plays that are international properties, and translation is a generally reliable, if not infallible, index of internationalization.

The development of my earlier manuscript into twins has left one problem to which there is no completely satisfactory solution. Even after the removal of the formal sections on modern drama, *Tragedy and Melodrama* still makes continual use of modern examples. Hence readers familiar with both volumes will find some overlapping which may seem less inevitable to them than it does to me. On the other hand, my sometimes hardy resistance to duplication may well give readers of *The Iceman, the Arsonist, and the Troubled Agent* a feeling that there are unwise lacunae: new sins of omission to add to those spun off by the sampling process. But incompleteness is a lesser evil than forbidding amplitude; it may become a virtue, indeed, by encouraging readers to go on into less fully surveyed areas for their own exploration of the generic terrain. Any readers who feel, however, that I err on the side of inclusiveness rather than insufficiency will want to practice their own omissiveness. It would make good sense to treat this volume partly as a reference work, reading the first several chapters to get bearings and thereafter proceeding selectively as different subjects arouse interest at one time or another.

Amid my different samplings of the last century there are recurrent references to still earlier plays, and chapter 2, in making basic definitions, depends largely on older drama. In part this practice reflects my desire to mitigate the risks in arguments dependent upon works about which there is not yet a firm critical consensus, and my grasping for the distance and detachment that are more probable with well-established pieces. More important, I want to treat old and new as fellow members of a dramatic continuum or community in which historical markings are less significant than persisting common traits. This runs counter to the still widespread view that the first duty of man in literary study is historical differentiation. (There is room for a historical approach to this ascendancy of history: what psychic needs of our own time account for the impulse to make history absolute?) Seeing an old play or a new play as a period piece is of course a valuable procedure, but it is dangerous if it becomes the only true way. Then it restricts us to an interior decorator's view of literature: the only issue in a literary work is its congruence with contemporary furnishings in an ensemble of what dates or has dated.

We cannot do without other approaches. My approach in this essay assumes the continued life of traditional forms in all generations of drama, even those apparently most innovative. It is possible to look at experimental plays as if somewhere within them were a substance imaginably recognizable to other eras, as if the most strenuous passion to "make it new" could not enforce a total discarding of established artistic modes. The most professional psychological dramas tend to have identifiable moral bearings; the most committed antipsychological dramas do not escape a sense of humanity in action. Dramatists simply do not get away, drift away, or flee from certain basic ways of looking at experience and hence from certain patternings that, with whatever variations and recombinations, become perceptible as generic forms. Some incidental evidence of the tenacity of dramaturgic habits, or of the survival of the old in the new, lies in the fact that many of our innovative plays call to mind the word *Jacobean*, which I use repeatedly. (We might say of our age that it has developed a Jacobean strain without ever having been Shakespearean.) This implies, not influence or imitation or revival, but rather a reappearance when one of our indispensable modes of insight, sometimes dormant, becomes active again. It goes without saying, of course, that the effort to identify lasting forms, especially where formal mutation is generally taken for granted, has to prove itself. If the effort succeeds, its service will be antisimplistic: we will have to accept some continuity where it is easier, and perhaps more congenial, to take discontinuity as a basic fact of life.

In examining plays from the perspective of generic form we try, not to label plays, but to see what formative tendencies are at work in them. If we have found central tendencies, then tracing them should shed some light on the plays, on the habits of the modern stage, and perhaps on the concept of generic form. We might indirectly serve this third end by stimulating others to seek out what criticism needs, that is, definitions that are precise without being imprisoning. Talking about tragic form, for instance, is an old game, and there are various ways of playing it. At one extreme there is the no-nonsense antitheoretical approach. Its implied platform is, "Come, come, we all know what tragedy is; let's not get tied up in rules and regulations and bylaws." This has an obvious appeal to which many are susceptible. Unfortunately it is of no help at all if we want to understand why certain generic terms that have great vitality do accurately describe some plays but not others. The opposite extreme is to elaborate a whole code of tragic differentiae, like the Renaissance Aristotelians (and some later ones). The middle ground, which I hope I am occupying, is to proceed from a central concept that is broad enough to manifest itself in a number of ways. I will articulate it in a metaphor that anticipates chapter 2: in tragedy we put ourselves in the erring man's place; in melodrama we put the erring man in his place, or, erring or not, are put out of our own place. These images embody several implications about essence and form; they should act either as clues to understanding or as spurs to the formulation of other distinctions between the tragic and the melodramatic.

The quest for generic form is, I suppose, explicative rather than evaluative. Since I take tragedy and melodrama to be neutral structures, however, I will make some effort to indicate whether a play comes in high or low on the scale of achievement within its own form. I do this with knowledge of the hazards, already mentioned, in judgments on works that have not yet had time to recede into the distance that cuts back emotional investments. But it is possible to simulate something of that distance by keeping up an awareness of two great countersources of fallibility: on the one hand, every age's resentment at the passage of things, the pique of the once novel at newer novelties; on the other, a more modern passion that often afflicts very lively criticism, the urge to be the first to lay the old aside.

The subtitle of the preceding volume, *Versions of Experience*, underscores my sense of continuities that make it natural to move back and forth between life and art rather than to separate them wholly from one another. There are parallels, interrelationships, reciprocal impacts. No one has ever doubted the impact of life on art; our present-day real-life melodramas of justice, those involving majorities and minorities, keep moving onto the stage. It is a truism to speak of dramas as affording, among other things, windows to the age in which they are written. It may be less clear that we can learn about the psyche of a period from its preferences among generic forms and themes. They let us gauge something of the self-understanding or lack of it in an age. For instance, what I have called the real-life melodrama of justice is often taken over and exploited by another real-life melodrama that is truly sinister: the one in which the pursuit of justice is the façade for a pursuit of power, and valid causes are hijacked by political gangsters. If such a perversion of conflict does not enter the theater along with the spontaneous conflict over justice, then we know that the age has not, or not yet, come to the kind of awareness required for its own safety. To shift to the other side of the picture: what goes on in the theater—the kinds of awareness, of formulation of reality—must be assumed, despite the continuing suspicion of Wilde's epigram that life imitates art, to have some impact on the consciousness of an age, however indirect and subtle. Influencing either many minds directly, or the minds of the few who mold the psychological conformations of an age, drama can contribute to an overly simple or an adequately complex sense of reality. We may legitimately speculate about the impact of a theater that often suggests the Jacobean but rarely, if at all, the Shakespearean. O'Neill harps on the need of illusion as a hedge against reality; Pirandello riddles about the identifiability of reality; Beckett inventively exploits his discontent with the cosmic establishment. It is reasonable to wonder how these reiterated views, in their movement through our imaginations, influence our nontheatrical patterns of thought and feeling. A wise man does not attempt to specify how or how much. But I find it appropriate to keep such matters in mind, rarely as the immediate subject of discourse, but constantly as a background for the estimate of the age through its habits in generic form.

My sense of theatrical practice as contributing, however intangibly, to the perceptiveness or imperceptiveness of a culture, is one of several matters that raised an occasional eyebrow among reviewers of *Tragedy and Melodrama*. There is no point in disagreeing with reviewers, but three quick allusions to comments of theirs may help clarify my objectives and my methods as I understand them. One reviewer has protested that with my concept of tragedy the word *tragedy* can be applied to fewer plays than it has customarily been applied to. My concern, however, is the precise use of terms; if this means that fewer plays can be described by one generic term or another, we should perhaps live with the reduction rather than wish that the larger number could remain unchanged. Another reviewer dislikes applying the term *tragedy* to an inferior play. Alas, he wants to go right on in the loose popular practice of using *tragedy* as a vague honorific term rather than as a definable neutral indicator of a structure than can be executed well or ill. Another reviewer was kind enough to call me a good "inside man" but regretted that at times, in his view, my theory got in my way. I would be fortunate if the first part of his statement were more accurate than the second. A student of drama wants above all things to put his finger on what goes on inside a play. It hardly needs saying, then, that he struggles, and he can only hope successfully, to make theory open the way to that end rather than block it.

On the few occasions when I allude to what I am writing I use, as I did in *Tragedy and Melodrama,* the word *essay.* It implies that the method is somewhat informal, that the procedure is exploratory rather than rigorously systematic, and that the approach represents personal choice rather than a dogma claiming infallibility. At the same time I hope that the personal means a steady eye rather than a rapid pulse, that the style is more objective than self-indulgent, more public than idiosyncratic, and more persuasive than willful.

PART I

Preliminaries: The Age and the Types

CHAPTER ONE

Modern Tragedy: Some Pros and Cons

I WILL begin by noting certain characteristics of a broadly conceived "modern" period (the twentieth century and some of its roots in the nineteenth)—those that seem to militate against tragedy, and those that enable us to expect the survival of tragic tone and structure. A survey of the antitragic and protragic implications of the age will reveal how much ground we have for looking at the theater in such generic terms. The picture is mixed: it neither refutes nor corroborates the oft-repeated assertion that tragedy is dead. Friedrich Duerrenmatt thinks that tragedy belongs, on the whole, to another day; Albert Camus believes that conditions are right for a renewal of great tragedy. Their views are worth attention; they will open the door to a survey of other pros and cons on the possibility of tragedy in our time. The survey, in turn, will serve to outline some working ideas about tragedy and other forms. After that I will look at the tragic or nontragic qualities of individual plays, most of them from the twentieth century, but also a few earlier ones that shed some light on modern theater. Trying to see what goes on in individual plays is the main business of the essay.

I. DUERRENMATT

In 1969, when he spent a week at Temple University, Friedrich Duerrenmatt answered many questions about his thought and its embodiment in his dramas. He made a number of observations, more or less incidentally, about tragedy and comedy. Like some of his other statements, his recorded words about the genres can be playful, epigrammatic, riddling, cryptic, as if he were checking solemnity by giving rein to a little ironic playfulness. One might apply to him Georg C. Lichtenberg's words about a contemporary, "He was running a little business in obscurantism." [1] But this would also have to be jesting—mainly a reminder to oneself that Duerrenmatt was not under oath, that obiter dicta do not make a system and need not even be consistent. Duerrenmatt says, for instance, that tragedy and comedy "are old concepts which have long ago become useless," but he uses both of them to define literary problems and his own work. He says that tragedy is "a much too narrowly conceived form" but adds immediately, "Strictly speaking, tragedy could only exist in classic periods"—thus using a narrow conception (as, of course, "strictly" reveals). He says that tragedy "presupposes a definite religion, a tragic religion" but does not define "tragic religion." [2] He says that "only comedy [that is, not tragedy] is possible in the world today" but describes a character of his as "a tragic figure . . . the modern man." [3] One might think that if man is tragic by being modern, tragedy would be the inevitable modern form, or conversely that if tragedy is impossible, modern man cannot be tragic. Duerrenmatt, however, is being characteristically modern by having it both ways, that is, conceiving of the tragic mode very tightly when he insists that it cannot be done now, and very loosely when he finds it indispensable to describe what goes on now.

For the nonfeasibility of tragedy today, Duerrenmatt provides a reason or two. In traditional tragedy "the powerful are always the tragic figures. Their power could be envisioned by the audience. But today power is too enormous, too automatic. We cannot see it anymore. . . . They are inhuman because they are so powerful and because their power separates them from other men. . . . [Nor can there be] a tragedy of the victims. . . . It is also inhuman to be a victim." He apparently accepts his interlocutor's summation, "the human and the tragic are contingent on freedom." He has already implied a definition of freedom in another assertion, "When we cannot have personal responsibility, personal guilt, we cannot have tragedy." [4]

In these utterances two themes are evident—the nature of tragedy and the nature of our times. The implications about the nature of trag-

edy are mainly traditional, and they are unexceptionable: the tragic has
to do with the human, not the nonhuman (that is, the sheer brutality
of men or events or natural cataclysms); freedom is essential because it
means the power to make choices, the very center of tragic action;
choice is the prime source of responsibility and guilt, a sense of which
is the necessary completion of tragic consciousness. In denying the tragic
quality both of exercising power and of being oppressed by it, Duerrenmatt is much more perceptive than the theorist who accepts all cruelty
and suffering as tragic. When he notes what is not tragic, Duerrenmatt
describes, without naming it, the alternative world of melodrama, that
is, the less complex though no less painful world of victors and victims,
of those who triumph and those who go down.

The power-wielder, however, may be tragic or nontragic: tragic heroes
are men of power, but not all men of power are tragic heroes. Lear is
tragic, Richard III and Tamburlaine are not. The tragic hero, as Duerrenmatt phrases it, can be "envisioned," "seen"; his interlocutor glosses
this by saying, of the nontragic men of power, that "we can't recognize
them, identify with them"; Duerrenmatt apparently accepts this in his
following gloss, "their power separates them from other men." The issue
here is manifestly the human representativeness of dramatis personae,
their ability to evoke the "there go I" of tragic participation; we refuse
this if the power-wielder seems "inhuman" by excessiveness or unbal-
ance, or by a narrowness of motive that invokes too little of the full
personality which we take to be "human." Lear's fullness is evidenced
in one way by his inconsistency; Richard III and Tamburlaine are too
consistent to be complete. Not that they are the less "real" or "true";
their reality or truth lies in the unilateral concentration of energy that is
the raw material of the melodramatic mode.

Though Duerrenmatt gives us a useful introduction to the tragic
mode, his brief observations on the present state of affairs are less helpful. It is hard to see that "today power is too enormous, too automatic";
surely it is no more so than the power of emperors and kings once was.
It is hard to agree that the powerful are "anonymous, inhuman," able to
be seen "only from a distance"; the multiplicity, ubiquity, and inde-
fatigability of our means of "communication" have made powerful
individuals so familiar that they are likely to seem, not remote and un-
imaginable, but petty and incapable of greatness. It is hard to think of
them as more separated from other men than Lear and Oedipus, hedged

by divinity as they were, and even in smaller worlds visible less often and less widely. It is the nature of democracy to reduce distance, not only social but moral.

When he talks implicitly of the nature of tragedy, Duerrenmatt is traditional; when he urges explicitly the antitragic nature of the present, he is being conventional. His words are reminiscent of the clichés about the largeness and impersonality of modern life, the forces that compress the individual and render him insignificant, the complexity that curtails personal responsibility. We need to ask whether the sense of helplessness or futility or external constraint that we permit ourselves has anything like the justification that there was for such sentiments in ages when gods and demons always threatened in daylight and shadow, when mysterious forces broke out in irrational intimidations, when royalty and nobility approached an absoluteness and unaccountability for which there is no modern counterpart in the Western world. If we lack an aptitude for tragedy, it is less that the world is one of great, inscrutable forces and small, weak men than that we indulgently let ourselves believe that it is. The attitude may be an unconscious device both for feeling irresponsible and for feeling sorry for ourselves. (In fact, in denying that tragedy is possible now, we may subtly be claiming for ourselves an easier world in which choices and self-knowledge are not called for.) These are familiar forms of sentimentality, which, like its alter ego cynicism, is antitragic by embodying an oversimple sense of reality.

II. Camus

If, then, we are to suppose that our climate will not nourish tragedy, we need to find valid grounds for the hypothesis. We need also to see if there are grounds for a hypothesis of another kind, since we can approach truth only by entertaining alternative options. In 1955, some years before Duerrenmatt visited Philadelphia, Albert Camus visited Athens to do a lecture, "On the Future of Tragedy." He argued that conditions in our own time are ripe for a resurgence of tragedy, tragedy of a Greek or Renaissance (English, Spanish, French) magnitude. In Camus's view, tragedy is begotten by a period of fundamental crisis— "a transition from forms of cosmic thought impregnated with the notion of divinity and holiness to forms inspired by individualistic and rationalist concepts . . . an evolution in which man, consciously or not, frees himself from an older form of civilization and finds that he has broken away from it without yet having found a new form that satisfies him." [5] In such an age there is a tension between values: ". . . the forces confronting each other in tragedy are equally legitimate . . . each force is at the same time both good and bad." The conflict is between "man and his desire for power" and "the divine principle reflected by the world"; man's "revolt" is "justified," yet the "order" against which he revolts is "necessary." We see "that there is an order, that this order can be painful, but that it is still worse not to recognize that it exists." Tragedy, he says, "is born in the West each time the pendulum of civilization is halfway between a sacred society and a society built around man. . . . Gradually, the individual rises against the order of things and against destiny." In Shakespeare "a kind of vast cosmic mystery . . . puts up an obscure resistance to the undertakings of its passionate individuals. . . ." [6]

What Camus sees in our own day is not the tail end of a revolt of the human against the divine or of reason against mystery (the usual formulations of our duality), but, on the contrary, a restoration of tragedogenic tension through a declining faith in the individualistic, rationalistic, and humanistic values that have been increasingly triumphant since the eighteenth century. He argues that "little by little the individual is recognizing his limits." Though "reason and science" have "transformed" the world, the result is "monstrous." This process, "rational and excessive at one and the same time," is "history," which, "at this degree of *hubris,*" now "has put on the mask of destiny." Man now wants to resist this destiny. "In a curious paradox, humanity has refashioned a hostile destiny with the very weapons it used to reject fatality. After having deified human reign, man turns once more against this new god." The process cannot be absolute: "We must keep alive our power of revolt without yielding to our power of negation"—the "price" for the functioning of "the tragic sensibility that is taking place in our time." We must also "create new sacred images." [7]

The two themes implicitly present in Duerrenmatt's words to his American audience are explicit in Camus's address to his Greek audience—the nature of tragedy and the nature of our times. In his analysis of the two periods of great tragedy, Camus is not altogether innovative; he extends to tragedy that tension between faith and reason (to use the simplest possible terms) which cyclical historians attribute to the apical phases of cultural life-history. Whether this tension is peculiar to periods of fundamental crisis, arising only with the surge of a new rationalism and being dissipated by the subsequent rationalistic triumph, is arguable; the tension of crisis, I suspect, is less a transitory phenomenon in time than it is an acute intensification of a kind of conflict that is permanently present in human make-up. In this view, tragedy is less a historical episode—though the number and richness of tragedies at a given time may reflect specific historical conditions—than an indispensable mode created by problems of belief and value that can never be wholly solved. At any rate, Camus puts his finger on the human dividedness which is the substance of tragic expression—a dividedness without which freedom would not be thought of, choice would not be called for, and responsibility and guilt would not be relevant. Though he speaks of dividedness in only one aspect, that of cultural transition, it also occurs, no less intensely, in community and personal situations that, if more limited in scope, still have human representativeness and resonance. Finally, Camus serves our purposes by stressing the ambiguity of good and evil in the tragic conflict, which embodies not good versus evil, but good versus good or a good-and-evil versus another good-and-evil. But here again Camus's sense of complexity needs to be extended: we may find a tragic opposition not only between one good and another, let us say, but between one reality and another. It is good to revolt, says Camus, but at the same time the object of revolt is also good. Camus is thinking of Prometheus. But take Macbeth or Phèdre, who also revolt—against the order that would nullify their passions—and whose revolt is not "good." But it is "real"; that is, it comes out of an eternal human reality that has to be dealt with. What such individuals do is "evil," but what prevents them from being vulgar as people, and nontragically simple as dramatic figures, is their consciousness of, and assent to, the order against which they revolt. Nevertheless, when Camus writes as if there were only one kind of tragic conflict, the tension that he describes is paradigmatic: it implicitly contains other modes of dividedness that produce tragic actions.

While Duerrenmatt's and Camus's views of the nature of tragedy are congruent, their views of our age are not. Duerrenmatt scarcely goes beyond sociological truisms; Camus tries to detect the deeper movements of the modern psyche in its quest for more valid, that is, more complex ways of comprehending reality and our relationship to it. As to Camus's view that a new tragic age may be imminent, it is tempting, but one cannot confidently assent or dissent. The movements on the surface of life are so multiple and quick-flashing that what one says as he writes may seem to have been refuted by the time manuscript becomes print. On the other hand, the underlying metamorphoses of "cosmic thought" are so massive as scarcely to be visible at all, much less predictable; they need the perspective of a century. Nevertheless, it is hard to question Camus's sense that there is some erosion of the individualist-rationalist-humanist hubris: what once was felt to be an ultimate modern dispensation seems now to have the good-and-evil quality of an order that, whatever its just claims upon us, also justly invites revolt. Whether this new suspicion of secular history as divinity will mean the discovery of true "sacred images" to be pitted against history in a new creative tension—this is not clear. We can challenge individualism, and come up with a valid order and utterly persuasive sanctions—or with tyranny. We can rebel against rationalism, and come up with the suprarational—or with the antirational or subrational. We can strive to look beyond the human, and come up with the more-than-human—or with the subhuman. Ahead one can visualize, maturing for birth, the divine or the demonic. The Hadrian of *Memoirs of Hadrian,* which brilliantly puts the intellectually contemporary into remote perspective, says at one point, "But our epoch is avid for gods." [8] Humanism has erred in not recognizing that the human completes itself by creating gods; the epoch becomes avid because of the nonfulfillment of this creative need. But an age can create true divinities or pseudo gods, and we cannot be sure which are being forged now. The ambiguity of the matter was foreshadowed in D. H. Lawrence's dark gods, which could symbolize, for one reader, a nonrational saving force, and for another, a destructive power. The whole point is that if Camus is correct in seeing a shift away from the secular trinity of modern times,* we cannot yet tell how it will swing—toward a redemptive concept of

---

* Hermann Broch sees the problem differently: as the need to create, so to speak, a secular trinity in a posttranscendental era. In *Dimensions of the Modern Novel* (Princeton, N.J.: Princeton University Press, 1969), Theodore Ziolkowski sums up Broch's position thus: ". . . in the absence of transcendental beliefs [men] attempt to elevate earthly phenomena to the level of absolutes—a process that Broch calls romanticism. They seek divine redemption in earthly love; they look for divine truth in the pitiful sects into which religion has dwindled with the collapse of a central authority. This flight from reality, however, necessarily involves guilt, for it represents an abjuration of man's basic metaphysical responsibility: that of establishing a new set of earthly values to replace those transcendental values that have disappeared in the breakdown of the old system" (p. 145).

order that will exist in tragic tension with the impulses dominant now, or toward an untragic civilizational disaster.

Certain popular phenomena seem to corroborate Camus's sense of a culture reaching toward a new "sacred order of things," such as some theologians envisage, and perhaps his sense of an emerging tragic consciousness of both "revolt" and "limits," of "liberty" and "necessity," of "human and historical ambiguity." [9] There are the reactions against scientific rationalism, the questioning of rational processes in the sociopolitical realm, the exalting of emotional responses, an inclination toward arcane revelatory mechanisms (for example, astrology), an exploration of biochemical sources of vision (neo-Huxleyism), the appearance of noninstitutional quasi-Christian words and gestures, a susceptibility to the attractions of alien religions and traditions, especially those of the Orient. Some of these phenomena have central bases, but most of them are on the fringe, and their ability to become less peripheral is uncertain; we perceive in them various degrees of the histrionic, much of the naïve, and as yet an emotional currency rather than a disciplinary power. Such phenomena might, in the length of time, help form a consciousness that embraced a true human contradictoriness, or simply take us toward a primitivism sentimental in concept and destructive in fact.

III. Antitragic Influences

The opposition between Camus's view that the soil is right for major tragedy and Duerrenmatt's that tragedy is impossible suggests a genuine inconsistency in the evidence. There are indeed phenomena—points of view, habits, aspects of style—which imply a nontragic or antitragic world, yet not all our conduct and attitudes lean in that direction. Duerrenmatt, it is true, speaks for many; announcing the death of tragedy is a frequent critical exercise. But if our climate is inhospitable to tragedy, the reasons are a little different from those sketchily presented in Duerrenmatt's observations. The central problem is rather the extent to which human duality enters into consciousness and thus combats the more simplistic views that hold in nontragic modes. For ease we tend always to fall back on inviting simplicities, which are available in large numbers. In our day, however, two of these especially help produce an air resistant to tragedy. One is the "little man" sensibility; the other is the indignation-and-blame pattern of life.

The "Little Man" Problem

When Elmer Rice named a hero Zero (there are a Mr. Zero and a Mrs. Zero in *The Adding Machine* [1923]), he gave both expression and impetus to the fashion of accepting smallness as the defining quality of modern man—a fashion that appears in literature and in daily life, and thus has a double effect. D. H. Lawrence must have been one of the first to put a finger on this smallness and its manifestations; indeed, he attributed it to the limiting influence of the very humanism which Camus, as we have seen, would later think had gone beyond appropriate limits. "As the imagination of divinity fails so does the imagination of the self. Lawrence's loathing of modern literature derives in part from a feeling that it offers us the spectacle of small selves in a godless universe, attempting to achieve significance through a psychological magnification of their most trivial feelings. . . ." [10] Lawrence's sense of modern literature is echoed in another critic's judgment on a distinctly modern art form, the movies. Pauline Kael had her say a few years ago, but her impression of filmgoers, or at least of the human attitudes manifested in them, is still valid: "The audiences at popular American movies seem to want heroes they can look up to; the audiences at art houses seem to want heroes they can look down on. Does this mean that as we become more educated we no longer believe in the possibilities of heroism? The 'realistic,' 'adult' movie often means the movie in which the hero is a little man like, presumably, the little men in the audience." [11] "Small selves" and "little men"—when an English and an American critic, a man and a woman, writing three or four decades apart, both hit on such terms, we can see how pervasive is the unconscious habit of feeling or being little. Eugene O'Neill and Tennessee Williams, whose writings have extended over half a century, must have sensed this habit, witness the number of ailing and insufficient characters they portray.

Littleness, as a matter of fact or belief, easily begets a sense of disadvantage or injury. Harold Rosenberg has written shrewdly of our "fantasy of being deprived"; in no literature outside the American, he insists, "is there so much suffering from ontological handicaps, the handicap of being an artist or an adolescent or a Jew or a Negro or a wife or a husband or of not having gone to Princeton or of having been changed into a G.I. The biographical perspective of our seriously intended novels (and of our plays, which try as hard as they can to be novels) strengthens this vision of injured being . . . constricted and wounded by 'interpersonal relations'. . . ." [12] Rosenberg's words do not date: it is easy to add new modes of felt deprivation—of not being a political insider, of not being a member of the "establishment," of not having power that will be felt by others, of not being able to change the world quickly. The obsession may be American, but in our times no sentiment is likely to observe national frontiers. The fantasy of "injured being" is represented with painful thoroughness in an English character, Jimmy Porter in John Osborne's *Look Back in Anger* (1956) (where, as in Edward Albee's *Zoo Story* [1959], self-pity is metamorphosed into verbal aggressiveness); but the work succeeded internationally and revealed the receptivity of an age to the small man with a large ache.

In 1932, shortly after Lawrence's death, Louis-Ferdinand Céline presented the plight of the modern little man in a crisp ironic formulation: "It's the nightmare of having to present to the world from morning till night as a superman, our universal petty ideal, the grovelling subman we really are." [13] Céline differs from most of the commentators in two ways: he spots the ideal of "a superman"—in contrast, I infer, with true greatness—as "petty" in itself, and he sees man as trying to mask his smallness instead of accepting it as final. More recently, however, Mary Renault, who has a fine moral imagination, presents men as "satisfied," or wanting to be satisfied, "with what they are." The author attributes the view to Plato and makes him condemn Euripides for telling little men what they want to hear. "But common men love flattery not less than tyrants, if anyone will sell it them. If they are told that the struggle for good is all illusion, that no one need be ashamed to drop his shield and run, that the coward is the natural man, the hero a fable, many will be grateful." [14] In the "century of the common man," then, it will not be surprising if the Platonic generalization is especially applicable. As Ruby Cohn notes, "aggrandizement of the Common Man is paralleled by reduction of the hero." [15]

"The coward is the natural man, the hero a fable"—the sense that this is what we like to believe is registered in a different way by John N. Morris in his study of various English figures, such as John Bunyan, who conquered neuroses and lived creatively. Morris argues that William James underrates Bunyan in a way that characterizes our own age: "We nowadays commonly resist or underrate or simply fail to perceive the heroic, as James does here: it makes us uncomfortable in its implicit reproach. Thus, we prefer to associate ourselves with Bunyan's weakness, with his neurotic misery which is so recognizably like ours, not with that strength of mind by which he achieved the wise sanity of which many of us in our own lives have despaired." [16] Acceptance of littleness or weakness can confer on life a comfortable kind of unity. Oddly enough, we may find a comparable unity in a situation which we ordinarily believe we do not like—being under orders. Carlo Levi describes a housekeeper charmed by the threat of bodily violence: ". . . she knew no greater happiness than that of being dominated by an absolute power." [17] A special case? Rather, I suspect, a representative example of the human fondness for feeling power, for being "ordered" by it as well as exercising it, since will-lessness, like willfulness, means a pleasurable escape from the choices that make tragic life.

These similar perceptions, by novelists and critics of four countries and two generations, help reveal the pervasiveness and the persistence of the sense, in modern man, that littleness is a principal fact of his nature. The sense of littleness—of weakness, incompetence, pleasurable subordination—is antitragic in that it means a one-sided view of reality; it implies no alternative value, and hence none of the tension of the tragic situation. To be little or commanded is to be outside a serious conflict of forces, claims, and desires, for conflict implies a vigor and direction incompatible with absolute smallness, that is, inadequacy and ineffectiveness. To be small is to lack inner room for the clash of motives and purposes by which the tragic figure is representative of human reality. When we think of tragic figures as large or great, we are of course thinking of moral, not conquistadorial, magnitude; as we have said, Lear is tragic, Tamburlaine is not. Moral magnitude implies, not success, but range, an embodiment at once of the passions and egotisms that drive men toward disorder, and of responsiveness to the transcendent commands and obligations that create order. If modern man is truly small, if in multiplying he has mysteriously shrunk in stature, then those who proclaim the death of tragedy have some grounds to go on.

The Indignation-and-Blame Pattern

The little-man sensibility contributes, ironically enough, to a kind of activity in the world that is no more tragic than the passivity implied in littleness. A sense of littleness may be gratifying emotionally either by encouraging self-pity, and hence a freedom from responsibility, or by eliciting pity for others. If one thinks of man as little, it is easy to move on to the next step: seeing little men as victims of unjust forces and lashing out against the forces. A cultivated sensitivity to victims may be socially meritorious, or it may serve to assure one of the justice of his own life. It may or may not, of course, create an adequate awareness of all the facts of life. I once knew a college instructor who dealt with American literature in terms of what he called "victimage," a term that students picked up readily. How far such a perspective would take one into the greatness of American literature is open to question. But surely it would give a fillip to the always ready impulse for indignation and blame, which in the 1960s became extraordinarily active both in the theater [18] and in American life. It would likewise help inflate the roles of "indictment" and "compassion," which at the right time may be socially beneficent but which are rarely the sources of major imaginative, that is, nontopical, nonpropagandistic, literature.

Experiencing indignation and affixing blame, though of value in the quest for justice, are ambiguous in that they may subtly tempt parts of the personality that are not at all devoted to justice. As F. R. Leavis has put it, speaking of Swift, "*saeva indignatio* is an indulgence that solicits us all, and the use of literature . . . for the projection of nobly suffering selves is familiar. No doubt, too, it is pleasant to believe that unusual capacity for egotistic animus means unusual distinction of intellect. . . ." [19] A comparable "indulgence" springs from what Reinhold Niebuhr calls "modern man's good opinion of himself," which "no cumulation of contradictory evidence seems to disturb." Hence man "considers himself the victim of corrupting institutions which he is about to destroy or reconstruct, or of the confusions of ignorance which an adequate education is about to overcome. Yet he continues to regard himself as essentially harmless and virtuous." [20] (When mankind's self-exoneration is concentrated as the self-esteem of an individual, he suffers from "that spiritual disease to which Goethe gave classic expression: self-absorption, a yearning for the infinite, isolation from the world out of a thwarted sense of one's own superiority and the corresponding unworthiness of the world." [21]) In the felt innocence that facilitates indignation, man can focus on himself as victim or on other parts of humanity as guilty. Franz Kafka and Hermann Broch both see man as guilty rather than innocent, but as foisting his own guilt upon others. Kafka asserts that the guilty man "does not normally do the single appropriate thing: accept his guilt freely. Instead, by a series of 'motivations' he projects his own guilt onto the world around him in an attempt to escape his own responsibility." [22] Broch sees this process in a metaphysical perspective: when he is "between two worlds," to use Matthew Arnold's phrase, man shirks the obligation to conceive and form a new order. "Instead of attempting to create new human values, [men] seek means of escape. Thus, on the one hand, they seize upon scapegoats, attributing the guilt for the breakdown of values to other human beings —a process not unlike Kafka's 'motivation.'" By this evasion man acquires guilt of his own, and he "multiplies this guilt by assigning it to other human beings, who become his scapegoats, or, in a religious sense, his Antichrist." [23] The state of mind which leads to the finding of scapegoats is countertragic: it makes too simple an arrangement of good and evil, a separation of them into different persons rather than a coexistence of them in the same being. Besides, the attributing of guilt to others has some side advantages: in detesting others' sins one releases his own passions, not always generous ones, under a mask of righteousness. One such mask is the air of saving others; behind it often lies a sharp aggressiveness, which in a salvation-bringing guise seems to wing its way toward a just target. Mary Renault describes a man of this type:

He would say of himself that he taught men to be free, to trust in themselves, to hold up their heads before men and gods, to bear no wrongs. . . . Yet he himself loved no man, for what in himself he was; a man was dead to Menestheus, unless he was a cause to fight for. . . . Menestheus, if someone was oppressive, would threaten and bluster long before he could perform, so as to be praised for hating evil: then the man grew angry, and hurt all those in his power to hurt; and Menestheus had more wrongs to shout about. Men who did good in quiet, without anger, he thought were spiritless, or corrupt. Anger he understood; but he had no kindness for men before the wrong was done, which would have kept it undone.

All custom he hated, whether it had outlived its use or not. He hated all obedience, whether to good law or bad. He would root out all honor and reverence from the earth, to keep one man from getting a scruple more than his due. Maybe there was only hatred at his core, and whatever he had found around him, that he would have destroyed.[24]

Obviously we need not insist that this brilliant portrait identifies the truth underlying every appearance of the indignation-and-blame pattern, but Menestheus' psychic contour is often observable in those who protest at others' evil. He helps alert us to ambiguities that may lurk in the pursuers of wrongs and the rescuers of the wronged. The animus against forces that seem oppressive or unjust can include a spectrum of emotions from love of justice to a pleasurable aggressiveness in need of an object, and from a warm sympathy to an exhilarating hot anger. It invites a spectrum of roles from being one's brother's keeper to wanting to find one's own victims, and from identifying actual evil forces to a kind of self-defensiveness against realities that one does not want to recognize as such. All of these styles are antitragic.

Some men need a cause, others take on responsibility. Since *responsibility* may be an important word for tragedy, and since it embraces various meanings, we need to distinguish between three sets of options that it offers. In the first of these, we can accept the notion of responsibility or deny it; in some people, the impulse to flee responsibility is so strong that they try to render the word impotent by calling it an "establishment" strategic device. If we do not take this tack, we have a second option: we can lay responsibility at someone else's door, or we can accept it ourselves. The former is one way of pursuing a cause; among intellectuals this often takes the form of abusing the culture generally—a somewhat more stimulating exercise than quietly living a redemptive life. If we accept responsibility, we again have an option: we can decide on a course of action toward some end, or we can acknowledge what we have done. We can say "I will take action against sinners" or "I have sinned." The former might, by a misconception of reality or oneself, lead one into tragedy; the latter is the completion of essential tragic experience.

In looking at such a range of actions and of underlying feelings, we are not trying to estimate better or worse, but are trying to see whether a given climate of feeling and attitude is conducive to tragedy. The climate is antitragic when it blinds us to the duality of motives in ourselves and others, or when it is dominated by a spirit of blame, of detecting and punishing wrongdoing, of assessing responsibility against others. In this climate we have "good" men—whether in fact they are really good men, or self-righteous men, or unhappy and disturbed men—against "evil" men, whether they are evil or are adjudged evil. This is a different thing from the tragic conflict of good and evil, or the tension between two goods or between two mixed choices, in a representative man.

The realm of emotions—indignation, righteous wrath, idealism, self-deception, hate begotten by hateful things without or by rancorousness within—that hold one in a nontragic posture of simple opposition is a wide one. The power of that realm is perhaps best summed up in an aphorism by James Baldwin: "I imagine that one of the reasons people cling to their hates so stubbornly is because they sense, once hate is gone, that they will be forced to deal with pain." [25] It is indeed true. Whatever its source, hate implies evil without and ordered wholeness within; pain implies discord within, the inevitable clash of motives in the sentient man. The wholeness is gratifying, even when men evoke one's hate; the pain is hard to bear, for, if one is mature and well, it cannot be released in outward blows. It marks the tragic condition.

When one considers the vastness of human energies deployed in campaigns against other persons—in prosecuting causes, in pressing reforms, in demanding change, in asserting rights, in opposing those who seek uncongenial ends, in uncovering misdeeds, in punishing miscreants, in anger at mistakes, in hatred of differentness, in irrational destructiveness aimed at all community, in the numerous outwardly directed activities that range from the therapeutic to the sickly revengeful—it may seem unlikely that the air of modern times can be in any way favorable to tragedy. Yet not all the evidence is on this side of the fence.

IV. PROTRAGIC ATTITUDES

The need to identify evil with other people is strong, in sick people or well, in those who feel little and victimized, or in those who strike out against oppressors. Jean-Paul Sartre catches this in No Exit (1944) when, in much quoted words, he defines "hell" as "other people." [26] But this self-regarding or self-justifying habit, which we may call heterophobia, also encounters opposition. The most effective resistance would come from the impact of Christianity as Duerrenmatt defines it: "Christianity as a revolution rightly sees the danger for man in his aggression. The emotional tendency to create the 'other,' who expands to the hated race, the Scapegoat, and ultimately leads man to fight. For Christianity the conquest of aggression is the task. Love is the highest good. One must stop constructing an enemy." [27] All efforts to modify heterophobia—and we find them, obviously, in secular as well as Christian attitudes—take a step toward tragic awareness: in discouraging hostility to the "other"—hated race or scapegoat or "enemy"—they encourage a turning from flaws abroad to flaws at home. The problem is to avoid being simultaneously hard on others and easy on oneself. Henri Peyre points to one rather subtle form of being easy on oneself when he thus characterizes the popular doctrine of the absurd: "the most blatant form of anthropomorphism: complaining that the world does not suit man's conveniences." [28] Though in formal doctrine the recognition of absurdity may be the *primum mobile* of moral energizing,[29] this is hardly true in less rigorous circles where the word is a cliché. As a cliché it is a variation on the romantic doctrine that man is blighted by an indifferent or hostile universe, such as appears in the work of Thomas Hardy and Samuel Beckett. Duerrenmatt also objects to absurdism, by implication because it is too simple, and goes on to point out a desirable substitute: "I am against the expression, 'The world is absurd.' I say only that the world is paradox." [30] Not only does this supply a more demanding concept; it emphasizes the contradictory that is felt by the tragic sense. It is only a step from blaming the world or the universe to blaming God. On this form of self-exculpation there is a sharp comment by Saul Bellow's Herzog, who exposes more than one cliché attitude of our era. Herzog points out that no great spiritual revolution has followed Proudhon's "God is *the* evil." What has taken place, then? "Our own murdering imagination turns out to be the great power, our human imagination which starts by accusing God of murder. At the bottom of the whole disaster lies the human being's sense of a grievance, and with this I want nothing more to do." [31] To reject the accusation against God—that rather facile ultimate blaming of the "other" that we find in O'Neill's *Beyond the Horizon* (1920) and Sartre's *The Flies* (1942)—is again to call us back to the tragic world where what is wrong cannot be attributed to agencies beyond ourselves. To reject "the sense of a grievance" is to give up the non-tragic sense of being victimized by the flaws of existence.

The sense of a grievance: this is an aspect of the widespread activity that we have already noted—finding and confronting opponents, whether to save the world or to destroy it. In such conflict the important thing is to assign guilt to others or to agencies outside ourselves. Yet Kafka and Broch, as we have seen, have pointed out that the guilt of others—of the world or of scapegoats in the world—is at least in part a projection of private guilt that we are endeavoring to elude. As long as someone with powerful claims upon our attention—claims such as those of major imaginative writers—can help keep alive the knowledge that the guilt is "our own," then an important precondition of tragedy survives. The guilt of others—or of institutions or of the cosmos (according to a sentimental metaphysics)—is a little too easy to see. The sight of our own guilt comes harder: tragedy demands a clarity that is not always easy. One link in the connection between the tragic and the free on which Duerrenmatt insists is that freedom, as Sartre has emphasized, is also a difficult burden. In part it is difficult because, in Kafka's view, it leads to the acknowledgment of guilt:

> *The Trial* is a book about guilt and freedom: the inevitability of man's guilt in the world and man's freedom to accept the responsibility for his own guilt. Guilt and freedom are inextricably intertwined. To be free means, for Kafka, to recognize and accept the fact of one's guilt. There is no such thing as a state of innocence. There is only the freedom of the man who recognizes his guilt and the animal state of those who have not reached that level of awareness or, having reached it, refuse to accept the fact of guilt. . . . [Joseph K.] is guilty from the moment he feels that he has been falsely accused; his sin, in the words of the paradox, resides in the very fact that he insists an injustice has been done unto him. The paradox has further important implications. Man is redeemed in the instant when he accepts the responsibility for his guilt, rather than feeling that he is being wrongly accused by a hostile world.[32]

The concept of liberty as the acceptance of guilt, which is also hinted at by Duerrenmatt, reveals something about innocence: that the conviction of innocence is itself imprisoning, since it shuts one off from a full sense of reality. Thus it has the effect of illness, and we may rightly call it the "innocence neurosis"; it is widespread enough to be disturbing. It is therefore significant that innocence is rejected by Kafka and in effect by Reinhold Niebuhr, who ironically notes man's strange faith in "himself as essentially harmless and virtuous." These views of Kafka and Niebuhr contribute to the moral climate which makes tragedy possible. Their words imply that man does act, for guilt inheres in what he does, not in what is done to him; thus he is not a little man, a weak man, a subordinate, a victim. Mary Renault's Plato attacks Euripides' representation of human beings (for instance, Medea and Phaedra) as impotent before their passions: "Men are seldom helpless against their own evil wishes, and in their souls they know it." [33] When we can think both that evil originates within and that man knows it for what it is and himself as the doer of it, we help maintain an atmosphere in which tragedy can be written.

We help maintain that atmosphere, too, if we call upon the idea of

tragedy to aid in placing persons and events of our day. Diana Trilling does that when, in discussing the Profumo scandal of 1963 in
England, she interprets Dr. Stephen Ward as its "small hero . . . perhaps in embryo its man of consciousness and therefore its sole victim to
rise to the level of tragedy." [34] Stanley Hyman argues that the writings
of Sigmund Freud "once again make a tragic view possible for the
modern mind." Hyman explains, "If we are serious, our reaction to this
bitter truth [suffering and death] is neither to evade it with one or another
anodyne, nor to kill ourselves, but to set out humbly through the great
tragic rhythm of pride and fall, so curiously alike in psychoanalysis and
literature. At the end of this hard road we can see faintly beckoning
that self knowledge without which, we are assured on good authority,
we live as meanly as the ants." [35] In "consciousness" and "self knowledge" is the crown of that life in which man does not assert his littleness and weakness, does not cherish himself as victim or nourish grievance, does not restrict himself to discovering and punishing the guilt of
others, however much opportunity for such blaming and penalizing the
world may offer, but rather chooses, knows that he has chosen, and in
final freedom accepts the meaning of his actions, bitterly painful as this
may be. When a Freudian sees in the world a renewed possibility for
experiencing "the rhythm of pride and fall" and thus for at least approaching self-knowledge, and when Camus sees in the world a renewed
possibility for the tension between conflicting and irreconcilable values
that holds in periods of great tragedy, their complementary views suggest
a modern atmosphere that can nurture tragedy and can compete with
that other atmosphere that inhibits it.

Tragic Myths

An openness to the tragic reveals itself in the frequency with which
the modern stage returns to ancient myths.[36] But the theater must also
find tragic materials in the present world, and an adequate imagination
can surely do this. The dramatist who can embody, in a representative
character, the "pride and fall" of white supremacy and the knowledge of
guilt that now, like that of Oedipus, comes to us long after the original
wrong actions, will write in the tragic mode. The writer who can embody, in a representative character, the pride and fall of the political
idealist subtly betrayed by self-righteousness and the love of power, will
write in the tragic mode. I suspect that our own era is producing mytho-

genic characters whose careers contain such themes in solution. There is, for instance, Huey Long, in whom a novelist and a biographer, both much honored for their work, have found tragic lineaments.[37] Long was a figure neither too little to be significant, nor too large to be visible, but of a breadth and complexity and representative contradictoriness to stir the tragic imagination.

If, then, there is much in the tone and quality of modern life to militate against tragedy and to corroborate those who affirm its death,[38] there are also apparently grounds for expecting its survival. Hence there is some justification for looking at a number of modern plays to see whether, besides the nontragic elements that may be expected, they also have anything of tragic characterization or structure. Rice's Zero has not influenced all subsequent characterization. Granted, on the stage there have been plenty of Willy Lomans, O'Neill Tyrones, and Williams dropouts from life. On the other hand, Duerrenmatt has been taking some little-man characters and investing them with a moral magnitude of a redemptive sort; he has turned erstwhile victims into maniacally vigorous revengers—Claire Zachanassian, Mr. Mississippi, St. Claude; he has shown one character, Alfred Ill, exercising freedom by renouncing a false innocence for a true guilt. Bertolt Brecht has a sense of victimizing forces, but he can also imagine strong characters making out under hard conditions—for instance, Mother Courage. Arthur Miller has turned from Lomans and those who fail to those who, as we can see in *The Crucible* (1953) and *A View from the Bridge* (1955), try to dominate their worlds. In Albee, even sick characters can exhibit almost heroic energy. Sometimes modern characters—for instance, in Camus's *Caligula* (1945) and *The Misunderstanding* (1944), and in Sartre's *Altona* (1959)—have a sort of frenzy that resembles the Jacobean; the resulting intensity is a long way from the drama of pathos. These samplings do not assure tragic achievement. They simply reveal the presence of some of the traits out of which tragedy can come.

CHAPTER TWO

Tragedy and Melodrama: Alternate Forms

IN SAMPLING the currents of modern life which carry us toward or away from tragedy, we have mentioned various components of tragedy and components of a nontragic or other-than-tragic form. On the tragic side there are freedom, choice, acceptance of guilt, tensions that pull men in opposite ways, humanly representative inclusiveness of personality, a sense of the ambiguity and contradictoriness in reality (of the good-and-evil in values and character), in sum, a fundamental complexity and a concern with the ordering of the self. On the other side there is a more clear-cut designing, usually a dichotomizing, of existence, with divisions between the good and the evil, the weak and the strong, victors and victims, the human and the inhuman; sometimes a sense of innocence accompanied by littleness, weakness, inadequacy, deprivation, grievance; sometimes a sense of innocence accompanied by the spirit of blame and indignation, the finding of scapegoats and the punishing of the guilty; in sum, a concern with ordering the world.

I. Basic Distinctions

The term for the one way of seeing life is, of course, tragedy; for the other, the most applicable and usable term is melodrama. This opposi-

tion of modes and of modal terms was, as far as I know, first given
utterance by Camus:

> . . . we can proceed by comparison and try to see, for example, how tragedy
> differs from drama or melodrama. This is what seems to me the difference:
> the forces confronting each other in tragedy are equally legitimate, equally
> justified. In melodramas or dramas, on the other hand, only one force is
> legitimate. In other words, tragedy is ambiguous and drama simple-minded.
> In the former, each force is at the same time both good and bad. In the
> latter, one is good and the other evil (which is why, in our day and age,
> propaganda plays are nothing but the resurrection of melodrama). Antigone
> is right, but Creon is not wrong. Similarly, Prometheus is both just and un-
> just, and Zeus who pitilessly oppresses him also has right on his side. Melo-
> drama could thus be summed up by saying: "Only one is just and justifi-
> able," while the perfect tragic formula would be: "All can be justified, no
> one is just." [1]

The general tenor of this distinction is excellent, and I want to qualify
it in only a detail or two. The conflict between right and right occurs
in one kind of tragedy, not in all (Lear against Goneril and Regan is
different from Antigone against Creon or, for that matter, Lear against
Cordelia). Likewise, the conflicting forces operate within character as
well as between characters; thus the conflict of good versus bad can be
tragic as well as melodramatic, and good-and-bad may be the contradictory truth of a character as well as of a "force." While Camus opposes both "drama" and "melodrama" to "tragedy," there is really only
one category on the nontragic side, and it is best called "melodrama." In
English, "drama" has so wide a meaning that it cannot comfortably be
restricted to a subgeneric structure; besides, to attempt to use it would
drive one into endless and frustrating efforts to identify nontragic plays
as "drama" or "melodrama." Camus really merges the two by using
"melodrama" as the over-all term in "Melodrama could thus be
summed up" and "drama" as the over-all term in "drama [is] simple-
minded." *

We cannot emphasize too much the fact that "melodrama" is not a
condescending term any more than "tragedy" is a laudatory term. Both
are neutral; both describe structures that correspond to forms of reality;
each structure may be executed with greater or lesser art. The neutrality
of "melodrama" is evident in our wide use of the term "popular melodrama," which implies a stereotyped and substandard version of a form

---

* "Simple-minded" is the wrong English word, since the context does not indicate disparagement. The opposite of "ambiguous" is of course "single-minded."

capable of better things. Melodrama exists because there *are* good and evil forces in the world, there are strong and weak, there are victors and victims; because actual grievances exist, blame and indignation may be justified, and there is guilt that can be discovered and punished; and finally because, with or without reason, hostilities, feuds, and hatreds persist. The critical problem is not the verisimilitude of the strife depicted by melodrama, but the adequacy of the depiction, the frequency of depiction that creates stereotypes, the maturity of the appeal made by the depiction, and the possible exhaustion of theatrical energies in the treatment of themes which, whatever their authenticity, still reflect only a part of human truth. We will come later to the problems of quality in both genres; for the time being we need only be aware of them as alternative modes of viewing experience—of recording it (in the sense that it is there) and of forming it (in the sense that the chosen perspective leads to one structure rather than another). In one we see evil as coexisting with good (Lear, Macbeth), and we contemplate it through the eyes of a doer with whom we are identified in the capacity for choice (of good or evil) and knowledge and self-judgment; in the other we see evil as independent, as out there, as a disaster (Richard III, Nazis, earthquakes, epidemics) that we contemplate from the vantage point of innocence, whether we simply suffer from it or contend actively against it. The latter is the realm which, because of its internal diversities, has not been known by an inclusive term (it comprises aspects of what Camus calls "drama," of "serious play," of "problem play," of "propaganda play," of "naturalistic tragedy," and, insofar as it envisages the triumph of good, even of "romance"), but for which "melodrama" is the rational designation.[2]

Our business here, of course, is not simply to divide plays up into two groups. The initial problem is the old one about which students of the drama cogitate with remarkable persistence: the state of tragedy in the modern world. In attending to this, we have to move on from preliminary hypothesizing about the art-producing qualities of the age and look directly at plays. In them we may or may not find the influence of a tragic view. If we do not, we might content ourselves with calling the play "nontragic." But if, contiguous to the tragic, differentiable from it though in some ways resembling it, there is, not simply an amorphous no-man's land of drama identifiable only by negatives, but an affirmative achievement of another form, we do better not to stop at a series of eliminations in the tragedy sweepstakes, so to speak, but to distinguish plays by positive characteristics, by their adoption of a perspective that makes for one modal organization or another. That is, melodrama is not the absence or simulation of tragedy but is a definite counterstructure. Hence, in trying to learn something about the vitality of tragic feeling and practice, we inevitably allude to the generic form of specific plays.

Tragedy and melodrama are contiguous in that both are ways of dealing with catastrophe; though in part committed to catastrophes of different make-up and origin, in the main they look in different ways at catastrophes that emerge from the human capacity for evil. Hence they may be mistaken for each other. They overlap. They are often found in the same play; there is a sense in which they may compete for the play. We do not often find either in pure form. But if we are to understand the generic mode that mainly organizes a play—or even the doubleness or irresoluteness in a play's interpretative angle of vision—then we need first to look at the pure forms more fully. Further, *tragedy* and *melodrama* are such popular words that they have become imprecise; when we use them as if they meant little more than "better drama" and "worse drama," or "drama of misfortune" and "drama of excitement," we fall sadly short of knowing anything at all about them. Thus we deprive ourselves of something we cannot do without—a grasp of basic kinds of human experience that have to be distinguished.

II. The Structure of Tragedy

In alluding to the realm of tragedy we have repeatedly spoken of "freedom," "choice," "guilt," and "complexity." What lies beneath them and gives them meaning is the fundamental human situation out of which tragedy grows, namely, dividedness. Only when he is torn between conflicting values and desires and hence conflicting courses of action can man exercise freedom, make choices, encumber himself with guilt, struggle with the complexity of existence. He is not W. H. Auden's "Religious Hero" who, having achieved "a passionate obedience in time," has "solved the conflict of divided consciousness." [3] He is rather the representative passionate man torn between modes of obedience and unlikely, by his choice, to settle a conflict that comes from roots deep in human nature. Tragedy expresses the "conflict within the self" that, according to Auden, "is perhaps a law of our being." [4] In Henry de Montherlant's view, which is unconditional, "it is man's nature to be attracted by opposites; it is his destiny always to be moving between polarities, between sensuality and chastity, for instance, between reason and unreason, between courage and cowardice. The central fact of human existence is inconsistency, an inconsistency that must be embraced, if one is to know the truth of life, for man will always shift urgently between animality and sublimity, in a dictated exploration of his own limitations." [5] We could add, between authority and willfulness, between obligation and irresponsibility, between love of power and sense of the possible, between recklessness and prudence, between desire for order and love of chaos, between subservience and subversiveness—all modes of the dividedness that is the ultimate source of tragedy. We must have some impulse to be blind to this dividedness, for periodically we are given reminders of its reality. André Gide, for instance, attacks the single-valued interpretation of humanity by "moralists and novelists" who, "enslaved" to François La Rochefoucauld's "pitiful way of looking at things," "stopped recognizing any alternative to egoism and have subjected all human impulses to its sway." That is, they falsified human nature by substituting one motive for a tragic inconsistency of motives. Gide also parallels Montherlant's affirmative statement by praising C. M. Saint-Evremond because he perceived "that man is 'wicked, virtuous, equitable, unjust, humane, and cruel.'" [6] Between Saint-Evremond and Gide, Baudelaire had put forward his dualism of "spleen" and "ideal"; this "was his way of designating the 'two simultaneous aspirations, one towards God, the other towards Satan,' which he found 'in all men at all times.'" [7] Oscar Wilde's Dorian Gray, with a touch of the rhetorical that usually afflicts Wilde characters when they take off the jester's mask, was to translate these aspirations into inner realities: "Each of us has Heaven and Hell in him. . . ." [8] Neither hell nor heaven alone would make the tragic hero— a truth which Camus has put with almost epigrammatic concision: ". . . revolt alone is not enough to make a tragedy. Neither is the affirmation of the divine order. Both a revolt and an order are necessary. . . ." [9] J. A. Bryant, Jr., finds the same basis of tragedy in different cultures: "Like Greek tragedy, Christian tragedy focuses upon a division in man himself. . . ." [10] His words, in my view, apply to all tragedy.

Types of Dividedness

Though we have offered, in passing, some examples of human dividedness—of inconsistent ends that attract man and inconsistent motives that impel him—we can make the idea of dividedness more concrete by identifying the basic categories of division. In the contradictions within the human spirit there are always at work, in one way or another, two powerful feelings, those of "I ought" and those of "I want." For the former, I will use the word *imperative;* for the latter, *impulse.* The imperative may be that of religious commandment, moral or civil law, traditional duty, filial piety, institutional obligation, commitment to justice, sense of mission, or urgency of conscience. The impulse may be love of power, love of profit, ambition, lust, hatred, all of the egoistic passions that want to defy controls, or the desires for fulfillment that would like to be sole arbiters of action and ignore all the contingencies of life. Imperatives imply limits and humility; impulses, license and pride.

Impulses may be "evil," as the universality of sanctions against them will testify (for instance, those against the desire to kill); they may be "good" (for example, a love that will lead one person to serve another devotedly); they may be neutral, needing a context to define their quality. A man may be divided between impulse and impulse, that is, two incompatible desires. This familiar human situation becomes tragic when impulses achieve a passionate intensity, or one becomes obsessive and carries a man beyond the safe borders implied by the other. Dividedness between impulses is conveniently exemplified in Henrik Ibsen. Rosmer in *Rosmersholm* (1887) wants to take a lead in local reform, but he is essentially a meditative idealist who cannot stand the sense of contamination that seems inseparable from the public activities of reform. Solness in *The Master Builder* (1893) wants to enjoy self-magnifying exploits of a demonic sort, but has only a partial talent for them; ordinarily he is protected against the daring venture by his counterimpulse, a need for a rather steady, nonexhibitionistic professional life. Joe Bonaparte in Clifford Odets' *Golden Boy* (1937) wants to conquer the world through boxing and to fulfill himself by becoming a violinist, but human hands are not adapted to the practice of both professions. Biedermann in Max Frisch's *Firebugs* (1958) wants to save his home from the arsonists, but he also wants to be well thought of by the arsonists. The experience of dividedness between impulses is likely to occur frequently in an age such as our own in which traditional imperatives have lost vitality and the replacements which are humanly inevitable have not yet assumed a compelling form.

The dividedness between imperative and impulse has a larger and fuller history, and it is so much a part of man's nature that it is bound to be a continuing source of tragic life. It will continue as long as passions are strong enough to drive men against powerful moral imperatives. If impulses or imperatives are weak, of course, the conflict may be nominal or resolvable in time. On the one hand, the passions may not be strong enough to set in motion a tragic course of events. In T. S. Eliot's *Murder in the Cathedral* (1935) Thomas, for whom the imperative is discovering and obeying God's will, is tempted by various forms of power, most subtly by that of martyrdom itself; but the temptations lack the passionate intensity that would give them even temporary control, and the resultant tone may be called "pretragic." On the other hand, an imperative may collapse or disappear, and the result will be disaster rather than tragedy: "Europe consented to Hitler," according to Auden, "because it had lost the sense of law which makes the recognition of an outlaw possible." [11] Like Europe, Hitler himself had no "sense of law," that is, no imperative that could make him a tragic figure; he was not divided, but all of a piece, and that in a pathological way. He is in the line of descent from Shakespeare's Richard III. In contrast, there is a sense of law in Macbeth; the passionate ambition that drives him to the throne does not blank out his painful knowledge of violated imperatives. Lear is not simply an insensate creature of vanity and arrogance; he knows, or has the power to know, that he is inflicting gross wrongs on child and country. Phèdre's unmanageable passion is no greater than her awareness of the imperatives that she is unable to live by. We intuit Dr. Faustus' acceptance of imperatives in the very intensity of his effort to deny them as his extravagant egotism drives him into a reckless gamble against heaven. Even a lesser figure like Pentheus in Euripides' *Bacchae* illustrates the split: ". . . bigoted and stiff-necked as Pentheus is, one must point up his integrity. That is the tragedy's core." [12] "Integrity" is the recognition of imperatives; "bigoted and stiff-necked" identify the impulse of self-righteousness.

The archetypal figure of the man caught between imperative and a violent self-assertiveness is Oedipus; obviously a man who totally accepts the imperatives against parricide and incest, he nevertheless yields to emotional pressures and takes incredible risks in a crucial confrontation. Mary Renault brilliantly imagines that confrontation and Oedipus' own judgment of it as he tells Theseus about it many years later:

"So. Did I not know that every man or woman past forty must be my father or mother now, before the god? I knew. When the redbeard cursed me from his chariot's road and poked me with his spear, and the woman laughed beside him, did I not remember? Oh, yes. But my wrath was sweet to me. All my life, I never could forgo my anger. 'Only this once,' I thought. 'The gods will wait for one day.' So I killed him and his foot-runners, for my battle-fury made me as strong as three. The woman was in the chariot, fumbling with the reins. I remembered her laughter. So I dragged her down, and threw her across her husband's corpse. . . .

"And later, when I rode as victor into Thebes, shaven and washed and garlanded, she met my eyes and said nothing. . . . I never told, she asked no questions. Never, until the end." [13]

We reveal ourselves by our interpretations of Oedipus. On the one hand modern antitragic propensities, which we sampled in chapter 1, entice us into making excuses for Oedipus: his actions were decreed by fate,[14] he was a victim of the gods (Jean Cocteau), he was a man of valor at the crossroads, and at the end he was a hero of truth suffering for his integrity. But the tragic spirit is not dead as long as the artist's imagination can make the Renault reconstruction of the key events. It catches both Oedipus' dividedness and his hubris (a subject to which we come shortly); hence it invokes what Clifford Leech calls "the idea that men somehow contribute to what happens." [15]

A statement by John Holloway provides a logical transition from the Oedipus type of dividedness to the third paradigmatic type: "Tragedy enters life at least as often because there is no right choice, as because when there is a right choice men choose wrong in preference to it. . . ." [16] While in the Oedipus story we saw an option between right and wrong choices, the "no right choice" to which we now turn offers several possibilities: two bad choices, two neutral choices, two mixed choices, or two right choices (this technical possibility comes into being only if either option is viewed in separation from the punitive powers held by the rejected option). Perhaps "two neutral choices" is the most appropriate term for the division between impulses at which we looked first. "Two mixed choices" is the state of affairs in the third paradigmatic dividedness, the split between two imperatives. Here the choice is mixed because in choosing one imperative man must reject another, and the rejection has its own penalties.

"The *dramatis personae* of Greek drama," Reinhold Niebuhr comments, "were . . . subject to conflicting claims upon their consciences which were not easily resolved." In Tom Driver's restatement, claims "upon the Greek [hero] are usually between two goods, or two necessities, rather than between a good and an evil." [17] Camus sees this kind of dividedness as the essence of tragedy, and he not only attributes it to Greeks and Elizabethans but believes it can produce great modern tragedy. I see it as active not only at cultural crises, when there is a dynamic equipoise between contending values before one competing force outweighs the other, but at all times because in confronting existence we inevitably espouse value codes that are not consistent with each other. God's due and Caesar's due are seldom neatly distinguishable. "Conflict of loyalties" is perennial: it implies a dividedness of an insoluble sort. One may be loyal to a country or an order of things or a chief and be equally loyal to a principle which the object of allegiance is supposed to embody but in some way does not. It is an ever-recurring situation in which the tragic potential will become actual if the protagonist does not fall short in passion and sentience.

One of the best known of all characters in this situation is Antigone, with her conflict between the pieties of kinship and the duty to civil authority; it is not so often noticed that Creon's situation is analogous to hers. Camus places Prometheus in this class, but there is a difficulty here in that, in Aeschylus' treatment of the myth, Prometheus scarcely feels conflicting imperatives; with a minor exception or two, he is the self-justifying revolutionary. On the other hand, Aeschylus' Agamemnon, returning from Troy, is of a somber meditative cast; one can imagine him, ten years before, suffering in the ambiguities of the public crisis in which he can fail as leader or sacrifice his daughter Iphigenia to an angry god. It is in such a light that Aeschylus sees Orestes, eventually accepting the obligation to avenge his murdered father, but knowing that vengeance takes him into another evil; his own sense of conflict is translated into civic and cosmic terms in the *Eumenides*. The problem for Hamlet, whose situation has remarkable resemblances to that of Orestes, is still more complex, so much so that we do not have generally agreed-upon definitions of it. Hamlet has violent passions, but he needs to operate under a clear moral imperative; the mandate to execute justice necessitates murders, but murder gives pause; the pressures make him want to escape from life, but he remembers God's "canon 'gainst self-slaughter." In Sidney Kingsley's dramatization of Arthur Koestler's *Darkness at Noon* (1951) Rubashov affords a striking example of dividedness between imperatives: his loyalty to the revolution is in growing conflict with his sense of the horrors committed by revolutionaries.

So much for examples of kinds of dividedness. I am not trying, however, to set up categories into which tragic characters may be dropped like letters into slots at the post office. The classes which I have described should serve, not as containers, but as expository devices that help render concrete the general concept of dividedness. "Imperative" and "impulse" (or, alternatively, "sanction" and "passion," "obligation" and "desire") are logically distinguishable kinds of motives; they are metaphors for contradictory sources of human action. Yet in the anomalies of experience they may drift toward each other with an illogicality that can be evicted only from the theoretical description of them. An impulse may become intransigent; it may find moral justifications; it may so act as to serve noble ends. In such ways it may become, or resemble, an imperative. And what starts as an imperative —a prescribed loyalty or obligation—may take on a spontaneity and emotional vitality that render it impulsive or passional. If we keep in mind such potential transfusions of identity, we should avoid the pat and the doctrinaire.

Dividedness and Hubris

While dividedness leads to the choices that signify freedom, it also is the ground of two other traditional ingredients of tragic experience— hubris and self-knowledge. Hubris ordinarily implies a self-glorifying aggressiveness, a rash assurance of beating the game, a reckless defiance of limits. The tragic hero is, whether grossly or very subtly, "the man who would be god." Baudelaire summarizes the tragic situation well, though he does not use the word *tragedy*: "Indeed, all men who refuse to accept the conditions of this life sell their souls. . . . Behold the man who wanted to become God, sunken in no time to a level below his own, by reason of inalterable moral laws." [18] Mary Renault gives a comparable account of an actor's portrayal of Pentheus, in

Euripides' *Bacchae*, as he is led on by the god Dionysos. Dionysos is "enchanting Pentheus with the hubris in his own secret heart. Once drunk on this sweet poison, he will know himself the one sane, righteous man in a wicked world. He has refused the little madness, to choose the great. . . . In the previous scene, [the actor Menekrates] had built up Pentheus' sincerity, his striving for order, and fear of the excess which makes men less than men. Now he showed a man better than his fate, a king in ruins, wrecked through a noble hubris—the belief that man can be as perfect as the gods." [19] When Baudelaire speaks of "men who refuse to accept the conditions of this life" and Camus defines "the constant theme of classical tragedy" as "the limit that must not be transgressed," [20] they are talking about the same thing. Hubris is denial of conditions and limits; these are implicit in the imperatives that represent one side of man's divided nature. Oedipus, Macbeth, Dr. Faustus, Beatrice in Thomas Middleton and William Rowley's *The Changeling* (1622), Annabella in John Ford's *'Tis Pity She's a Whore* (1633), Koestler's Rubashov—all know what limits are set to their actions, and all of them, in an unmanageable exuberance of passion, violate these limits; they literally "transgress."

But if hubris is the I-can-get-away-with-it spirit of a man who knows both desires and limiting imperatives, and who lets the desires have sway, it may be difficult to interpret as hubris the choice made by the man who is divided between two imperatives. A forced choice as hubris? Here, indeed, tragedy reflects an intransigent vein of reality that does not conform to the natural but ingenuous preconception that guilt does not attach to a choice made as a value judgment or as an act of conscience. In this difficult area Camus makes two enlightening observations: "For the chorus [in classical tragedies] knows that up to a certain limit everyone is right and that the person who, from blindness or passion, oversteps this limit is heading for catastrophe. . . ." At this point it might seem that "blindness or passion" eliminates the kind of deliberate choice that we are talking about. But Camus finishes the sentence thus: ". . . if he persists in his desire to assert a right he thinks he alone possesses." [21] That is, to commit oneself to a single imperative is in effect to assert a transcendent right, to spurn the limit imposed by the other imperative that has to be felt in the divided situation. It is perhaps tantamount to self-righteousness, which does indeed appear in Antigone. Camus says a little later, "what is punished is not the crime itself but the blindness of the hero who has denied balance and tension." * "Blindness," then, is not simple ignorance or unawareness; it is the undervaluation of the imperative in conflict with the imperative one obeys. Hence, hubris is the implicit claiming of sole authority for the principle one acts by; it is the self-aggrandizement of having the right god while others are content with minor or nonvalid divinities.

But if the counterdivinity is authentic (and it cannot be otherwise in a conflict of "imperatives"), this will appear in sanctions against the man who, with whatever force of conviction and conscience, has asserted the unconditional claims of the loyalty he chooses. (The irreconcilable conflict of imperatives, and hence the vulnerability of the man who has made his choice, are beautifully symbolized in the hostilities, partisanships, and punitive angers of the Olympians, which are sometimes read as mortal frailties and rather solemnly reprehended.) The divided man can, of course, make his choice with full awareness that there are no perfect choices, and thus accept the consequences: Orestes does this, and in so doing he acknowledges the tragic truth of life. In contrast with this is a particular modern sentimentality: the flight from consequences, which, if it goes far enough, will be a disastrous misprision of reality. In our day the cries for "amnesty" from people who in heeding one imperative have violated another are a form of this sentimentality. To choose a loyalty and demand immu-

---

* Page 304. In another essay in the same volume Camus makes a remarkable statement about a characteristic modern denial of balance and tension: "But the Europe we know, eager for the conquest of totality, is the daughter of excess . . . we extol one thing and one thing alone: a future world in which reason will reign supreme. In our madness, we push back the eternal limits, and at once dark Furies swoop down upon us to destroy. Nemesis, goddess of moderation, not of vengeance, is watching. She chastises, ruthlessly, all those who go beyond the limit.

"The Greeks, who spent centuries asking themselves what was just, would understand nothing of our idea of justice. Equity, for them, supposed a limit, while our whole continent is convulsed by the quest for a justice we see as absolute" ("Helen's Exile," p. 149).

If Camus is correct, the Nemesis of which he speaks would seem to be operating through the massive antirationalities which we glanced at in chapter 1. This is apparently implied in another remark by Camus a page or two later: "While the Greeks used reason to restrain the will, we have ended by placing the impulse of the will at the heart of reason, and reason has therefore become murderous" (p. 151). No wonder Auden defined the twentieth century's "Worst Sinner" as the "deliberate irrationalist" (Greenberg, *Quest for the Necessary*, p. 72).

nity from the costs is one form of believing that "men can be as perfect as the gods," of believing that life is but a melodrama of triumph.

Dividedness and Self-Knowledge

Dividedness is a source, not only of hubris, but of self-knowledge,[22] for self-knowledge is primarily concerned with the imperfect choices that are hubris in action. Dividedness is what there is to know; we assume unity in ourselves and find that it is not so. The unity that we assume is that of goodness, and we find that not so. We cannot bear the knowledge of total evil in ourselves; that means cynicism or despair, neither of which is tragic. (One might, of course, follow Jean Genet and embrace evil as the ground of sainthood, but that is no more tragic than less heterodox avenues to sainthood.) It is not likely that we shall have to bear the knowledge of total virtue. Rather we know dividedness: that we are not all of a piece, that we can make wrong choices, that we are vulnerable to the consequences of any choice. Oedipus learns that despite a flight into salvation abroad, he did commit parricide and incest; Lear must say "I did her wrong"; Antigone knows that she cannot escape civil penalties; Rubashov knows that in his loyalty to revolution he has become an evil man; and Duerrenmatt's Alfred Ill acknowledges the old evil deed that in his civic success he had almost managed to forget. This is the ultimate completion of the tragic rhythm; it alone gives us the sense that the experience has come full circle. "Oh light! The cry of all the characters in classical tragedy who come face to face with their destinies." [23] Hadrian defines "the true birthplace" as "that wherein for the first time one looks intelligently upon oneself. . . ." [24] Kafka, as we have noted, sees knowledge of one's own guilt as the source of freedom. Auden makes a similar point, though with a unique moral specification: "It is only when he is forced into self-knowledge, compelled to learn that his own rebellion is conditioned by the forces he is rebelling against, so that his most intense desires are untrustworthy, that he becomes a free agent." [25]

These are different ways of making the important point that the tragic is not the disastrous, that tragedy is not the dramatic embodiment of despair, but rather a testimony to the on-going of the qualities of spirit on which life depends. Penalties reveal order; acceptance of guilt, moral awareness; the alternatives are chaos and stupidity or grossness. If a hero dies, "in dying nobly he may reveal to others a kind of commitment without which the human cosmos is doomed." [26] Duerrenmatt concurs in Immanuel Kant's "magnificent statement": "The tragic thing about life is that the 'Not,' misery, alone can make man do what he could do better by reason," and Duerrenmatt adds, "Man doesn't shine in happiness . . . but in the catastrophe." [27] (There is no reason to read "tragic thing about" as "regrettable thing about" rather than as "tragic value in.") Camus complains that "too many people confuse tragedy with despair" and quotes D. H. Lawrence with approval: " 'Tragedy,' Lawrence said, 'ought to be a great kick at misery.' This is a healthy and immediately applicable thought." [28]

The burden of such statements is that in tragedy, suffering and death have meaning and value, there are moral sequences rather than discontinuities, all is not absurd and pointless, and what is essential survives catastrophe. Of the different tragic events that testify to an order in life, that assert continuity rather than stoppage and a blank, the central one is the achievement of self-knowledge. When this occurs in a deeply representative being such as the tragic hero, his experience affirms the human openness to and recovery of the kind of wisdom that creates a durable and endurable community.

It is the most difficult wisdom to come by, since it is founded on the knowledge that is hardest to bear. No one should fall into glib homilies on the theme "Know thyself." When man does know himself, he does so in anguish. Three major modern dramas advance the notion that self-knowledge cannot be borne, that it destroys men if they do not flee from it—Ibsen's *The Wild Duck* (1883–84), Maxim Gorki's *The Lower Depths* (1902), and O'Neill's *The Iceman Cometh* (produced, 1946). Ibsen and O'Neill both present the partisans of self-knowledge very unsympathetically. Though O'Neill nowhere else treats the theme as brilliantly as in *Iceman*, it seems always to lurk not far from the surface of his thought. The sudden deaths that come out of the theatrical side of Ibsen tend to dispose of his characters before they have come to, or come to terms with, self-knowledge.

III. The Quality of Tragedy

Tragedy, as I have already emphasized, is a neutral generic term; it can apply to great plays or more limited ones, to plays that are successful or seriously flawed. One difficulty here is that the preceding theoretical account attaches tragedy to the deep roots of emotional and moral life; with such origins, tragedy may seem to be profound by definition, incapable of drift into failure or triviality. But a cathedral may be ugly, and a cottage handsome. To achieve the technical structure of tragedy is one thing; to achieve excellence or greatness is another.

There is, for instance, a problem of magnitude of substance. While the tragic conflict is essentially one of inner life, one man's inner life may be much more resonant than another's; the more it opens out into general human significance, the further it is on the way to one kind of greatness. Dr. Faustus, for instance, might seem doomed to only coterie significance because he is an intellectual; but Marlowe has framed his dreams of power and glory with such intensity and rightness that they embody everyman's fantasies. The more usual way of enlarging the private experience is to conceive of it as echoed or reflected in public life. The plague in Thebes symbolizes the general significance of Oedipus' actions: a moral order is at stake. In the parallel situation in Duerrenmatt's *The Visit*, Alfred Ill accepts his guilt but the moral plague in Guellen gets worse; the spiritual restoration remains private, a contrast to public life, and the result is satirical power rather than tragic magnitude. Aeschylus gives the Orestes story the widest possible range by externalizing the private dividedness into a cosmic struggle for the soul of Athens; though there are different judgments of the success of this procedure, it is difficult not to feel that fundamental matters are being probed. In *Lear* and *Macbeth* the essential dividedness is in the hearts of kings, but the royal choices infect whole kingdoms; the national disasters symbolize the public, reverberating force in the passions of representative men. In Sartre's *Altona*, Franz von Gerlach, son of a German industrialist, is horrified to find in himself evidences of anti-Semitic sadism, and for a while the play tries to draw us into an empathic sense of him as everyman; but this reaching toward magnitude is defeated, finally, when human dividedness cedes the stage to a trite lecture against capitalism.

If in one play the dividedness of tragic existence may be purely private or of limited resonance, in another it may be so managed as to fail to invest the character himself with magnitude. It is not easy to conceive and present a character in whom divergent motives operate simultaneously and vigorously, who has a convincing doubleness, and who inflicts or undergoes suffering but is not destroyed. John Webster, who had exceptional skill in the melodramatic portrayal of human life, essayed dividedness in Bosola in *The Duchess of Malfi* (produced about 1614), but Bosola remains minor because he is now one thing, now another; we hardly sense in him the actual conflict of the different motives that lead to different kinds of conduct at different times. In Tennessee Williams' *Cat on a Hot Tin Roof* (1955), Brick Pollitt exists in a kind of stasis in which the conflict is postponed; continuous sedation is a substitute for self-confrontation. In O'Neill's *Days Without End* (1934) John Loving undergoes an apparently shattering conflict between faith and skepticism, but he reaches a too easy resolution; he seems hardly scarred. Something of the same sort goes on in Quentin in Arthur Miller's *After the Fall* (1964).

Without the power of self-knowledge, the awareness of different options, dividedness does not exist. Hence the innocent flamboyant arrogance of a Tamburlaine, which ministers to fantasies of power buttressed by immunity, and the uncomprehending monotonous humiliation of Arthur Miller's Willy Loman (a mercantile Tamburlaine manqué), which ministers to fantasies of weakness that beget self-pity, belong to another realm than that of tragedy. But the moral intelligence that helps constitute tragedy may not be successfully imagined by the dramatist: a self-judgment may be hasty, mechanical, histrionic, even self-indulgently protracted. The self-judgments imputed to the Cardinal in Webster's *Duchess of Malfi* and to Chance Wayne in Tennessee Williams' *Sweet Bird of Youth* (1959) are unconvincing codicils; they are not prepared for by the drama of the preceding lives. Equally untragic is the man who has undergone a moral crisis and then steps out of it to observe it as if it were a work of art. Speaking of a man who had experienced a conspicuous reorientation of his religious life, Eric Voegelin once remarked, "He likes to contemplate himself in the posture of convert." Camus spots a comparable self-consciousness, that of conspicuous penitence: "But too many people now climb on to the cross merely to be seen from a greater distance. . . ." [29] Without at all intending to do so, Oscar Wilde, writing to Lord Alfred Douglas, imparts a theatrical quality to the confessional aspect of self-knowledge: "A man's very highest moment is, I have no doubt at all, when he kneels in the dust, and beats his breast, and tells all the sins of his life." [30] This is the kind of thing that almost literally happens in English "domestic tragedy," in which the didactic impulse of the dramatist can render self-knowledge histrionic: in Thomas Heywood's *A Woman Killed with Kindness* (1602) and Lillo's *The London Merchant* (1731) the protagonists hold on to their self-accusations lovingly, as if fascinated by their role as cautionary spectacles. We can say that they lack the awareness of their own motives that we expect in tragic intelligence.[31] Or we can say that they cling to a fantasy of embodying special significances, whereas a true coming to knowledge is the destruction of a fantasy. This is what literally happens at the end of Albee's *Who's Afraid of Virginia Woolf?* (1962) in a low-keyed dialogue which in my view increases the spaciousness of the play.

The Styles of Conscience

In the Albee play the closing dialogue is in marked contrast with an older copiousness of speech that we have come to distrust, so much so that to some modern readers even Oedipus' long speech after he blinds himself seems excessive. The problem for the writer of tragedy is to mediate between the laconic and the loquacious. He must find a middle ground between the grudging and the excessive, or between the non-tragic Iago, who will never say one word more, and the quasi-tragic treason-trial penitents' volubility in self-castigation. Verbal styles are a clue to styles of conscience. Since conscience is literally a knowing, the styles of conscience belong to the problem of self-knowledge and its relation to tragic magnitude.

There are two or three modern versions of what is called "conscience" that are outside the realm of tragic activity. One version claims various exemptions for the individual; because of conscience he is freed from obligations that otherwise hold for the community generally, and he tends to expect freedom also from the penalties that, as we have seen, normally follow any choice of an imperative. In another version, conscience is invoked in defense of a will that, by the nature of will, is hypersensitive to the exactions of any authority; what emerges is that spirit of "independence" which instinctively resists any kind of accommodation to institutional ordering and governance. The habitual objector may wish to protect a private domain from anything that seems like encroachment, or, on the other hand, his conscience may push him into opposition, not simply to the official, but to other wills and consciences that are oriented differently from his own.* All these exercises of conscience—if indeed it is admissible to apply *conscience* to an impulse which looks toward a privilege or toward a combative assertion of the self against other selves—have nothing to do with tragedy; their world is that of melodrama, in which the conflict is with other forces, one's own rightness is assumed, and the risk is self-righteousness rather than self-incrimination. The "melodramatic conscience," then, serves the self. It may mean a sense of wrong done to or by others, but it cannot turn to one's own wrongdoing, which is the field of the tragic conscience. The tragic conscience implies, not the joy of rectitude, but the suffering of guilt. We can see it struggle into being in Lear, who lives as long as he can in blaming his daughters.

Thus we have two kinds of "conscience"—the polemic type focused on one's own rights or on the wrongdoings of others, and the evaluative type by which one knows his own wrongdoing. Though the latter is necessary to tragedy, it can actually develop a kind of antitragic redundancy. This hyperactive conscience is akin to the "sickly conscience" that appears in several forms in Ibsen dramas; it can make too much of suffering. If freedom is, as Kafka said, the acceptance of guilt, here we have a kind of libertinism of guilt. We see a hypertrophy of conscience in Ibsen's Rosmer and Rebecca; their self-examination verges on the neurotic, and the tragic potential keeps melting away. There is something of this in Richard II and a great deal of it in the less complex Henry VI, in both of whom the latent tragic is not quite actualized. It is what Franz von Gerlach in Sartre's *Altona* does not

* In an obiter dictum Lord Byron, commenting on Lady Jersey, notes an ironic ambiguity in the spirit of independence: ". . . she is independent in her principles—though, by-the-bye, like all Independents, she allows that privilege to few others. . . ." This is in *Lady Blessington's Conversations of Lord Byron*, ed. Ernest J. Lovell, Jr. (Princeton, N.J.: Princeton University Press, 1969), p. 37. Compare, in O'Neill's *The Iceman Cometh*, the comment of Don Parritt, a young revolutionary, on his mother, a lifelong revolutionary, "She doesn't like anyone to be free but herself" (IV). Eugene Goodheart says of Lawrence: "Throughout Lawrence's work there is the fear that the doctrine of spontaneity and freedom will be perverted by those for whom freedom is an excuse for self-indulgence and the coercion of others" (*The Cult of the Ego: The Self in Modern Literature* [Chicago: University of Chicago Press, 1968], p. 177). The narrator in Camus's *The Fall* constantly talked about freedom: "With that keyword I would bludgeon whoever contradicted me; I made it serve my desires and my power" (p. 97). Much the same insight is expressed from the opposite point of view by Oliver in George Santayana's *Last Puritan* (New York: Charles Scribner's Sons, 1936), p. 581: "The world is full of conscript minds, only they are in different armies, and nobody is fighting to be free, but each to make his own conscription universal."

really find his way out of, what Harry Monchensey in Eliot's *Family Reunion* (1939) has to find his way out of, and what Julian in Albee's *Tiny Alice* (1964) is in danger of falling into. Any aspect of the tragic process, that is to say, has its own hazards; the conscience which leads to self-knowledge can take a drama off into case history or be an essential component in its greatness.

The Problem of Forgiveness

Self-knowledge includes, not only not fooling oneself about what is going on, but enduring what one knows rather than succumbing to an excess of conscience or falling into a nontragic despair.[32] The tragic hero has strength but is not merely stoic. His moral posture has been put epigrammatically as forgiveness of oneself—a special version of the aphorism *tout comprendre, c'est tout pardonner,* which has its own risks. Though *After the Fall* is not Arthur Miller's best integrated or tonally best controlled play, it contains some sharp insights, one of which occurs in Quentin's significant speech that closes the play: "And the wish to kill is never killed, but with some gift of courage one may look into its face when it appears, and with a stroke of love . . . forgive it. . . ." The risk lies in "a stroke of love," which may suggest an ease that there cannot be, until we remember that to forgive is not to do away with or dismiss as inconsequential. What is forgiven stays there, be it an evil impulse that recurs or an actual deed that is never quite forgettable. True forgiveness is a painfully difficult action, for it means living with a knowledge that may be agonizing or horrifying, always threatened by it, and yet resisting the temptation to indulge in a continuing destructive self-blame. Dorothy Richardson wrote in *Pilgrimage:* "From hell, heaven is inaccessible until one has forgiven oneself. So much, much more difficult than accepting forgiveness. Not God, but we ourselves, facing the perspective of reality, judge and condemn. Unforgiven, we scuttle away into illusions. But, all the time, we know. We are perambulating Judgment Days. . . . If one could fully forgive oneself, the energy it takes to screen off the memory of the past would be set free." [33] This psychological state in its extreme form is nowhere better exemplified than in Sue Bridehead in Thomas Hardy's *Jude the Obscure* (1895). The untragic opposite of such untragic masochism is a quick absolution that is in effect a stopping comfortably short of knowledge. The comic heroine of Joyce Cary's *Herself Surprised* (1941) catches herself in this and thus moves into a valid central self-knowledge: "If I went to the bad at last, it was not the fault of the times, but of myself. It was . . . because I did not remember my weakness and study my faults, and because I forgave myself too easily for those evil deeds which always took me by surprise." [34] Eddie Carbone in Miller's *A View from the Bridge* (1955) suffers much but avoids the pain of forgiveness by refusing to admit that any action of his needs forgiveness. Like Macbeth, he is able to divert the energies of open self-confrontation into conflict with adversaries, so that self-defense can replace self-recognition.

A convincing action of self-knowledge, of conscience, of the self-forgiveness that surrenders the right to punish without either slighting or burying the punishable facts—this is the final element in the fullness of character that can produce tragic magnitude. In the words of a critic of Bernard Shaw, "the great heroes of tragedy, Sophoclean or Shakespearian, also come to self-awareness." [35] I would stress the word *great*; self-awareness is the seed of greatness because it is the elusive, recalcitrant end of the most painful struggle and growth; it is the ultimate achievement of personality, and it does not come to a little man. In C. P. Snow's *The Masters* (1951) a character is defining the kind of largeness that the master of a college should have: "I want a man who knows something about himself. And is appalled. And has to forgive himself to get along" [36]—a man, in other words, who has the qualities that could make the tragic hero. The idea that tragic magnitude is a function of completeness of character is well summed up in Shaw's words: ". . . the greatest man is the completest man, he whose eyes are as good as his ears, and his head as his hands. . . ." [37] To say that the eyes and the head are indispensable is to stress the power of understanding; as it grows, we come closer to greatness.

IV. The Functioning of Tragedy

Without adequate self-knowledge in the tragic hero, tragedy has difficulty in working as it should. Clifford Leech puts "the ultimate effect of tragedy" concisely: it is "to sharpen our feeling of responsibility, to make us more fully aware that we have erred as the tragic figures have erred. . . ." [38] But this feeling of responsibility, this full awareness, does not come to us as a "message" which the drama delivers like a postman, or as a lesson outlined on the blackboard; it is not communicated literally by the developing action, as in a charade, nor is it a sort of "answer" arrived at in time by accurate reassembly of the scrambled parts of a puzzle; it is not a preachment, an injunction, an exhortation, a warning, or a threat. It is simply an inseparable part of the imaginative experience; it exists as what I have elsewhere called "feeling knowledge"; it characteristically belongs to us without being articulated at all,[39] except perhaps in retrospective meditation. In Leech's words, "to encounter *Lear* fully is to have made a major advance in self-knowledge and in knowledge of the world." [40] To "encounter fully" is not to examine carefully or analyze studiously but to participate deeply, to be drawn into the full drama by a sympathy approaching or becoming identification. One is not watching a demonstration but spontaneously and recreatively entering into a life. It is by finding himself doing the unexpected, the unimagined, the unthinkable, perhaps even the unforeseen admirable that the spectator comes into self-knowledge. The truth was expressed long ago by Lucian: "When every spectator becomes one with what happens on the stage, when everyone recognizes in the performance, as in a mirror, the reflection of his own true impulses, then, but not until then, success has been achieved. Such a dumb spectacle is at the same time nothing less than the fulfillment of the Delphic maxim 'Know thyself,' and those who return from the theater have experienced what was truly an experience." [41]

While the suspension of disbelief, or of its sibling, the rejective impulse, appears to be a part of normal human equipment, the spectator does not automatically "become one with" all kinds of characters: he shies away from the ridiculed, the satirized, the perverse, the stupid, the vicious. Instead of embracing them, he points at them. We need hardly consider his being drawn in by those who are virtuous from the start, since they, presumably, could contribute little to his self-knowledge. The problem is rather his identification with those whom he may want to reject precisely because he intuits their power to reveal him too fully to himself. What he cannot comfortably resist is representativeness, especially as it appears in dividedness, since in tragedy its most characteristic form is the original one named by Aristotle: that of the "good man" with the "flaw." We can generalize these preliminary considerations thus: the narrower and more limited the character, the greater our tendency to separate ourselves from him; the broader and deeper he is, the more easily we feel kinship with him and yield ourselves to him. That is, we accept our own fullness of being; hence we are drawn to, and into, the complete character; then he inducts us into implications of fullness which we have not acknowledged. As we have already seen, the crucial mark of fullness is intelligence, that is, the kind of awareness that makes self-knowledge possible. We do not concede our identity with people of restricted insight, of insensitivity to cardinal issues; hence we cannot, except with small segments of ourselves that are hardly effective in adulthood, become one with Tamburlaine or Willy Loman, whereas we can find a common center with Dr. Faustus or Miller's John Hale.

The power of the sentient being to arouse our concern, that is, to draw us into his own life, has been very well put by Henry James in the preface to *The Princess Casamassima:*

. . . the figures in any picture, the agents in any drama, are interesting only in proportion as they feel their respective situations; since the consciousness, on their part, of the complication exhibited forms for us their link of connexion with it. But there are degrees of feeling—the muffled, the faint, the just sufficient, the barely intelligent, as we may say; and the acute, the intense, the complete, in a word—the power to be finely aware and richly responsible. It is those moved in this latter fashion who "get most" out of all that happens to them and who in so doing enable us, as readers of their record, as participators by a fond attention, also to get most. Their being finely aware—as Hamlet and Lear, say, are finely aware—*makes* absolutely the intensity of their adventure, gives the maximum of sense to what befalls them. We care, our curiosity and our sympathy care, comparatively little for what happens to the stupid, the coarse and the blind; care for it, and for the effects of it, at the most as helping to precipitate what happens to the more deeply wondering, to the really sentient.[42]

"We care . . . little for . . . the stupid, the coarse and the blind": that is, we separate ourselves from them, we do not participate in their lives. On the other hand those who " 'get most' out of all that happens to them . . . *in so doing enable us* as readers . . . *as participators"*— a key word—"also to get most." Thus, in Lucian's words, we "have . . . truly an experience." By being at one with those who, in coming to self-knowledge, represent the full scope of tragic engagement, we "see ourselves for what we are," as Cleanth Brooks puts it, and thus complete the full scope of the tragic function.

Empathy and Illusion versus Distancing and Instruction

In the view presented above, the audience responds to tragedy by experiencing empathy, not by receiving prefabricated instruction transposed into dramatic dialogue. The relation between drama and theatergoer or reader is quite different from that which Brecht envisaged in his "Lehrstücke"—instructional plays—and indeed attempted in his drama generally. In the one, we are drawn in; in the other, we are supposed to be kept out—"alienated," held at a distance by a cordon sanitaire of technical devices. In the one we proceed through imagination into "feeling knowledge"; in the other, we are propelled by essentially allegorical pressures into an understanding of the lesson. In view of the enormous influence of Brecht in recent decades,[43] we may seem to have in the theater itself a powerful antitragic force. This is at least partly true. The kind of lesson to be found in instructional drama ordinarily concerns, not the man within but the world without—society, its institutions, the "establishment," politics, economics, culture. The pupils in orchestra and balcony are invited to discover the flaws in bodies, forms, and attitudes outside themselves, or at most, perhaps, to ponder an opinion that they have held. They are invited, not to understand their own moral nature, but to consider the imperfect nature of the social order. If such a response is secured, it is clearly that of a nontragic realm.

What has been accomplished by Brecht, by those whom he has influenced, and by others who take the theater to be a handmaiden of social or philosophic thought is the present-day revival, in sociological dress, of the medieval morality play. Characters are conceived of, not as autonomous and hence rather unpredictable beings, but as carefully designed and controlled instruments of explication and exhortation. But the ironic thing about the original morality plays was that, like *Everyman*, they often tended to become, not simply illustrations of doctrinal soundness and right choices, but the depiction of struggles between alternative choices; that is, they drifted toward the realm of tragedy. The dramatist set out to preach orthodoxy and found himself portraying the anguish of man for whom being orthodox was not as easy as following the rules of carpentry or leatherwork. This shift of role in the writer happens at any time when the conceptual dramatist turns out to be also the imaginative dramatist, when the artistic impulse begins to press the evangelical. Fortunately it often happens today. When it does, the audience is not held off, but is drawn imaginatively into human experiences.

It is theoretically questionable, in fact, whether any man who is artist despite himself can fend off the wily human imagination and prevent it from finding its way through a barricade of songs, vaudeville skits, interruptions by an emcee, explications by an omnipresent *raisonneur* (the Doctor of the moralities), improbable names of characters and places, harangues to the audience by the actors, chic reminders, ubiquitous and often tedious, that what goes on is only a play—and, beyond the barricade (the overturned furniture of the illusionist drama), finding some genuine inducement to empathy. In *The Balcony* (1957) Genet uses various means—most notably the closing speech— of telling the audience that preachment rather than illusion is his end: and what he is preaching about is that man has an insatiable need of illusion. The illusion to which man is most addicted is that in the theater, and despite itself the theater seems unable to quell that illusion. So far, at least, the theater is not suicidally forcing itself into a wholesale conversion to forum, pulpit, and hospital for supposedly therapeutic revels of a nontheatrical formlessness. It is now a truism that in Brecht himself the illusionist regularly triumphed over the propagandist, and in his audiences empathy over cool study-hall detachment. We do not remember *Mother Courage* (1937–38) as a treatise on war and economics; we remember a full, energetic character in whom skeptical realism almost reaches tragic proportions. We do not remember *St. Joan of the Stockyards* (1929–30) as an anticapitalist tract; rather we have images of human hypocrisies and, in the title character, of a strange mingling of motives that defeats the end she has chosen to serve. In Frisch's *Firebugs* we remember Biedermann, not as a personified study of a class style, but as an autonomous character in whom our own guilt and follies are at work. Cleanth Brooks observes that when one "comes to estimate the achievement of the serious writers of our times" he looks for "something more inward than a tract— something deeper and more resonant than a tirade against a particular abuse. One looks for an image of man, attempting . . . to act like a responsible moral being. . . ." [44] Brooks alludes to critics, of course, but behind the formal activities of the critic lie the fundamental expectations and inevitable responsiveness of the theatergoer, his imaginative openness to the "image of man."

In sum: if dramatists can succeed in turning plays into treatises and audiences into pupils, they can indeed create an antitragic atmosphere. But if the dramatist is really the artist who has to use stage instead of pulpit, he will be unable to prevent the illusion of human truth and hence the empathy through which the tragic experience is realized.

V. The Structure of Melodrama

In tragedy, dividedness is inner; in melodrama, it is outer. In tragedy, one potentiality in man is pitted against another; in melodrama, man is pitted against another man, or against certain other men, or a social group or order, or a condition, or even against events and phenomena. In melodrama, one attacks or is attacked; it is always a kind of war. One may be fighting against injustice or for survival. In tragedy, good and evil are a private matter, whatever their public repercussions; in melodrama, they are a public matter, though they may have private repercussions. In tragedy, two alternative but incompatible goods may struggle for the soul; in melodrama, they struggle in society or in the world. But in melodrama we tend to conceive of the struggle as between good and evil; we convert the other man's good, which we do not embrace, into an evil so that we may have the vigor to contend against it. The good and evil may be absolute; it is always possible to find acceptance of some forces as divine and others as demonic. Or the good may be pragmatic; to condition oneself for combat, one ignores one's vices and expands one's virtues into all of one's being. A man can fight effectively only as the good man; if he simply finds goodness out of reach, he elects evil as his good. He battles against someone or something else because he is good, or if he is the victim of irrational attack, he is good by definition. Edward Alexander alludes to "that great tenet of ritualistic liberalism: namely, that oppressed people are incapable of doing wrong." [45] One might call it a tenet of melodrama, in life or on the stage. If stage melodrama ignores the tenet, it will move toward tragedy; we see a touch of this in the stage version of *The Diary of Anne Frank* (1955) when the Jewish victims of the Nazis at one time turn on each other. On the whole, however, the apparently accepted goodness—of the oppressed or of any victims—is less an absolute than it is a by-product of our withholding of an inappropriate scrutiny. We know far more about the vices of the Greeks than about those of the Trojans. We do not inquire into the moral stature of victims of storms, earthquakes, holocausts, accidents in industry and transportation, riots, mob action, tyranny, invasions, crooks, perverts, criminals, or maniacs. Disastrous events are different from tragic events in that they happen from the outside and do not offer a choice; hence they do not introduce the issue of moral significance that is central in tragic actions. Victims are, for all practical purposes, undivided; they do not invite their disasters (and if they do, they are not victims).

Dramas of disaster are a regular kind of melodrama. Disaster means victims (waiting for the end, or for Lefty, or for Godot, or just waiting; even, perhaps, struggling), in the main to be pitied, since they do not often embody complications that modify our responses. We see victims of nature in John Millington Synge's *Riders to the Sea* (1904) and of human nature—its primitivism—in Eugène Ionesco's *Rhinoceros* (1960); of society in the plays of Ibsen's "middle period" (for example, *An Enemy of the People*, 1882); of political forces in Brecht's *Private Life of the Master Race* (1934 ff.), Robert Sherwood's *There Shall Be No Night* (1940), Lillian Hellman's *Watch on the Rhine* (1941), Max Frisch's *Andorra* (1961); of evil men in Webster's *Duchess of Malfi* (1614) and of greedy men in Henry Becque's *Vultures* (1877); of revenge in a long series of plays from Thomas Kyd's *The Spanish Tragedy* (*ca.* 1585–88) to Duerrenmatt's *The Visit* (1956). There is another special kind of victim whom we may call the victim of the self: the person who cannot cope with human situations any more than he could with a hurricane, who goes to pieces before life generally, as in Gorki's *The Lower Depths* (1902), Williams' *The Glass Menagerie* (1945), and O'Neill's *The Iceman Cometh* (1946), or who goes to pieces in a crisis, as in O'Neill's *Emperor Jones* (1920). In *The Infernal Machine* (1934) Cocteau tries to make Oedipus a victim of the gods, but what might be a first-rate melodrama turns into a second-class tragedy as Oedipus becomes a figure of excessive vanity and defective intelligence.

In dramas of disaster the perspective is that of the victim. If on the other hand we use the perspective of the stronger character who in his strength makes victims, the result is the drama of triumph, another familiar type of melodrama. This is the type most susceptible of simplification and popularization, for it tends by its nature to sidestep the moral maxim that power corrupts, and hence to provide images of power and incorruptibility; in various media it can display virtuous and effective politicians, detectives, doctors, and other conventional good guys disposing of conventional bad guys. In *Yellow Jack* (1934) Sidney Howard, developing a medical theme, uses this structure but tries not to oversimplify the situation. A more sophisticated melodrama of triumph is Marlowe's *Tamburlaine*, where there are no sympathy-evoking ends to palliate the adventures in pure power. A subtler kind of triumph appears in Thornton Wilder's *Skin of Our Teeth* (1942): here mankind does not so much defeat the powerful antagonists of his race—ice age, flood, and war—as achieve the quasi victory of survival. In *Macbeth* and *Richard III*, too, we are gradually brought to the point of view of men who might remain anonymous bystander victims but who gain identity in a struggle against unjust rulers.

We looked first at the victims of disaster because, in both life and drama, it is they who are most likely to be confused with tragic figures; the difference is that the tragic figure is an agent who brings on or contributes to his catastrophe, whereas the melodramatic figure is simply the recipient of catastrophe which originates elsewhere—in things or in other people. Then it was a natural step to the other end of the dramatic spectrum, where, in drama as in life, the tone is that of triumph. Obviously, however, the alternative outcomes and the alternative roles of victor and victim neither exhaust the melodramatic possibilities nor essentially identify the melodramatic mode. The common element in those who succeed or fail (or do something of both) is of course their undividedness—the fact that they either have no inner conflict, or subordinate it to conflict in the world, or, in the fairly frequent pathological cases, project it into the world in search of what we may call "therapy by combat." They have a real wholeness or a quasi wholeness. The dramatist may portray them as truly integrated or may disregard the humanly expectable splits, either because he is unaware of them or because they are not relevant in the convention within which he is working. In the world or in the theater, wholeness—I use this term to indicate the melodramatic oneness, whatever its origin or nature—is the working basis of external conflict. Not only is it demanded by conflict, it also demands conflict: one's being is taken over by a singleness of conviction or passion that naturally expresses itself in action against what implicitly or openly stands in its way.

The Realm of Melodrama

A good deal of daily life belongs to the realm of melodrama, to the extent at least that this life involves competition and rivalry, that is, stresses between rather than within people. Ordinarily this is low-key enough not to have theatrical utility; for the stage it needs heightening and concentrating in special episodes and crises. There is such ritual heightening in all kinds of athletic competitions, where the theatrical quality is demonstrated in the tendency to call them spectaculars, to translate the opposing players into heroes and villains, and to resist the detachment called for by a "sportsmanship" which seems ever to have harder going. It occurs also in politics, where all combatants turn their campaigns into forays of good against evil, and where much turns on the histrionic devices by which a contestant can heat up his audiences into uncritical partisanship.

Commonplace competitiveness is heightened, again, in the special conflicts produced by public situations: this or that group fights to compel a community or nation to adopt a program or pattern of life (desegregation, conservation, legalized abortion, tax reform). This is the large melodramatic realm of causes: on the affirmative side, one fights for the institutionalization of virtues and, on the negative, against vices deemed to threaten or inhabit institutions (on the stage, the accusing finger points at societal origins of vice in George Lillo's *London Merchant*, materialism in Odets' *Awake and Sing* [1935], capitalism in Brecht's *St. Joan of the Stockyards*, the church in Rolf Hochhuth's *Deputy* [1963], the gods in Sartre's *Flies*). The fighter detects wrongdoing, assigns guilt, imposes punishment, whether he opposes crime syndicates or the unsyndicated crimes of those who have betrayed trusts. On the one side are all the energies of reform; on the other those who equate it with subversion or simply do not believe in it (the idea of reform by fiat is satirized in Dorothy Sayers' *The Devil to Pay* [1939] and in Duerrenmatt's *An Angel Comes to Babylon* [1954]). Thus we enter the huge realm of problem plays, of social diagnosis or propaganda; this form of melodrama has had a vigorous life from the eighteenth century through Ibsen's middle period to our own day.[46] Indeed,

Ibsen's first major admirer, Bernard Shaw, wanted to equate this type of melodrama with the whole of drama. He wrote thus in 1902: "Drama is no mere setting up of the camera to nature: it is the presentation in parable of the conflict between Man's will and his environment: in a word, of problems." [47] "Man's will" versus "environment": it names the conflict between undivided man and all his antagonists—individual, societal, cosmic, from the conventions in Shaw to rascals in Sean O'Casey and an inscrutable universe in Beckett.

In the conflict of programs, the personal spirit is sometimes distilled from the total ferment. Then the personalities of individuals and even of houses become evil; the result is the feud, one of the most intense and clear-cut of melodramatic situations (for example, the Montagues and Capulets, York and Lancaster in the Wars of the Roses). When the spirit of punishment takes on a peculiar virulence and overflows the institutional channels meant to contain the private passion that substitutes *lex talionis* for the law, we have the melodrama of revenge. As Electra and Orestes work toward their revenge for Agamemnon's death in Giraudoux's *Electra* (1937), Clytemnestra chides them: "What kind of children are you, turning our meeting into a melodrama?" (II. iv). She uses the word disparagingly, but it is the right one. The melodrama of revenge has been a staple of myth and history and stage from Euripides' *Medea* to crimes of passion in all the daily papers, from *Hamlet* to the alienated and destructive who seek revenge on society because it exists (Schmitz and Eisenring in Frisch's *Firebugs*). It echoes from generation to generation in the extraordinary family line of Tantalus, Pelops, Niobe, Atreus, Thyestes, Aegisthus, Agamemnon, Orestes, and Electra, where everyone so acts as to evoke revenge from god and kin. In Giraudoux's *Electra*, the Beggar says of Orestes and Electra: "Look at those two innocents! What will be the fruit of their marriage? To bring to life, for the world and for ages to come, a crime already forgotten, the punishment of which will be a worse crime?" (I.xiii).[48] Crime-punishment-crime—it is a good shorthand for that sequence of retaliations which makes exemplary melodrama unless it is turned into tragedy, as indeed it is in Orestes, by the emergence of an understanding sensitive to the moral quality of action taken.

The ultimate activities of the aggressive spirit that appears in reform, punishment, and partisan life are revolution and war, and here, of course, melodrama is at its fullest. Revolutionaries are locked into a self-righteousness, and defenders of institutions into an inflexible resistance, that forbids self-knowledge; in wars, both sides claim God's support and thus forestall the dividing conscience that would be a severe operational handicap. There is no tragedy in revolution or war per se (though a dramatist may endow a participant with a tragic consciousness, as Carl Zuckmayer does with General Harras in *The Devil's General* [1942–45]). The recurrence of revolutions and wars indicates, then, how extensive the stage of melodrama is. That sense-of-an-enemy of which war, in its actuality or in its moral equivalents, is an outcome is dramatized repeatedly in Shakespeare; it appears vividly in Christopher Fry's *Sleep of Prisoners* (1951), especially in the character named David King, and in Wilder's *Skin of Our Teeth*. The latter even notes, ironically, the pain of returning from war to peace.

In the second part of the twentieth century there is some disposition to treat revenge and war, the basic forms of melodramatic action, as aberrant and perhaps obsolete; the legal infliction of penalties, or at least of some penalties, appears to some observers to be punitive and revengeful, and we recall a war to end wars. One would not willingly predict whether history will support or disappoint the hopes of terminating such societal methods of dealing with apparent misconduct at home and abroad. But it is observable that some antipunitive forces would like to punish the punitive, and that large numbers of antiwar people use highly warlike means against those assumed to be prowar. (It is other people's wars, it sometimes appears, that are to be warred against.) Commitment is called for, rationality is decried, force is extolled. The spirit out of which melodrama comes seems unimpaired.

The Future of Melodrama

If that spirit manifests certain distortions in our own day, still all the normalities of human nature argue the continuance of a field for standard melodrama. To some writers commitment will always mean not the commitment of self to literature but the commitment of literature to the self, that is, to the causes that quicken the heart. These are never likely to be in short supply; the most utopian innovations that we can foresee will not wholly eliminate, if indeed they will lessen, the occasion for problem plays and propaganda plays. All the new models of societal mechanisms and institutions may not eliminate the human capacity for, and the attractions of, wrongdoing. At least as long as we can discern evil in other men, in groups, or in institutions, we will have the grounds for melodramatic action, in life and on the stage. It seems unlikely that Richard IIIs, Iagos, Lovelaces, Cencis, Fagins, Maulers, Schmitzes and Eisenrings, Gletkins, Caligulas, and the pigs on animal farms will go into a decline. The obsessed like Electra, Captain Ahab, Stavrogin, and the Mannons appear to be permanent human phenomena. So, too, on the other side of the fence, the Talbots, Edgar and Albany, Cordelia, Prospero, Squire Allworthy, Prince Myshkin, and, in a different way, Akki, Übelohe, and Bérenger. In other words, until we are all good, when we will neither need nor have literature, or until we all are troubled only by the evil that originates in ourselves, when we will have only tragedy, the world will offer stimulus for melodrama.

Aside from being a probable and at times a necessary response to the world as it is and as we expect it to be, melodrama offers an enticing emotional satisfaction. This is another reason why it is not only an enduring form but is likely to be cheapened and to usurp, in our consciousness, a larger domain than it should have. What melodrama makes possible is a sense of undividedness, of unified feelings. Inner conflict, of whatever kind, is the most painful of all experiences, whether it sticks to us as a chronic low-keyed affliction that we can neither cure nor succumb to, or flares up in acute crises of tragic dimension. In life or on the stage, melodrama annuls or deadens or displaces that conflict: through it we become, in effect, all one, all feelings and energies outward bound, united toward a goal or against an evil. There is no shilly-shallying, no agonizing over alternatives. The unifying force may be indignation, excitement, valor, hopefulness, channeled energizing, sheer aggressiveness; or, if one is responding to a serious threat, it may be fear, hatred, desperation, love of survival. The oneness within makes it easier to contribute to, and in turn is reinforced by, the oneness without, the union of the like-minded: the satisfaction of being on a moral bandwagon, of being "with it," of feeling "solidarity," of cooperating in a crusade or a quest for salvation; or the reassurance of fellowship in the face of disaster, as experienced in Act I of *The Skin of Our Teeth* or the later acts of *Richard III* or in London during the bombings of World War II. The need for the strengthening, the stimulating, the exhilarating may lead not only to fighting for causes, but to creating them, just as it may encourage an addiction to stage-works that set forth an "indictment" or reveal "compassion," which, however worthy socially, do not often create very substantial nontopical literature.

The agreeable oneness within is attached primarily to the pursuit of an end, but it is capable of subtle variations as the quest succeeds or fails. The joy of triumph is the most obvious of the melodramatic satisfactions; given our habits in fantasy, it is in danger of being too easily come by, and we are most likely to be suspicious of it. The joy of survival is a soberer affair; whatever its ecstasy of the moment, the costs are present in imagination, the residue of suffering in memory. One does not want to be a victim, but the empathic fellowship with victims may be profoundly gratifying; one's imperfections do not count then, and one may easily drift into the ascetic luxury of self-pity. Failure itself has a delicate underground appeal, the invisible teasing seductiveness of nonfeasance, passivity, cessation. Despair, which we have noted is not tragic, may seem the least inviting of the melodramatic experiences. But it may entice us with its own paradoxical triumph: in its way, with its declaration that all is intolerable, it undermines all other triumphs, and insinuates that failure to despair is crass. It was Harry Monchensey's peril; Eliot did rescue him, but a little late.

VI. The Quality of Melodrama

Melodrama has a role, then, because of the way things are in the world, and because of the way things are in human nature. Like tragedy, it may carry out its role with varying degrees of art. It slips more readily into the facile because man's impulse to think well of himself renders him, whatever disciplined exceptions there may be, susceptible to the imaginative experience wherein his vices disappear because he is a partisan against oppressive men or defective principles. Hence the stereotypes that account for the popularity of "popular melodrama." But nothing in the melodramatic perspective predisposes it to facility. The desirability of inner oneness to all men does not mean that it is easy to portray singleness of being convincingly. Doing that is what leads to one kind of melodramatic excellence. The "humors" characters, the men accepted as evil (such as Renaissance machiavels), the men accepted as good (such as the eighteenth-century men of sentiment) are not often able to survive beyond their own times. To embody the evil of the world in characters who live on in human imagination in different ages, to catch its inner core of threateningness, to depict the enduring spiritual lineaments of a malice and destructiveness that lie behind any age's conventional formulations of depravity—this takes something like genius. It is there in Richard III and in Iago, in Goneril and Regan, in Blifil; in Pecksniff and Murdstone and Orlick; and in our day Orwell appears to have caught it in 1984 and *Animal Farm*. Harold Pinter is admired for a mastery of the ominous; this sense of his achievement may last. The difference between inferior and superior melodrama is the difference between the connotations of "villain" and the connotations of "evil man," or on the other hand between "good guy" and "good man," between, in a word, popular conventions and moral reality. It is apparently as difficult to dramatize successfully the man of undivided character as it is the man of profound doubleness.

If melodrama can achieve distinction, on the one hand, through the intensity and power that come from authentic undivided characters, it can also succeed by investing characters with a dividedness of appeal that elicits a certain dividedness of response.[49] "Dividedness of appeal" is to be distinguished from the "dividedness of being" of tragic characters. The latter, as we have seen, is a split between different motives or impulses within the character; he himself feels this split, and we are asked to experience it with him. Dividedness of appeal does not modify the characteristic singleness of being in the melodramatic protagonist; he is not drawn between alternatives and does not choose one rather than another. But as he pursues his single course single-mindedly, he appears to us in different perspectives that evoke different responses. Compare a man who pursues a "good end" by "good means" with a man who pursues a "good end" by "bad means." The former may simply be a too good character in popular melodrama; or he may be a genuine hero, as in, let us say, a dangerous feat of mountaineering, a polar exploration, or scientific experimentation. But suppose he completes an experiment, which is of accepted theoretical or practical value, by using vivisection, subjecting human "guinea pigs" to questionable methods, or misappropriating funds: we then have one type of "divided appeal" and, presumably, of invitation to divided response. Conversely, a character may pursue ends that we do not approve but in the pursuit of them may exhibit admirable qualities—independence, perseverance, bravery. Or he may exhibit qualities that we do not expect to find together—bravery and foolish vanity, malice and integrity, perceptiveness and mendacity. In thus appearing to us through different perspectives he inhibits conventional shapings of reality and stock responses; he embodies, at his own level, the contradictions in the world, and this kind of inclusiveness of character is one form of magnitude in the play. Through dividedness of appeal the dramatist catches something of the dividedness of existence,* not as a dilemma in the consciousness of the hero, but as a diversity of attributes that the spectator can see in him.

This kind of melodramatic excellence appears in different ages. The title character in Sophocles' *Philoctetes* has a strong claim on our sympathy because he has experienced severe suffering and has a genuine grievance, but he so clings to both as to be almost irritating. Euripides' Hippolytus behaves with magnanimity in keeping Phaedra's secret but is complacent and self-congratulatory in his chastity; Alcestis is the heroically generous wife in dying for her husband, but she also assigns great credit to herself and saddles Admetus with a lifetime of emotional debt. Marlowe's Jew of Malta is presented as a villain, but since nearly all of his victims are as bad as he, or even worse, he elicits something more than the most obvious univalent response. Chapman's Bussy D'Ambois appeals to us both because he is an independent spirit and because he is a victim of smaller men, yet his very independence becomes a wearying egotism and aggressiveness. In *The White Devil* (1611) John Webster takes a pair of adulterous murderers, Brachiano and Vittoria, and gives them a resoluteness and spirit that would become heroic opponents of evil. Vendice in Cyril Tourneur's *Revenger's Tragedy* (1607) has every justification for revenge but turns an understandable retaliation into sadistic orgies. The title character of Montherlant's *Master of Santiago* (1945) combines a pure idealism with a repellent arrogance. In *The Firebugs* Frisch takes two "underprivileged" and needy men, who look like conventional objects of human sympathy, and converts them into cunning destroyers of the community; to avoid clichés, Pinter in *The Birthday Party* (1958) presents the social pressures upon the artist in the guise of two gangster-like figures who are the least expectable voices of convention and conformity. On the other hand there are good characters in the Don Quixote tradition that

---

* Though a sense of dividedness may appear by definition to exclude conventionalities, that is, simplistic orderings of experience, there are, ironically, clichés of dividedness. One of these is the whore with the heart of gold: one does not admire the profession but approves a virtue in the professional. But in this fantasy of male self-interest the dividedness is only nominal after all: the realities of the profession are blotted out by the dazzling warmth of the professional.

reappears in different guises in Tennessee Williams, Duerrenmatt, and Ionesco: in this mode of divided appeal, moral quality is seen in company with confusedness, incompetence, silliness, drunkenness, and so on, so that one is not given a tritely irresistible model of virtue.*

By such instances of divided appeal and response, melodrama seeks excellence: it captures the dividedness of the world or by fresh means restores complexity to aspects of reality that have been taken for granted, that is, felt in a singleness that at least in retrospect seems illusory.

VII. Oppositions and Combinations

Tragedy and melodrama are complementary ways of apprehending the disunities of life. In one, we are aware of a conflict in consciousness; all the dualities are focused there, and we go through the experience of trying to resolve them by choices that can rarely be made with impunity. In the other, we see the dualities outside ourselves in contentions between forces which represent alternative singlenesses in action; we are likely to think of the forces as good and evil, and empathically participate in struggles that go on to triumph or destruction. The more mature and skillful the presentation of these struggles, the greater our sense of authenticity in the good and the evil, or, alternatively, the greater our sense that the singleness in the competitor, though not an optical illusion, embraces an aggregate of elements more divided than unified in appeal.

Melodrama may be seen as a detection of others; [50] tragedy, as a detection of oneself. In one, the implied theme is the salvation of the world; in the other, of oneself. The better melodrama is, the more it should enhance knowledge of the world; tragedy fails if it does not lead one into self-knowledge. Ideally, melodrama should protect us against thinking too well or too ill of the world; but because it is sometimes tendentious and wants to make us partisans rather than contemplators, it may succeed in making us laud or condemn this or that in the world.

* The dramatist, of course, may not succeed in defeating the spectator's strong impulse to reduce dividedness of appeal to a more manageable singleness, and to find that apparently inconsistent attributes are, after all, "only" this one or that one. In this mood the spectator will easily find a simplifying clinical term for Don Quixote, and will tend to think of him only as someone who cannot safely be left to his own devices. The reductive use of Marxist and Freudian views is very familiar. Most skepticism of doctrine-oriented interpretation springs less from the skeptic's allegiance to some other faith, or from his belief that the interpretation is not true, than from his sense that a partial truth is claiming to be an exclusive truth.

The melodrama of ideas—or "philosophic melodrama," as Eric Bentley calls it [51]—wants to convince us that one intellectual stance is good, another bad (too simply done, this can separate ideas themselves into good guys and bad guys). In leading us to know ourselves, tragedy protects us against thinking too well or too ill of ourselves, against thinking we are safe or thinking we are lost, against embracing nineteenth-century complacency or twentieth-century disillusionment, against viewing ourselves sentimentally or cynically. Yet we are not always eager for that protection; self-knowledge is taxing; salvation is high-priced. We may be blind to the subtle and hard-earned reassurance that comes through tragedy, resist knowing our complicity in the errors or the forthright evil of which the tragic hero is capable. We instinctively prefer outer enemies to inner ones, evils that can be pointed at to evils that must be lived with—even those, such as natural disasters, for which there is no remedy. Melodrama is alluring; as tonic or tranquillizer, it unifies. It may be that our tendency to use the generic term disparagingly reflects an unarticulated resistance against an unacknowledged seductiveness.[52]

To describe the experience offered by melodrama I will use the term *monopathic*; of the tragic experience, *polypathic*. In the former, man has oneness of feeling—as competitor, crusader, aggressor; as defender, counterattacker, fighter for survival. He may be assertive or compelled, questing or resistant, obsessed or desperate; he may triumph or lose, be victor or victim, exert pressure or be pressed. Always he is undivided, unperplexed by alternatives, untorn by divergent impulses; all his strength or weakness faces in one direction. The monopathy of combat and victory is self-evidently pleasurable, an exhilarating form of a desired unity. But the monopathy of the victim, of defeat, of decline, of fading away or out—this too has a charm, though it may not be visible to the naked eye. In this monopathy man is good, for misfortune blots out the discreditable; impotence in evil frees him from the labors of conquest; and beneath these more evident gains lies the strange teasing impulse to submit, to acquiesce, to be passive, to give up, to embrace the tranquillity of nonstruggle and the quietude of death. During the 1960s it became conspicuous in the phenomenon of opting out or copping out; yet some guilt is attached to it still, for the exit-prone person must blame his defection on the defects he flees. Thus he enjoys the double monopathy of goodness and withdrawal.

Tragedy is polypathic in that we have to experience the conflicting impulses of the divided man. We cannot be simply indignant, triumphant, hopeful, hopeless, bitter, challenging, defensive, goal-bound, or victimized, for contradictory emotions force themselves upon us. We have Macbeth's driving ambition and his painful knowledge that the steps to his goal are evil; we have Lear's illusion of being scorned and his punitive wrath, and his latent sense of being viciously foolish; we make Faust's proud boast that he can beat the game, and share his inexorable realization that the rules still hold; with Cordelia we may choose to knuckle under and save skin, or to keep pride, pain father, and lose land; with Hamlet to combine revenge and a grudge-murder, or to combine integrity and filial undutifulness; with Solness to be dutiful, safe, and stodgy, or to seek glory and be suicidally rash; with Alfred Ill to become a guilty wanderer and escape the malicious and self-seeking, or to acknowledge guilt and then be used by a cunning revenger and a ruthlessly self-serving town. The polypathic experience is complex, troubling, burdensome, as gaining knowledge must be; the monopathic may be exhilarating, pacifying, or cathartic. Timon and Coriolanus come close to offering us the latter because their dominant sense of grievance is virtually unqualified by a grasp of their own contributions to their troubles.

Melodrama, monopathic as it is and thus likely to produce stereotypes, can actually approach the polypathic in one of its modes—that in which an unexpected putting together of discordant elements creates dividedness of appeal and response. We see something of this in *Coriolanus:* the hero's rule is integrity, but in practice he is stubborn and undisciplined. Different phases of his personality call forth "mixed feelings." But such mixed feelings, which make greater demands than does the apparently more univocal personality of say Brutus, are still different in kind from the empathically experienced conflict in a divided character struggling with counteroptions.

Unmixed and Mixed Types

In looking at individual plays in terms of these two theoretical types, we find either-or and both-and situations. *Richard III* is clearly melodramatic, as are virtually all problem plays and revenge plays; *Dr. Faustus* is undeniably tragic. The two modes may be combined: [53] the tragedy of Oedipus is the melodrama of Thebes. In some plays, two modes seem to be struggling for control: it is possible to describe *Richard II* as a tragedy which slips into melodrama, or as a melodrama which pushes toward tragedy. There is a similar situation in Miller's *After the Fall*, in which Quentin's laboring toward self-understanding rather fitfully holds its ground against his almost equal love of finding others to blame. Most tragic heroes try to live in a melodrama, and their efforts seem to urge their creators to follow the same course. Lear would rather blame his daughters than know himself; one can imagine him, in a modern anti-illusionist version of the plot, stopping the show to urge the playwright not to drive him into a tragic misery far worse than that of being furious at his willful daughters.

Clifford Leech sees "a tragic element" in Pinter's *Caretaker* (1960) and in certain plays by John McGrath and Tom Stoppard, though they "refrain from appearing to offer the minimal affirmations that are basic in tragedy." He adds, "Tragedy here, as characteristically in drama of the 1960s, is an undercurrent but, I believe, a determining one." [54] Though Leech's view of tragedy is somewhat different from mine, his words accurately describe a recurrent situation: a play may lack a tragic structure but still may contain a "tragic element" or what I would call a "tragic accent." Even such wielders of power as Duerrenmatt's Nebuchadnezzar and Mr. Mississippi fall short of a total singleness. O'Neill's Orin and Lavinia Mannon feel some impact of alternative values: though they drive toward disaster as if in revengeful destruction of themselves, they occasionally desire, or even make some effort toward, a salvation outside their doomed house. The main characters in a play may forge ahead in a melodramatic quest, while a single individual suffers with a tragic awareness. In Miller's *Crucible* the community is relentless in its extirpation of witchcraft, but the Reverend John Hale can think of himself as a murderer. In a somewhat similar way the townspeople in Frisch's *Andorra* can save their skins by acquiescence in evil, while the Teacher can know what is going on and can acknowledge his own grievous share in it (exactly like the Teacher in Duerrenmatt's *Visit*).

The Choice of Modes

Besides these written dramas, with their diverse modes of both single and divided appeal, there is, as I suggested in chapter 1, an unwritten drama inherent in our racial situation. Though I have set forth the tragic potential, the situation is one which can work itself out in either tragic or melodramatic terms. In a sense, the world can make the kind of choice a dramatist makes when, sensing either latent salvation or latent ruin in the materials for drama, he elects one perspective or the other. The initiating deed—the enslaving of men—has been committed, whether in blindness or in subconscious choice (perhaps like that of Oedipus at the crossroads: ". . . this one doesn't count"), and the plague is on the city. But what was done long ago is now alive in the consciousness of all, white and black, and all may choose modes of response to evil done. Whites have come slowly, and not very willingly, to tragic self-knowledge, to a sense of guilt, and their problem is to follow this route, if they can, to the end. Authentic sense of guilt leads to expiation, which human willfulness always makes difficult. But if whites can move from authentic self-knowledge to authentic guilt to authentic expiation, they will create a state of affairs in which blacks can forgive: this course of events would reflect, finally, the kind of moral recovery that rounds out the true tragic rhythm. But if in the strange unyieldingness and self-defensiveness which can afflict even well-meaning people, whites do not bring about the moral atmosphere in which forgiveness is possible, or if the blacks in their turn cannot bring themselves to forgiveness, which is as hard for those sinned against as expiation is for sinners, then the only role left for blacks is to be punitive and retaliatory. They will then act out a melodrama of revenge, and this will beget an answering revenge by whites. The melodrama of revenge will pass on into the melodrama of the feud, and the end will be total disaster. In the theater the melodrama of disaster is an imitation of men in action, and it provides defining terms for the actions of men.

The world's power of choice in the black-white situation is, as I have said, analogous to the choice of mode which the dramatist can make when his theme is wrongdoing. He asks for the melodramatic response if he sees evil actions as the work of undivided people whom we look at from an external point of view as objects. He asks for the tragic response if he can imagine evil actions as the work of divided people whose sentience makes it possible and indeed necessary to use their point of view. There are some themes, granted, which seem to offer him no choice: the broad realm of natural, accidental, gross, and impersonal disasters cannot be looked at tragically (in the sense that a man cannot really choose not to be a victim of an earthquake, a storm, a poor driver, a defective plane, a riot, a war). There is, too, a realm of human evil in which the dramatist appears to have little choice—the evil done by passionate men without the sentience that might divide them: the envious, the haters, the greedy, the lustful, the retaliatory, the malicious and destructive; the obsessed, the monomaniacs, the mad. These men are realities; they must be portrayed, but they cannot be seen as tragic, any more than their victims can be. Still, in the raw material of human conduct, the dramatist has vast room for choice: there are many men whom his imagination can see either as limited and single-natured, or as endowed with a consciousness of alternatives and the ability to make choices. If he sees the former, he writes melodrama; his field is the straightforward doers of evil and especially their victims, without whom evil is an abstraction. If he sees men of actual or potential understanding, he writes tragedy; his field is the dual-natured people whose evil, however much it brings misery to others, in the end ricochets upon themselves and comes home to them in their consciousness. To illustrate the choice possible to a dramatist: Shakespeare might have construed Macbeth simply as a coarse regicide, so mad for power as to know no restraints. In that case we would see Macbeth from without, an evil to be fought against as best men might, not as a profoundly troubled man torn between imperatives and desires known to every man. If it were possible to think of all doers of evil as knowing not only their own lusts but the limits that constrain men, all drama of evil would be tragic. But all men do not have an awareness in the light of which they may be understood to be, and understand themselves to be, responsible for their own doom. Hence melodrama coexists with tragedy.

Modes of Response

The coexistence of the modes is not only a fact of life but a characteristic of individual dramas. These require an especial flexibleness in the reader. But if he needs to be on guard against the too rigid generic expectations which come to us almost instinctively, he needs also to be aware of a certain excessiveness of response that can undermine the right functioning of either mode. Indeed, by distinguishing kinds of response we can make a final distinction between the modes themselves. We can discover, at least as a theoretical possibility, a "normal" and a hyperbolic or pathological way of placing oneself in respect to tragic and melodramatic experience. We can say, of a tragic action, "There go I"—and if we do not say it or feel it, we have not entered the experience properly. We can say, of a melodramatic action, "There go real people" —and if we do not, we may be failing in a necessary suspension of disbelief. These are the expectable "normal" responses. But, overly self-conscious, we might also say of a tragic action, "There go I alone"—a hypertrophy of guilt that forbids recovery, or an egotism in vice that is prerequisite to a secretly desired self-torture. And we might likewise say, of a melodramatic action, "There goes the world" or "There goes everybody else"—a hypertrophy of innocence that forbids a feeling knowledge, or an egotism in separateness that assures a freedom from all troubling involvements.

Overresponse of this kind may be rare. Confused response is probably more frequent, and hence more of a problem. If we do not distinguish between the two modes—that in which the doers and victims of evil are different men, and that in which they are the same man—we diminish our sense of reality. If we simply disparage melodrama, we cut ourselves off from an awareness of kinds of evil and good that the world does produce. If, without using the term, we use exclusively a melodramatic point of view—that is, divide the world into evil and good— we see men, and ourselves, too simply. If we apply the term *tragedy* indiscriminately to all kinds of catastrophe—those that strike men from without and those that men bring on themselves—we confuse two radically different kinds of experience, a confusion that cannot be thought harmless. We may expect of life that it will cast us at times in a melodramatic role, at times in a tragic. If we are to act responsibly, we need to know one from the other, to avoid the temptation of trying to stay in one role all the time, and to enact only the one that is called for. In a different way the same calls are made upon dramatists and theatergoers.

CHAPTER THREE

The Plays and the Approaches

AFTER a preparatory look at some aspects of the modern spirit and their possible impact on drama, and at aspects of dramatic genres that endure in various times, we now turn to the individual plays that are the testing ground of all theories of form. True, in chapters 1 and 2 there are allusions to fifty or so plays of the last century, but these are rarely more than brief illustrative comments. A full picture of generic form in operation requires a more detailed examination of a number of plays.

How arrange these plays? It might seem almost automatic to split them up under such captions as "Variations of Tragic Form" and "Variations of Melodramatic Form." Such an ordering would have manifest advantages: contrast and neatness. Perhaps, indeed, too much contrast and neatness. The procedure would imply a sharper separation than ordinarily occurs, it would make it difficult to deal with generic mixtures in a single play, and it would seem to mean distributing plays into bins rather than seeking out the formal properties which make a work one kind of thing or another kind of thing or a combination of several things. Alas, there are similar objections to the exclusive use of any one of several other procedures that come to mind. An organization entirely in terms of playwrights would imply the full treatment

[63]

requisite for generalization; this could be done for only a few playwrights, and others would have to be skimped or omitted. The method would also be hostile to the sampling that makes possible a larger, more varied, and more revealing spread. A purely chronological approach would imply a historical survey that I do not aspire to and a fullness that would limit criticism to assertion rather than demonstration. A purely thematic approach would have to ignore the fact that themes are not always isolatable or fundamental.

What I elect to do, then, is to use three different perspectives—first that of authorship, then that of chronology, and finally that of theme. This should make for variety, it should be conducive to a sampling method, and it should help discipline the taxonomic tendency that may threaten the study of formal differentiations. The different approaches will test differently the theories of tragic and melodramatic form, and the helpfulness of the theories in shedding light on individual plays. Finally, each approach has its own utility. The inspection of the works by a single author can show how much he sticks to a given perspective and hence to a certain generic pattern, or, conversely, how much he alters the point of view and thus writes in different modes; this should be a useful way of characterizing him as a dramatist, as well as a significant way of seeing how generic theory works in practice. The inspection of chosen segments of time might reveal fluctuations in the use of generic structures and thus lead to conclusions of a historical sort; or it might establish that in shorter periods of time (that is, something less than a century) there is no historical pattern, that the basic forms persist without quantifiable changes, and that variations seem to be a matter of chance rather than results of, or clues to, a history to which meaning can be ascribed. Finally, tracing a chosen theme through a number of plays makes clear how different points of view lead to different generic organizations of material; it becomes unmistakable that theme does not predetermine form, but that form interprets theme.

The three approaches are not wholly separable; the use of each tends to rely at least in part on another. I will look first at the work of a half-dozen individual dramatists (chapters 4–9); for each of these the material tends to organize itself chronologically. I will then take up certain plays in a chronological pattern (chapter 10); here the thematic tends to catch the eye as a secondary way of organizing the material. Thence I will pass on to the final topic, a series of plays in which money is either a central or an important theme (chapter 11); here the search for modal variations will bring out some differences that can be described chronologically.

While the arrangement of these different quests is arbitrary, there is some advantage in coming last to the thematic perspective. Most themes are not bound by time; the money theme is conspicuously universal. In using it, then, we are reminded, as we need to be, of the links between our times and other times. Most themes are amenable to various generic interpretations; the money theme is conspicuously so. In using it, then, we can see the affiliations as well as the differences among the tragic, the melodramatic, the comic, and the satirical. There is a clear profit in such a historical and formal opening out into the whole world of drama, since our chosen area is not separable from it.

PART II

Place and Persons: Three Americans

Foreword

I N APPROACHING a set of plays through the gate of authorship we can hardly avoid having a double goal: what goes on in the plays and what goes on in the playwright's mind. The plays are differentiable, but they are the product of a single transforming imagination. In dramatizing different themes, one imagination might act with essential uniformity in different works, as did Sophocles and Racine, or with great multiformity, as did Shakespeare. One thing that we should learn in trying to discover the generic nature of a dramatist's body of plays is, then, the imaginative style that dominates them, or the variation in imaginative styles of which the dramatist is capable. We should see whether his career as a whole shows definite alterations, whether the dramatist tends at different times to use one perspective or another. Thus we may come upon some additional means of placing him critically. If, however, we fall short of firm conclusions about the dramatist himself, we can hope to gain some insight into individual dramas.

Our best subjects, obviously, should be dramatists whose work has been influential or who have, as far as we can tell now, a fairly assured position in the theater or who have been writing long enough to provide a substantial body of work. Eugene O'Neill, Tennessee Williams, and Arthur Miller may be forgotten in time, but at present they make a strong claim on our attention. O'Neill dominated the American theater from 1920 until the 1940s, and Williams and Miller the theater of the next twenty-five years; and their most striking successors have yet to accumulate a body of work that would permit secure generalization about them. Through O'Neill, Williams, and Miller we should manage an adequate sampling of the American theater of this century.

I use "American" rather as a convenience than as a designation of a theatrical reality that can be distinguished from other national or regional realities. The ways of looking at reality that lead to different generic structures are human characteristics that tend to function in the same fundamental way regardless of place and time. Even in the more visible matters of convention, idiom, and style there are few national borders today; indeed, for five hundred years all national borders have been easily crossed by the theater. The three Americans whom we look at in this chapter belong also to the European theater, just as the three Europeans in Part III are very familiar to English-speaking audiences.

We are primarily concerned with plays in which the tragic may be supposed either to dominate or to lurk. This appears to be a straightforward quest. But our approach involves different, even apparently inconsistent, attitudes because an expectable human contradictoriness renders the situation with regard to "tragedy" ambiguous. Duerrenmatt, as we saw in chapter 1, both denies the possibility of tragedy in our day and uses the term *tragic* to describe contemporary or modern problems. He did not invent this practice of seeing at the same time the actuality and the impossibility of the tragic: it is a widespread habit. Some critics speak of tragedy as a thing of the past; many noncritics find tragedy all around us (the newspapers daily report what they call tragedies). On the one hand there is a kind of purity of thought, especially in those sectors that derive aesthetic forms from historical particularities rather than from human constants; on the other hand we find not so much an impurity as an imprecision of usage, in which terms reflect vague feelings rather than differentiations of experience. If we deny the possibility of tragedy, we foreclose the question of whether in fact tragedies are written or plays have tragic ingredients; if we apply the word *tragedy* to all kinds of human misfortunes and their representation on the stage, we lose all sense of the nature of tragedy and hence, as I proposed earlier, the power of making essential discriminations. In one case, the mind is too nearly closed; in the other, it is too nearly wide open. We need to find a flexible middle ground which does not accept a priori either a doctrinaire deficiency or an excess without doctrine. In the quest for a reasonable mean we have to resist extremes that take too easy a way out of the complications of experience. In this resistance we may have to insist, at one moment, that here are indeed tragedies and tragic accents, despite denials of their possibility, or, at another moment, that these are not tragedies though they have often been called so. In these rather contrasting responses the critic may seem self-contradictory or perverse. He can only hope that he does not seem so.

CHAPTER FOUR

Eugene O'Neill (1888-1953)

E UGENE O'Neill's characteristic vein is, in the popular sense of the word, "tragic": repeatedly his stage turns to woes, declines, failures, literal or living deaths. Often the inadequacies of his characters give them the air of "victims," and as soon as we use this word, we may wonder whether the characters are really tragic. Yet we find that O'Neill victims are rarely, if at all, innocent victims of outside forces—of hostile nature or of hostile society or of the recurrent catastrophes that disturb existence. They are, finally, victims of themselves; what happens to them comes out of character, not out of misfortune or irrational event. One cannot say that much without saying that O'Neill's sense of human experience is tragic. What is more, his way of conceiving character is generally that of the tragic writer: he sees a central dividedness, a clash of motives, discrepancy between the desired and the possible, the uneasy cohabitation of two personalities in one person. His sense of disunion in the individual is at times so strong that, to signalize one fragmented identity, he can use asides that express the true sensibility, masks that denote one phase of personality, or even two separate beings on the stage. Finally, many of his main characters feel at least some impulse to come to self-knowledge. More often than not, then, O'Neill is working within the realm of tragedy, and we need to see how steadily he remains in that realm and how far he penetrates it.

The truth is that in several characteristic ways he drifts out of that realm. O'Neill's passion for completeness—witness his interminable stage directions—leads him into very long plays that become novelistic; not that a novel cannot be tragic, but O'Neill's inclusiveness becomes epic, the crucial heights of experience flattened out by all the details of a record which in the end is simply the chronicle of a rise, decline, and fall. History can become tragic only insofar as we look at some critical moment abstracted from the full course of events; the descent into debility which terminates all chronicles is not tragic because it is not earned or avoidable. Again, O'Neill's passion for his subject sometimes attaches itself to the conceptual form of the subject, and the drama then becomes allegorical; with O'Neill, the conceptual and the experimental usually go hand in hand, the experimental leads into the expressionistic, and the expressionistic, as we have seen, is really the modern dress of the allegorical. In this mode, he rather demonstrates a meaning by character than creates a free character who first arouses the empathic imagination and whose meaning yields only to contemplation. Reuben Light in *Dynamo* "illustrates" the insufficiencies of machine-worship, though he also has some plausibility as a character.

On the other hand, when O'Neill is intuiting character rather than working out a proposition, the reality that impinges on his imagination habitually, though not exclusively, takes two special forms. In one, there is an excess of tragic potentiality, and the dividedness becomes schizoid; the split is pathogenically enlarged, and the character is or becomes ill. In the other, there is a defect of tragic potentiality. The split is between demands and capabilities; the protagonist fails, not through a hubristic assault upon unbreachable ramparts, but through not being up to the obstacle course of existence. Time and again O'Neill finds illness or weakness as the central human truth; when a dramatist thus fixes on the failure of personality, the result is melodrama of disaster. Though he paints several counterpictures of triumph, O'Neill's dominant sense is that of human incapacity; for him, this is ultimately manifested in man's inability to bear the truth about himself. Man is less inclined to discover his own imperfections than to rest in blame of others, or even of God. O'Neill's evangelists fail—Lazarus in *Lazarus Laughed* fails to evoke in men a durable, saving sense of immortality, and Hickey in *The*

Iceman Cometh fails to evoke an acceptance of self-knowledge. Hickey is mad; if he converted men, they would be destroyed, for illusion is their Rock of Ages. *Iceman*, in which doctrine and passion are most successfully fused in dramatic unity, is a key play for our purposes: in it O'Neill sums up ultimately his most persistent view of man as lacking the strength to encounter either life or himself. Hence we may suitably take it out of its chronological position among O'Neill's works and use it as a starting point.

I. "The Iceman Cometh": The Problem of Self-Knowledge

In *The Iceman Cometh* (copyright 1940, produced 1946) O'Neill looks squarely at the central crisis of tragic experience and declares that it is humanly unbearable. A group of has-beens, representing all walks of life in America and other countries, now live on drink and on talk of "tomorrow" (one man is actually known as "Jimmy Tomorrow") in a dismal rooming house and bar run by a man with the heavily allegorical name of Harry Hope. They anticipate the visit of Theodore Hickman, a high-pressure salesman whom they know as "Hickey"; he comes in periodically for a binge and prodigally sets up drunken parties which are the high points of their lives of sponging and of clinging to illusions about both past and future. This time, however, instead of dispensing joy by whiskey, Hickey announces a grander program of aid: he is going to bring them the "peace" which he himself has just found. The price of it is the surrender of "pipe dreams" (one of the central symbols in the play): he presses the inmates to sober up, get out of the asylum and into the world, and thus flee the illusions which, he argues, are a source of guilt and suffering to them. The trip outside—Hickey knows that it will be brief—will change their lives by making them see that they are living on illusions, on gratifying visions of the past and mirages of the future, and will thus free them from a fundamentally distressing falseness. *Veritas liberabit:* from guilt, and for peace. However, it does not work that way: trying to be sober and making a bluff at reentering the larger world outside fantasy are so hard on the inmates that they become despondent, sullen, suspicious, and quarrelsome to an almost murderous degree. Only after Hickey has gone for good do they again begin to drink easily, find that liquor again "works" for them, tell stories, and fall amiably back into the lies which are the foundation of their community. It is a powerful denial of the ability of man to endure self-knowledge.

The same denial is made with equal force by two other main lines of action. It turns out that Hickey, the persuasive salesman of self-knowledge, has found his peace by murdering a faithful wife whose forgiveness of his endless sins has burdened him with guilt. In the course of telling this story Hickey learns a new fact about himself, that he had always hated his wife: as a result of this discovery, he suddenly finds himself without illusions and, despite all his doctrine, without peace and so wants "to go to the Chair" (IV).[1] O'Neill's moral blow, which makes excellent theater, is a double one: the know-thyself man not only is a slick scoundrel, a murderer, and really a madman, but has deceived himself just like everyone else. Finally, Hickey's case is ironically paralleled in various ways by that of young Don Parritt, a revolutionary who has betrayed his revolutionary mother to the police "because," as he learns while listening to Hickey tell his tale, "I hated her" (IV). He commits suicide. Like everyone at Harry Hope's, he cannot live with true knowledge of himself.

In these different ways, then, O'Neill asserts the impossibility of the key action on which tragedy depends. He thus denies the possibility of tragedy: he gives man a choice between the melodrama of disaster and the melodrama of survival-by-illusion. In a number of details the picture of life in Harry Hope's place, which includes a brothel, strongly anticipates Genet's later picture of the brothel as a "house of illusions" in *The Balcony* (revised edition, 1962). But the striking difference between O'Neill's drama and Genet's is that in *The Balcony* the men are only visitors, for a brief time enjoying a masquerade (as Pope, Judge, General, and so forth) which is the first phase of sexual play, and then returning to the ordinary world of activity. As Irma, the "Queen," says of them, "When it's over, their minds are clear. I can tell from their eyes. Suddenly they understand mathematics. They love their children and their country."[2] But O'Neill's people have taken permanent sanctuary in their house of illusions, and "clear minds" are for them the one impossible state. O'Neill's antitragic manifesto is limited in one way, however: his characters do not finally convince us that they are the world. Rather they seem constricted, ill, living in an enclave around which, though we do not see it, there is a less sodden and decayed world, the one they cannot face. If this is true, then *Iceman* says only that, given this assemblage of dropouts, the stronger life of tragedy is not possible. Yet it speaks with such intensity that it is difficult not to feel that it is O'Neill's judgment of humanity at large.

The Iceman Cometh provides, then, a logical point of departure for an inspection of O'Neill's other plays and a name for one modern idiom.

II. Four Early Plays: Two Basic Patterns

In his first five years of writing full-length plays O'Neill produced four plays that naturally fall into two revelatory pairs—*Beyond the Horizon* (1920) and *All God's Chillun Got Wings* (1924), and *The Emperor Jones* (1920) and *Desire Under the Elms* (1924). Though both *Emperor Jones* and *All God's Chillun Got Wings* have black protagonists who fail in their programs of life, the plays are based on entirely different conceptions of character. *All God's Chillun* is really a successor of *Beyond the Horizon*, and Jim Harris is a black-skinned Robert Mayo: both men are weak idealists who muddle into taxing ways of life and gradually erode away pathetically in a bleak moral climate. Their careers provide the pattern for human disintegration that O'Neill would later trace in a number of different variations. On the other hand, the title character of *Emperor Jones* and the leading figures in *Desire Under the Elms* are strong, aggressive characters of much greater tragic potential. From these two introductory pairs of plays, O'Neill might have developed in either of two opposite directions.

"Beyond the Horizon" and "All God's Chillun Got Wings"

Beyond the Horizon initiates the main lines O'Neill would follow in what we may call, quite neutrally, his quasi-tragic plays. Here we see the decline into misery that, along with the impotent dragging on in misery of those already there, most characteristically expresses O'Neill's sensibility. Robert Mayo, with his "touch of the poet," [3] his consumption,[4] and his longing for distant scenes, is an earlier Edmund Tyrone, and the family wretchedness is a sketch for that of the Tyrones in *Long Day's Journey into Night* (1940). O'Neill spares nothing that can contribute to an atmosphere of suffering and failure.*

---

* Robert Mayo's parents die, his father of grief, and the death of Robert's young daughter is another turn of the always active screw of torment; his wife's mother is an intolerable nagger, Robert ruins the family farm because he is a hopelessly incompetent farmer; his wife Ruth comes to hate him and sinks into an apathetic

As in Chekhov's somber comedy, *The Sea Gull,* a central motif is that of the star-crossed lovers. Everyone takes it for granted that Andrew Mayo and Ruth Atkins will make a match of it and take over the farm while Robert romantically wanders over the globe in fulfillment of his dreams. But Robert also loves Ruth, she responds with what they both take to be love, and under the spell of this "bigger dream" (I.ii), Robert renounces travel and becomes a farmer. Andrew, still in love with Ruth, goes to sea. Robert's incompetence as a farmer helps cure Ruth of her romantic infatuation for him, and husband and wife "look into each other's eyes with something akin to hatred" (II.i)—an early appearance of a motif that O'Neill would use repeatedly later. Ruth now tells Robert, "I do love Andy. . . . I always loved him" (II.i). But Andy returns from a voyage and reports that he has long since got over the "foolishness" of thinking he loved Ruth. In these reversals there is a somewhat heavy irony that dwindles off into pathos. Robert's trite question when the original triangle developed, "Why did this have to happen to us?" (I.ii), helps create the impression of an irrational chance that is making a quite untragic mess of people's lives.

Yet O'Neill also makes Robert say, of the loves at cross purposes, "so senseless—and tragic" (I.ii). Though this is the loose popular use of the word, there is a way in which O'Neill does move toward a tragic view of Robert. A stage direction says that Robert "betrays the conflict going on within him" (I.i) when Ruth, having avowed her love, presses him to give up the dream of distant horizons for love on the farm. This is a possible version of the tragic division between impulses; yet the issues are so circumscribed—a vague dream versus domestic life—that the drama does not open out as it would if there were a moral component or, let us say, the kind of pressures that affect an Ibsen idealist. Robert's problem comes a shade too close to the kind of dilemma explicated in advice-to-the-lovelorn columns, and the conflict is resolved almost as easily as if Robert were following well-meant counsel. True, he makes a bad choice that not only ruins his life but contributes to the misery of other lives. Yet it is a choice made in simple innocence; it seems to be the choice of the greater good instead of the lesser; though it is an

slattern, and Robert dies. Robert's brother Andrew, the better disciplined, less imaginative Mayo who succeeds at sea and in business, is suddenly revealed, despite all the probabilities of character, as a speculator who is almost broke—the final evidence of O'Neill's determination to leave no possible hint of well-being undemolished.

error, it has in it none of the active self-deception and willfulness that often accompany self-aggrandizement. Robert passes through the stage of recrimination to the degree of self-knowledge which lets him admit that he has been a failure as a farmer and has dragged Ruth down; but his self-understanding is never directed toward the fundamental error of misconceiving, if not actually his emotions, at least their significance for the ordering of his life. Nor, indeed, has O'Neill chosen to approach the situation in these terms. Shortly before his death, in the posture that belongs to melodrama, Robert can still insist that Ruth and he "can both justly lay some of the blame for our stumbling on God" and can rather oracularly call Andrew "the deepest-dyed failure of the three" (III.i). Despite a certain struggling for lucidity and charity at the end, Robert remains too insignificant a person; we see the inevitable final collapse of someone whose weakness has been emphasized more than once (I.i; II.i). What we have is less a tragedy than the disaster of an inadequate personality reminiscent of Hardy's Jude Fawley, whose melancholy story, as well as that of Sue Bridehead, is more than once suggested by an O'Neill plot. Finally, in decor and conduct there is a persistent dinginess that cannot contribute to tragic effect.

Though *All God's Chillun* continues with the decent, aspiring husband who cannot live up to his hopes, it is a more complex, less prosaic play than *Beyond the Horizon*. Not only does it explore the difficulties of interracial marriage, but Jim Harris' white wife, Ella Downey, has a streak of vindictive husband-hating that makes Ruth Atkins seem only a conventional nagging wife. After Jim and Ella are married, their private life continues the public tensions that O'Neill has already shown us in the street life of a biracial section of New York. Yet here, just when we seem to be coming to the heart of a sociological melodrama—the pressure upon individuals of forces that lie outside their own character—the play leaves its documentary premises and moves into an inner life that is not, or at least need not be, of racial origin.* True, there is persistent talk of "black" and "white"; Jim keeps wanting to be whatever is meant by words that Ella first applies to him, "the

---

* The various whites and blacks who make the first half of the play essentially sociological disappear; in the second half there are only four characters, of whom one, Jim's mother, makes only a brief appearance. Jim's sister does have an important role, but she leaves two-thirds of the way through. Thence on, the stage belongs entirely to Jim and Ella and their small private world, a microcosm largely outside of social history.

whitest of the white" (I.iii; II.i, ii).[5] But just as in *Othello*, of which such passages are reminiscent, the word play uses literal facts mainly for their symbolic suggestiveness; in the end *All God's Chillun* is hardly more of a drama about interracial marriage than *Othello* is. Jim is less "a black" than he is a particular kind of person—a man of ambition partly impeded by his own awareness of being black, but ruined in the main by fanatic devotion to an inferior woman. Jim is the man who must love and who defines himself in devotion to another, and Ella is a woman torn between her own kind of love and the irrational impulse to destroy what she loves. Their fault is in themselves, not in their societal stars. This is dramatically much better than making them racial figures.

Yet while O'Neill is drawn from social document and history to the larger canvas of nontopical humanity, he is likewise driven, by a force that appears in play after play, to cut back that canvas and thus reduce its representative powers. In *All God's Chillun*, as in many of his plays, O'Neill's protagonists are hardly of tragic scope. Like Robert Mayo in *Beyond the Horizon*, Jim Harris is a descendant of Jude Fawley. For such men, few things ever go right; they are sweet, generous, and loving, but they have some defect of stamina and judgment which would make their survival dubious in any but ideal conditions. Their devotedness conceals what is little less than a craving to be victimized,* and they characteristically find either a woman who is openly destructive or one who pursues her own ends with a hardiness that may be destructive in effect (in the women the line of descent is from Hedda Gabler). In contrast with the pathos of Jim's fidelity and his failure as a law student, Ella Downey approaches the tragic in her split between an affectionate reliance on him and a savage wish to have him fail and to keep him down. On the one hand she "needs" him; on the other hand, with uncontrollable malice, she calls him "dirty nigger."

Though O'Neill may be putting a finger on unacknowledged or unrecognized attitudes that complicate race relations,† he really goes

---

* It is characteristic of this type, in brief moments of rebellion, to blame heaven. Jim closely echoes Robert Mayo when he says, "I don't see how He's [i.e., God] going to forgive—Himself" (II.iii). But a moment later he slips from melodramatic blame into a pathetic retraction and a prayer to be made "worthy of the child You send me for the woman You take away" (II.iii). The move from indignation to pathos is logical: from the melodrama of blame to that of the poor fellow.

† It is possible to interpret the latter part of the play as a symbolic version of interracial relations. The white "loves" and "needs" the black but wants to play

beyond this and identifies in Ella not only the hatred of any superior quality, especially that of which one is a beneficiary, but the leveling destructiveness that may be at variance with its possessor's own best interests. Whatever the occasion that brings it out,* she has a basic nastiness and malice, and her alternate struggling with this and yielding to it are in the tragic realm. The difficulty is, finally, that Ella is simply a sick woman. Her illness infects Jim; she passes through frenzy into a whimpering second childhood (when the first is hardly finished), and Jim from general weakness into grateful servitude. At the final curtain they are playing games in a childish fantasy that Osborne might have borrowed for the ending of *Look Back in Anger.* Here is another imagining of the regression which is central in *The Emperor Jones* and *Long Day's Journey* and even in *Strange Interlude,* of the drawing away from the world into a private sickbed reality as in *Mourning Becomes Electra.* Regularly in the early plays O'Neill reveals the preoccupation with the human inadequacy, the psychic or moral sickness, that would mold his career as a playwright and keep pushing him back from the attainable tragic form toward the drama of disaster.

"The Emperor Jones" and "Desire Under the Elms"

On the other hand, the title character of *The Emperor Jones* and the three principals of *Desire Under the Elms* are strong and active people; if one comes back to these plays after reading a good deal of later O'Neill, he is relieved to find protagonists of resolution and will. Jones is in some ways a traditional tragic hero—the man of hubris, the overreacher, the vain conqueror who feels that he can beat the game. *Desire Under the Elms* starts as a heavily ironic comedy on an ancient subject: aged husband (Ephraim Cabot) and young wife (Abbie), with everyone but the husband knowing that his grown son Eben is the father of the new baby whose birth is being celebrated. But it develops as a

the role of an irresponsible but all-powerful child worshiped by an "Uncle Tom" or "Negro Mammy," who is to be kept always in a subordinate position. The black makes this attitude possible by accepting the role, grateful for whatever morsels of devotion, or whatever kind of devotion, come his way. All this is rather subtly conveyed. However, the play does not really aim at such allegory.

* Ella's earlier ambivalence about blacks comes through as an expression of, rather than a source of, the schizoid personality that always appears in her relations with Jim. A childhood sweetheart of Jim's, she goes through a phase of being openly antiblack; she consorts promiscuously with unsavory whites, has a child by and is deserted by a tough prize fighter; and then, disillusioned and broke, she marries Jim, who has always been the faithful friend and admirer in the background.

virtually Jacobean revenge melodrama in which O'Neill gives full scope to his sense of the resentful, the rancorous, and the retaliatory in human beings; then, in this generic melange, two of the energetic and aggressive characters take on a tragic quality.

To Emperor Jones, O'Neill attributes "an underlying strength of will, a hardy, self-reliant confidence in himself that inspires respect" (p. 175); [6] Jones can boast, "From stowaway to Emperor in two years!" and reply, when told he is lucky, "But I makes dat luck . . ." (i). Here is something of the hero who incorporates mankind's tragic dimension: the characteristic impulse to vent the ego upon the world—in forthright exercise of talent, in violent assertiveness, in triumph through brilliance that denies all limits. Jones is quite different from the more frequent O'Neill characters who dissolve before reality, whose discords are rooted in disability. *The Emperor Jones* is in contrast with another one-acter, Synge's *Riders to the Sea*, where outer nature continues to triumph over beings who simply go mechanically on their way, targets without resources to preserve themselves. It has some parallels with greater plays in both tragic and melodramatic realms. Like Richard III, Jones has nightmare visions of men whom he has done in. Exactly like Macbeth, he is terrified of supernatural visitants but endeavors to reestablish his manliness by protesting the normal areas of fearlessness: "I ain't skeered o' real men" (v). But in the realm of political entrepreneurs, he reminds us less of Macbeth than of Richard III and even, at a large remove, Tamburlaine. In the end, Tamburlaine falls when his physical being gives out, Jones when his nervous system is not up to the strains put upon it.

Yet if in the context of O'Neill's heroes, Jones is at least an active, affirmative being, in the context of tragic heroes generally, he lacks stature. He is simply a racketeer; he has none of the moral perceptiveness that for half the play keeps Macbeth in terrible inner conflict. True, he falls at one point (v) into prayerful self-accusation that resembles the onset of remorse, but he achieves instead a mechanical tabulation of misdeeds intended to appease "Lawd Jesus" and secure better protection against the terrors of the forest; it is the suppliant's gesture of humility rather than the self-judgment issuing from a new moral alertness that re-creates the order violated by the original act of hubris. Instead of expanding and becoming capable of new understanding, the consciousness of this hero keeps on shrinking until all that is left is a primitive sensibility dominated by superstitious terror. In the end we have, with a surprising irony, a new version of the O'Neill hero crumbling before stresses of existence, diminishing until he is destroyed.

In one sense the play touches on the old problem of the discrepancy between ambition and talent. This discrepancy can become the tragic dividedness if the ambition takes on the coloring of a characteristic hubris, and the talent is an image of the morally possible. But this seldom happens. Talent is most often simply the degree of formal adequacy to task. Inadequacy is pathetic, not tragic; and for that reason Jones's decline is no more than pathetic. Further, the decline in the world does not paradoxically coincide with spiritual recovery; instead, the decline is total, embodying as it does a regression into a hysterical primitiveness. As soon as we become aware of the pattern of backward movement through anthropological time, we realize that Jones exists, no longer as a moral being, but as an illustration of some special mechanisms of personality. The failure of his sophistication, which might be given moral significance, becomes simply the breakdown of inadequate psychic equipment. One other aesthetic element militates against tragic effect: O'Neill's tireless insistence on the idiosyncrasies of uneducated speech means that verbal farce is always uncomfortably close.

In *Desire Under the Elms* the family antagonisms make vigorous melodrama; unlike many O'Neill characters, the Cabots are energetic, and they really "desire." The stage directions and the dialogue that present the hatred between Ephraim Cabot, the hard, driving farmer and tyrannical father aged seventy-five, and his sons, aged thirty-nine, thirty-seven, and twenty-five, are full of such words as "vindictive," "spite," and "hatred"; * the mutual hostility reaches a climax when Ephraim marries thirty-five-year-old Abbie,† and a triangle involving Ephraim, Abbie, and Eben, the youngest son, develops. Abbie, who has married Ephraim only for the farm, clearly dislikes him, feels attracted

---

* References are to the text in volume 1 of the three-volume edition. Eben feels "vengeful passion" because he believes that Cabot killed his mother (Cabot's second wife)—"he was slavin' her to her grave" (I.ii). Ephraim's attitude to his sons is, "I've sworn t'live a hundred an' I'll do it, if on'y t' spite yer sinful greed!" (I.ii).

† Of the marriage Eben says, "with vicious hatred," "It's jest t' spite us" (I.iii); and the two elder sons, "with sudden vindictive anger," decide to loaf and drink until the bridal pair reach the farm (I.iii). They resolve on a better life in California, and Eben buys their share of the farm with gold stolen from Ephraim.

to Eben, and starts wooing him; though he feels an answering attraction, he is hostile to her as a rival claimant for the farm. His offishness and combativeness lead Abbie into an ancient pattern of revenge: * she tells Ephraim that Eben "lusts" for her, and then has a hard time fighting off Ephraim's determination to "end" Eben (II.i). In Eben the conflict between desire for and antagonism toward Abbie is resolved when Abbie plays mother to Eben—an early instance of O'Neill's sense of the mother-mistress ambiguity in sexual life—and Eben concludes that loving Abbie is a filial duty: "It's her vengeance on him" (II.iii), that is, his mother's vengeance on Ephraim. Here O'Neill skillfully elaborates the revenge pattern, revealing the self-gratification behind the façade of obligation. Ephraim then makes Eben think that Abbie has been using him, and Eben determines, in a fury, "I'll git my vengeance too!"—on both Abbie and his father (III.ii,iii). To prove to Eben that she loves him, Abbie kills their baby (who would inherit the property); Eben, horrified and infuriated, shouts, "But I'll take vengeance now! I'll git the Sheriff!" (III.iii). The tricornered recriminations and threats of violence are the climax of forceful revenge melodrama. Then they fade out, Eben acknowledges his own complicity in the death of the baby, and his new self-understanding—Abbie and he are taken off together by the sheriff—works toward a final tragic note.

The tragic developments—the act of violence and the acknowledgment of responsibility—come late in the play, and it is possible that the young lovers achieve a too easy serenity at the end. Hence the final tragic note may seem an uneasy codicil to a work that is essentially a revenge melodrama. Yet, in the context of O'Neill's plays generally, what is remarkable here is the strength and vigor of the protagonists. For once we do not have ailing people, people in retreat, people who cannot stand the truth, people who regress, people whose inadequacy leads them to drink, dope, disease, fantasy, and self-enclosure. They oscillate between the egotism of revenge and the tragic egotism—between getting even with the world for a real or imagined slight and getting ahead of a world in which they seem to have special immunities. They are much closer to birds of prey than to lame ducks, to the large figures that represent mankind in its hubris than to the smaller men whose incapacities make them seem only deviant and pathetic. At this

---

* Here, of course, O'Neill uses the myth that appears in the stories of Joseph and Potiphar's wife and of Phaedra and Hippolytus, but he makes many alterations.

point O'Neill seems to be discovering the kind of character out of which major tragedy can come.

III. Allegorical Plays: The Problem of Faith

Within a few years, however, O'Neill turned toward the novelistic (*Strange Interlude* and *Mourning Becomes Electra*) and the allegorical —modes not likely to carry to further depths the tragic potentialities of *The Emperor Jones* and *Desire Under the Elms*. Four allegorical dramas, our business in the present section, are in an expressionistic style that technically can encompass tragic effect. But for fullness of character, they tend to substitute symbolizations of emotive, psychic, and conceptual elements abstracted from the human complex, and thus to appeal to the spirit of dissection and identification rather than to the instinct for empathy. Three plays came out in a rush—*The Great God Brown* (1926), *Lazarus Laughed* (1927), *Dynamo* (1929)—and the fourth, *Days Without End*, appeared not long after (1934). In this series of morality plays, characters wear masks that denote phases of personality, literally act out metaphors that define them (for example, love of a machine), or appear on stage as two simultaneously present entities. We are asked to attend to the meaning rather than the free functioning of character; the dramatist less represents conduct than underlines what the conduct represents, less intuits character than interprets it, less creates meaningful figures than invents figurative beings. As a writer of moralities O'Neill is repeatedly concerned with problems of belief, with "life" and "love" as values that may be symbolically expressed by laughter, and with a Mephistophelian destructive negativism as a principal threat to spiritual well-being. The problem is whether O'Neill's sense of character can evade his diagnostic intentions.

"The Great God Brown"

In *The Great God Brown* O'Neill uses two dualities, one essentially melodramatic, the other potentially tragic. The former is that of two high-school friends, Billy Brown and Dion Anthony. Billy is the well-organized, handsome, decent, friendly, extrovert, success-bound All-American boy; Dion, "dark, spiritual, poetic, passionately supersensitive, helplessly unprotected in [his] childlike, religious faith in life" (Prologue),[7] is the artist or martyr or saint who opts out of the world in which Billy assumes a managerial role. If this is a version of the bourgeois-bohemian confrontation that haunted Thomas Mann, O'Neill gives it freshness and force, partly through the paradoxical love-hate relationship of the two types (a frequent O'Neill theme), but principally through his picture of the duality in Dion Anthony, whose name suggests both Dionysus and St. Anthony. In him O'Neill reveals an almost Joycean sense of the convergence of mythic beings and of the subterranean ties between apparently independent personalities, and in presenting him O'Neill relies most heavily on the use of masks. The unmasked Dion—the "real face" (Prologue)—is "shrinking, shy and gentle, full of a deep sadness," troubled, unsure, inquiring, unprotected by attitudes, joyful in love, and in love able to say, "O God, now I believe" (Prologue). This personality develops throughout the play, "more strained and tortured, but . . . more selfless and ascetic" (I.i). To give an impression of unmasked Dion, O'Neill presents him as reading the Bible and Thomas à Kempis, praying, believing or seeking belief,[8] painting "in an endeavor to see God!" (I.iii), and uses such words as "pure, spiritual and sad," "an ascetic, a martyr," "spiritual calm and human kindliness," "gentler, more spiritual, more saintlike and ascetic" (I.iii; II.i,ii). He finds a strengthening friend in "Cybel," a prostitute who, unmasked, is Cybele, the Mother Earth type who appears more than once in O'Neill (I.iii; II.i); but his "heart-broken cry" of "Mother" to her is no more sustaining than is a prayer of "ascetic fervor" (II.i). When he finally dies, the others see his "Christian Martyr's face," which leads Billy Brown to say contemptuously, "So that's the poor weakling you really were!" (II.iii).

Billy, however, admires Dion's mask: "Say what you like, it's strong if it is bad! And this is what Margaret loved, not you" (II.iii). Margaret is Dion's wife, the mother of his three sons, a faithful, courageous sort of All-American woman who in high school had been fascinated by Dion and had chosen him over Billy Brown, a "good loser" (a version of the basic triangle in *Beyond the Horizon*). Though Billy is not always the most perceptive person in the world, he is entirely right about the mask; Margaret has never known the "true" Dion and has actually been frightened by occasional glimpses of him; O'Neill's originality has been to make her responses almost the opposite of those of Margaret in Goethe's *Faust*. For the mask Margaret has loved is a "fixed forcing" of Dion's "own face . . . into the expression of a mocking, reckless, defiant, gayly scoffing and sensual young Pan" (Prologue). He is always

ironic and detached; and it is O'Neill's perceptiveness to identify this
as the alter ego of the saint-artist-believer. In the midst of a prayer Dion
"suddenly claps his mask over his face again with a gesture of despair
and his voice becomes bitter and sardonic"; he addresses God with a
jaunty sneer (Prologue). As a lover he woos Margaret with an "ironic
mastery" of romantic rhetoric; he speaks as "the Great God Pan," and
after a nocturnal episode announces "Great Pan is dead" and treats
"mockingly" Margaret's statement that she is "ashamed" (Prologue).
Seven years later, after marriage, the mask (like the portrait of Dorian
Gray) is "older, more defiant and mocking, its sneer more forced and
bitter, its Pan quality becoming Mephistophelean," and it "has already
begun to show the ravages of dissipation" (I.i). As husband he is cease-
lessly ironic, especially about himself, but Margaret continues to be devoted in the maternal * way that O'Neill emphatically imputes to both
her and Cybel. Nearly broke because of dissipation, he thinks with
"diabolical, ironical glee" (I.i) of working for Billy Brown; Cybel calls
him "Kid Lucifer" (I.iii); and when she mentions Brown, Dion automatically puts on his mask, "now terribly ravaged. All of its Pan quality has changed into a diabolical Mephistophelean cruelty and irony"
(II.i). As he sinks toward death, the "mocking irony" of his masked face
"becomes so cruelly malignant as to give him the appearance of a real
demon, tortured into torturing others" (II.iii). He thinks of himself as
a Pan who, "forbidden the light and warmth of the sun . . . became
the Prince of Darkness" (II.iii).

In Dion and his mask O'Neill struggles in an almost frenzied way to
embody different potentialities of the more sentient, more imaginative,
more creative kind of man, who can be seeker or scorner, believer or
destructive skeptic, ascetic or debauchee, saint or devil. In this portrait there is a kind of arranged inclusiveness that prevents Dion from
really coming through as a character; one senses him less as a tragically
divided person than as a symbolic confluence of alternative possibilities
which coexist until the end, one chosen by some men, the other by
others, in accordance with need and context. Dion is less a saint flawed
by unbelief, or a splendid skeptic flawed by a martyr complex, than he
is a compendium of all the impulses that may be found in Everyman

---

* Once she thinks alternately of Dion as "my Daddy-O" and as "my little boy"
(Prologue). In play after play O'Neill shows himself fascinated by the coalescence
of the maternal, filial, and erotic, as experienced by the woman or sought by the
man; and some of his men also play a compound role analogous to this.

on his contemplative-imaginative-aesthetic side. He is most a person, and least a symbolic container, in his antagonism to Brown, the managerial type; but when Cybel tells Brown that women love Dion because "He's alive!" (II.i), and Dion describes himself as "life's lover" and Brown as "unloved by life" (II.iii), and finally declares "I am love!" and hence the object of Brown's bitter envy (II.iii), we pass from a drama of character to a laborious melodrama of ideas. The allegorical drift becomes more emphatic when Dion, dying, bequeaths himself to Brown; when Brown, putting on Dion's mask, is accepted as Dion by Margaret and makes her such a newly vigorous lover that she is happy as never before; and when Brown, exhausted by the strain of the dual life, made manic by being Dion and sharing his duality, and comforted like Dion by Cybel (who indeed calls him "Dion Brown"), finally dies much in the manner of Dion. The movement to allegory is complete when Cybel tells a police officer that the dead man's name is "Man!" (IV.ii) and recites a short prose lyric on the theme, "Always spring comes again bearing life!" (IV.ii). Death is a phase of life; the final message, for which there has been no dramatic preparation, is the cyclical return.

Yet in spots the oppressive meaning is shoved aside by the pressure of a recurrent O'Neill sense of character. Twice O'Neill calls Dion's mask "Mephistophelean"—the same adjective that he would apply to James Tyrone in *Long Day's Journey* and *Moon for the Misbegotten*, and the same concept that would shape Loving in *Days Without End*. As a dramatist O'Neill was haunted by the thought of skeptical mockery as a destroyer of the human personality; it is close to the center of his imaginative energies, so that his destructive characters of this stamp not only earn the label "demonic" often applied to them but also tend to take over the play. Hence the formal banishment of despair in *The Great God Brown*, as well as later in *Days Without End*, seems a willed alteration of the outcome demanded by the pressure of characterological evidence, rather than the earned rediscovery that is the difficult final phase of the tragic rhythm. If we doubt Cybel's seasonal lyric "Always again! . . . Spring again!" we have even less ground for believing in Billy Brown's ability to assert, while dying, that "the laughter of Man returns to bless and play again in innumerable dancing gales of flame upon the knees of God!" (IV.ii; compare John Loving's words that close *Days Without End*: "Life laughs with God's love again!"). The real dramatic strength is in the no-saying diabolic characters, the faithless, faith-annihilating, desperate beings who ever turn blackly inward and downward. Even at the rare moments when he asserts a new life for them or beyond them, O'Neill seems still the dramatist of spiritual disaster, just as he will be later in the compulsively black plays like *The Iceman Cometh* and *Long Day's Journey*.

"Lazarus Laughed"

While the theme of the Mephistophelian destroyer is the bridge between *The Great God Brown* and *Days Without End*, the bridge from *The Great God Brown* to the immediately following *Lazarus Laughed* has at least four strands: the use of masks, the Dionysian value, the Cybelian proclamation of the eternal springtime renewal, and the Billy Brown view of laughter as the symbol of hopeful life. *Lazarus Laughed* makes a full formal statement of the idea of the good that was rather hastily tacked on in the final scene of *The Great God Brown*. In experiencing "death" Lazarus has learned that though men may die, there is no death for Man. (In Athens, significantly, Lazarus is taken for Dionysus—a nice leap of O'Neill's syncretistic imagination.) Not only does Lazarus preach this inspiriting doctrine of immutability, but he presents it symbolically by a talent for laughter which has a remarkable effect on people; they laugh, too, and this manifests the power of salvation working in them. In using this dramatic device, O'Neill teeters on a razor's edge of risk between brilliance and bathos; while a crowd's breaking into laughter as evidence of spiritual conversion is fraught with the danger of unsought farce, still individual styles in laughter are skillfully used to reveal moral composition, and "infectious laughter" is an original symbol of the power of a charismatic personality actuated by a salvationary idea.

Lazarus Laughed is a philosophical melodrama,* and the contending forces are ones which a quarter of a century later would become clichés of popular psychology. Hackneyed as "on the side of life" and "on the side of death" have become, they maintain here a certain freshness that belongs to the work of the heuristic rather than the echoic imagination (in contrast with *Strange Interlude*, where O'Neill seems posi-

---

* One might also call it an allegoric panorama or, in cinematic terms, a "colossal" allegory. It ranges over the ancient world at the dawn of Christianity, from Israel to Athens, Rome, and Capri; its main characters are Caligula, Tiberius, Mary, Martha, and Lazarus; and there are large choruses of Nazarenes, Orthodox Jews, Athenians, and Roman legionaries, senate, and populace.

tively to have discovered banalities). Inflicting pain, torturing, killing, all evidences of fear—these are the hallmarks of the death-oriented mind; and O'Neill exercises a great deal of dramatic ingenuity in representing the force and pervasiveness of this cast of mind, as well as of the Life-Love-Laughter way of believing and energizing. Lazarus' doctrine keeps swaying men, from anonymous crowds to individual rulers, toward a happier, easier, more generous way of life. As they go from antagonism and skepticism toward belief and the surprised discovery of a new well-being, and then often into backsliding and the old hostilities, and on into vindictiveness or uncertainty or renewed hope, we are aware of a conflict of motives and possibilities pushing men now in this direction, now that. Yet we are hardly drawn into an action centered in a divided representative personality; rather we see an almost impersonal assemblage of personalities representing the vagaries of an idea in the body of mankind. Lazarus, with his mystic vision of deathlessness, shines on serenely, a symbolic luminousness emanating from him to astonish men; all that happens to him—even, at the end, death by fire —does not cut off the gentle equanimity and the power to laugh that always move men and that even shake the cynicism of Tiberius and Caligula. O'Neill has written a chronicle of an evangelical doctrine held with passion and professed with coercive genius.

Despite the frequent intensity of episodes, and the often brilliant detail of an expressionistic quasi history that anticipates Frisch and Duerrenmatt, *Lazarus Laughed* is fundamentally abstract in conception; when drama elaborates creed, it can hardly be kept from being talky, and this drama has, in its later parts, an air of long-drawn-out argument. True, the argument is about a human conflict that could be given a tragic formulation; this is approached in the dividedness of Caligula's response to Lazarus, in his mingling of triumph and remorse at the death of Lazarus; but he is a secondary figure, and a grotesque one at that, a sketch for the complex being that Camus would produce two decades later.

"Days Without End"

The allegorical bent in *The Great God Brown* and *Lazarus Laughed* continues most markedly in *Days Without End*, which has a comparable dualism and carries the expressionistic presentation of divided character to an ultimate form. The superficial story is simple enough: a disillusioned John Loving breaks away from the Catholic Church but in the end recovers a saving faith. In the underlying morality play, the virtues and vices contending for John Loving's soul are familiar psychic forces. On the one hand there is the impulse toward faith and belief, to take things on trust, to love freely, to forego the questions that destroy the capacity for spontaneous joy—in a word, to escape from a doubting and accusing ego. O'Neill treats this as a basic part of human equipment, a part that may, however, be damaged and deformed. When, despite his prayers, both his parents die in a flu epidemic, John Loving, a devout fifteen-year-old, revolts against faith and church; however, the rest of his life is a series of alternative faiths—atheism, socialism, anarchism, Marxism, Buddhism, and finally, in a happy marriage, a devotion to his wife on which all of his existence seems to depend. (Compare, in Miller's *After the Fall*, Quentin's loss of belief in "some final saving grace! Socialism once, then love. . . ." [9]) On the other hand there is the central vice: the doubting, skeptical, destructive spirit insistently rational in manner and assumptions, yet ultimately committed to laying bare the illusory character, the meaninglessness, of any faith or belief, to annihilating whatever stands as a barrier against despair, be it religious devotion, secular faith, personal love, or even courage or stoical endurance. Wherever it turns, this spirit finds *nada*. Here again O'Neill anticipates what would become a hackneyed literary practice, tracing Loving's sick nihilism to a trauma [10] (his parents' death) that left him with a shattering sense of betrayal; to forestall other betrayals, he denies the reality of any emotional or psychic support that might some time give way. At once preventive and revengeful, his nadaism is clung to and indeed extended in every direction, until suicide is the logical end. His conflict includes even the love-hate nexus which O'Neill had already used in *Beyond the Horizon* and *All God's Chillun* (and which would become another cliché of later writers). John Loving feels that his life depends upon his wife Elsa's love; yet with the dark side of his nature he wants not to be at the mercy of love, and he makes a subtle, and all but successful, effort to kill it and Elsa. Her death would be the first step in his suicide.

In presenting John Loving, *Days Without End* carries on from *The Great God Brown* in two notable ways. Though the word itself is not used, the destructive side of John Loving is clearly "Mephistophelean"; at the very end, before the cross, his negative spirit sums up in

Goethian terms, "No! I Deny!" (IV.ii).[11] There are several suggestions of the demonic in the cynical component of John Loving, and his wife Elsa's response to this component is quite like Margaret's response to Faust's sinister friend.* Again, *Days Without End* gambles on a striking expressionistic device for presenting split character to the audience; it goes beyond *The Great God Brown* by actually having two persons on stage to objectify contrasting phases of personality. "John" is the naïve, honest, believing or wanting-to-believe component, "Loving" the cynical denier,† the voice of despair and death. However, while we see Loving as a separate body, other characters do not see him; they simply hear his words as if spoken by "John," and "at times one or another may subtly sense his presence" (I). Loving's face is "the death mask of a John who has died with a sneer of scornful mockery on his lips" (I)—a reminiscence in this play of the death-in-life theme which dominates the slightly earlier *Mourning Becomes Electra*.

The very substance of the drama is the division of forces in John Loving. Hence, like its early forebears, this morality is in "the realm of tragedy"; its own special mark is the severity of the conflict between "John" and "Loving." But the brilliant method of turning phases of personality into different dramatis personae has a price: it pushes the divided character toward the schizoid state which is the pathological condition of tragic man. The character actually seems broken apart, and it is difficult, not so much to put the pieces together logically, as to sense a unitary being with disparate impulses. John Loving is now one,

* John Loving at one time feels that "he really had given his soul to some evil power" (III.i) and that "something outside him, a hidden spirit of evil, took possession of him" (III.i). Elsa always shrinks from her husband's cynical style (in contrast with Margaret—a coincidental name?—who in *The Great God Brown* is attracted to that energetic and aggressive side of Dion which goes on to become Mephistophelian and denying). Even Elsa's friend Lucy Hillman is shocked when, in an adulterous act which she is glad to commit with John Loving, she finds in him, not sexual passion, but a revengeful love-killing spirit.

† One wonders if O'Neill knew S. N. Behrman's *The Second Man* (produced, 1927), in which the male lead, a gay and insouciant writer (played by Noel Coward in the first English production), laments the presence of "someone else inside me— a second man—a cynical, odious person, who keeps watching me, who keeps listening to what I say, grinning and sophisticated, horrid . . ." (London: Martin Secker, 1928, II.i). In an epigraph Behrman attributes the term and the concept to Lord Leighton, the painter. However, what is little more than a momentary brake on romantic and sentimental feeling in Behrman's play becomes, in O'Neill's, a destructive total disbelief. Incidentally, the "John" character in *The Second Man* discovers the hate-love ambivalence that O'Neill develops much more fully: ". . . I wanted to hurt you. I hated you, Monica. . . . But all the time . . . I loved you. You were inside of me. I was desperate—to tear you out" (III).

now the other; his situation is not unlike that of Bosola in *The Duchess of Malfi*, yet Bosola, despite all his abrupt shifting from one role to another, is a whole being in a way that John Loving never quite is. The play demonstrates division schematically rather than dramatizes it as a not altogether transparent disturbance of complex but integral character.

Again, the excessive clarity of the dividedness serves to reveal weaknesses in the imagining of John, the "good" component in the tragic hero. Loving's vindictive nihilism comes through as a powerful and relentless force, energized by the dominant inclination of modern sensibility, which, though not unopposed, is strong in O'Neill. John, on the other hand, is a rather naïve and boyish chap, meaning well, hopeful, enthusiastic, hastily utopian, lacking both the stable central simplicity and the trained maneuverability of mind that are the best bulwarks against corrosive skepticism. He seems rather a setup for Loving, and we have little confidence in his ability to endure the battering of Loving's Everlasting No's. The drama does not give us a sense of recuperative powers in John Loving, and we seem inevitably on the way to another O'Neill drama of disaster. O'Neill perceives the crisis of personality very much like Hardy, who in Sue Bridehead offers a precociously early gauging of the cost of a hypertrophic rationalism, of the crushing strain felt by a personality deprived of nonrational supports. Sue and Loving both exalt reason and call religious faith "superstition." Then, in crucial scenes of amazing similarity, Sue and John Loving both seek out a church and kneel at the foot of the cross. The trauma of death, which once undermined John Loving's belief, now undermines the disbelief of both of them. Sue, however, is smitten with guilt and rebounds into a self-flagellating hyperreligiosity; John Loving, whose despairing nihilism was self-punitive and self-destructive, now finds a restorative faith. The question is whether "John," on the edge of the abyss, really had enough strength to come back and defeat "Loving."

John Loving's hair-breadth recovery affords less the tragic sense of continuity, of the agonized illumination that saves catastrophes from meaninglessness, than it does the gratifications attendant upon the last-minute rescue, before catastrophes have taken place, in the truly popular melodrama. The action demonstrates, of course, what Father Baird calls "the grace of faith" (IV.i).* We can simply settle for the

---

* A still sharper turnabout is that of John Loving's wife Elsa, who, a virtual suicide in her "despairing bitterness" at "Loving's" murderous vindictiveness, sud-

meaning, as in the morality. But there is one way out of the characterological problem (our suspicion that John Loving is too far gone for recovery)—the phenomenon of conversion.

O'Neill has certainly a grasp of this psychic reality, for he made partial use of it in The Great God Brown and dramatized the difficulty of it in Lazarus Laughed. In a sense he is doing here what he refused to do three years before in Mourning Becomes Electra, writing a conclusion in the spirit of The Eumenides. The term "Oresteian conversion" will do for the psychic event that closes the play, for the vindictiveness personified in "Loving" has some resemblance to that of the Erinyes; each dramatist gives objective being to the force that distorts the personality, and the final action is the freeing of the personality from that force. However, if O'Neill is belatedly utilizing the rich materials of The Eumenides, he also attenuates the Oresteian conversion. For Aeschylus depicts the Erinyes as both changing and enduring; though they have a new function, they still exist, and their ministry is not one without danger to those who disregard them. They represent a permanent fund of energy, and it must continue to make itself felt in the human soul. In Days Without End, on the other hand, "Loving" is miraculously beaten down by "John" ("as if some invisible force crushed him down" [IV.ii]), and finally rolls over beneath the cross, a corpse. Aside from the awkwardness of this physical death of a segment of the personality, John seems to be getting out of it too easily. All the "Loving" energy is evaporated, and John Loving is home free.

As an artist contemplating the problem of human salvation, O'Neill is a kind of manic-depressive: in such plays as The Iceman Cometh and Mourning Becomes Electra he can do nothing but despair, and then in Days Without End can have his chief character soar up from the depths to an "ecstatic mystic vision" and declare "Exaltedly," echoing the hero of Lazarus Laughed, "Love lives forever! Death is dead!" (IV.ii). On the one hand the tragic tone is crushed under incurable misery, on the other it floats away on the breezes of triumph.*

denly bursts out of a "half-coma," decides to "forgive" her husband, and promptly is on the road to health (IV.i).

* The characteristic tragic ending is like recovery from a plague; it is a recovery, but great damage has been done, and whoever survives is marked by it. That is what the action of Days Without End seems to require, but O'Neill's ending is rather like recovery from a childhood illness, with everybody surviving unmarred. The total salvation that comes along in due course appears in a different way in Fry's Sleep of Prisoners, where there is a kind of "epic survival" of trials.

"Dynamo"

If *Days Without End* was chronologically the last of the allegorical series, its predecessor *Dynamo* already prefigured a move back to the realistic mode. Though one central action—Reuben Light's worship of the dynamo—is entirely a metaphor for a central idea, the dramatization on the whole is naturalistic rather than conceptual. The action turns on a question which obviously would not leave O'Neill at peace— the problem of faith, skepticism, and the religion of rationality which penetrates the whole allegorical series. But Reuben Light experiences the problem rather than represents it; as a personality he is molded not only by ideas but by the sexual ambiguities that were touched on by *Desire Under the Elms* and that strongly interested O'Neill in the late twenties and early thirties. Reuben, a minister's son, feels the dangerous impact of his father's narrow and vindictive Protestantism, of their neighbor Ramsey Fife's equally narrow and vindictive atheism, of Ada Fife's coquettishness, of his mother's jealousy of Ada, and of his own oedipal attachment and its jealous possessiveness. The sex problems make *Dynamo* a link between the immediately preceding *Strange Interlude* (1928) and the immediately following *Mourning Becomes Electra* (1931); Reuben to some extent anticipates Orin Mannon. *Dynamo* is likewise a link between the other allegorical plays and the later Tyrone plays through the Mephistophelian skepticism which appears slightly in Fife, the atheistic electrician, and with greater intensity in Reuben when he is disillusioned by his mother (she sides with his father against him) and revolts against the parental brand of Christianity. Mrs. Fife is an amateur version of the Great Mother played by Cybel in *The Great God Brown.*

While *Dynamo* has these various ties with other O'Neill plays, its strongest thematic connection is with *Days Without End.* Reuben Light is an earlier John Loving who rejects his original faith,* but in *Dynamo* the stress is upon the new disbeliever's need for a new faith.

---

* The allegorical series consistently makes evident the religious awareness that was an important element in O'Neill's sensibility. He has always a strong sense of man as a worshiping being, whether man seeks an Earth Mother divinity or a transcendental reality; but O'Neill has an equally strong sense of all the powers of skepticism and negation that cut man off from visions of salvation (a theme that Tennessee Williams touches on for the first time in *The Milk Train Doesn't Stop Here Anymore*). Repeatedly the latter leads to despair.

Whereas John Loving would rush from one quasi-religious ism to another, Reuben Light plunges from Christian belief into a scientific rationalism that quickly takes on a religious aura. Reuben hardly has time to experience the strains of pure rationalism—another O'Neill theme—because he instinctively shifts from a Christian to a scientific puritanism. For him, electricity is God, and the Dynamo is "her" Divine Image on earth; [12] the "her" refers to the "great Mother," also imaged by Mrs. Fife and in Reuben's mind associated with his own mother. He literally worships the Dynamo; he expects that it will make a revelation or give a "sign" to him; he prepares himself for it by flagellation; like a saint in the desert, he feels that he must conquer his physical desire for Ada.

In the Dynamo scenes in Act III there is a good deal of expressionistic brilliance; O'Neill finds a fresh, extraordinary way of dramatizing the power of the religious impulse. To this he imparts a tragic dimension by stressing the ignorance and self-deception of the protagonist, who has an imperious sense of rightness that he relentlessly imposes on others. In his need to discover the fount of truth Reuben believes that he is freeing himself from old errors and falsities, but unknowingly he is transferring an old pattern of belief—in which the basic flaw is a sense of transcendent powers conferring privileges upon himself—to a new vision of reality. However, instead of finding a tortured way through catastrophe to enlightenment, Reuben simply advances in his infatuation until he plunges into final disaster. While still hoping for a "miracle" from the Dynamo, Reuben, kissing Ada "just once . . . to prove I'm purified" (III.ii),[13] yields to his passion for her, feels with horror that he has "betrayed" the Great Mother, shoots Ada, and, imploringly embracing the "Mother," is electrocuted, his final sound a "moan that is a mingling of pain and loving consummation" (III.iii).

As so often in O'Neill, the potential tragic hero dwindles into the sick man who is destroyed by his own weakness or his dissociation from reality. The divided man becomes the schizoid who goes to pieces. Once he has rebelled against home and faith, Reuben appears to be an addition to the small group of vigorous O'Neill heroes—Emperor Jones and Eben Cabot. In arrogance and the appearance of strength, Reuben seems the erring man who might make his way through deep troubles to a better wisdom. But the disaster of the personality that always haunts O'Neill's imagination overtakes Reuben, and the final note is one of disintegration. Instead of the drama of tragic rashness we have the history of pathetic illusion, ending, Ibsen-fashion, in theatrical sudden death. In that, *Dynamo* looks backward and forward to many of the realistic plays.

IV. Epic Dramas: Natural History and Inferno

During the "allegorical period" O'Neill was also writing very long plays—*Strange Interlude* (1928) and *Mourning Becomes Electra* (1931)—and was at work on the epic "Tale of Possessors Self-dispossessed." [14] Length and comprehensiveness, which one would ordinarily note only as an aspect of technical experimentation, are interesting to us here because they reveal that in some part of himself O'Neill was instinctively the historian, the man who wanted to lay out the entire record in documentary detail rather than compress it into a dramatic précis that would only imply a history while staying formally within the intensities of a crux. Imagine a play that took Lady Macbeth from a teen-age trauma through a gamut of desires, dissatisfactions, and disasters or near-disasters into middle-aged quietude and indifference! Whatever the concentration, passion, or frenzy possible to some of the episodes, a dogged inclusiveness militates against the tragic; the heights and the revelations are so submerged in the details of ordinary experience that one has, in the end, less a drama than an unusually animated entry, or series of entries, in a biographical dictionary. The divisions of the soul are flattened out into temperamental biases for which, in turn, one finds empirical accommodations. Given ten years to contemplate supplanting Duncan, Lady Macbeth might have fallen into castle or bedroom politics and discovered a surrogate queenship without running into deadly all-or-nothing moral confrontations. Making the empirical accommodations that go with less concentrated historical existence, one can, with luck, get by for a long time; what he faces, finally, is not moral nemesis, the oedipean tragic reckoning, but simply the passage of time, the debilities that take the game away from him. Instead of the smash-up emblematic of the tragic clashes within human nature, there is a gradual wearing out of parts. Whereas in several O'Neill plays the end is the discovery of eternal recurrence, in *Strange Interlude* the end is the cessation of occurrence. The combative heart slacks off into the inaudible beat of weariness. True, we have a final glimpse of young lovers in the next generation, but the note is less that of the new burgeoning of life than of ironic duplication, less that of spring song than that of W. Somerset Maugham's *The Circle*.

"Strange Interlude"

The panoramic, which goes allegoric in *Lazarus Laughed*, goes naturalistic in *Strange Interlude*: O'Neill spreads out the natural history of Nina Leeds from her twentieth year into something like old age (though only about twenty-five years elapse), and of three men who make up her psychological and marital entourage. There is a good deal of both exposition and post-mortem discussion; often the talkiness is tedious; much of the time the discontents displayed are closer to the petty than to the grand. Not that Nina entirely lacks the makings of the tragic heroine—if not of a Lady Macbeth, at least of a Queen Margaret in *Henry VI*. O'Neill begins the record, as Tennessee Williams was often to do in his studies of more singular and perverse individuals, with a trauma: the war death of the pilot Gordon Shaw, whom Nina loved and could never forget. In particular, she could not forgive herself for having become neither his wife nor his mistress. After a bout of penitential promiscuity—a surrogate giving of herself to wounded veterans in a hospital—she embarks on a therapeutic marriage to Sam Evans, a young advertising man (a Billy Brown type) who is devoted to her as a superior being. Up to this point Nina seems mainly another of the ailing characters, lacking in tragic strength, that often attract O'Neill. But another disaster—the late and unprepared-for discovery that there is hereditary insanity in her husband's family and that she dare not risk having a child by him—rather surprisingly converts her into an aggressive, calculating, and deceiving woman. She stays married to Sam, persuades Dr. Ned Darrell to father her child, and emotionally hangs on to Charlie Marsden, a novelist fifteen years older than she; thus she rejoices in having three men—husband, lover, and father—and spends the rest of her life managing this trio and, in a later action, trying jealously to break up her son's love affair.

Here is an aggressive attempt upon the world, even a small world, that could have tragic dimensions; but the result is little more than a frittering life of annoyances, jealousies, and failures to catch up with elusive happiness. None of Nina's men seems any the worse for being only a minority stockholder in her emotional corporation,* and Nina, far from coming into a serious confrontation of what she is and has been, stops at the sad comment, "[all are] gone. They're all dead" (IX),[15] and sinks back into being a happy little girl, snoozing in the arms of the desire-less paternal lover, "dear old Charlie" Marsden. We have only a cyclic decline, not the profound but representative violations of order that constitute tragic reality. Erosion is no more tragic than disease.

O'Neill introduces some ethical ideas, but toys with them rather than discovers dramatic depth through them. Old Mrs. Evans' theory—"Being happy, that's the nearest we can ever come to knowing what's good! Being happy, that's good! The rest is just talk" (III)—is given some testing during the action, and does not fare very well; but no counter-idea of the good has much dramatic force. Dr. Ned Darrell shifts between scientific detachment and passionate engagement, and on the whole does better with the former. When at a crucial moment a character wants to reveal a basic truth of family history, he is thwarted by another person's commandeering of the dialogue; the dimension of the play is reduced when the action is influenced, as it is more than once, by someone's conviction that vital facts are best concealed. Ignorance of relationships makes possible several rather obvious ironies, for example, Gordon Evans slapping Ned Darrell, who is really his father (Oedipus enraged by Laius at the crossroads).

O'Neill toys with psychological situations with which he would do more later: for a while Nina experiences the battle of skepticism and the need of belief which would receive fuller treatments in *Dynamo* and *Days Without End*. Her relations with her platonic and paternal older

---

* Something (perhaps his generally naturalistic posture in this play) leads O'Neill to see in these three men certain deficiencies of will that make them on the whole manageable in, and hence apparently uninjured by, this relationship. Since they do not have a strong impulse to a greater wholeness of living, the situation somehow lacks the moral dimension which one feels it ought to have. That dimension is remarkably apparent in a film that on the face of it looks simply like a gay fantasy—Alec Guinness's *Captain's Paradise*. In this a ferry boat captain, going back and forth between two ports, keeps a wife in one port and a mistress in the other. This is not simple philandering; rather one woman represents a quiet home life, and the other a night-clubbing, caper-cutting existence, to both of which the captain is equally addicted. His life has attained the same theoretical perfection as Nina's. But his two women are not content to remain as single-natured allegorical figures, and the captain loses both. On the other hand, a woman's skillful management of a trinity of men is ironically portrayed by Becque in *La Parisienne* (1885). But in contrast with Nina's rather somber self-regarding possessiveness is Clotilde's cool virtuoso worldliness.

lover foreshadow the father-daughter incest of *Mourning Becomes Electra*. Nina's equipping herself with father, husband, and lover in the persons of three devoted males is a heavily literal working out of O'Neill's sense of the triune nature of sex relationships; more often he reverses the perspective and notes men trying to find mother, wife, and mistress in a single woman (for example, *Desire Under the Elms, The Great God Brown*). The psychological drama tends to be mechanical: Sam Evans' business success fluctuates in exact ratio with his confidence as husband and father; jealousies and hostilities are spotted with systematic thoroughness; the "death wish" is called to our attention periodically. Though O'Neill came early to this "modern" sense of personality, he did not so encompass it in his art as to achieve more than historical novelty; rather at this point he looked at psychological phenomena in a way that gives us, for all his pioneering, a sense of banality. One wonders whether his fate as an innovator in tragic form may not be like that of Lillo. Where he is most effective is in his revival of an ancient device, the aside, and his expressionistic use of it to set forth thought and feeling inconsistent with the words spoken for the hearing of other characters. There is much vitality in the dramatized split between what a person says to himself and what he says to others, between the naked ego and the relatively conventional personality in a social context. Yet what comes through is rather the normal duplicity of existence than the critical dividedness which, since one cannot choose both alternatives, is the genesis of tragedy.

"Mourning Becomes Electra"

Mourning Becomes Electra (1931), which translates into modern American idiom Agamemnon's return from Troy and the succeeding events in his family (the Mannons at their New England Mycenae after the Civil War),* takes in much less territory than *Strange Interlude*. The greater compression helps invigorate and intensify an ingenious, though sometimes laborious, transposition of myth into modern terms of motivation and sensibility. Into the speech, flat and prosy as it tends to be, O'Neill has got a pressure and vehemence that make

---

* The characters are transposed as follows: Agamemnon, Ezra Mannon, a lesser northern general; Clytemnestra, Christine; Aegisthus, Adam Brant, a ship-loving sea captain; Orestes, Orin Mannon; Electra, Lavinia Mannon.

for authenticity.* In modernizing, O'Neill makes some key omissions, and what he does not see (and for that matter, what he sees) in the Mycenaean myth is a key to his way of dealing with tragic materials. For instance, he omits the Cassandra figure and the solid strength of the returning conqueror; Ezra shrinks into a minor commander who is almost pathetically trying to break the wall between Christine and himself, and who seems a sad little victim. In motivating Christine's animus against her husband, O'Neill uses two devices that work against grandeur of effect. He omits the sacrifice of Iphigenia and substitutes a "sacrifice" of Orin: General Mannon had made him go to war,[16] where Orin had suffered almost fatal head wounds. Hence Christine's maternal resentment serves mainly to illustrate the mother-son affinity (an old O'Neill theme), which is pushed very hard in scene after scene. Even before this, we find, Christine had been disgusted by Ezra on their wedding night and had never forgiven him. Not only does this history render her romantic passion for Brant questionable, but it is a comedown from the queenly vindictiveness of Clytemnestra.

O'Neill tends to constrict the legend by naturalizing it in clinical terms, especially of types of sexual conduct that, however universal, have here got out of hand and disturbed the personalities. He employs mother-son, father-daughter, and brother-sister patterns of incestuous feeling, and introduces incest implicitly into Christine's liaison by making Captain Brant (the Aegisthus figure) a first cousin of Ezra Mannon. Orin's head wound gives him a psychic shakiness which, added to his oedipality, means that under stress he will not find purgation through misery but will simply get sicker and sicker. This world closes in upon itself; instead of convincing us of its representativeness, it keeps circumscribing its relevance.

Ironically, this movement away from largeness takes place in characters who are tragic in conception. They are virtually all divided characters. Their divisions are of the peculiarly modern sort; they feel the pressure of clashing impulses, hardly at all that of imperatives. Lavinia

---

* This survives various awkward procedures in which characters clumsily reveal what they are supposed to hide, slip into verbal betrayals and only too obviously endeavor to change the subject, drop objects that are picked up by unfriendly finders, appear surprisingly at crucial moments, engage in unsubtle eavesdropping and espionage, and are heavy-handedly made to feel very accurate premonitions. The mechanical keeps jostling the spontaneous, the naïve encroaches on the knowing, the contrived interrupts the sure sweep of feeling; yet after four decades the dating is not so extensive as to undermine our sense of substantial, if limited, performance.

keeps talking about her "duty" to her father, but we are to see this as a rationalization of her strong, if unrecognized, sexual feeling for him. Whereas Orestes felt both the obligation to avenge the murder of his father, and the counterobligation of filial piety, Orin's motive is jealousy of his mother's lover; and Lavinia's interest in the death of Brant, though less visible because of her own self-deception, is of the same kind (Brant had intensified Lavinia's hatred of her mother by loving her mother instead of her). Yet if the motivations are mechanical, the Mannon actions take on a moral complexion by becoming unsatisfactory to the agents; quite aside from the agonizing quest for security (the Macbeth vein), the Mannons crave something more durable than the catharsis of destructive jealousy and hate. They have a sense of impending judgment. Their feeling of guilt goes hand-in-hand with a dream of "love" and "life" elsewhere, outside; each has the possibility, or the hope, of a saving relationship with another—Christine with Brant, Orin with Hazel Niles, and Lavinia with Peter Niles (when they are on stage, the Nileses create a sense of a well world utterly different from that of the Mannons). But though the Mannons yearn for salvation through the love of these others, they are even more strongly driven by the family heritage, with its mixture of perverse love and vindictive hate, of jealousy and of tensions that break out into violence, its severity and willfulness that sometimes appear as "duty," its sense of immitigable punishment, of threatening and inescapable ghosts. (The talk of "the past," "the house," and "the dead" * is remarkably like that in Ibsen's *Rosmersholm*.) They cannot find tragic purgation; they turn inward and downward.

O'Neill's treatment of guilt reveals his antitragic perspective. For the Mannons, guilt is only a chain, or, as Orin puts it, the "darkness of death in life" (Part III, Act II). Yet the ability to know and to feel guilt is a mark of tragic sentience; without it, a character is villain or moral vegetable, too limited to be intrinsically interesting. Furthermore, it is a possible avenue to well-being; it is that coming to consciousness of one's history through which one may enter into a new history. It is that acknowledgment of the past that holds out some assurance of a future.

---

* Repeatedly in the stage directions O'Neill describes characters as looking like death masks, an idea of ailing human appearance that he uses in a number of plays. The "death" and "life" antithesis is a cliché that seduces O'Neill more than once; here the details of the drama are concrete and lively enough to diminish our sense of banality.

Orin contributes to the suicide of his mother by killing her lover Brant, then is divided in what he wants to do after murder. On the one hand he can tell Lavinia that their only way to salvation is to "Confess and atone to the full extent of the law!" (Part III, Act II), and he can write a family history as a part of "man's feeble striving to understand himself" (Part III, Act III); on the other hand he wants to use this history to keep Lavinia from marrying Peter Niles and then to bind her to himself through the guilt of incest. Though he longs to "confess to [Hazel's] purity" and "be forgiven" (Part III, Act II), the obsessive involvement with his sister prevents his putting his longing into effect, and he commits suicide. Lavinia is equally split. She complains bitterly of Orin's "stupid guilty conscience" but adds, like Rebecca West to Rosmer, "You're becoming my guilty conscience, too!" (Part III, Act II). On the other hand, "There is nothing to confess! There was only justice! . . . You're too vile to live! You'd kill yourself if you weren't a coward" (Part III, Act III). And again: "I'm not asking God or anybody for forgiveness. I forgive myself!" (Part III, Act IV). At the end, however, after she has driven her lover away and turned to the house: "I've got to punish myself! Living alone here with the dead is a worse act of justice than death or prison! I'll never go out or see anyone! . . . I'll live alone with the dead . . ." (Part III, Act IV). While Orin has chosen death, Lavinia has shut herself up in a living death. The tragic division has found a solution only in illness; the normal contradictoriness of life has led to a clinical flight from life—into the grave and the hospital. The vindictive need to punish others has metamorphosed into the need to punish oneself, the soul on the road to light has become irretrievably fixed in the darkness of self-flagellation. (Thirty-five years before, Hardy pictured this outcome in Sue Bridehead; twenty years after O'Neill, Duerrenmatt saw it in Mr. Mississippi.) Illness is not tragic; what we have here is again a drama of disaster, the disaster of personality, with all the intensity that the narrower form can generate.

The world of the play keeps closing in, as we have said, cutting itself off from the full human cosmos. This is symbolized not only in the last and best remembered action of the play, Lavinia's shutting herself in the house for good, but in the incestuous longings that cut off the outer life where salvation might lie. Here, in this drawing back into sickness, death, and death-in-life, is O'Neill's sharpest departure from Aeschylus: what O'Neill did not comprehend in Aeschylus, or chose to reject, was the *Eumenides*, that imaginatively structured third drama in which Aeschylus made every effort to "open out" the myth, to bring it into the widest stream of significance, to catch all its reverberations for humanity at large. Orestes is caught, not in an infantile emotion, but in a terrible conflict that has to be debated on the Areopagus, and evokes strife among the gods; the closeness of the vote attests to the almost equal strength of the claims upon a humanity gifted with the sentience to respond to them. Though he never imagines that he can act without suffering, which indeed becomes illness, Orestes is unwilling to accept his immense act of penance as everlasting, but struggles, literally and symbolically, to turn from the agonized payment of a debt and return to ordinary life. Finally, Athena's persuading the Erinyes to accept their new role as Eumenides is an extraordinary symbolic drama, for through it, as Maud Bodkin has shown,[17] we understand the conversion of primitive energy, without its simply becoming innocuous, from a destructive to a beneficent function. This may be considered a turning point in the history of human potentiality.

It is just this turning point that O'Neill does not reach. *Mourning Becomes Electra* stays in that narrow, stern, unalterable region in which, once man comes under the hand of the Erinyes, he is always under the hand of the Erinyes. He falls into the egotism of permanent disaster. As Orin sums up, "The only love I can know now is the love of guilt for guilt which breeds more guilt—until you get so deep at the bottom of hell there is no lower you can sink and you rest there in peace!" (Part III, Act III). It carries on, to a more desperate misery, the quest for punishment of *Strange Interlude*, the pathetic vital inadequacy of men in *Beyond the Horizon* and *The Great God Brown*, the oppressive closing-in that afflicts the protagonists of *The Emperor Jones* and *All God's Chillun*; it anticipates the pitiable in-turning wretchedness of *Long Day's Journey* and *Moon for the Misbegotten*. But the perspective of *Mourning Becomes Electra* is most interesting in its kinship with that of *The Iceman Cometh*, which O'Neill would write within a decade. The two plays are complementary in the antitragic bias. In *Iceman* O'Neill implicitly argued the impossibility of tragic experience: man cannot bear self-knowledge. He must therefore live in illusion,[18] protected by a cordon sanitaire from the monstrous infection of truth. For once that infection has reached him—as in *Mourning Becomes Electra* —it will be so terrible that it will kill him or make him a lifelong invalid.

In O'Neill's hopeless view, man has only two choices with regard to the evil blight of self-knowledge—total immunity or total contamination, ignorance or ruin.

Iceman dealt with derelicts, *Mourning* with aristocracy. *Iceman*, we noted, has some remarkable similarities to *The Lower Depths*. *Mourning* is the lower depths of the upper crust, the Inferno of those privileged to know something of what they are, but sharing with all degrees that corruption of the will that tyrannizes over O'Neill's field of vision. It is Christine Mannon who says, "Now I know there is only hell!" (Part II, Act V). The play as a whole supports her: there is only an Inferno, no Purgatorio. This is the dark record of total catastrophe, not the tragic account of experience. But as melodrama of disaster, it has the massiveness of total conviction.

V. Final Decade: Sagas and Disaster

Mourning Becomes Electra, which echoes much from earlier dramas, in various ways announces what O'Neill would be doing in his final decade of work.[19] It is true that in the next five years he twice wrote plays of spiritual regeneration, whether we think of them as kinds of comedy or as melodramas of triumph—*Days Without End* (1934) and *A Touch of the Poet* (1936). In four other major plays, however, including his most admired ones (*Iceman* and *Long Day's Journey*), we can see the essential lineaments of *Mourning*: the novelistic length and the sense of inescapable disaster. It is interesting that O'Neill turns to chronicle and even saga (*A Touch of the Poet* and *More Stately Mansions* both deal with Melodys and Harfords, and *Long Day's Journey* and *Moon* both with Tyrones) just when his vein of metaphysical inquiry is petering out: he exemplifies the logical move from belief to the record, from supratemporal truth to the facts as they followed one another in time. Too, the chronicler and the prophet of doom are related: O'Neill sees no promise of salvation in history.

"A Touch of the Poet"

Only in *A Touch of the Poet* does man, so to speak, find salvation. Indeed, the play is rather a secular version of *Days Without End*. In each play a husband, driven by one side of his make-up, all but destroys his wife and himself, and in each play he finds the psychotherapeutic method that saves the day for self and family. John Loving has to triumph over skepticism and yield to a saving faith, Con Melody to triumph over a romantic self-glorification and yield to a saving acceptance of facts; John Loving must acknowledge himself a Catholic, Con Melody must acknowledge himself a commonplace Irishman. While John Loving is all but destroyed by "Loving," his Mephistophelian spirit of denial, Con Melody all but ruins himself by imagining that he is a sort of Wellington plus Don Juan, but above all a Byronic hero.* In effect, the Byronic hero is a Mephistopheles whose contemptuous skepticism stops short at the self and turns suddenly to self-pity. Both personae foster an egotism that raises a dangerous barrier between man and reality. Finally, O'Neill uses the death imagery that almost obsesses him to present the victory of the enduring elements in the personality over those that imperil it. "Loving" dies literally, and "Major Cornelius Melody, one time of his Majesty's Seventh Dragoons," is repeatedly described, after Con Melody has seen through the fantasy of his own greatness, as "dead." [20]

The dramatic problem is the same: both conversions afford a relief that we usually find pleasant, but neither is completely convincing. Melody comes around suddenly after a traumatic beating in a brawl; it is as if his opponents had "knocked some sense into him." But before this we have seen little in Major Cornelius Melody to prepare for his metamorphosis into Con Melody, the contented barkeep and jocose fellow-spirit of barflies. As if aware of the problem, O'Neill gives Con an occasional anguished glance back to the old role, and, still more subtly, endows his daughter Sara, who had always scorned his pretensions, with a disturbing ambivalence about his shift of role: beneath her scorn lay a pride in what she felt was his real distinction, so that Con's very denial of affectation seems to Sara to take him too far down into ordinariness. In despising his new unpretentiousness, she reveals the same kind of aspiration that had led him to live so much of his life in a legendary past.

This persistence of not altogether coherent motives shows O'Neill shunning the absolute answers of total destruction and monochromatic salvation—that is, the melodrama of disaster and that of triumph. Thus it is relevant to a consideration of his role as a tragic writer. For it sug-

* Interestingly enough, O'Neill transfers the self-adulatory note of "I have not loved the World, nor the World me" passage from the Irishman in *Touch* to the New England upper-middle-class pair, Deborah Harford and her son Simon, in *More Stately Mansions* (II.ii).

gests a working toward solutions that are not all black or all white but rather gray: the real blackness of events is relieved by a light of knowledge that distinguishes tragic experience from pure disaster; or, conversely, the light of salvation is shadowed by the old unsaved state, still incompletely rejected.

"Long Day's Journey into Night"

After embarking on the giant series, "A Tale of Possessors Self-dispossessed," O'Neill "interrupted work on the Cycle plays to write *The Ice Man Cometh* . . . , [and] *Long Day's Journey into Night.* . . ."[21] The interruption involves, however, not an essential discontinuity, but a return to the mood of *Mourning Becomes Electra*: the sense of overwhelming disaster. In this return, O'Neill continues with Irish families:[22] from *A Touch of the Poet* on, all his full-length plays but one[23] are concerned with the Melodys and the Tyrones. *Long Day's Journey* (1940) is consistent with the other plays of the period: the Irish family is rocked by conflicts between and within individuals; whiskey is needed to convert the nightmare of fact into the dream of glory; and characters express themselves, directly or histrionically, by quoting verse.* *Long Day's Journey* revives a concept of evil that O'Neill had used in *The Great God Brown* and *Days Without End*—the "Mephistophelean" spirit of rational denial: James Tyrone, Jr., is often driven by that spirit, and he is literally called "Mephistophelean," as he is in the sequel, *A Moon for the Misbegotten* (1941–42). *Long Day's Journey* follows *Mourning Becomes Electra* and *The Iceman* in using physical boundaries to symbolize the disastrous separation from a larger world of possibility. Lavinia Mannon shuts herself in the family mansion; Harry Hope's failures cannot safely go beyond the walls of the saloon; the Tyrones' summer home is like a prison, for, though nominally free, the Tyrones are bound by it in feeling and action (the Harford home and the summer house in Deborah's garden would have a

---

* The first character formally credited by O'Neill with "a touch of the poet" is Robert Mayo in *Beyond the Horizon*. In *A Touch of the Poet* the phrase is repeatedly applied to Simon Harford (I.iv); this prepares for the ironic application of the phrase to himself by Con Melody when he is renouncing his earlier pretentious life as "a lord wid a touch av the poet" (IV). In *More Stately Mansions*, Sara Melody, now Mrs. Simon Harford, expresses remorse for her bad influence on Simon, "the dreamer with a touch of the poet in his soul" (III.ii). In *Long Day's Journey* Edmund Tyrone is said to have "the makings of a poet" (New Haven, Conn.: Yale University Press, 1956), Act IV. Quotations are from this edition.

similar function in *More Stately Mansions*). Again, *Long Day's Journey* has a tie with *Mourning* and *Days Without End,* for it reveals, within domestic walls, a mixture, indeed an easy interchangeability, of love and hate that makes for a ruinous tension. Among the Mannons, the only alternative to family vindictiveness is incestuous attraction. Mrs. John Loving is indispensable to the well-being and life of "John," but "Loving" cannot bear the idea of loving her and wants to do away with her.

At one point or more, each member of the Tyrone family protests his love for parent, child, or brother, but the devotion is almost drowned out by a constant stream of quarrelsomeness, abuse, invective; like the Mannons, the Tyrones are held together by family bonds, but with most of them, most of the time, the style is one of self-interest and self-justification. Edmund says, of their mother, "It's as if, in spite of loving us, she hated us!" (IV). But the love-hate paradox is developed most overtly in James, the elder brother, who acknowledges that while he wants his younger brother to succeed as man and writer, he also wants him to fail and has tried to make him fail: "That part that's been dead so long. That hates life. . . . Can't help it. I hate myself. Got to take revenge. On everyone else. Especially you" (IV). (A little later he adds, "Feel better now. Gone to confession"—his central experience with Josie Hogan in *A Moon for the Misbegotten.*[24]) James has a more sharply accentuated version of a dividedness that runs through the family. Yet what might be a tragic split, with the possibility of recovery after the temporary derangement of the good man, deepens into a permanent malady.

Repeatedly O'Neill is fascinated by illness, by the irreparable disaster of body or spirit. The Mannons are victims of a malaise that leads all but one to death, and that one to death-in-life. Harry Hope's protégés are so ill in spirit that they can only feed on fantasies, and the man who purports to be their physician is an all-but-demented revenger (and like "Loving" a wife-destroyer). The Tyrones are virtually all ready for one kind of pathologist or another. The father, an actor, has a sense of failure as an artist, and appears always to have had alcoholic tendencies. Edmund has tuberculosis, and will escape from the house only into a sanitarium. James is an alcoholic and a sardonic ne'er-do-well. The mother is a drug addict, whose most recent effort at a cure has, like earlier ones, failed.

Into this untragic record of catastrophe there enter periodic notes of tragic self-recognition. At times the mother is aware of herself as a "lying dope fiend" and of the true import of her style with husband and sons (II.ii; III). At one point the father can acknowledge his failure as an actor and understand the reasons for it (IV). James can articulate his envious hatred of his brother, as we have seen, and note the parallel between his being unable to give up liquor and his mother's inability to do without morphine (IV). But at no time is there a painfully earned self-knowledge which then becomes a determinant of action and a molder of personality. Occasionally the truth breaks in as if by accident—*in vino veritas*, perhaps, or under some emotional stress—but it makes an essentially unwelcome intrusion, after which it is ignored, fled from, or rejected by the host whose defenses have been unexpectedly breached. The moral situation, indeed, is almost identical with that in *The Iceman Cometh:* no one can stand the truth, and everyone takes almost any means he can, either to get away from it or to erect in its place a quasi truth—an illusion, a memory, or a combative stance in which an accusatory ego begs its own merit. As the play goes on, Mary Tyrone sinks ever more deeply under the influence of her drugs; Edmund speaks of "a bank of fog in which she hides and loses herself" (IV); the final scene of the play is centered on Mary, now completely alienated from the others by dope, living in a world of dreams and memories. But dope is to her what drink is to the others and to Harry Hope's henchmen. Again Edmund voices the mood of the play: "We are such stuff as manure is made on, so let's drink up and forget it" (IV). Except for rare moments, Tyrone and James can manage illusions about themselves; Edmund does not do that, but his need is for a veil over actuality—the veil of drink or fog. Edmund interprets the fog explicitly: "The fog was where I wanted to be. . . . Nothing was what it is. That's what I wanted—to be alone with myself in another world where truth is untrue and life can hide from itself. . . . I'm talking sense. Who wants to see life as it is, if they can help it?" (IV).

This is the antitragic vein that we have seen persist from one O'Neill play to another. *Long Day's Journey* is antitragic in another way; the knowledge that the characters find unbearable concerns less-than-tragic matters—a knowledge not of large characteristic wrongs, but of ordinary insufficiencies; not of enormities, but of pettinesses; not of willfulness but of will-lessness.[25] Granted, James says he wanted to ruin his brother Edmund, but this seems to have been a transitory rather than a driving motive. Finally, the characters' greatest energy appears in a standard manifestation of the melodramatic spirit: the discharging of blame and indignation at others. The inner need to condemn is released again and again in abuse and excoriation: the air is full of charges of stinginess, inconsiderateness, selfishness, laziness, deceitfulness, cheating, drunkenness, promiscuity, ostentation, lying, spying, cheap cynicism.[26]

"A Moon for the Misbegotten"

A Moon for the Misbegotten (1941–42), in which old-style plot surprises somewhat diminish an effect of tedious talkiness, continues the history of James Tyrone, Jr., from *Long Day's Journey* (and advances the Hogans, who appeared only in a minor reported action in *Journey*, to dramatic majority). More important, O'Neill again shows his preoccupation with the "damned soul" that governed *Mourning Becomes Electra* and *Days Without End* (and influenced *The Great God Brown*). He again gives centrality to the character with a destructive "Mephistophelean" [27] side; like John Loving in *Days Without End*, James alternates between moods of straightforwardness, simplicity, and trust, and, as the stage directions keep reminding us, of "sneering" and "cynical" disillusionment—between tears and jeers, the poles of the unstable temperament that always fascinates O'Neill. In exploring a new course for this divided character, O'Neill reveals the religious background that influences many of his plays: he gives a major role to a secularized confession-for-forgiveness that shaped episodes in *Strange Interlude*, *Long Day's Journey*, and *Mourning Becomes Electra*. In *Mourning* Orin Mannon, whose troubles were rooted in his special attachment to his mother, can cry to his fiancée, Hazel Niles, "I want to confess to your purity! I want to be forgiven!" (Part II, Act III). In *Moon* James Tyrone, who "Ever since Mama died" has been "dead" (and he has reverted to an earlier alcoholism), believes that if only he could explain his life, and her responsibility for it, to his dead mother, "She'd understand and forgive me . . ." (III). Orin Mannon so suffers from the Mannon in-turningness that he cannot turn outward to Hazel; but James finds a tenant-farmer's daughter, Josie Hogan, who actually encourages him to cathartic autobiography and who says later that Tyrone wanted "to confess and be forgiven and find peace for a night" (IV).[28]

"Peace for a night" is what Tyrone gets; it is more plausible than John Loving's total victory over his despair (O'Neill's *Paradiso*), and at least it alters the bitter descent of the Mannons into total misery (O'Neill's *Inferno*). Yet *Moon* is not a *Purgatorio*. Tyrone's kinship is finally with the Mannons; not only does he call himself dead, but Josie, who loves and comforts him, also acknowledges that he is "dead" (IV). In him O'Neill portrays a man without will; he has less will than John Loving and the Mannons of earlier plays, less than the Melodys and Harfords in the cycle plays, all of whom could act vigorously, some of them murderously. He is like the Tyrones in *Long Day's Journey* and the barflies in *Iceman*; indeed he carries further the ineffectuality of the heroes in *Beyond the Horizon* and *All God's Chillun*. For all of his tragic division, he lacks the tragic hero's power to act. His problem is not excessive pride but absence of ordinary pride. His pathetic oedipality is once again a mark of O'Neill's despair.

Further, the confession itself, which might be a good dramatic version of tragic enlightenment,* is carried away from the tragic by O'Neill's characterization of Josie Hogan. Here we are constantly on the edge of the romantic and sentimental. For Josie, a very large and very strong farm worker, has not only beautiful breasts but much womanly wisdom and a *belle âme*; she can be coarse, earthy, vulgar, but gentle, subtle, enduring, and compassionate. Distantly echoing Abbie in *Desire Under the Elms* and Cybel in *The Great God Brown*, Josie is Earth Mother as Virgin Mary, the harlot as madonna. Somehow, being sustained by her all but converts Tyrone's final descent into a triumph. What is more, she is that rare creature of the romantic male imagination who may give herself to many but whom the individual male envisions as faithful to himself alone—a distant, rural, unschooled cousin of the Cleopatra who, a cut-glass reflector of the self, turns the plain light of self-knowing into the prismatic luster of self-love.

---

* O'Neill rather successfully gets dramatic tension into the long confessional scene by having Josie uncertain whether she wants to seduce Tyrone with marriage in view, or simply yield to him, or love him romantically, or comfort him maternally, and by having Tyrone respond to Josie with a medley of oedipal reliance, sentimentality, sensuality, and the desire that she not be common. O'Neill makes profligate Tyrone rather laboriously show revulsion toward the world of tarts and "tramps"; what he puts his finger on is a kind of Puritanism of feeling that may underlie or coexist with promiscuity.

"More Stately Mansions"

Though *Moon* apparently occupied O'Neill's final working moments,[29] *More Stately Mansions* (1938–41) had most of his attention in his later years. Of the works of this period, it was the last to reach production (1962). We cannot judge it as a work of art, since the very long printed version, which represents about half of the typescript text, was arranged by others.[30] Yet, despite the new directions in which it partly moves, in the main it continues with old preoccupations and perspectives.

What is new is O'Neill's initiation of the historical panorama of nineteenth-century America. Simon Harford, planning to be a radical political writer, gets into business, finds he has a talent for it, and goes on to become a megalomaniac tycoon. O'Neill is at his most acute in detecting a power-loving entrepreneur lurking within the utopian idealist, and is hardly less so in tracing the development of Simon's megalomania. This appears in private life as the passion for a great mansion and in business life as an insatiable acquisitiveness that becomes madly speculative and makes disaster, we surmise, inevitable. (His career has some remarkable resemblances to that of Uncle Teddy Ponderevo in H. G. Wells's *Tono-Bungay*; O'Neill Americanizes Wells's social history.) Simon is in the tradition of the strong O'Neill characters such as the Emperor Jones and the Cabots, and in this sense he looks more like a tragic hero than most of the men in the intervening plays. Unlike many O'Neill heroes, he has a real case of hubris. He has Napoleonic fantasies,[31] and to his love of victory he adds a passion to humiliate his victims that makes him something of a Tamburlaine in the business world. Yet he surpasses Tamburlaine in tragic capacity because he is also a divided character. As he himself says, Simon "lives split into opposites and divided against himself" (I.iii). Again, "as if at last I must become two selves from now on—division and confusion—a war—a duel to the death—" (II.i). He comes to feel that he must "choose one or the other" of his "conflicting selves" as "the one possible way he can end the conflict and save his sanity" (III.ii). Here, of course, is the threat of that illness that is so often the untragic end of O'Neill's heroes.

Simon is split between Rousseauian idealism and Hobbesian realism, between the dreamer and the wolf in the American character. But beneath this historical formulation we see an old O'Neill duality of character—the naïve-hopeful-creative on the one side, and the Mephistophelian-cynical-destructive on the other—that has already appeared in Dion Anthony, John Loving, and James Tyrone. Since in dealing with this obsessive phenomenon O'Neill has recorded one miraculous recovery and several disasters, it is difficult to expect a new move in a more tragic direction now. In fact, O'Neill's problem with Simon is made clear by the way in which Simon's wife Sara defines the savable side of him: ". . . the dreamer with a touch of the poet in his soul, and the heart of a boy!" (III.ii). While such words conceivably might define an admirable union of the artist and the innocent man, they hardly do that here; just as the "good" side of the O'Neill hero is always less impressive, so in this context the words applied to him simply suggest immaturity. The split in Simon, indeed, has another dimension which looms so large in the play as to supersede both the social history of America and the tragic history that Simon at least enters on: he is split between wife and mother. Yet it is more complex than that: he is ridden by the mother-mistress-wife problem that O'Neill explores or mentions in play after play, and he gets confused about the roles played by both wife and mother. Simon takes his wife into business partnership and converts her into a mistress whose favors he buys; the relation between prostitution and entrepreneurial adventurism is underlined heavily. At other times he feels that mother and wife have merged; they seem to be one person, or at least indistinguishable. Into this potpourri O'Neill has poured another motive: to an ambiguous heterosexuality he has added the war of the sexes. Simon fights against the mother-wife pair, and they gang up against him. But Simon plays one against the other, and is remarkably adept in forming an alliance now with his wife, and now with his mother; thus the drama often moves in terms of three different two-party alliances against the third party. The new Wellsian in O'Neill has not made too much headway against the old Strindbergian.

This medley of unfused, though not unrelatable, themes and motives * might, in the course of the strenuous reworking which O'Neill

---

* There is, for instance, a dream theme that might be an extension of Joseph Conrad's theme. In becoming a Napoleon of business, Simon has got too far away from the dream; his mother, on the contrary, is always tempted by dreams that take her away from reality entirely. Sara fluctuates between the two positions. Again, the "greed" of business is interpreted as an alternative to love, a consequence

always did, have become integrated. But even in what we have, we can discern familiar O'Neill habits of mind and ways of dealing with character. There are the complex intrafamilial infighting, the oedipal yearning, the in-turning, the regressive, the final air of illness and failure. For all of his Napoleonic achievements, Simon Harford turns out in the end to have the ineffectuality of the Robert Mayo of long before; like Orin Mannon he cannot get free of a son-mother attachment; like Emperor Jones he goes backward, not through ethnic, but through personal, history. While his mother, Mannon-like, has entered a symbolic summer house to solve a conflict by a madness that she regards as sacrificial, Simon becomes a little boy calling "Mother" (as Dion Anthony did to Cybel long before). His wife Sara closes the play by saying, "Yes, I'll be your Mother, too, now, and your peace and happiness and all that you'll ever need in life! Come!" (III.ii). The ending gives us, as O'Neill's endings so often do, a disaster of personality, the pathos of failure. If there is to be any salvation, it will come from without, from the wife-mistress-mother as nurse. Instead of the tragic recovery we have, though in psychological terms, the melodramatic rescue. Later, Tennessee Williams would be drawn to the same structure of experience.

VI. Integrity in Disaster

Whatever the impact of the Monte Cristo tradition upon him,[32] and the theatricalities which he instinctively devised, O'Neill had always integrity of feeling. Nicola Chiaromonte calls this integrity "romantic" and continues, "The use he makes of the stage is romantic, displaying, declaiming and proclaiming there his problems, or I should rather say dreams and nightmares of problems, including the most romantic of all, the dream he never fulfilled, of reaching the heights of tragedy." [33] Those heights could not be scaled by integrity in the feeling that found its best formal expression and therefore its maximum effectiveness in The Iceman Cometh, where the essential O'Neill is most powerfully articulated. For here more than anywhere else he relentlessly dramatizes a conviction that is antitragic—the conviction

of the failure of love. But Simon appears to identify love only with a child-mother relationship; we seem to have an option only between being a jungle-fighter and being mother's boy. Incidentally, when Simon is exploring his childhood in dialogue with his mother, and is searching for what has been lost, there is a good deal of talk of a "door" and a "garden"; the images are remarkably like some of the key images in Eliot's Family Reunion (1939) when Harry is going into his past with his Aunt Agatha.

that man cannot bear self-knowledge, and that man needs the crutch of illusion. But nearly everywhere else he does dramatize what underlies the flight from truth in *Iceman*, namely, a fundamental weakness of being before the exactions of life. Weakness may be immaturity or maladjustment or active disorder; this is the sense of life that permeates *Mourning Becomes Electra* and *Long Day's Journey*, which join *Iceman* as the most characteristic O'Neill. These develop with greatest force the intuition of reality that governs the lesser plays such as *Beyond the Horizon*, *All God's Chillun*, and *A Moon for the Misbegotten*. A "historical" drama like *Strange Interlude* records man's slow decay in time. Three of the four allegories present man's failure to find an alternative source of strength (*Lazarus Laughed*) or the sheer destructiveness of his divisions (*The Great God Brown*, *Dynamo*). Of the stronger heroes, Emperor Jones develops less as a tragic character than as the embodiment of a primitiveness incapable of contending with critical stresses; Simon Harford has divisions which he cannot solve except by a return to infantility; only Eben Cabot retains his hardiness and seems up to a sense of reality. Two heroes triumph—John Loving in *Days Without End* and Con Melody in *A Touch of the Poet*—and thus create melodramas of victory. O'Neill occasionally moves toward this extreme, much more frequently toward the other, hardly at all toward the more complex tragic form with its small restorative victories-in-defeat. His spontaneity and energy are most conspicuous when he dramatizes man's illness and failure, his decline and loss; despair is his métier. His men and women do not undertake too much; rather they can take on too little. O'Neill's characteristic field is the kind of failure that we have called the disaster of personality. In many ways he moves toward tragedy, but his instinct is for the pathos of insufficiency, the melodrama of disaster. To say this is simply to identify the modal form embodying a given intuition of reality. At his best he executes that form with great power.

CHAPTER FIVE

Tennessee Williams (1914——)

ONLY about a half-dozen years elapsed between O'Neill's last complete play and, in the late 1940s, the first major successes of Tennessee Williams and of Arthur Miller. It is easy to think of the three together, for their thematic similarities are more marked than the patent differences among them. Their chief common ground is the portrayal of men and women who suffer disaster, who destroy themselves or move toward self-destruction, or are the victims of maladjustment, debility, or outright malady. For the most part, however, O'Neill and Williams are closer to each other than either is to Miller. Failures of personality are a special theme of O'Neill and Williams; but while Miller first achieved fame with a drama of a man who failed, he has moved on to deal with stronger characters. However, O'Neill and Miller do share a suspicion of would-be saviors, while Williams develops a considerable interest in savior-figures who succeed, either straightforwardly or ambiguously. Despite their common interest in characters who collapse or fail, O'Neill and Williams go about the subject differently. O'Neill's people, as we have seen, are self-conscious, striving, attuned to problems and ideas. Williams' people, to whom we now come, are more given to undefined feeling than to thought, and their troubles originate more often in faulty neurological mechanisms.

I. Early Dramas: The Weak and the Strong

In Williams' work the sufferers who do not make the grade have an air of illness or something close to it. The early plays deal with hypersensitive characters who, from weakness or disability, either cannot face the world at all or have to opt out of it. Laura Wingfield in *The Glass Menagerie* (1945) cannot meet the ordinary problems of life; Blanche DuBois in *A Streetcar Named Desire* (1947) lacks stamina to bear up under the stresses that experience brings. Laura stays at home for good; Blanche ends up in a sanitarium. Williams' early predilection for the structure of melodrama appears in another way in his male protagonists, who face the world vigorously and in their own ways seem headed for triumph; Tom Wingfield escapes from financial constraint and family burdens to travel and write, and Stanley Kowalski, endowed with sexual virility and a keen sense of how the world goes, is ready to charge over all obstacles. So we have the familiar dualism of victors and victims.

But *Streetcar* has other convolutions that come out of a less simplistic imagination. There is the paradoxical attraction, for a moment at least, of opposites: Stanley, carrying the no-longer-resistant Blanche into the bedroom, tells her, "We've had this date with each other from the beginning!" (III.iv). The sexual common ground points up a world of imperfect choices: in Blanche, sexuality is allied with indiscriminateness, sentimentality, a decayed yet not wholly unattractive gentility, in a word, the end of a line, the collapse of a tradition; in Stanley, with a coarse new order, vigorous but rude and boorish. Stella, Stanley's wife and Blanche's sister, has to make a choice: she cries in bitter grief for the sister, but chooses Stanley, whose "maleness," as Williams' master D. H. Lawrence * might call it, is evidently meant to compensate for

---

* In *The Glass Menagerie* (New York: New Directions, 1949) Amanda Wingfield is made to say "that hideous book by that insane Mr. D. H. Lawrence" (I.iii) and to become, in part, a Lawrence villain by opposing "instincts" and supporting "Superior things! Things of the mind and the spirit!" (I.v). Williams and Donald Windham coauthored *You Touched Me!*, a "romantic comedy" based on Lawrence's story of the same title, and produced in 1945; it is a rather gay theatrical version of the Lawrence melodrama of admirable body (lower-class boy and middle-class heroine) against villainous spirit (spinster and clergyman). *I Rise in Flame, Cried the Phoenix*, "A Play in One Act about D. H. Lawrence," was published in 1951 and again in 1970. Williams' preface, dated 1941, not only expresses admiration for "probably the greatest modern monument to the dark roots of creation" (*Dragon Country* [New York: New Directions, 1970], p. 56) but also shows criti-

conspicuous narrowness, gaucherie, and arrogance (though the arrogance is modified in turn by his dependence on Stella). What is notable here is Williams' complication of the basic Lawrence melodrama, which, as in *Lady Chatterley's Lover* and *St. Mawr*, tends to put sexuality and all the other virtues on one side, and nonsexuality and the vices on the other.

With Blanche, Williams goes a step further away from the univocal record of disaster. The crucial trauma in her life was the discovery that her young husband—"Blanche didn't just love him but worshipped the ground he walked on!" (III.i) [1]—was homosexual, and the shock of his consequent suicide. This might be simply something that happened to her. But Williams is feeling his way into personality rather than stopping at bad luck. He makes Blanche say, of her husband's suicide, "It was because, on the dance floor—unable to stop myself—I'd suddenly said— 'I know! I saw! You disgust me!'" (II.ii). Here is a flash of something new: Williams transcends the story of the victim and finds complicity, or tragic guilt, in the heroine. It is evident that Williams wants to give this episode major importance, for he has the "Varsouviana"—the music for the dance from which Blanche's husband broke away to shoot himself—played at key moments throughout the drama. And here several problems arise. If we grant that the music attaches to her sense of guilt rather than simply to the whole shocking experience, still the effect is lyric rather than dramatic: it creates an indefinite feeling rather than establishes a definite development of consciousness. Blanche speaks almost no additional words on this central experience; it remains a wound, the center of a morally static situation, in which it is not clear whether

cal detachment with respect to Lawrence's work. In Williams' Lawrentian works several shifts are worth notice. Lawrence's lower-class potent males have a sort of innate gentility, whereas Williams has not, for the sake of doctrine, purged Stanley Kowalski of his vulgarity. *Summer and Smoke* (1948), instead of simply deriving soul from body, attributes to the soul an independent restorative function. *The Rose Tattoo* (produced 1950), a comedy, avoids the frequent Lawrence melodrama of the elect and the nonelect; here all are elect and their need is simply to divest themselves of mistaken ideals that temporarily obstruct salvation by the body. In writing the script for the film *Baby Doll* (1956), Williams made more conspicuous the Lawrence element in the Boccaccian one-act play of ten years earlier, *27 Wagons Full of Cotton*: in the film, as in *You Touched Me!*, sexual competence is accompanied by other virtues—somewhat at the risk, indeed, of making a Lawrentian Merriwell out of Silva Vicarro, the lover who is at once good businessman, imaginative playfellow, and philosophical commentator. But then in *Cat on a Hot Tin Roof* there is, in spite of the importance of sex in the lives of the central characters, something close to a reversal of Lawrence doctrine: sex does not produce, but is wholly dependent on, the integrated personality.

a sense of guilt persists as much as does a sense of shock and privation. At any rate, infinite regret, plus an infusion of self-pity, provides Blanche with no way of coming to terms with the disaster that borders on tragedy; when there is no reordering, shock becomes illness, and illness eventually triumphs. By the end *Streetcar* has drifted back to the history of the victim, with its seductive appeal to the strange human capacity for sinking luxuriously into illness as an aesthetic experience. Yet its claims on the feelings are divided enough to prevent an unqualified monopathic structure.

"Summer and Smoke"

In *Summer and Smoke* (first produced in 1948; subsequently revised) Williams appears to be making a more definite move toward a tragic complexity in his major characters, and then again to be drawn to a kind of theatrical effect that takes him away in a different direction. Almost from the beginning we are aware of divisions within two characters whose repeated confrontations provide, on the face of it, the principal dramatic tension—Alma Winemiller, a minister's nervous and genteel daughter, evidently in her mid-twenties, and her neighbor and friend from schooldays, Dr. John Buchanan, who in this Mississippi summer seems about to give up medicine, which he temperamentally shrinks from, for gambling, drink, and debauchery. Alma, believing in "culture," the finer things, ladies and gentlemen, noble actions, and above all in the primacy of the soul (that *alma* is Spanish for soul is carefully brought out in the dialogue), upbraids John for choosing the lower instead of the higher, for preferring worldliness, fleshliness, and deviltry to medical salvation for others, and for thus being false to himself. He, in turn, denies the soul, affirms the body, and taxes Alma with confused ideals, artificiality, hysteria, and self-delusion. In some ways quite like a medieval body-and-soul allegory (that is to say, a melodrama of concepts), *Summer and Smoke* is complicated, on the surface level, by the fact that there is attraction between Alma and John, indeed on her side a very strong one, and then, at the level of personality, by the conflicts within each of the two, and particularly in Alma. The play is more hers than John's, and we are given a fuller and more immediate view of the clash of her ideas and ideals with her basic impulses, a clash that is making her into a textbook neurotic. Her split is first articulated when John tells her that she has "palpitations" because she has a *doppelgänger* who is "badly irritated" (i).[2] Alma herself is made to speak in terms that, from our point of view, are very significant: she tells John that she is "one of those weak and divided people" that contrast with "you solid strong ones," and she repeats that she is "a weak and divided person who stood in adoring awe of your singleness . . ." (xi). Though Alma is hardly right in thinking John "single" (she is more accurate in scene vi when she calls him "confused, just awfully, awfully confused, as confused as I am—but in a different way") and in identifying dividedness with weakness, nevertheless her key terms "singleness" and "divided" point to antithetical realities that are the issue in *Summer and Smoke.*

That Alma is "divided" and John "confused" is the groundwork of tragedy, and indeed here the potential is great. The situation is significantly like that in Samuel Richardson's *Clarissa,* where the intense struggle between Clarissa and Lovelace coexists with a strong attraction between them. What happens to Richardson's pair is that each of them resists his own doubleness and so fanatically preserves an inadequate singleness (she her ideal of chastity, he his will to conquer) that both are destroyed.[3] For a while it appears that Williams is sensing and tracing such a destructiveness, which is a familiar form of tragic hubris. But he decides not to follow through; the only violence is among minor characters (John's father is shot by the father of Rosa Gonzales, John's other-side-of-the-tracks girl); and the mode becomes essentially comic when therapeutic adjustments are made before any passion gets out of hand. The parallels are extraordinary as each instructs the other, and Alma sums up, "You've come around to my old way of thinking and I to yours . . ." (xi). John acknowledges the soul by becoming a medical hero, and does a turn for the body by marrying a floozie's gay and sprightly daughter, a morsel sent to Newcomb College and there made more colorful by new wiles rather than sicklied o'er by the pale cast of thought. In the improbable final scene Alma picks up a traveling salesman in the square, and they make off to a night club. She seems to have said a permanent farewell to her soul.

A situation that could lead into troublesome depths and irreversible plunges is smoothly planed off into a neat symmetry of reversals; a dramatist who is consciously experimental falls back into an old theatrical device used by both Ibsen and Wilde.* What Williams does here is not dissimilar to what he did a little earlier in *A Streetcar Named Desire*, that is, rely on an "effect" that turns him away from character. In *Streetcar* it was the repetition of a dance melody that substituted for a full verbal exploration of consciousness; in *Summer and Smoke* it is the surprise of an ordering of parts that precisely inverts a previous ordering. Not that a balance of elements is always an artifice; it could hardly seem so in a day when we have learned to see analogy as a frequent and admirable device of structure. But structural equations need to be somewhat elusive, to entice us to discover them behind a resistant surface; when a symmetry calls attention to itself, we suspect that it is imposed on the human actuality.†

Not until *Cat on a Hot Tin Roof* (produced 1955) did Williams again use the tragic perspective. In the meantime there were *The Rose Tattoo* (produced 1950), a comic variation on the recurrent D. H. Lawrence theme, and *Camino Real* (produced 1953), called a "pageant" (Block 16),⁴ and, with the opening lines of Dante's *Inferno* ("In the middle of the journey [*cammin*] of our life") as epigraph, committed to an allegorical method, which, as often in more recent theater, subordinates individual lives to archetypal patterns of experience or traits of personality represented by large mythical figures.‡ Yet *Camino Real* has some relevance for us in that it is essentially a drama of disaster: over it hangs the sense of death—of bodies and hopes and dreams—and of all the lesser simulacra of death that are in the human calendar; and

---

* In *Rosmersholm* Rebecca West, who represents the will ruthlessly seeking its ends, comes to believe in Rosmer's ideal of nobility, while Rosmer loses faith in his mission to ennoble men. At the end of *Lady Windermere's Fan* Lord and Lady Windermere have essentially reversed their attitudes to Mrs. Erlynne. On the other hand, Williams uses a symmetrical structure very effectively in *Period of Adjustment* (1960), a "serious comedy" in which two married couples who are breaking up are in the end restored to at least a working harmony; the duplication emphasizes the spirit of compromise which is at the basis of the comic structure.

† In some analogous events Williams is much less obtrusive: in parallels between two generations, between different women inviting traveling salesmen, different men calling taxis for Alma. Symbols, which are in good supply, vary in subtlety: temperature, dress, statuary, fireworks, sleeping pills. This is true of most of his plays.

‡ Williams himself says that "its people are mostly archetypes of certain basic attitudes and qualities" (Foreword, p. viii). He adds, very soundly, that "symbols are nothing but the natural speech of drama" and "when used respectfully, are the purest language of plays" (pp. x, xi). Perhaps "used respectfully" should mean giving them a dignified reticence instead of making them take the role of human beings in the dramatic arena.

the mood is one of the morning after, of wearing out, of *où sont les neiges d'antan* and of *post coitum triste,* and, in Dante's figure, of "a dark wood where the straight way was lost." There is an occasional touch of the paranoid that melodrama may entail: Esmeralda, the Gypsy's daughter, utters the symbolic cry, *"They've got you! They've got me!* Caught! Caught! We're caught!" (Block 6). But we are asked to feel not so much resentment and blame as sadness at the way things go, and Williams vigorously resists the tonal dangers of this structure when at the end he makes Don Quixote, who apparently has authority, say, *"Don't! Pity! Your! Self!"* (Block 16). The drift toward the nostalgic and pathetic is held in check by lively ironies of fact and word, by novel and ingenious detail, and by brisk epigram: "We're all of us guinea pigs in the laboratory of God. Humanity is just a work in progress" (Block 12). Nevertheless, despite the epic and panoramic frame, the picture is one of limited dimensions, as it must be when depth yields to spread.

II. "CAT ON A HOT TIN ROOF"

Cat on a Hot Tin Roof (1955) carries on, after eight years, from *Streetcar,* and in some ways also from the slightly later *Summer and Smoke.* In Brick Pollitt there is the inner split that is central in the earlier protagonists, but it is far more intense than those of Alma and John in *Summer and Smoke.* Brick is the product of the same kind of unrelenting imagination of inner discord that created Blanche Du-Bois. Indeed, his case history has some remarkable resemblances to hers: glamorous youth, the critical trauma that again involves homosexuality and the rejection of a homosexual, alcoholism, disintegration (with the possible loss of the great plantation as an accompanying symptom of decline), all this in a charismatic personality in which charm is the element that longest resists decay. This degree of likeness in key characters helps outline the differences in the plays taken as wholes. Whereas in *Streetcar* hope lies in Stanley and Stella, with their hearty sexuality and insouciant energy, in *Cat* Williams all but demolishes the fertility myth: Gooper and Mae, with their six children, are made vulgar and grasping plotters, realistic versions of the quasi-human worldliness that is done expressionistically in Goldberg and McCann in Harold Pinter's *The Birthday Party* (1958). Such hope as there may be attaches to the title character, Margaret or Maggie, who, in her desperate struggle to save her husband Brick both for herself and for the plantation, and the plantation for them, might be merely a slick popular heroine. She is much more than that: she is, among other things, an embodiment of the Shavian life force, and that means that she is not so plain and simple as she manages to look. She had some complicity in her husband's downfall, since, in a calculated risk, she had broken up his ambiguous relationship with his best friend, Skipper; her devotion to Brick and the plantation is clearly interwoven with her passionate desire not to be poor again, her cool quest of advantage, and her detestation of Gooper and Mae; she can match them in laying strategic traps for the favors of Brick's parents, and in all the ruthless family in-fighting. So she is a person, not a cinematic madonna to the rescue. Still, insofar as the play is hers, it is concerned with a battle against outer forces by a character of what we have called pragmatic wholeness; win or lose, she herself is not looked at tragically, for, though she has some keen perceptions about herself—"[I've] become—*hard! Frantic!—cruel!!*" . . . "I'm not good," and "I destroyed [Skipper]" (I)[5]—her fight is not to discover herself or order herself but to escape from being a victim.

In terms of her vigor, of the frenzy of her struggle, and of the magnitude of her role, the play is Maggie's; after all, she is "the Cat." Yet Williams is pulled in two different directions, one toward the portrait of the strong competitive woman (the line that descends from Lady Macbeth through Ibsen's Rebecca West), the other toward inner conflict that has tragic potential. On the one hand there is all the tension that derives from Maggie's gladiatorial finesse and daring and her thrusts in various directions; on the other hand, there are the larger-looming problems of character that lie in Brick and in his powerful father, Big Daddy, whose presence alone marks a big jump ahead from *Streetcar*. The protracted confrontation of father and son takes up most of the long Act II, almost half the play in its original form. Bound by affection, they offer a sharp contrast: the mild, quasi-clearheaded pseudo serenity of the son, steadily drinking toward the inner "click" that signifies "peace"; and the violent boisterousness of the older man, ironically euphoric in the illusion of a reprieve from cancer (a faint reminiscence of Oedipus' certitude that he has defeated the malign oracle), triumphant, planning new triumphs, among them straightening out Brick.

Yet there is another bond: the old man's cancer, which will kill him, is paralleled by the thing in Brick's mind that Margaret literally calls "malignant" (I). (Symbols flow from Williams: trying drunkenly to repeat a youthful exploit, Brick gets a fractured foot that is analogous to the broken spirit partly due to the ending of football glories: he uses a literal crutch that also defines the role of alcohol for him.) A less tangible, but dramatically more important, bond is a concern for "truth," or, perhaps better, an incomplete invulnerability before it when the other uses it, therapeutically or punitively, as a flail. In the drama of self-knowledge, where tragedy has its roots, Williams appears to be again of different minds. Up to a point Brick does not muffle his sense of fact: he can say, "I'm alcoholic," he acknowledges, "I want to dodge away from [life]," and he defines, "A drinking man's someone who wants to forget he isn't still young an' believing" (II). Though these recognitions seem to go far, they do not "hurt," and that they do not is part of the dramatic evidence that there are still deeper levels of truth to be known.

The gradual revelation of these deeper levels, with an increase of pain that suggests a saving remnant of sentience in Brick, makes extremely effective drama. What is revealed cannot be defined simply; in a long interpolated note Williams inveighs against " 'pat' conclusions, facile definitions" and rightly insists, "Some mystery should be left in the revelation of character . . ." (II). Brick is tensely and even explosively resentful of the view, partly held by Maggie and, it appears, by Gooper and Mae, that his relationship with Skipper was homosexual; he calls it "friendship," his experience of the "one great good true thing in [a man's] life" (I), and he passionately elaborates his notion to Big Daddy (II). He resents, too, Maggie's view that he and Skipper carried their college relationship on into professional football "because we were scared to grow up," were hanging on to adolescent dreams of glory.* We can argue how much of the total truth is represented by each of these views; what is clear is that, however we assess the mixture of ingredients, Brick was inhabiting an idyllic Eden at whose breakup he began his determined push into a surrogate realm of alcoholic peace. Maggie surely has authority when she comments, "life has got to be allowed to continue even after the *dream* of life is—all—over" (I).

As the history is slowly set forth, Brick claims for himself the virtue of honesty; yet his stance is on the whole the pretragic one of defensiveness and blame—blame of a mendacious world and particularly of Maggie: he punishes her by refusing to have sexual intercourse with her.

---

* Football is also used to symbolize immaturity in Miller's *Death of a Salesman*.

She had destroyed the idyll by putting it into Skipper's head that his feeling for Brick was homosexual and thus destroying him. But at this moment Big Daddy, skeptical, puts on the pressure and elicits the fact that, when Skipper had phoned Brick to make a "drunken confession," Brick had hung up. Big Daddy charges, "we have tracked down the lie with which you're disgusted. . . . This disgust with mendacity is disgust with yourself. *You!*—dug the grave of your friend and kicked him in it! —before you'd face truth with him!" (II). It is at this point that we sense the "two minds" in Williams. Big Daddy presses for the ultimate recognition of truth, and his great strength and passion apparently establish this value beyond question. Then Big Daddy himself is challenged a little later when Brick retaliates by letting it slip out to him that he has not escaped cancer, as he supposes; on the contrary, he is really dying of it. But the truth that Big Daddy has to face is that of physical fact, not moral act. Brick, confronted with the latter, cries, "Who *can* face truth? Can *you?*" (II). And insofar as Williams doubts the human ability to face truth, he is of the same mind as O'Neill in the anti-tragic *Iceman*, where an anesthetic Lethe of alcohol is all that makes existence endurable. It is the reversal of George Eliot's requirement, "No opium." Eliot may have had an illusion of strength, but she could imagine the tragic situation rooted in power to endure. In Brick what we find, on the contrary, is the disaster rooted in weakness. He reflects that sense of human incapacity to endure that has appeared in a good deal of modern "serious drama." Dr. Faustus was the man who tried to be God; Miller's Quentin would castigate himself for entertaining the illusion of divine power; but Brick simply found himself accepted as a "godlike being" (I) and then went to pieces when one worshiper challenged another's purity.

Again, however, Williams has an impulse to go beyond the disaster of personality. He is not willing to let Brick be simply a victim, a good man destroyed by the actions of others. For what Big Daddy, acting as prosecutor, establishes is that Brick "dug the grave of [his] friend and kicked him in it" and that that is the source of his malaise. If this does not impute to Brick the hubris of the "overreacher," it at least makes him a man who does evil instead of one who simply suffers evil. We need now to see whether the play continues to regard him as a man of action or simply settles for his passivity and disintegration. It is here that Margaret's efforts to stir him into a resumption of sexual intercourse—including her final theatrical public claim that she is pregnant—take on great dramatic significance. For his rejection of sex is not only a symptom of illness, of one kind or another, but also, as we have seen, a punishment of her; and punishing her is his means of declaring that the guilt is hers, and of keeping his eyes off his own guilt. It is the old story from *Lear* to O'Neill's *Iceman*, of the man living in a melodrama of blame and resisting the tragic self-confrontation. To resume intercourse would be to declare Margaret innocent of his charges against her, or to forgive her, and thus to make possible his acknowledgment and understanding of his own role—in Skipper's death and in his and Margaret's subsequent misery. Williams has imagined an active tragic role for him. The problem is whether Brick can advance beyond the relative comfort of the melodrama he has created for himself, and beyond that, whether Williams is able to conceive of him as transcending the rather familiar role of the sad young man going under.

Again it appears that Williams is of two minds or at least that he was capable of being of two minds. For he wrote two versions of Act III, his own original draft and then, at the urging of his director Elia Kazan, a second one which was used in the first stage production.[6] While both versions end with at least a touch of the-lady-or-the-tiger ambiguity, the first gives little ground for supposing that Margaret can win her battle against Brick's punitive and even self-righteous detachment. In the second version Brick is a little less laconic, gives a touch of support to Margaret's game of publicly claiming pregnancy, and views with admiration her final tactic of throwing out every bottle of the whiskey that he relies on. There is a little more reason to think that he may take the critical step and break out of his own rigidity. Though even here Margaret retains the line, "Oh, you weak, beautiful people who give up . . . ," still she is now permitted a stronger assertion of her own will to rehabilitate him. However, Williams has more of his heart in the first version: a subtly more urgent dialogue conveys this, and besides, Williams is explicit in his prose comment. He cannot, he says, believe that "a conversation, however revelatory," even a "virtual vivisection," can effect much change in "a person in Brick's state of spiritual disrepair."

In rejecting the dramatic convention that a moment of revelation, even a brutally fierce one, can be the equivalent of a conversion, Williams is perhaps unconsciously seeking ground for sticking to the disaster of personality—the history, not of the person of hubris and of eventual insight, but of the person who cannot cope and cannot face the record. Yet in speaking of Brick's decline, Williams twice applies to it the word *tragedy*, another evidence of his persistent attraction to the form.* In *Cat*, surely, he reveals a further tendency to get away from, or at least to modify, the pathetic story of collapse. His central character is the man who himself committed the originating deed and who is on the edge of acknowledging his own guilt. Williams catches Brick at a less irremediable stage of collapse than he does Blanche in *Streetcar*, he almost eliminates the element of the victim that is a bona fide part of Blanche, he gives more authority to the protagonist's crucial rejection of another (Blanche's injury to her husband we see in her own memory only after she has become an undependable witness). And in Big Daddy and Margaret there is a spontaneous emphasis on discovering the truth that is hardly present at all in *Streetcar*. Both of them are also potential tragic characters.

"Sweet Bird of Youth"

Four years later, in *Sweet Bird of Youth* (1959), Williams, consciously or not, makes Chance Wayne a variation on Brick Pollitt—the charming young man who achieves a premature glory and then, when it fades, himself fades into dope, drink, ruthlessness that is a pointless by-product of ego-saving, low-grade racketeering, immature exhibitionism, cinematic dreams, scheming, and fakery. Chance has had, also, a fund of energy and unscrupulousness that would make him much closer to the traditional hero than Brick was. Yet he has been successful only as a stud, so that in his failure he can be figuratively described, in the stage direction, as "faced with castration." Suddenly in his final half-dozen speeches this character starts speaking of himself with wisdom: he is "nothing," by the "level-of-rot" measure he is "ancient." "I lived on something that time. . . . Gnaws away" (III).[7] Here, with the

---

* It appears to have been active in his imagination from the beginning. A stage direction near the end of *The Glass Menagerie* refers to the mother's "dignity and tragic beauty." Again near the end of *Streetcar* Williams uses a stage direction to attribute to Blanche DuBois, now mentally ill and about to be taken to a sanitarium, "a tragic radiance." He gives the subtitle, "A Tragedy in One Act," to *Auto-Da-Fé*, which deals with another character whose inner stresses have driven him out of his mind. He theorizes about the "tragic sense" in his preface to *The Rose Tattoo*, a comedy, and in the foreword to *Sweet Bird of Youth* he speaks of his satisfaction when "a work of tragic intention has seemed to me to have achieved that intention, even if only approximately, nearly."

active man's self-knowledge, Williams pushes on into the technically tragic in a way that he only tentatively approached in *Cat*. Interestingly, he uses a stage direction to insist that "Chance's attitude should be self-recognition but *not* self-pity—a sort of deathbed dignity and honesty apparent in it." Perhaps the use of the insistent stage direction is a symptom of Williams' own subconscious disbelief in this degree of illumination in Chance. There are several problems here. The most important is that Chance has appeared both so shallow and so preposterous that the self-recognition is hardly plausible in terms of character. Williams felt that Brick, in *Cat*, had disintegrated so far that signs of recovery were inadmissible; though Chance is not alcoholic, he suffers from a multifaceted degeneration, including loss of a kind of dignity and single-mindedness that Brick still held on to, that would much more effectually bar a moral pullback. The ending, then, falls into the sentimental.

The sentimental effect is enhanced by another aspect of the method: Williams makes Chance almost an allegorical figure of youth or of the loss of youth (the epigraph is Hart Crane's "Relentless caper for all those who step / The legend of their youth into the noon"), a subject on which characters arbitrarily make many expository remarks. Adult readers are likely to regard the A. E. Housman elegy as the fitting tune for the departure of youth, and to resist the view that the passage of time is tragic, or is a palliative of the falsenesses by which Chance has become a "monster" (the term that his traveling companion, a decayed actress but less muddleheaded person, applies to both Chance and herself; she is a Blanche DuBois who has caught herself just as she is going down the drain). Hence it is exceptionally difficult for brief speeches plus lengthy stage directions to confer dramatic or moral validity on the loss-of-youth theme. At best pushing this theme is a poor substitute for tragic self-confrontation, which is the expectable consequence of Chance's treatment of his girl (he has not killed her, as Othello did Desdemona, but reduced her to a kind of death-in-life). Then at the very end Williams has Chance, not judging himself, but coming forward and, like the Doctor in the morality play, addressing the audience: "I don't ask for your pity, but just for your understanding—not even that—no. Just for your recognition of me in you, and the enemy, time, in us all." At best such a lecture is untragic. But here it is doubly unfortunate because it bluntly demands what it has to earn imaginatively: identification. And in doing so it invites all men to think, not of the quality of man, but of an "enemy"—to assume, that is, the traditional melodramatic stance that justifies an enlarged blind spot for the self. There are, of course, real enemies to be faced, but to include time in that category hardly escapes the bathetic.*

III. MELODRAMAS OF DISASTER

Except in comedies, such as *Period of Adjustment* (1960) and *The Night of the Iguana* (1961), Williams has not again approached characters in terms of crisis, enlightenment, and possible reordering. In both *Orpheus Descending* (1957, a reworking of *Battle of Angels*, 1940) and *Suddenly Last Summer* (1958) he images the destroying of men by horrors and furies, whether these are hardly interpretable irrationalities, or intelligible as symbols of the darker side of a man or of men. *Orpheus* takes as its theme the community's savage ways of excommunicating or destroying "outsider" types, whether natives or visitors, those who inherit

---

* Self-pity by people who imagine themselves the victims of time may be becoming fashionable. This mid-twentieth-century sentiment vitiates the characterization of sixteenth-century Pizarro in Peter Shaffer's *The Royal Hunt of the Sun* (1964); Pizarro's continual self-righteous indignation against the hostile passing of time undermines a treatment of him that could be tragic, for Shaffer realizes that Pizarro's "lifetime of . . . rejections" simply lets in "the flood-tide of meaninglessness." If Shaffer had been able to trust to a direct imagination of character in such terms, he would have been on much safer ground; but he further presses down the action under the weight of other anachronistic ideas, most of them undergraduate clichés even by 1964—the "joylessness," the "anti-life" attitudes, and the "denial of man" in both the Inca religion and Christianity. When a writer feels superior to the institutions he depicts, and regards all attachments to them as "neurotic allegiances," he starts with an inadequate view of man that inhibits the full imagination of character. Hence *The Royal Hunt* becomes insubstantial spectacle. (The quotations are from Shaffer's "A Note on the Play" in the formal program of the Old Vic production that opened in London late in 1964.)

An appropriate way to deal with passage of time and loss (or revival) of illusions appears in Eugène Ionesco's *The Chairs* (1952), in which a husband and wife, both nonagenarians, commit suicide after acting out, as in a child's game, a scene of social success. The effect is one of immense pathos, sharpened by the irony of make-believe. Ionesco subtitles the play "A Tragic Farce," using both terms, one suspects, with his tongue in his cheek. However, cf. Richard N. Coe's serious discussion of the implied duality of mode in "Eugène Ionesco and the Tragic Farce," *Proceedings of the Leeds Philosophical and Literary Society, Literary and Historical Section* 9, Part 8 (1962):219–35.

G. B. Shaw, according to a recent critic, strongly resisted the now popular pathos of time. In *The Unrepentant Pilgrim* (Boston: Houghton Mifflin, 1965) J. Percy Smith writes: "It is perhaps his refusal to allow the grim fact of devouring Time to turn his gay courage into lugubrious stoicism that makes him so irritating to sad-eyed realists who prefer the sweet way to despair" (p. 256).

There is a firm, nonbathetic, almost tragic treatment of aging in Ray Lawler's *Summer of the Seventeenth Doll*. See chap. 10.

something of the "wild" that is not yet "sick with neon." Two of these are women who, like Blanche DuBois, are scarred by past injuries but, unlike her, survive to fight back and meditate or practice different revenges against the cruel and malicious local society. It is this society that is identified with the nether world, with Death and Demons; and the Eurydice character, Lady Torrance, believes that she is returning from it to "life" when she finds herself pregnant by the Orpheus character, Val Xavier, a strolling guitar player.[8] Carol Cutrere flaunts outrageous conduct to let the town "know I'm alive," and the sheriff's wife, putting her "visions" (whether imaginary or willed or hysterical) on canvas, gains a reputation as a "primitive" painter. The cast is one of Williams' largest, and the situation has numerous ramifications; in the medley of conflicts we see evil almost entirely as an outer threat to the major characters, and almost never as the genesis and material of self-understanding. But a certain melodramatic brilliance hangs over the portrayal of hostilities and revenges.

Again in *Suddenly Last Summer* (paired with *Something Unspoken* under the general title of *Garden District*; the common element is a tyrannical woman operating in a context of New Orleans "Garden District" values) Williams presents the outer destructive force, and the weaker beings who are its actual or potential victims or who have a built-in readiness for destruction. Mrs. Venable, a powerful old woman who can push poor relatives around, centered her life in a relationship with her son Sebastian, still a virgin at forty, whose poetic gift she believed she had always protected, whose eccentricities she humored, and whose false steps she corrected. We see her recalling all this after his death, as she is trying to destroy, or at least by surgery render innocuous, Sebastian's cousin Catharine (by promises of support for research Mrs. Venable is trying to bribe a young experimental neurosurgeon to do a lobotomy on Catharine). Catharine was traveling with Sebastian at the time of his death, she had been "disturbed" in the past, at the time of the play she is on a family visit from a sanitarium, and her state of mind is in part connected with her memories of Sebastian's death. Mrs. Venable, who is murderously jealous of Catharine ("He was mine!"), wants to suppress Catharine's "hideous story" of Sebastian's death: he was killed by a mob of naked, starving Spanish children and partly eaten. On the face of it there is the "oedipal situation": Catharine says, "I failed him" (just as Blanche DuBois said, "I'd failed him in some

mysterious way"), and reports that "something had broken, that string
of pearls that old mothers hold their sons by like a—sort of a—sort of—
umbilical cord . . ." (iv; one recalls the title of Sidney Howard's play
produced in 1926, *The Silver Cord*).

Yet Williams may be doing something more than replaying, even with
his own ingenious variations, a familiar tune. For he has left the story
ambiguous, and it is not clear whether the oedipal relationship is primary or secondary; it is by no means evident that Mrs. Venable is
wrong when she avers that she "held him back from . . . *Destruction!*"
(iv).[9] Sebastian's impulse to find destruction may be an expression of
his filial situation, a projective multiplication of his mother into inescapable harpies in the cosmos; or it may be anterior to all else, a thing in
itself which draws his mother, repellently willful as she is, into a role
not so simple as it appears—that is, a hypnotic energizing of him without which he might not have survived to forty. Beneath a fine front
suitable to "Renaissance princes," as Mrs. Venable puts it, Sebastian
has shown some odd interests and almost clinical weaknesses. At the
end he manages to invite, to contrive as it were, a death resembling a
scene of destruction that he had witnessed years before and had been
strangely fascinated by—that is, the destruction of newborn sea turtles
by carnivorous birds on the "blazing sand-beach" of a Galapagos island
(the Spanish children who destroy him are regularly described in bird
images). Besides, there are all sorts of symbolic echoes and parallels: of
St. Sebastian, St. Catherine of Ricci (Catharine's "vision"), the search
for God, the jungle (with psychological and social implications).

But all the cornucopia of actual and suggestive materials is gradually
subdued to one final effect: the climactic revelation of the mode of
Sebastian's death. With skillful theatricality Williams produces a shock
of horror; then an abrupt curtain. The principal character, so to speak,
was dead before the play started, and even alive did not have a consciousness through which we come to understanding; he is another of
the somehow inadequate beings who, like Brick Pollitt, seem fated only
to slide down, or even subtly construct, a chute into the waste barrels.
Mrs. Venable remains a "whole" woman: all energies lavished on aggres-
sively defending a position which she neither questions nor regards as
questionable. Catharine continues the frail line of descent from Laura
Wingfield through Blanche DuBois (and in some ways even the "fugi-
tive kind," Carol Cutrere): sweetness, shock, illness. From the pathos

of victims, the grotesque horror of events, and the hardly modified fierceness of the competitor, Williams makes almost no move toward the tragic form. But he reveals considerable skill in the melodrama of shock.

The Night of the Iguana is focused on one more in the steady line of Williams characters who have had a rapid slide downhill and who lead a touch-and-go existence on the border line between hospitalization and a very shaky survival outside. The Reverend Lawrence Shannon, forced out of the pulpit by misconduct and a "breakdown" (as often in Williams, we hardly know which is prior), now barely manages to hang on either to his job as conductor of vacation bus tours or to his mental health. He is another sick man with an early trauma, this one related to punishments for masturbation; among other symptoms, he has a vengefulness which, somewhat like that of Spandrell in Aldous Huxley's Point Counter Point, leads him to seduce, or accept seduction by, teenage girls and then punish them by verbal and even physical blows. In the course of the action he does some rather sturdy self-inspection, noting among other things that in seducing women on his bus tours he always first "ravages" them by "pointing out" the "horrors" of the tropical land they are in; and at the end he apparently finds a solution appropriate to comedy, that is to say, a workable arrangement in the world: joining forces with a lusty widowed innkeeper to run a hostelry in which, as hosts, they will each make special contributions to the entertainment of guests of the opposite sex. (Thus his errant sexual prowess will be rendered socially beneficent by institutionalization.) But even this retrieval of quasi strength out of weakness, or of a modus vivendi out of maladjustment to life, depends upon the therapeutic ministrations of Hannah Jelkes, a fortyish virgin who travels around the world with a ninety-seven-year-old grandfather. She supports them, under exhaustingly difficult conditions, as they go, but she has still energy and generosity and understanding enough to establish with Shannon a "communication" that has restorative value for him. Out of "Maggie the Cat," for whom trying to save Brick Pollitt is hardly distinguishable from saving herself, Williams has distilled a special being who approaches secular sainthood.

IV. The Theme of Salvation

The savior or nurse figure is a relatively late arrival in Williams' characterology, and it underwent several metamorphoses between *Period of*

Adjustment (1960) and *The Milk Train Doesn't Stop Here Anymore* (1963). In *Period of Adjustment* there is a literal nurse who marries another of Williams' ail-and-retreat figures, this one afflicted with a disabling psychosomatic palsy. She not only takes on the assignment but cosmicizes her role: "The whole world's a big hospital, a big neurological ward and I am a student nurse in it" (III, almost at the end).[10] Her words summarize a good deal of the Williams world—a world of human disasters unless someone comes to the rescue.

Hannah Jelkes in *The Night of the Iguana* is a more sophisticated, though still romantic, version of the nurse. But the savior or helper figure becomes most interesting in *The Milk Train Doesn't Stop Here Anymore*, in which Williams employs much more indirection and ambiguity. The savior cannot save, in any ordinary sense, for here the patient is dying, and the only issue is the style of dying. *The Milk Train*, which Williams acknowledges "[has] been rightly described as an allegory and as a 'sophisticated fairy-tale,' " [11] belongs roughly to the class of *Camino Real* of ten years earlier, though the roving panoramic style of *Camino Real* is replaced by a central focus on one character. She is a crass, wealthy old woman, a Mrs. Goforth ("it's my turn now to go forth," Williams makes her pun heavily in scene vi).

Here again Williams is on the *sic transit* theme that repeatedly attracts him, this time portraying a furiously fighting doomed person, like Big Daddy in *Cat on a Hot Tin Roof*, rather than the person who wilts away or seeks death. The treatment of a person dying amid opulence, protected by a gunman and savage dogs on a presumably impregnable height overlooking the Mediterranean, might remind different readers of Ivan Bunin's "The Gentleman from San Francisco" or Hugo von Hofmannsthal's *Everyman* or George Kaufman and Moss Hart's *You Can't Take It With You* or Aldous Huxley's *After Many a Summer*. Sissy Goforth, after a highly profitable career starting in a Georgia swamp and moving through the musical comedy stage to six husbands (a "Little Me" who has developed into a Claire Zachanassian of Duerrenmatt's *The Visit*), seems to think that you can take it with you; her heraldic device is the griffin, presumably an allusion to the mythic function of guarding gold in Scythia. There is a good deal of satire of that excessive love of property [12] which reduces all other love to multiple sexual episodes; even on her deathbed Sissy, naked, summons a young man into her bedroom, with an ironic intimation of at least optical carnality. But though Sissy is a "dying monster," as her secretary Blackie calls her (an echo of *Sweet Bird of Youth*), she is more than an object of satire, for Williams also endows her with a brute sense of fact (within limits), an overwhelming candor (outside of specific areas of self-deceit), a blunt vulgarity not without its charm, and a passion for not being taken in.

The person who she thinks is intent on taking her in is a man in his thirties, Christopher Flanders, who has a number of times become a steady guest of well-to-do old ladies about to die and hence has become known as the "Angel of Death." This is Williams' latest, and most complex, version of the nurse or savior. Sissy sees in him only a hippie, a professional sponger, a pretended artist using "moral blackmail" on people who lack the "robust conscience" to throw him out as he deserves. The known facts about this partly mysterious figure make her estimate of him understandable, and he offers her assistance with a death-bedside manner that helps justify her doubts and scorn. Yet she does not want to lose him to a more vigorous old moneybags, the "Witch of Capri." Her doubleness of view either reflects or helps establish doubleness in him. In one stage direction, Williams refers to "the ambiguity of his character," and it appears that he could be an old ladies' con man ("you're suffering more than you need to," he tells Sissy, and he offers "agreeable companionship"), or "a saint of some kind" as Sissy jeeringly puts it (v), or a spiritual picaro, or something of all of these. Sissy sneers at his "list of suckers" (v), and in a final burst of self-assertion she rejects him with "This milk train doesn't stop here any more" (vi); this, along with her "I want to go forth alone," is quite convincing. On the other hand, she holds on to his hand as she dies. In using the term "Angel of Death" Williams may have in mind Azrael, which means "God has helped," for Chris says of his initial experience of this kind, "I had helped a dying old man to get through it," and his "Hindu teacher" replies, "You've found your vocation . . ." (vi). Chris tells Sissy, "you need somebody or something to mean God to you. . . ." It is possible that Chris is the bringer of "The Hidden God," to borrow Cleanth Brooks's title. When all the action takes place in a little world where, as Blackie says, "Everything signifies something" (ii), one notes Chris's name, the "Christ-bearer," and remembers that he arrives at

Sissy's on foot, carrying an impressively heavy sack (it contains metal-working tools for making mobiles). He has some of the markings of Julian in Albee's *Tiny Alice.*

We have, then, ambiguity on both sides. Sissy is a heartless old miser, ruthless and paranoid; but her "fierce life" when dying and her tough grasp, if not of the whole human heart at least of the ways of the world, are not contemptible. She cannot let Chris go, but so suspects him that she half starves him while trying to use him. She may be a true stoic, a solitary endurer in a final scorning of illusions; or she may be a cheap-skate trying to get needed help for nothing; or in her sardonic skepticism she may be utterly confused both about herself and him. Chris's epigram may have authority—"you're nobody's fool, but you're a fool . . ." (vi) —or he may be skillful in working on her. Seen in the light of Sissy's combined attraction and repulsion, her need of help and her fear of quackery, Chris remains an ambiguous being who may be a professional "free loader" or a groundless consolation or a necessity or a blessing or the bearer of a "sense of reality" that is "disturbingly different" and hence has undeservedly made him, as he puts it, "a leper" (v). The opulent world formally rejects him, crying fraud, but still clings to him, as if he were a man of indispensable vision—poet, artist, or prophet, false or true.

As a drama about the ways of dying, *Milk Train* belongs to the morality plays that are remarkably frequent in the modern theater, and as such it is peripherally related to tragedy. On the face of it, Sissy Goforth's struggle against death is rather like a melodramatic struggle against an omnipotent adversary raised to a level of significance and dignity; there is none of the pathos that such an action is likely to evoke. One of the bars against pathos is the uncertainty within Sissy herself; hence we may say that she has something of the tragic dividedness, even though it is present only because of the last-minute intrusion of motives that she hardly identifies or understands. There is not the primary split that is at the center of *Everyman,* the archetypal play about dying. But Williams is writing for a different world, and in *Milk Train* he avoids the errors of *Sweet Bird of Youth*—the sentimentality and the histrionics that the subject of death easily drives us into.

In general, we might reasonably think of Williams as experiencing a tension between fantasies of catastrophe and fantasies of salvation. Fantasies of catastrophe produce dramas of disaster; those of salvation may lead him to another basic structure of melodrama—twice, we note, with a *dea ex machina*. In *Milk Train* Williams works in another manner, that of allegory; here his interest is neither in catastrophe nor in the success or failure of the savior type, but in the complex attitudes of the affluent society toward the equivocal figure, artist or religious guide, who is both pensioner and alleviator. If the dramatic focus is on the sick or disintegrating character who simply follows his sad downward course, or whose strongest act is to be the beneficiary of someone else's supporting clasp or cool hand on fevered brow, then the direction is not a tragic one. Nevertheless Williams shows himself also able to imagine the relatively well or strong person or that in-between figure who has had to struggle for wellness or strength. The last of these, Hannah Jelkes in *The Night of the Iguana*, is moving toward dramatic centrality. If such a character were to gain the center of the stage, it would be a move away from dramas of disaster.

V. Last Plays

In the shorter plays to which Williams turned in the later 1960s, however, there are no major new developments; the collection entitled *Dragon Country* (1970) [13] works mainly from familiar Williams motifs. There are, of course, some emphases that belong to the later rather than the earlier work. One play has an explicitly, another an implicitly, Christian context. The scenes are not in the world of plantations and permanent homes, as in *Cat* and *Streetcar*, but in the world of hotels, bars, and boarding houses, as in *Night of the Iguana*. The dramatis personae may be transients or permanent residents, but even with the latter, their existence has much of the uprooted, the peripheral, the hanging on. Various people are on the edge of death, or hold out poorly against it, or are done in, or endure a sort of death-in-life. Against the nonsurvivors or the marginal survivors are ranged a few tougher types—crass or ruthless or simply gifted with more vitality. More than once there is a familiar melodramatic contrast of the weak and the strong, with overtones of the D. H. Lawrence dualism (the volume includes one very early play, *I Rise in Flame, Cried the Phoenix*, in which the characters are Lawrence, Frieda, and Brett) and of the allegorical shaping of experience toward which Williams' imagination occasionally turns (in addition to the life-versus-death [14] presence in various plays there is, in two of them, a generalized rendering of the fate of "the artist"). None of these materials looks naturally toward the tragic; the kind of words I have used implies rather an absence of the individuality and human stature essential to tragic quality. Yet Williams has used the word *tragedy* of two of the plays, and in two others he conceives of a character in terms that could lead to a tragic structure.

True, when he does use the word *tragedy* he is being suggestive rather than literal, and ironic rather than solemn. In 1966 two of the plays in *Dragon Country*—"The Mutilated" and "The Gnädiges Fräulein"—were produced in a double bill with the program title of "Slapstick Tragedy." Here is an echo of the old concept of the sorrowing clown and the jest that barely conceals grief. The "slapstick" in these plays is the loud verbal conflict between the characters—in both plays two women who belabor each other with heavy irony, suspicion, abuse, threats, and even blows, but who need, or can use, each other and hence grudgingly find an accommodation.[15] "Slapstick" implies that the blows do not hurt, but in these plays they do; survival has a price. "Tragedy" implies the presence of something harsher than farcical shenanigans, but the nonfarcical belongs less to tragedy than to disaster or potential disaster. In "The Mutilated" we are more aware of the needs of the two women who abuse each other; in "The Gnädiges Fräulein" the personalities are cruder and more calculating. The former is basically pathetic comedy; the latter relies strongly on the grotesque, and the tone is dominantly satirical.

"The Mutilated" is about little people—a lonely woman, an aging streetwalker, sailors, customers at a bar. The title character, Trinket, is a woman who has had a breast removed; the sense of being "mutilated" is a horror that hangs over her, makes her forgo sex, and leaves her vulnerable to a blackmailing crony, Celeste. The mutilation is symbolic as well as literal, however; "we all have our mutilations," Celeste says (i); and death in one form or another is just around the corner. The basis, then, is the pathos of human insufficiency and vulnerability. But at Christmas the two women find a way of making up the quarrel which is at the center of the action, and even manage to sense a visitation by Our Lady. It is their experience of "the miracle" promised by carolers whose carols, sung periodically throughout the play, are charming in their union of freshly imaged faith and delicate irony.

Thus the pathos is modified by the slender comedy of spirit: the momentary triumph of wholeness over mutilation. A gentle irony hangs over the triumph and forecloses the sentimental. However, what remains most vivid is the conflict that dominates most of the play—the harsh idioms of hostility among various characters, but especially Trinket and Celeste, the "pair of old bitches" as Celeste describes them (i). In all these plays Williams has a good ear for the recriminative and vituperative style.

"The Gnädiges Fräulein" portrays an intrinsically tougher world of calculation and profit-seeking, with the two women who want to use each other combining the ludicrous and the sinister. Molly the boarding-house keeper wants a puff in the paper for which Polly writes; Polly wants a good news story from the boarding house and gets stud service from an Indian inmate there. The satirical keeps welling up through the surface farce. Besides, Molly and Polly have a common victim, the title character: an outcast from "show biz," she is treated like a workhouse inmate by Molly and is regarded as good copy by Polly. Thus the satire of crassness, as often, involves the melodrama of the victim.

But what dominates the play is the grotesque. This appears chiefly in the terrifying aggressiveness of the "cocaloony" bird, a "sort of giant pelican" who combatively invades Molly's rooming house, scares the people, and snatches a fish caught by one of them. At an offstage dock, we learn, the Fräulein has to compete with the cocaloony birds of the area for the unsalable fish tossed out by fishing boats; thus she pays her way in Molly's place. The struggle is desperate: the cocaloony birds have gradually stripped the Fräulein, plucked out one of her eyes and then the other, and half scalped her. Every time she appears on the stage she is bloodier and more nearly naked—a Williams horror story that inevitably reminds us of the end of Sebastian in *Suddenly Last Summer.** While Sebastian was an eccentric courting disaster, however, the Fräulein is struggling for survival. Since the word *competition* is used, the tale is really a fierce parable on economic rivalry and its threats to plain subsistence (there is a casual reference to the Mafia and "the Syndicate"). But still deeper than this is another theme that recurs in Williams: the fate of the original artist both in the commercialized theater

---

* Williams seems mildly haunted by an image of people-and-birds, people as victims of birds, or people victimized as birds. In "The Mutilated" there is a "Bird-Girl" in a freak show, and Celeste reports that she once had this role. Speaking of the present Bird-Girl, "poor Rosie," Celeste voices one of the best ironic remarks in the volume: "If she was a bird, the humane society would be interested in her situation but since she's a human being, they couldn't care less" (i).

and in the outside competitive world. The Fräulein, we learn, got black-balled in show biz when her innovations in a performance infuriated a "trained seal," and he beat her. Ever since, she has battled desperately for a marginal subsistence, her life as fish-catcher analogous to her role on stage. It is as if an original playwright was driven out of the theater because of his originality, had to write commercials for a living, and was then hated by the pros in this grosser field. Viewed reductively, this is the old romantic melodrama of the innovator victimized both by his fellow professionals and by society generally; yet it is translated into fantastic terms that create a satiric melodrama of originality and force. The expressionistic voice gives freshness and toughness to a theme that could spawn the trite and the sentimental.[16]

Hubris and Dividedness

Three years later, in "In the Bar of a Tokyo Hotel" (produced, 1969), Williams returns to the subject of the artist and his fate, this time the overt theme. The expressionistic appears in some of the details, but the general procedure is realistic. The artist is still in part a victim, but there is a new element in that he is in some sense also a victim of himself. Here, then, Williams moves into the realm of tragedy.

Mark, the painter, is a febrile and almost hysterical version of Ibsen's master-builder Solness—endeavoring to control a new style, sensing a dangerous breakthrough of old limits and all limits, terrified, exhausted by the intensity of a struggle that is imaged as a sensual conflict, as if canvases were women to be sexually subdued by force. Like Solness, Mark dies at the end, not in a sudden theatrical accident, but in a climactic dissolution prophesied from the beginning by a fantastic physical and spiritual debility. Mark's own view is that he is worn out by wrestlings with problems of creation; as he says, "An artist has to lay his life on the line" (i). In Mark's striving to go beyond limits there is a tincture of the Faustian. After his death his wife Miriam argues that he has erred by not staying within "the circle of light," which is "our existence and our protection." She rejects the "romantic" view that "the circle of light is the approving look of God" (ii), but she has managed to get it expressed and thus to set loose in our imaginations the idea of the artist as actuated by a demonic drive. What we sense here is a version of the tragic passion to exceed human limits.

Disappointingly, this possibility is not realized. For one thing, we have only Mark's word for the intensity of his aspiration, and the play does not make him a reliable witness. We do not see enough of Mark's consciousness to be sure that his striving is hubristic, an assault on limits that, like Faust, he cannot ultimately deny. For another, it is by no means clear that he is not deceived about his breakthrough or is not just sick. Though we are told that he has been a successful and productive painter, he is, during the action of the play, so emaciated and feeble as to be almost a caricature. In this lack of robustness he seems a distant echo of Brick Pollitt, of Shannon in *The Night of the Iguana*, and, in his off-center nervous organization, of Sebastian in *Suddenly Last Summer*. Here is a recurrent Williams problem of a lack of tragic stature in a character who is potentially tragic.

But Miriam is not going to play Maggie the Cat or Hannah Jelkes to what she calls Mark's "tyrannical dependence" (i). Indeed, her intention to withdraw support from him is implicitly a murderous act; if she is truly the bitch that he calls her, then we have a melodrama of evil woman and her victim. The play is rather, I believe, a more complex melodrama with dividedness of appeal: neither is wholly justified against the other. The life of the play is the intensity of the conflict between them. At the same time there is an ironic balance between them: Mark lusts after art, Miriam lusts after other men.

Insofar as Mark is "the artist" and the subject is "the creative life," there is a touch of the allegorical which has occasionally cropped up in Williams since *Camino Real*. It appears again in "Confessional" (copyright 1970), where there is much talk of "birth" and "death," in one speech called "holy miracles" and "holy mysteries" (i). Death is introduced most ingeniously in the fact that Leona, the strong woman in the play, is on a quarrelsome drunk in ritual mourning for her brother on his "deathday." We are meant to feel these abstract themes in the heart of the action. The play is in part a documentary on kinds of vitality and nonvitality (an echo of the old Lawrence strain in Williams), and at the same time on kinds of sexuality. The result is a panorama of types of psychological subsistence in which the habitual is varied by cathartic binges.

The allegorical had a strong hold on O'Neill too, and "Confessional" reminds us of O'Neill in more ways than one. The scene is a bar which is reminiscent of Harry Hope's place in *The Iceman Cometh*; though in no way so far gone as O'Neill's, the characters lead a limited, in-turning life—an unfrocked M.D., a whimpering, disintegrating whore, a middle-aged short-order cook who barely makes a living, a weary homosexual, a self-centered male hustler (a more limited Chance Wayne); the stage directions are lengthy and novelistic; periodically one character or another, spotlighted, addresses the audience in a "confessional," a rather mechanical revelatory device such as O'Neill used more than once. It is more a theatrical self-exposé than an essential coming to knowledge in a tragic manner. But this is the right style for these characters, who, as often in O'Neill and Williams, have a limitedness or weakness that is not the raw material of tragic life.

The possible exception is Leona, the vigorous, combative, promiscuous hairdresser who tells people off, levels with herself, combines a tough mother-earth good sense with a passion for sentimental music, and is always ready to defy loneliness and hit the road in her trailer when the joys of the current stand run out. Not only does Leona have the strength for a tragic role; she is specifically defined in terms that we have seen more than one dramatist apply to tragically conceived characters: "She's got two natures in her" (i). But the "two natures" are less divergent passions than they are moods which alternate. Leona may be easy to get on with, or very quarrelsome, but in either phase she is completely unified, not disturbed by a conflicting impulse. Rather than divided, she is remarkably well held together, despite shifts in emotional state. Indeed what might in a truly complex character be dividedness of appeal is here rather an easily agreeable mingling of dissimilar elements —itself a kind of cliché. But at its best the treatment of her manages a subdued pathos laced with irony.

The Williams Mode

Williams has not again come as close to the tragic structuring of character and experience as he did in *Streetcar, Cat on a Hot Tin Roof,* and *Summer and Smoke.* The vigorous characters in these plays do continue to appear, in many variations, in the dramas up to 1970; likewise the weak and disintegrating characters, victims sometimes of others, sometimes of their own fragility. But the life of the play is rarely in the inner discords of strong characters who in hubris or error make choices that lead to catastrophe. What especially attracts Williams is the built-in liability to disaster, and he often infuses a remarkable vitality into the portrayal of characters with limited powers of survival. Death and a deathlike state frequently hang over the heads of people troubled either by their own inadequacies or perversities, or by the malice that comes out of the needs or perversities of others. The death theme is treated most complexly in *Milk Train*, with an ambiguity that lies less in richness of character than in the meaning that attaches to action; the complexity is more in symbol than in passion. In that play, Chris Flanders is from one perspective the artist, the figure who appears in two of the recent short plays: we regularly see the artist in a tense conflict with others, more often than not victimized, yet keeping to his last as best he may. Williams is consistently good in representing the spirit and style of hostile confrontation, the drama of counterforces and counterpurposes. When he internalizes his drama, he is on the road to tragedy.

CHAPTER SIX

Arthur Miller *(1915 ———)*

ARTHUR Miller provides the best materials for the present kind of criticism when he moves away from the view of reality that was most frequent in O'Neill. We should not of course deny certain resemblances to or influences by O'Neill. These are especially apparent in Miller's first major play, *Death of a Salesman* (1949): a fundamentally naturalistic method, with some infusions of fantasy; theatrical innovation; a sense of motives that are unseen or not understood; a family where mutual attachment is hardly distinguishable from mutual blame and recrimination; and, above all, a central character whose weakness and incapacity restrict him to a course of pathetic decline. The disintegrating protagonist might also have come from Tennessee Williams, though in Williams' hands Willy Loman would have had a flamboyant self-destructiveness rather than an unchangeable habit of knocking his head against a wall of unapprehended actuality. But *Death of a Salesman* does not represent the mature Miller. He became more independent, more forceful, and more deeply imaginative in *The Crucible* (1953), *A View from the Bridge* (1955), *After the Fall* (1964), and *The Price* (1968).*

---

* I am omitting *All My Sons* (1947) from formal consideration. It is an over-plotted play in the well-made tradition, with an uneasy marriage between theatrical

I. THE TURN FROM MERE VICTIMS: "THE CRUCIBLE"

For my purposes, *Death of a Salesman* is useful chiefly for its employment of a point of view that Miller was to give up, namely, that of the victim. Willy Loman is a victim of inadequacy and obsolescence, and hence his story is essentially a pathetic one. He is a victim, too, of mistaken dreams, and in this lies the possibility of tragedy, that is, of the heavy knowledge of what has been mistaken. But this means a capacity for new wisdom, whereas Willy is never perceptive enough to know what the trouble has been; he continues as a victim of ignorance. Finally, Willy is specifically defined as "the salesman"; he illustrates a circumscribed type of employment rather than opens out toward the inclusiveness of everyman. For these reasons, then, *Death of a Salesman* is a rather closed-in affair. Miller is not yet going for the bigger game that would later bring out his best talents: the protagonist is still only a man to whom things happen, who is not capable of even a belated understanding, and who is seen in a vocational and technological rather than a broadly human context.

Miller therefore rightly thinks of *The Crucible* and *A View from the Bridge* as new departures. In these plays he was, in the first place, formally rejecting a certain kind of drama: ". . . I was tired of mere sympathy in the theater. The spectacle of still another misunderstood victim left me impatient." [1] This is a significant moving away from a smaller theme, from the kind of melodramatic mode that easily becomes sentimental. Words like *sympathy* and *victim* imply sufferers from action which originates elsewhere rather than initiators of decisive action. In dismissing characters whose role is bearing blows, sinking down, and failing, Miller is deliberately turning to the stronger principals of *The Crucible* and *A View*. Hence he begins to open the door to tragedy.

The opening of that door is implied by another comment: "In *The*

sense and problems of conscience. It almost proceeds on the assumption of television drama that a sudden disclosure of concealed fact, resisted by some and sought by others, will neatly package up various emotional problems; hence it hardly avoids an air of gimmickry. Focus tends to wander as new issues are continually introduced, and some are left hanging. Yet the issues show Miller becoming interested in problems of character that extend beyond clichés. One of the leads, Joe Keller, might be described as an Uncle Ben (from *Death of a Salesman*) who is finally pushed, somewhat abruptly, into a quasi-tragic role—self-recognition and suicide.

Crucible I had taken a step, I felt, toward a more self-aware drama"
(p. vi). If "more self-aware drama" means "more self-aware dramatis
personae," the step is indeed toward a tragic concept of character. Still
there is some ambiguity here, just as there is in some other words of
Miller: the play "must call up a new concept, a new awareness" (p. vii).
This might mean either that the action itself entails a conflict of ideas
as well as an exercise of pure feeling, or that, like an editorial or a treatise,
the play should effect an alteration of ideas. The ambiguity may exist
in Miller's own intentions, for *The Crucible* moves in different artistic
directions. In the "commentary" interpolated into the printed text of
The Crucible [2] Miller is sometimes the imaginative contemplator of the
complex human disaster in seventeenth-century Salem, sometimes the
twentieth-century moralist exposing a racket—as when he reduces the
Devil to "a weapon designed and used time and time again in every age
to whip men into a surrender to a particular church or church-state"
(p. 31). When he writes out of such simplicity, *The Crucible* sounds
like what even an admiring critic calls "a polemic" and "a modern
morality play," and the characters tend to become "dramatized points
of view." [3] Indeed, in treating the devil and witches as a put-up job to
safeguard the establishment, Miller might have been borrowing from
Sartre's *The Flies*, which similarly applied an ancient story topically
(Sartre's topic was the occupation of France by the Nazis, as Miller's
was the occupation of America by McCarthyism). Sartre's lesson is put
affirmatively—Orestes gets rid of the Furies and undermines the theocracy; and Miller's is put negatively—John Proctor denounces the witch
business and is done in by the theocracy. The two plays represent opposite ends of the spectrum of melodrama: the hero as victor, and the
hero as victim. Despite a good deal of ingenuity in detail, however,
Sartre's is closer to pure demonstration; Miller is ambiguous, as we have
said, and the case-making ideologue is challenged by the dramatic ex-
plorer.

The basic pattern is that of the good man destroyed by the forces of
evil. As the man of integrity opposing an erring system, John Proctor is
made to speak, more than once, like an independent twentieth-century
rationalist. The official eradicators of witchcraft, on the other hand, are
legalistic, bigoted, and even vengeful. The artistic execution, then, is not
unlike that of the popular theatrical confection by which the audience
is easily gratified because, while the décor affords an agreeable novelty,

all habits of feeling and thought are given a familiar workout. The audience can simply be for "freedom" and against "tyranny." Yet *The Crucible* is superior melodrama. For one thing, there is the sheer tension of events—the public disclosure and misinterpretation of skeletons in domestic closets, the creeping monstrousness of nominal justice, the valiant struggle against injustice, the frail hope of rescue by Mary Warren's testimony, the combat among the girls as rival witnesses, the disastrous loss of Mary Warren, the perilous interweaving of a calculation and a hysteria that are not always distinguishable, the final agonized uncertainty in John Proctor's mind. All this is saved, in the main, from the taint of theatrical manipulation by pictorial completeness: Miller dramatizes all the elements in the psycho-social context that contribute to the catastrophe—the medley of private and secular passions, the literal acceptance of witchcraft, the excitement afforded by it, the use of it for self-defense, its relation to some men's sense of status and institutional order, its role as an instrument of resentment and revenge. That is, he has enforced a sense of community disorder too far-reaching to be produced by the machinations of a mere villain; the play creates a genuine terror of encroaching and enveloping evil—one of the maximum possibilities of the melodramatic mode. If the characterization had a little less of the tendentiousness that has often been noted (and perhaps overemphasized) and if the language were less prosaic,* *The Crucible* might come within the *Duchess of Malfi* range of drama.

Miller fell short, someone has said, by not treating witchcraft historically as an aberrant aspect of a faith that had a creative role and that cannot be reduced to the mechanisms of repression. The idea is that he could have made a stronger attack on "intolerance" by attributing official injustice to "good and conscientious men." [4] In this point of view *The Crucible* is merely a satire which might have been made fiercer, but the words point incidentally to the tragic potential in the story, that is, wrongdoing by good men. Now, though it is aesthetically easier for a writer to point the finger of blame, and though there is a

---

* Miller occasionally writes speeches with an imagistic vitality that O'Neill, with his much more pedestrian style, hardly ever achieved. Most often it is Proctor whose lines take on poetic life. "Were they born this morning as clean as God's fingers? . . . but now the little crazy children are jangling the keys of the kingdom, and common vengeance writes the law" (II). "Aye, naked! And the wind, God's icy wind, will blow!" (II). "Now she'll suck a scream to stab me with . . ." (III). "I have made a bell of my honor! I have rung the doom of my good name—" (III).

tendency to admire Miller for doing just that, the fact is that he repeatedly moves toward the tragic view. Miller can picture a community
overflowing with the rancor by which everyman may absolve himself,
and yet also imagine more than one person with the moral capacity for
self-judgment. Rebecca Nurse can not only question "the seeking of
loose spirits" but can take the harder step: "Let us rather blame ourselves . . ." (I). Elizabeth Proctor can suggest, "we have been too hard
with Mr. Parris" (II), and, much more emphatically, say of herself as
wife: "I have sins of my own to count. It needs a cold wife to prompt
lechery" (IV). As the constant speaker of truth and as the victim of
legal injustice, John Proctor could be a wholly simple figure; but Miller
has chosen to extend him beyond allegorical status by bringing in the
affair with Abigail and making him feel guilt on this account; by giving
him a rashness that, like Kent's in *Lear*, contributes to his own difficulties; by putting him at one time in the Antigone conflict between the
law and family loyalty and at another time in the conflict between the
desire to live and the hatred of the lie by which life may be purchased.
The basic conception is tragic. Yet the conception does not determine
the execution, for, as we see in our response to Alfred Ill in Duerrenmatt's *The Visit* (another drama of disorder in the community), a man
under the gun can hardly be a tragic hero: to judge himself, a man must
be free, not the victim of others' judgment.

Since Miller goes so far toward the tragic treatment of Proctor, we
think of the tragic possibilities in the men of authority. Deputy Gover-
nor Danforth, however, remains only the rigid voice of the bench, with
no hint of a future like that of Judge Gaunt in Maxwell Anderson's
Winterset (whom, one suspects, Miller would have done so much better
than Anderson did). Of the Reverend Parris, Miller writes in a closing
note: ". . . [he] was voted from office, walked out on the highroad,
and was never heard of again" (p. 140). The words "walked out on the
highroad" somehow suggest Oedipus, and we suddenly see in Parris a
remarkable drama: the spiritual head of Salem sets out to cure the
plague in the town, and finds the cause in himself. That is not the way
Miller did it, but the fact is that he came very close to doing it with
another minister, the Reverend John Hale. Hale enters with a debonair
confidence that he will make dark things plain; like Oedipus he inter-
rogates; like Oedipus he can imagine evildoing in characters who we
know are innocent. He asks, "Were there murder done, perhaps, and

never brought to light? Abomination? Some secret blasphemy that stinks to Heaven?" (II). Such Theban echoes continue when Hale begins to alter his idea of where guilt lies and then exclaims in horror, "There is blood on my head! Can you not see the blood on my head!! . . . I count myself his murderer . . . what I touched with my bright confidence, it died; and where I turned the eye of my great faith, blood flowed up" (IV). Here is one of the fundamental tragic ironies: the good intent has an evil issue, and he who has worked or aided evil knows what he has done. But Hale is a secondary character; it is not "his" play; and, though he partly modifies it, he does not determine the tone.

Miller hovers on the edge of tragedy, then, by choosing strong characters, by beginning to complicate them, by introducing self-awareness. Thus he raises *The Crucible* in the melodramatic scale, makes it more than propaganda against socio-political wrongs. There is a real evil, and there are real victims, but we perceive in the dramatist something subtler than the black-and-white imagination not sensitive to the grays of more complex experience.

II. The Turn to the Private Disaster: "A View from the Bridge"

In going on from *The Crucible* to *A View from the Bridge* Miller shifts emphasis from the societal to the personal catastrophe—another step toward tragedy. In *A View*, Miller says he wanted to create in the audience a "desire to stop this man and tell him what he was really doing to his life" (p. vii). The "desire to stop this man," it is worth noting, might be a response to a conventional danger in "popular melodrama" or to a serious impending disaster or to an action of tragic scope. We might want to stop an ignorant driver speeding toward a washed-out bridge, that is, a catastrophe unrelated to his moral make-up. Or we might want to stop a driver riding for a fall because he is reckless, arrogant, or obsessed. This latter character is the one Miller was striving to depict in the 1950s, for the words "what he was really doing to his life" describe a man endangered by forces from within rather than perils from without. The verb form is significant too: "was . . . doing" means that things are not too far gone and that there is still room for choice.

Miller might have structured differently the events of his waterfront story. He might have worked out a quite traditional romantic conflict of several kinds: that of the young lovers faced with a more than usually sinister family opposition—a Romeo and Juliet struggling against an incestuous father Capulet; or that of the admirable but extralegal young immigrants ("submarines") contending with the technicalities of the immigration laws. Significantly, Miller adopted another focus, one which meant a different form. He chose the perspective, not of the young couple who could be victors over or victims of Eddie Carbone, but of Eddie Carbone, who was ultimately to victimize others, yes, but most of all, himself. Miller sticks to the perspective without deviating. Eddie not only holds the stage most of the time, but he also dominates the scenes in which he is not present.*

In focusing the drama on the man who destroys himself while trying to control others, Miller elected a tragic pattern of experience. Hence he needed a protagonist of activity rather than passivity, one whose own energy and initiative determine his fate and that of others. Unlike Willy Loman, who destroys himself by a mechanical repetition of unbreakable patterns, Eddie Carbone breaks out of the patterns where safety and order lie and forces the issue. He is not a lugubrious cipher, but an aggressive, headstrong man who, like traditional tragic heroes, would impose his will on the world around him. We see not his weakness but his hubris. Yet it is not the hubris of a Tamburlaine, the zestful undivided man, the born winner. Eddie Carbone is less grand than Tamburlaine, but more significant: he is caught in the tragic opposition of impulse and imperative. His passion for his niece both opposes an ancient taboo and threatens his husband-wife relationship with Beatrice. However, Eddie has in him nothing of the pure villain such as Count Cenci, of the bold opponent of taboos such as Ford's Giovanni, of the maniacal accepter of perverse love such as Orin Mannon, or of the romantic who can put his marriage behind him. Hence the tensions between husband and wife remain secondary expressions of the conflict that becomes overt in Eddie's hostility to Rodolpho as Catherine begins to be attracted to him. Since Eddie has the lover Rodolpho in his power (as one of several "submarines" liable to deportation for illegal entry), he resembles the villain who could foreclose the mortgage or otherwise put on legal or

---

* There are scenes between Beatrice and Catherine (I), between the lovers Catherine and Rodolpho (II), between the arrested "submarines" and a lawyer (II), but what takes place in them is determined by the actions and spirit of Eddie. The physical actions of the arrest of the immigrants by the authorities, and of the revenge sought by Eddie and those arrested, actions likely to expand into independent sources of melodramatic tension, are decently held down to their role as extensions of actions in the moral realm—Eddie's betrayal of the guests in his house.

quasi-legal pressure. But the potentially melodramatic becomes tragic because Eddie is forbidden, by the Italian longshoreman's code, to use his power; there is a moral obligation to protect the "submarines," a taboo against revealing their presence. So Eddie's passion brings him into conflict with two taboos.* He is an Antigone in reverse: Antigone, faithful to the unwritten law, is destroyed by civil law; Eddie, nominally faithful to civil law, is destroyed by one unwritten law (while trying to violate another). Again, Eddie's case offers a rather sophisticated variant of the love-versus-honor tradition: he gives up honor for a "love" that is both forbidden and unattainable.

That we can think of such analogies argues that Miller was not deluding himself in saying that the play demanded a "larger-than-life attitude" in its actors, and was correct in speaking of "the mythlike feeling of the story" (p. ix). Myth offers the most significant analogy: Eddie is a version of the Phaedra who loved her husband's son Hippolytus. In both the Greek story and the modern one the incest would be technical; the need to retaliate for a rejection, whether overt or implicit, leads to dishonorable conduct; indeed, in Racine's version of the theme Phèdre is specifically jealous of Hippolytus' fiancée Aricia and barely pulls back from a plot to ruin her. Yet to carry the comparison so far is to reveal that it can go no further: Euripides' Phaedra and Racine's Phèdre both know from the beginning the nature of their passion and the canons that oppose it; their very awareness of what they are doing is at the heart of the struggle. Irrational urgency and agonized understanding possess them equally and give full dimension to the drama.

Eddie Carbone, plainly, is a lesser breed of tragic hero. He is never willing to know, or capable of knowing, what he is up to. He must translate every emotion into terms that reflect his authority, his good intentions, his honorableness, his "responsibility" for his niece. Catherine must yield to him because he is benevolent and all-knowing (Miller rightly substantiates Eddie's claims up to a point; only an Eddie who knows the ways of the world could say "most people ain't people"). His theory of unquestionable paternal wishes helps conceal the nature of his

* Miller's ability to complicate characters appears to a lesser extent in other dramatis personae: Beatrice fluctuates between a devoted and innocent wife, and a knowing protector of the lovers who at last tells Eddie the truth; the "submarine" Marco senses Eddie's irrationality but tries to preserve the situation; but a far more interesting personality is that of Catherine, who loves Rodolpho but who, before Eddie's betrayal of the immigrants, can so little bear to oppose Eddie that her response to him seems to have a sexual tinge.

desires. When his wife asks hard questions, he can duck all answers by insisting "I want my respect." When he is attacked by jealousy of Rodolpho, he simply invents good reasons for hating him: Rodolpho does not "respect" Catherine or Eddie, Rodolpho is homosexual, Rodolpho wants to marry Catherine only to gain American citizenship. When he has betrayed the immigrants, Eddie chooses to regard himself as a victim of defamation; he acts as if his "name" had been lost by others' words rather than his own deeds. When Beatrice, after trying to tell him the truth about his honor, goes on to try to tell him the truth about his love, his only reply is an incredulous and indignant "That's what you think of me—that I would have such a thought?" (II).

Miller dramatizes the intensity and relentlessness of the pursuit of self-ignorance; for Eddie Carbone self-knowledge is as unavailable as for O'Neill's heroes it is unbearable. Here Eddie falls away from the tragic magnitude that he has when, with mythic overtones, he is doubly caught between an imperative and a destructive passion. Up to a point there is always something fascinating about the mechanisms of self-deception. But the clinging to delusion, however authentically human, finally sinks into obtuseness, and obtuseness begins to stir impatience rather than sympathy. The man who has unknowingly erred falls characteristically into blaming others, as Eddie does, but the mark of the errant man's stature is his coming to know where blame must lie; if he never discovers this, his failure of intelligence is alienating, since our oneness with ignorance is tenable only when ignorance is a temporary failure of knowledge. These are different ways of saying that the tragic experience afforded by Eddie, while far greater than that afforded by Willy Loman, is limited by the limitations of his own personality.

III. The Turn to the Reflective Hero: "After the Fall"

It is almost as though Miller tried to escape these limitations in *After the Fall* (1964). The move from Eddie Carbone to Quentin is the move from a man whose passions inhibit understanding to a man whose efforts to understand are more evident to us than his passions. Quentin keeps asking himself hard questions and hacking his way through obscurities to such answers as may be come by. The principal materials for his diagnostic self-interrogation are his relation to his parents and brother, to his first and second wives, and to various other women, one of whom may become wife number three. The fact that both wives undergo psychoanalysis is appropriate, for the play as a whole is the analysis of Quentin: ". . . the action takes place in [his] mind, thought, and memory. . . ." [5] His inquest into things past takes the form of statements about, meditations on, and for the most part reenactments of key events, all addressed to an invisible listener occasionally permitted, for the sake of variety, to interpose unheard replies or questions. The multileveled stage is Quentin's mind, and all the people who enter his history are actually or implicitly present on it, visible or invisible, and "in abeyance" or "alive" (I). When they talk or in some way catch our eye, they are active in Quentin's memory or consciousness, sometimes for a brief puzzling or clarifying flash, sometimes for an extended episode formally acted out.

The drama of the mind ordering itself utilizes a spontaneity of consciousness which creates an air of great disorder. Segments of the past leap or wind into the present by some associative stimulus that makes the flow of events seem haphazard. This simulation of nonrational processes both forces the audience into experiencing the inner life of a mind struggling to find its own order, and permits the audience to make connections among disparate experiences as Quentin himself is making them. We see different wives making similar complaints to Quentin, his mother attacking his father in a way that seems meaningful in his own life; phrases and words like "separate person," "innocence," and "power" take on imaginative life by appearing in separate contexts; and, in trying to understand himself and human nature, Quentin recurrently finds purely personal memories interrupted by images of the 1929 crash, of anticommunist investigations in the 1950s, and, most conspicuously, of German concentration camps.

In making us share a psychiatric enlightenment, Miller has dispensed with plot in the ordinary sense; tension inheres in episodic conflicts rather than in an over-all advancing action. The sense of an evolving general situation, so well achieved by tight structure in *The Crucible* and *View from the Bridge*, is largely gone. Quentin's self-study, presented in intermittent action, creates an air of private problems inadequately transmuted into art,* and hence the reader finds himself pushed,

* With all allowance made for dramatic concentration, some things happen too fast to be plausible—most conspicuously the transformation of Maggie from Miss Life-Giving Sex to Miss Death Wish. Characterization appears to have yielded to portraiture or quasi portraiture.

despite all good resolves, into the familiar biographical readings of *After the Fall*. We have the sense of simply being pitched into painful family life, as we do in O'Neill's *Long Day's Journey*. Once biography takes over, tragedy is improbable; as we saw several times in O'Neill, tragedy inheres in a crisis, not in an entire life.

Yet the play differs from the O'Neill analogue in that Quentin labors toward a tragic sense of reality. He struggles from a simple view of life toward a more complex one, from a sense of grievance to a sense of guilt. He wants to avoid a melodramatic view when a melodramatic view is not appropriate. This comes out early in Act I when Quentin says, "I don't know how to blame with confidence," and Felice, to whom Quentin is a sort of inspirational guide, attributes to him the view that "No one has to be to blame!" Yet here we run into another problem: this rejection of the melodramatic view hardly outweighs the dramatic evidence of a Quentin who does blame rather confidently. There is something uncomfortable about the way in which he keeps criticizing "my women," using his praise of Holga and Maggie as a means of attacking other women, and clinging to his sense of betrayal by his mother.* Though he abuses those who take advantage of Maggie, in time he accuses her of wanting to make him her murderer and of seeking his "destruction" (II). Quentin's diagnosis of others may actually be sound, but his self-interest and self-protection are persistent, almost more spontaneous than the formal eschewing of blame. Quentin's self-absorption is conspicuous (perhaps more so than Miller intended). His father is not altogether wrong when he says accusingly, "What you *want!* Always what you *want!*" (II). Quentin seems somehow to be a recipient of love rather than a participant in a mutual enterprise. Despite eventual alterations in attitude, he spends much time receiving the "blessings" of Felice and Maggie, somewhat complacently observing Holga's tears for him, and making her assure him that she loves him.† Yet he can also

---

* "These goddamned women have injured me!" Later, "All my women have been so goddamned sure!" Holga, his latest love, pleases him because she alone seems not "to be looking for some goddamned . . . moral *victory*" (I)—as by implication all the others had been. Maggie was "someone who—could not club you to death with their innocence!"—the relief of one who believes he has been a victim. "This woman's on my side" (II)—as if all the others had been opponents. All this is too close to grievance and self-pity.

† Felice blesses him for some psychic boon that made it possible for her to have a cosmetic operation on her nose (I, II)—a matter where the bathetic and the farcical compete. Maggie's blessing is in Act II. Holga weeps (I, II), and

say, "I am bewildered by the death of love" (II), and much more important, he can at last put his finger directly on the issue of character which the reader has feared might never come to the surface: "And I wanted to face the worst thing I could imagine—that I could not love" (II).*

Here again we see Quentin turning toward a tragic sense of reality. To sum up this discussion thus far, *After the Fall* struggles to be a tragedy, but it is impeded by two forces: the strong biographical tendency, the historical inclusiveness that works against dramatic concentration; and the heavily egocentric quality of the protagonist, who, with an insistent self-regard at times almost fatuous, seems to resist the author's effort to will him into the tragic stature earned by self-understanding. Nevertheless Miller keeps pushing Quentin toward self-knowing. He learns to suspect himself of different vices of self-serving, from lying to treachery; † he must even acknowledge, "I know how to kill" (II). Aside from such special acts of awareness, he wrestles continually with moral problems identified by key words that act as leitmotifs. One such word is *power:* Quentin uses it repeatedly, first as a word of felt but unclear significance, then as a definition of an erring quest.‡ The power theme is merged with another theme that is introduced quite imaginatively. Quentin finds that when standing between two lamp fixtures on his hotel-room wall he can stretch his arms out and touch the fixtures (I). Eventually, just when he is again entertaining an old thought— "the power to change her!" (that is, Maggie)—he realizes that the posture is that of the Crucifixion (II). The dialogue makes a great deal

replies affirmatively to his question, "You love me, don't you?" (I). He defines Maggie as "all love," and she agrees (II).

* It is interesting that, working from wholly divergent premises, Miller and T. S. Eliot alight on some of the same problems. The fear that he could not love is the central difficulty of Edward Chamberlayne in *The Cocktail Party* (1949), and Harry Monchensey in *The Family Reunion* (1939) has to live with the fact that potentially he is both wife-murderer and matricide, as does Miller's Quentin (II).

† He can suspect himself of cruelty, doubt his good faith, ask whether he demands of women an impossible "simple-minded constancy" (I), acknowledge that he has "lied" to Maggie, "brought the lie" into their relationship, and can "lie" about it to the Listener (II). He can spot himself as a false friend (I), acknowledge his rejoicing when another's death relieves strain on himself, and learn that you can "turn your back" on friends "in your own—blood-covered name" (II).

‡ He feels "power" in leaving his family and apparently in leaving Holga (II). He is gratified by the power to "influence" a woman's "life," first with Felice, then with Maggie, with whom his feeling, he sees later, becomes the sense of "power" to "transform somebody, to save!" (II).

of the image of Quentin as savior.* While Miller imagines Quentin as tempted by the role, he also imagines Quentin's moral wit as wholly reliable here, and Quentin is persistent in his disavowals.† The most resonant passage comes when Quentin is explaining to Maggie the story of God's raising Lazarus from the dead: ". . . God's power is love without limit. But when a man dares reach for that . . . he is only reaching for the power. Whoever goes to save another person with the lie of limitless love throws a shadow on the face of God" (II). Quentin's implicit identification of himself as the man who would be God, which has been well prepared for, makes him a highly representative figure. We sense in him, indeed, an interesting distant echo of Faustus, especially Dorothy Sayers' Faustus, who would like to relish the divine power of transforming humanity. When Miller's imagination is at its best, his characters suggest mythic figures.

There is another myth operating in the play; it appears in the insistent leitmotif of innocence, a subject which obsesses Quentin.‡ He wants to have it both ways, to be free of guilt and still to enjoy a godlike power that cannot be exercised without guilt. Yet just as he spots his own love of power, so Quentin becomes wiser about innocence. He not only recognizes his lack of innocence (II), but questions the value of innocence itself, as if dissociation from evil were a denial of full humanity: § "—is it altogether good to be not guilty for what another does?" (I). What is more, he faces his own complicity in apparently alien evil. From the beginning he has struggled to interpret the concentration-camp tower that, as a part of the stage set, is permanently embedded in his mind. Only in the last minute of the play does he reach his

* Act II has many such passages. Maggie for a while speaks to Quentin "with timid idolatry"; Holga makes him think of himself as "adored again"; Maggie assures him, "—you're like a god!" "He saved me," cries Maggie, and Quentin uses the same word, though in a different context, to her: "I saved you twice. . . ." This is just after she has assured him, "no man was ever loved like you." Maggie also calls him "a king" and wants "like a castle" for him. There is another version of this in some words of Holga that exemplify the bathos into which the play occasionally falls: "I love the way you eat! You eat like a Pasha, a grand duke!"

† ". . . there is a fraud involved; I have no such power" (II). "Why did I lie to her, play this cheap benefactor . . ." (II). ". . . the lie that she had to be 'saved'!" (II).

‡ He recognizes that he has had a craving for "innocence" (I); then he revolts against pretended innocence, or innocence used as a weapon (II).

§ Quentin first forces the issue upon a legal client of his who has just "taken the 5th Amendment" before a congressional committee. He asks the indignant client, "if the tables were turned, and they were in front of you, would you permit *them* not to answer? Hateful men that they are?" (II).

final interpretation: "Who can be innocent again on this mountain of skulls? . . . My brothers died here—but my brothers built this place; our hearts have cut these stones!" (II). This acknowledgment of guilt —so close to the event, a considerable feat of the moral imagination— is the tragic complement of an early passage in which Quentin describes the easier, more exhilarating days of melodramatic feeling: "Remember —when there were good people and bad people? And how easy it was to tell! The worst son of a bitch, if he loved Jews and hated Hitler, he was a buddy" (I). And this remarkable rejection of a simpler doctrinaire world, of a monopathic partisanship, is put in terms that utilize the innocence myth and point to the title of the play: of that rejected world, the Quentin of the more difficult polypathic present says, with a sharable tinge of regret, "Like some kind of paradise compared to this." "Paradise" will not do. Quentin's ultimate knowledge is that "we meet unblessed; not in . . . that lie of Eden," as he puts it with a jarringly polemic note,* "but after, after the Fall, after many, many deaths." Our ultimate knowledge is the denial of innocence and the acceptance of our human liability to evil, our kinship even with that evil practiced by our enemies. This knowledge of original sin can lead to salvation: to know the worst is to be able to love and forgive. Though the note of hope for fallen man runs some risk of the facile, it is a significant antidote to the untragic despair which began to appear in Ibsen, which was almost standard fare in O'Neill, and which has been much affected in more recent thought. By the end of *After the Fall* Miller has earned the insight that knowledge is the perfecting of tragic experience, that the most appalling knowledge can be borne, and that in that sense tragedy implies, not a terminal catastrophe, but, after error, revision and continuity.

After the Fall constitutes, then, a quite perceptive essay about tragedy. It is an "essay" in that the meanings are established pedagogically rather than dramatically. The body of the play has two components: one is analogous to the rerunning of video tapes made in the past, the other part to an interpretative commentary in the present. Quentin is the commentator—retrospective, interrogative, cogitative, and finally instructive. Passions did spin the plot; but the analytical mind weaves the conclusions. Quentin is less the purged sufferer, struggling through pas-

---

* Calling Eden a "lie" seems to have come out of some unexamined aversion, for it creates logical confusion in the metaphor: if Eden is false, then the Fall is meaningless.

sion into enlightenment, than he is a moral docent, lecturing Maggie as well as understanding himself (there is about him an uneasy touch of Merriwell as psychiatrist), and somewhat too obviously, and even protectively, generalizing himself with such statements as "And I am not alone, and no man lives who would not rather . . ." (II). The faint aroma of the professorial in Quentin means that he is not the fully imagined man of pathos that Miller achieved in Willy Loman, or the man of passion that he realized in John Proctor and, for that matter, in the Reverend John Hale, and especially in Eddie Carbone. There is not the same freedom and boldness, the capacity for the big move or leap; rather there is a somewhat pinching constraint.* Nor is there the large, sweeping dramatic structure, despite the glimmering presence of the Faustian man-who-would-be-god; rather there is a series of theatrical ingenuities. So we have a sense of artistic diminution in this play, and it brings to mind a term like "essay."

Quentin does have, however, a reflective and theoretical intelligence not given to any of his predecessors. Through him Miller reveals a way of thinking about character that can produce the tragic hero: a sense of the self-corrective impulse, of the need to find the truth and to struggle for conduct that accords with it. At the core of Quentin's self-knowing is the renunciation of innocence, a moral action of such importance that it provides the title of the play. Here Miller advances further in the direction which he chose when, in the introduction to A View, he finally put behind him the "misunderstood victim." Now he takes a man who might think of himself as a victim—of parents, of women, of political injustice, and, by extension, of the grossest evil of his own times—and refuses to let him assume the role of victim. The rejection of innocence, as a personal act, eliminates the idea of oneself as victim; as a theoretical act, it eliminates the victim as concept. Hence Miller has diagnosed what I have called the "innocence neurosis," and has made the major decision not to let his protagonist fall into its allurements. And if Quentin as an individual has not entirely escaped from the characteristic styles

---

* One is never quite free from discomfort at a certain subtle persistence of self-regard in Quentin, even at times when he is explosively deriding himself. This may be the result of total reliance on his point of view, through which it is difficult to mediate convincing self-placement. A character like Quentin really needs to be seen from without. The tendency of Quentin's drama to become "a life" implies that the materials would be more successfully handled in a novel. A novel with third-person point of view would, or at least could, put Quentin in better perspective.

of the innocent man, still Miller has inferentially renounced the relatively easy modes of blame and indignation. Without innocence one must forgo the indignation which, if it is in control, "subvert[s] tragedy to melodrama." [6] But Miller does more than take the negative steps which simply protect tragedy against "subversion"; he is at pains to achieve a tragic execution of the dramatic materials. For it is his aim to have Quentin not merely forgo innocence but rather discover in himself the guiltiness that belongs to the human condition. Quentin can almost say what Robert Penn Warren's Jerry Beaumont said, "But that innocence is what man cannot endure and be man, and now I flee from innocence and toward my guilt." [7]

IV. Return to Older Themes and Form: "The Price"

We might approach Miller's latest play, The Price (1968), either as a full development of the depression-family theme briefly introduced in After the Fall, or as a return to the stubborn, self-willed, closed hero of A View from the Bridge. Though these links with earlier plays do catch the eye, what is more notable is that, after much experimentation and in a strongly antitraditionalist period in the theater, Miller turns to an Aristotle-cum-Ibsen kind of production. Its theatrical skill flows from a sense of complexity in the human issues and from an awareness that such complexity comes gradually to light only under the pressure of conflicting needs in the characters. Three of the four characters belong to a family—Victor Franz, his wife Esther, and his brother Walter; there is only one scene, a Manhattan apartment; and the action takes place in a few hours. As the tensions become sharper, their ancient roots are revealed, step by step, and we see the present impact of new knowledge of old deeds. What is more, in their need to justify themselves, the brothers want the deeds of long ago to conform to a sense of them that they have long held; they want old facts to support their salvation now. As often in Miller, there is considerable thematic richness in the generally straightforward dialogue; in a different kind of study one might follow up the themes of stasis in life, of the rat race, of forgiveness, of dream and belief and illusion. There is less of the symbolic than in Ibsen, though one character, the eighty-nine-year-old secondhand-furniture dealer, Gregory Solomon, has a strongly symbolic role. Old enough to be out of such competition, Solomon, "still driving" (II),[8] contends vigorously over "the price" for the elder Franzes' furniture, which must be disposed

of now, long after their deaths, because the apartment building in which
they lived is to be torn down. As Solomon bargains with the brothers
over the furniture, so they bargain with each other over their actions as
young men, over their conduct to their long-dead father, over the prices
once paid by sons—paid in their lives and still to be paid for truth or
for the maintenance of self-images. As Walter says, "We invent ourselves, Vic, to wipe out what we know" (II). Age does not stale the
contentiousness, the suspiciousness, the self-protectiveness of brothers
who need to extract some profit from the disposal of the past.

As the apartment house is torn down, so does the "house of Franz"
lose its façade and have its interiors exposed. The elder Franz had been
ruined in the 1929 crash. Victor had pitied him and supported him; this
had meant leaving college, where he had shown some promise in science,
and taking a dependable job on the police force, from which he is now
about to retire. (His wife Esther is more eager than he for a new life.)
As Victor sees it, Walter had selfishly gone his own way, becoming a
well-to-do doctor; through indifference or guilt or snobbery Walter has
not communicated with Victor for many years. It is the ancient story of
two sons quarreling over a patrimony, here an intangible one; over their
merits, their fidelities, their finding favor, to speak, in the eyes of God.
Walter does show up for the furniture sale: not only is he willing to have
Victor take all the profits, but he wants to help Victor find a job that
will use his talents better than police work has done. But Victor is so
full of a sense of Walter's misconduct over the years that he interprets
Walter's proffered assistance as a bribe to make him forget injuries.
Surface courtesy yields to challenge and accusation; justifications lead to
new facts. The second half of the long Act II develops a remarkable
continuity and increase of tension as successive revelations about the
Franz family not only complicate the past but heighten the pressure
which the brothers feel in the present. Walter's view is that theirs had
been a loveless family which knew only the spirit of competition; that
even after the crash their father had had some secret resources and with
an effort could have made out on his own; that he, Walter, far from
ducking a "responsibility," had saved himself from the clutches of a
paternal racketeer and only in later years from the psychological marks
of the harsh Franz life; and that Victor had been "exploited" and
victimized by the father. But this theory deprives Victor of the image of
his life as a history of virtuous sacrifice; he insists that he saved his

father's faith in things and people. Walter retorts that Victor could not face the nothingness of the Franz life: "You don't want the truth, you want a monster" (that is, Walter) (II).

This cursory summation does not do justice to all the layers of unconscious motive implied in counteraccusations and responses. The confrontation, which is sustained with great vigor, has excellent melodramatic life, and it affords in an exemplary way the melodramatic virtue of dividedness of appeal. The simplicities immanent in the situation are all gone. Walter, the potential "bad guy," has undergone something like a tragic experience: fierce competitiveness led to a crack-up, and the crack-up was followed by an apparent new wisdom about self and family. Victor, the "good guy," appears to have needed his sacrificial role, to have used it as a weapon against Walter (Esther tells Victor, "You can't bear the thought that he's decent"; Walter's version of it is, "To prove with your failure what a treacherous son of a bitch I am! . . ."—II), and to be utterly unwilling to alter his sense of himself as filial hero playing Aeneas to his father's Anchises. Yet Esther, in attacking her husband, speaks also from disappointment in their lives and from her desire to use Walter as a stepping stone to better things; and Walter's fierce laying bare of Victor's soul, convincing as it is, springs also from his need to maintain his own moral position. The ambiguity appears even in the supporting character Solomon, who mingles the understanding of a Solomon with the calculation of a skillful dealer. In all the characters, then, there is an indeterminacy that reflects skillful use of the melodramatic mode.

Walter sees Victor as "sacrificing his life to vengeance" (II), a half-truth which is useful in enabling us to see a subtle echo of the old revenge drama. Here, as in revenge drama, each person clings desperately to a singleness that he needs—and yet comes across to us not singly but dividedly. Miller has caught the rigor with which human beings cling to roles, their need for a consistency that is not consistent with reality. So they—we—fight off the tragic experience, the inner awareness of a contradiction, the living with it. After Walter leaves, Esther says, "It always seems to me that one little step more and some crazy kind of forgiveness will come and lift up everyone" (II)—an ironic commentary on the unforgivingness that rules at the end.* In forgiveness one con-

---

* Interestingly, *After the Fall* also introduces the theme of forgiveness near the end. There the theme comes in only verbally and so risks the sentimental. But tone

cedes something of one's position, one's "rights" that imply retaliation, one's untouchable singleness. Here, Miller reveals how strongly the "good man" resists this concession. Miller makes superior melodrama out of man's determination to be melodramatic rather than tragic.

V. MILLER'S CONTRASTING TENDENCIES

There is no risk of overneatness in asserting that Miller's two plays of the 1960s, *After the Fall* and *The Price*, reveal two contrasting tendencies in the playwright—one toward the tragic interpretation of experience, one toward the melodramatic. Quentin struggles to escape from blame of others and defense of self and to achieve an understanding of self and a coming to terms with the facts that it might be more comfortable to deny; each Franz brother, but especially Victor, wants to keep the other in the wrong, since another's wrongness establishes or enhances one's own rightness. In *After the Fall*, the action turns on a resolution of internal conflict; in *The Price*, on the strenuous maintenance of outer conflict.

Writing at the time of *After the Fall* and trying to look ahead, one might reasonably have predicted that Miller would go on to a greater mastery of the tragic form. He had seemed to be moving, more or less regularly, in such a direction. In *Death of a Salesman* he wrote pathetic drama, the history of an undivided character experiencing pitiable obsolescence. In *The Crucible* he turned to more vigorous characters who cause suffering rather than uncomprehendingly suffer, he portrayed an evil rooted in human nature overwhelming the community, he made advances toward complexity of motive, and he began to discover inner division. In *A View from the Bridge* he first focused attention directly on a potentially tragic central character—the divided man who cannot

aside, Miller is exploring a theme that has considerable relevance for generic form. He sees the relation between being unable to forgive oneself and being unable to forgive others; in either stance, one is locked in a kind of solitary cell that cuts one off from the potential fullness of one's own nature. One keeps punishing oneself or punishing others, perhaps both simultaneously. In either case one lives in a melodrama of revenge, against oneself or others, and denies the openness of tragedy. In expository speeches by the characters, *After the Fall* is more hopeful; in total dramatic effect, *The Price* takes a tougher line.

There are other verbal or dramatic ties between different Miller plays. In *The Price*, Victor's hurt feeling that only Walter has earned "respect" is reminiscent of Eddie Carbone's demand for "respect" in *A View from the Bridge*. Victor and Walter might be Willy Loman's sons twenty-five years later. The recollections of the impact of the 1929 crash on a family with two sons develop more fully certain hints in *After the Fall*.

stop short of the aggressions that, ministering to the ego, rebound ruinously upon the doer. Miller does not quite complete the route to tragedy, for Eddie Carbone clings furiously to his innocence. That innocence is what Quentin in *After the Fall* learns to abjure, and in his turning from innocence to guilt we see Miller taking the final step into the tragic form. Yet an oversupply of talkiness and episode, of under-assimilated raw material, makes the play fall considerably short of excellence. One might have expected that Miller would go on to master the tragic structure. Yet in *The Price* he returns to a view of man as self-defensive antagonist in whom duality of being is replaced by a certain duplicity in maintaining a longed-for singleness.

Generic form, of course, is always a reflection of the dramatist's way of reading human nature. Miller offers two characteristic readings. In one, he sees man as erring and then understanding; thus Biff in *Death of a Salesman*; several characters, most notably the Reverend John Hale, in *The Crucible*; Quentin in *After the Fall*; and perhaps, though rather ambiguously, Walter Franz in *The Price*. On the other hand, Miller has a powerful sense of man's unconscious need to lock himself in a position and blindly to maintain it, as if obsessed, against every painful force that might free him. It is the kind of rigidity—image-preserving, accusing, punitive if the means are at hand, ultimately self-destructive— that we see in Othello before light dawns, and in Lear before his therapeutic madness. Willy Loman simply cannot break bad habits; the would-be saviors of Salem cannot escape from their preconceptions about the strategies of evil. Eddie Carbone mistakes a forbidden passion for a moral imperative that justifies the violation of other imperatives and makes him see the truth as a monstrous lie. Like Eddie Carbone, Victor Franz must cling to the image of himself as the hero of a noble mission; he obstinately rejects flaws in himself or forgiveness for his brother.

Miller gets some of his best dramatic life from the portrayal of these characters who with utter stubbornness refuse the pain of a genuine salvation and succumb to the flattery of a false one. He catches a basic passion of man—to live on in a melodrama and escape tragedy. But above all things, Miller does not conceive his inflexibles simply: in their humanity they win our sympathy, and they appall us. In catching this duality melodrama is at its best.

Afterword

I F WE NOW glance back at O'Neill, it is difficult not to think of
Hickey's judgment in *The Iceman Cometh:* "There's a limit to the
guilt you can feel. . . ! You have to begin blaming someone else,
too." Whatever Hickey's credentials as spokesman, his "limit to the
guilt you can feel" seems an authentic statement of an O'Neill credo:
self-knowledge is a terrible burden that must be relieved by illusions
about oneself or blame of others. This self-saving blindness Miller sees
at times as possessing man wholly, at other times as yielding to man's
openness to light. Where O'Neill thinks man can survive only by choosing self-protective ignorance, Miller presents him as either instinctively
self-protective or as potentially self-corrective. For O'Neill, the truth
cannot be borne; for Miller, it may not even be recognizable as truth, or
it may lead to salvation. The Miller of the latter view has, of course,
better materials for tragedy. His hero can have more range, a more
flexible strength; he is no less likely to fall, but after the fall he can
wean himself away from dreams and acrimony.

O'Neill works regularly within the realm of tragedy; Tennessee
Williams often does. Both, that is, use the divided character who, caught
in a conflict of imperatives and impulses, prepares his own catastrophe.
They do not spend time on the melodramatic figure that Miller would

formally renounce, the "misunderstood victim." Yet more often than not for them, the divided character resembles a victim: the cause of catastrophe is some inability to cope—less an outburst of hubris that demands a return to measure, than a corruption of will or a decay of spirit that leads to being overwhelmed as if by an enemy. What O'Neill and Williams repeatedly see in man is incurable weakness or illness. Once or twice O'Neill imagines a healing by faith, and Williams has been developing some interest in what we might call the faith healer. But their dominant tendency is to imagine human beings too far gone— crumbling rather than crashing, dwindling rather than diving, less contriving a tragedy than falling into the disaster of personality (Blanche DuBois, Brick Pollitt, the Mayos, the Mannons, the Tyrones, the Hopemen), turning within, fading out, or dragging on with the medicaments of abuse, drink, drug, or dream. Occasionally there is the excess rather than the deficiency, the energetic overreaching that is potentially tragic —in the Cabots, in Emperor Jones, in Simon Harford, and indeed somewhat in Brick Pollitt. Even in these, though there are some notes of the anagnorisis and recovery that can fill out the full tragic range, there is the familiar pressure toward certain effects of melodrama: the pathos of erosion and the horror of disorder and disintegration. When Miller writes melodrama, however, his characters are dominantly strong rather than weak; they attempt to rule life rather than cave in before it. When this energy is combined with the ability to endure self-understanding, they are the human materials of tragedy.

It would be tempting to go beyond these descriptions into genetic accounting. Though that will not be possible for quite some time, we do recall the symbolically divergent backgrounds of these three leading American practitioners of serious drama, tragic or quasi-tragic: the Irish Catholic, the Episcopal,* the Jewish; northeastern and theatrical, southern and ecclesiastical, metropolitan and commercial. In some sense each of the three draws material from his own background, each finds problems in his own heritage and experience: one in New Englanders, the Irish, the theater; one in the clashing sensibilities of the South; one in the politics, economics, and family life of the big city. As yet we have only fragmentary evidence on the way in which each man's personality and history have put pressure on his imagination and account in some way for the profound anguish and sense of doom in O'Neill, for the dis-

---

* Williams has now (1970) become Catholic.

order verging on the bizarre and the sensational in Williams, for the pressure of the expository and homiletic in Miller. In all of them we sense a need for the catharsis of disturbing personal and family history. Of the three, Miller seems spontaneously to try to enlarge or transcend the private: he uses Jewish themes only incidentally, making them representative rather than particularizing them; he endeavors to read the demonstrably personal in large human terms; he overcomes the temptation to the polemic mode; he turns his eye deliberately away from the victims of others to the victims of themselves; and focuses on the strength that men bring either to protecting themselves or to enduring new light.*

* These conclusions are supported, in the main, by Miller's long one-act play, *Incident at Vichy* (1964), although on the face of it they may seem to be contradicted. *Incident at Vichy* presents the reactions of a group of men, nearly all Jewish, rounded up at Vichy in 1942 as Nazi anti-Semitism spreads further into France, and awaiting the hearing that will send them to slaughter in Poland. It amplifies a study of the concentration-camp theme that appears symbolically in *After the Fall*. Mainly a melodrama of disaster executed with maturity and detachment, it records the diverse reactions of victims who can neither make choices nor have hope—their incredulity, rationalization, self-reassurances, courage, terror, self-insight, and their irrational hopes both for personal safety and for general salvation. The heightening tension of a cruel and desperate situation is done very well; even in the didactic passages, which are of some extent, it is generally maintained by differences of opinion. In such passages it becomes clear that Miller wants to universalize anti-Semitism rather than stop at the polemic which is inseparable from the subject: the character who comes closest to being his spokesman, the Jewish psychoanalyst Leduc, says, "And Jew is only the name we give to the stranger, that agony we cannot feel, that death we look at like a cold abstraction. Each man has his Jew; it is the other. And the Jews have their Jews" (New York, 1965, p. 66). Leduc, speaking with great passion to Von Berg, the "decent" Austrian aristocrat who also has been grabbed by the Nazi-and-collaborator dragnet but who will probably survive the hearing, demands that Von Berg accept his own complicity in, his own responsibility for, the Nazi ethnic murders which he believes he abhors. It is here, then, that the play turns from the central melodramatic mode toward the tragic mode: Von Berg, when he gets his white passport to safety, gives it to Leduc. On the one hand, Von Berg acknowledges guilt and performs an expiatory act (he will doubtless be killed); on the other, a stage direction refers to Leduc's "awareness of his own guilt." (Here are two different versions of that action late in *After the Fall* in which Quentin acknowledges as "brothers" both the victims and the murderers in the concentration camps.) What Miller has done is to approach evil, not entirely as the deeds of some "other" who touches us not, but from the point of view of the person who, though he himself has not performed the evil deed, has the moral sentiency which enables him to recognize his participation in it. To picture the survival of that ability—under conditions where self-survival might blot out every other motive—is to introduce the "tragic continuity," the missing element in the melodrama of disaster.

PART III

Place and Persons: Three Europeans

Foreword

THOUGH O'Neill had an allegorical period lasting a half-dozen years and Williams wrote several dramatic fables, O'Neill, Williams, and Miller work predominantly with a sense of character that we can call "anthropomorphic." They conceive of each character as a human being who is as complete as they can make him. When we turn to Bertolt Brecht, Max Frisch, and Friedrich Duerrenmatt, we run, more often than not, into a kind of character for which we need a different term—"logomorphic" or "ideomorphic" or "semamorphic" or "pathomorphic." Like many recent playwrights these three Europeans depart from a traditional sense of personality (and for that matter, of plot). The model on which the character is formed is not a probable man, however narrow or imperfect, but a part of a man—a mood, a need, a passion, an obsession—or an aspect or habit or tendency of society, or the dramatist's interpretation of a historic disturbance or a nonhistoric reality. The model on which actions are formed is not an imaginable pattern of conduct, the externalization of a fully developed personality in either ordinary life or emotional or moral crises, but the outrageous, grotesque, "mad" gesture or movement or deed that ignores all convention or expectation or even literal possibility to express totally the value or meaning or motive embodied in the character. We have the

[167]

impression of watching counters in a startling and uninhibited game of ideas, with its own esoteric rules.

Such expressionist drama, whether puzzling, provocative, or shocking in the fantasy of spirit or method or décor, is a theatrical analogue of nonrepresentational art. Nonrepresentational drama has given up, as if it were worn out, the representing (or "imitating") of men in action and finds its being in a tension among constituent parts. In drama these parts are not colors, lines, masses, or textures, but urgencies, *idées fixes*, hypotheses, emotional and psychic and intellectual forces—that is to say, "abstractions" from "nature," which, in the dramatic cosmos, is the full human personality. Like painting, drama disintegrates "nature" and reassembles the fragments in new compositions upon arbitrary principles that, till novelty has sunk in and become custom, create an air of simple distortion of reality. Tempting as it is, however, the analogy ends there, for drama rarely seeks to be purely nonrepresentational; rather its counters are representative in a new way—of themes, states of being, moral styles, special visions, essences, unseen realities. Since these are ordered by an attitude meant to be communicated to the audience, we sense another analogy: the speaking art which on the one hand behaves like abstract painting, on the other behaves like nonartistic speech-making. It becomes explicative and minatory discourse; the stage is chosen by people who would once have found themselves in forum or pulpit. The expressionistic characteristically tends to become the instructional (that is, allegory in modern dress). Maybe there is an inner affinity between the two: the artist working with full human character has no time to make points, and the character itself includes the range of choices that pictures a moral world; but the artist who works with segments of personalities or with personified ideas finds himself inevitably having special accents, and the very absence of wholeness leads to explanatory or even hortatory gestures. Conversely, an artist may start with points, gestures, or accents, and find partial personalities to be their dramatic agents.

The theatrical success of expressionism implies not only a weariness with realism but also a receptiveness to the doctrinal use of the stage; ironically we supersede realism by going back to prerealistic forms, though we deck them out in novel fashions. A secular age does not turn its back on sermons, or at least not on preachers and prophets; it likes them in unexpected places, disguised. The theater is rich in sermons, and in that respect it resembles the church where it was born and lived for centuries. But the vocabulary is strange, upsetting, enigmatic. The pulpit conundrum is the Platonic form unconsciously imitated by many expressionist writers—Pirandello, Camus, and Sartre, for instance, as well as the three to whom we now come.

To include such writers in a consideration of tragedy may seem perverse or precious. Aside from their allegorical bent, they have other characteristics which might seem to rule them out. Brecht is not only committed to the didactic, whether in exposé or exhortation, but with the "Verfremdungseffekt" endeavors to proscribe the empathic response which helps differentiate the tragic and melodramatic structures. In character he wants an epideictic singleness, not a sharable doubleness or many-sidedness. All these dramatists are satirical, often bitterly so, and satire is quite alien to tragedy. Frisch calls one of his plays a "farce," and Duerrenmatt describes several of his by the term "comedy." So we seem to be caught in a dilemma. If we say that, in spite of everything, the plays of these writers are indeed tragedies, we risk the pedantry of sheer contradiction; and if we say that they are not tragedies, we risk the pedantry of proving what no one is disposed to question.

But the situation is not hopeless. Expressionist plays, to repeat, have much in common with morality plays. Morality plays tend to fall into the realm of tragedy, for their dramatic issues originate in counterclaims within the morally aware person, that is, inner divisions and the kind of self-knowledge that is the end toward which, however reluctantly, unintegrated beings must move. Hence we can hardly look at morality plays without observing how far they tend toward tragedy. Further, though all three dramatists can agitate topical matters, their dramas become, in different ways, nontopical. Brecht is most strongly committed to political doctrine, yet he cannot always bind reality in ideological fetters. His characters often gain independence; he had well-known troubles in preventing empathic responses to them. Once we find ourselves imaginatively joining them instead of intellectually observing them, we may legitimately ask whether the experience afforded is tragic or melodramatic or something else. Duerrenmatt and Frisch are not advancing some contemporary doctrine or other, or using their characters to illustrate a social or political theory; rather they are using, as motives of action, the kinds of value that in all times destroy or preserve. Duerrenmatt not only calls one of his plays a "tragicomedy," but attributes to comedy—that is, to what he calls comedy—an order-creating function that all but usurps the role of tragedy. His jests lead naturally into the grotesque, and his grotesque turns on those driven, obsessive, frenzied beings reminiscent of Jacobean figures twisting on the border line between melodrama and tragedy. Frisch has fewer jests, but he likewise uses the grotesque, in which a surface incredibility magnifies horrors that have deep roots. Now and then each man gives an essentially tragic form to a character, making him a divided sufferer who moves into, or approaches, self-knowledge.

In examining some expressionist plays, then, we are not running head-on against all probability but are assuming that the conventional accounts of them are not exhaustive. If we find the plays in the main neither tragic nor melodramatic, still the perspective may be helpful in characterizing them. On the other hand, it would be illuminating to find evidence of a traditional sense of human reality in an innovating drama that seemed to have discarded older formulations or altered them beyond recognition.

To choose three rather than five or seven European dramatists for examination is obviously to provide a convenient parallel to the three Americans. Since we have to be selective rather than inclusive, there is something to be said for a limit of three and for these three. Like O'Neill, Williams, and Miller, they belong to an international rather than a regional theater. Like the Americans, they are or have become professional theater people; they are not to be thought of simply as writers who have also made use of the theater. So each one has a body of work which permits some conclusions about him as a dramatist. With Brecht, as with O'Neill, we have a completed canon. Just as O'Neill influenced Williams and Miller, so Brecht influenced Frisch and Duerrenmatt. But in Europe as in America the later men diverge both from their predecessor and from each other.

CHAPTER SEVEN

Bertolt Brecht (1898-1956)

D ESPITE his ideas on "epic theater"—surely the best known of all modern dramatic theory—Bertolt Brecht did not consistently succeed in keeping the audience in the role of detached observer and learner. It is most difficult to exclude an audience from emotional participation when the dramatic materials, by their nature, encourage participation. This was often the trouble for Brecht, since he had a strong sense of where the enemy lies and of who the victims are. Hence he naturally offered a melodramatic experience, which can come, though it need not do so, from a rather slender characterological base. A viewer or reader of *The Private Life of the Master Race* (1934 ff.) does not remain dispassionate and studious; only one kind of feeling is open to him, and he has it in abundance. This series of episodes, however, is a superior instance of the melodramatic genre, for in depicting victims it refrains almost entirely from the more obvious effects such as pathos, and goes instead into many subtleties of response to the political disaster pressing in upon the Germans.

In more than one play Brecht, in translating ideas into stage people who are to act them out, gives a character his head, so to speak, and lets him so develop that he becomes a human, as well as a semantic, being. We are "with" him. Eric Bentley noted this long ago and argues that Brecht wanted to get "sympathy *and* distance";[1] my point here is that in a certain kind of play the distance is reduced much more than may be intended. *The Caucasian Chalk Circle* (1944–45) is a romantic fairy tale spiced with tense adventures (a long pursuit); we know which side we are on. We are not much held off by the announcer, who succeeds only in becoming tedious in actual production, nor by comic irony and an almost Shavian turning upside down of expectations. On the contrary there is a quite marked traditional suspense as a disreputable village clerk, characteristically "in rags and tipsy" (v), becomes by fabulous means a judge whose folk-wisdom sets back arrogant and grasping lords, gives have-nots a break, and creates "a brief / Golden Age that was almost just" (vi).[2] All this is very pleasant, whether or not it was supposed to work in just this way. The characters are often picturesque in detail, their normal straightforwardness little tinged with ambiguity; there is little, if anything, to complicate a rejoicing in the triumph of unlikely underlings over social and political racketeers.

In pointing to Brecht's tendency to engage sympathy as well as create distance we have alluded to one play of mid-career and one that belongs to a later period. From this we might conclude that the willingness to let the imagination of character escape from the doctrinal will was a new thing, slowly learned with the passage of time. This surmise, however, is only partly true. For one thing, there is not really a Brecht period that we could think of as postdoctrinal; it is simply that the didactic becomes less overt and hence shares the stage with other materials that invite either empathy or a more complicated response to dividedness within the character. For another, there is what we might call a predoctrinal period that extends up to the late 1920s; in the works of these years we see Brecht looking at human personality with a spontaneous sense of its mingled motives and resistance to straightforward formulations—with an awareness of reality that is the foundation of greatness. Then we see him clamping down on this and enclosing himself, or trying to enclose himself, within a doctrine of virtue and vice by which the inner landscape of character, untroubled by uncertainties of terrain or mirages or destructive floods, is easily mapped by the socio-political rules. If we glance, then, at a few representative plays selected from Brecht's various periods, we can see the alterations in the dramatic substance that reflect his initial free sense of human nature, his new sense of mission, and finally a relaxation of the rules whereby the definition of goals for men yields to a sense of complexity in man.

I. SEVERAL EARLIER PLAYS

Drums in the Night (1922)[3] is a romantic drama, embodying the kind of feeling that would later reappear in *The Caucasian Chalk Circle;* but while in the latter play the romantic is an instrument of an underlying didactic intention, in *Drums in the Night* it is at the center, modified only by realistic and sometimes cryptic detail that inhibits the sentimental to which the materials are liable. Anna Balicke is a sort of Juliet, whose parents, a war profiteer and his equally calculating wife, want to marry her to Frederick Murk, a slick and vulgar man with good prospects in the business world. Anna has already been made pregnant by Murk, and she has used pepper in a futile attempt at abortion (Act II is entitled "Pepper"). But emotionally she has remained tied to an earlier lover, Andrew Kragler, who has been away four years in military service and reported dead. In a traditional romantic coincidence Andrew turns up on the day of the Anna-Murk engagement party. Andrew is less a Romeo than an Othello, however; his service in Africa was full of wonders, though of a surrealistic, nightmarish sort where the romance is less that of adventure than that of Gothic horror. Like a romantic in a Victorian novel, Anna tells Andrew that she cannot be his, but she does not say why; like a romantic victim of love, Andrew contemplates drink, suicide, and an escape into revolution (the Spartacist coup of January 1919). But Anna romantically catches up with him and confesses; he survives his shock, accepts her, rejects the revolutionaries, who try to keep him from her, and off they go together.

Anna might have been portrayed as caught in a conflict between the feeling of duty (to Murk) and the duty of feeling (to Andrew), but her hesitancy is minimal, and we soon see her in the right choice of romantic comedy. Yet the play has none of the banality that this bald synopsis implies, for a fresh, imagistic, often pungent, and often allusive style transforms the bare plot with folds of moral and metaphysical drapery. Andrew says of himself: "Seasick on a sea that swarms with corpses but doesn't suck me down. Rolling southward in the dark cattle cars: nothing can happen to me. Burning in the fiery oven: I burn hotter myself. A man goes mad in the sun: not me. Two men fall into a water hole: I

go on sleeping. I shoot blacks. I eat grass. I'm a ghost. . . . If you have
a conscience, the birds shit on your roof. If you have patience, the
vultures will get you in the end. Everybody works too hard." [4] This
Romeo-Othello has benefited from Renaissance and twentieth-century
reading; oddly, the final note of dawn after a dreadful night is not unlike
that in Christopher Fry's otherwise quite different *Sleep of Prisoners*.
Finally, if the play as a whole avoids much of what is expectable in
romance, the ending avoids what is expectable in the later Brecht: the
lovers are not deflected into the style of formal, public socio-political
revolt (against the Balicke-Murk world, whose grossness is strongly
satirized), but are faithful to the style of the private, romantic revolt of
feeling (against Balicke plans for profit and marriage). Brecht later
repudiated this effect.[5]

Brecht tackles a much more resistant subject in *Jungle of Cities*
(1927). This is less a drama examinable in terms of structure than it is a
literary tour de force in which unlike elements are yoked together but
not really fused, so that a persisting incoherence balks efforts at critical
definition. It may be best thought of as a symbolist poem in which
Brecht's adventurous imagination did not cope altogether successfully
with the unification of highly diverse materials and with the functioning
of the symbols. Hence Anselm Hollo's conjecture that the play "is, perhaps, . . . a poetic re-creation of Brecht's own season in hell" [6] makes
sense. It is as if Brecht were suffering through conflicting imaginative
experiences in which he intuited an ultimate unity but for which he
could not find, in objective drama, a common base and direction. The
parts have their own genuine urgency, and that is the life of the play.
Perhaps, in a season in hell, one is more likely to feel the series of blows
than the underlying order.

Brecht takes the Verlaine-Rimbaud homosexual affair (an intense,
quarrelsome relationship that ended when Verlaine shot and wounded
Rimbaud), transfers it to Chicago (here the senior participant is an
Oriental lumberman, Shlink, and the younger is George Garga, a native
of the "flat country"—Ohio, it turns out—who has come to Chicago
with his family and works in a bookstore), translates it into gunman-
gangster idiom (plus touches of the frontier), and attaches to it some
side actions in a vein of tough urban realism (drinking, whoring, family
tensions) or in reversal of popular expectations. To take the latter first:
George's sister Marie, instead of being the stereotyped victim of seduc-

tion, loves Shlink but cannot attract him; then when Shlink, urged by George, makes moves toward her, she shrinks from this as from a sale (v) and gives herself to a sailor; then gets money from Shlink and perversely insists that she is a "whore" (vi); then gets rid of the money she makes as a whore but adds, "I don't feel any easier . . ." (ix). There are no cliché actions here, and Marie's speeches often image great anguish; but they give an effective impression of misery rather than create a tangible character.

The symbolism in the Shlink-Garga relationship has familiar bases, but the detail is novel. Marie says of the two men: "Loving, hating: how they bend us down, how low they make us" (ix). Garga has already referred to Shlink as "my Infernal Bridegroom" and to himself as "his little bride" (v). But before this we have seen Shlink, with a bevy of henchmen who resemble bodyguards, enter the bookstore where George works, and talk in the tough style of a gangster who might be the trigger-man for a rival entrepreneur. Yet in time it appears that he is trying to give money to George; he does shortly make over to George his lumber business, the first of two such gifts. He helps take care of George's family, proposes to his sister Marie, and makes possible George's marriage. This strange wooing, however, is at the same time a subtle but fierce competition. Shlink: "I declare war on you! I'll begin the fight by shaking the foundations of your life" (i). Of Garga, "he's a good fighting man," and to Garga: "So you're really joining battle." Garga: "Yes, I am"—and Shlink gives him the lumber business (ii), "just for the privilege of insulting another man," as Garga puts it (iii). Others refer to each as the victim of the other (ii, iv). There are many such variations in this paradoxical feud, which at one time Garga calls a "tremendous debauch" (ix); it reaches a paradoxical resolution when Garga, declaring that he has had enough of it, takes a very damaging action against Shlink, and Shlink's death is apparently caused by Garga's withdrawal from what has been called a "metaphysical battle" and "metaphysical action" (v, x). The use of the word *metaphysical* indicates that the action is essentially symbolic; as such it tends to disengage us as successfully as Brecht's most self-conscious instructional devices in the *Lehrstücke* which he was about to undertake. Yet in a struggle as abstract as this one becomes, the verbal and actional details still create a melodramatic vigor which would be more expectable in a less disembodied conflict. Despite the human fuzziness of the motivation, however, Brecht is letting go with that side of himself essential to his greater work: the exploration of humanity rather than the explication of doctrine.

II. INSTRUCTION AND INVENTION

When Brecht began writing Marxist *Lehrstücke* in the late 1920s, he obviously did not lose his artistic talents, but he often hid them under the bushel of dogma. He is always inventive; the question is whether the inventiveness serves a predetermined end or begins to get loose on its own and thus to flourish as the free imagination which could convey a penetrating sense of human reality. He is closest to being a party agent in *The Mother* (1931); he widens the canvas considerably with the analysis of Nazism in *Roundheads and Peakheads: Rich and Rich Make Good Company* (early 1930s); then in *The Private Life of the Master Race* (later 1930s) Nazism grows from a political aberration to a human disaster.

The Mother, adapted from Maxim Gorki's novel *Mother* (written in the Adirondacks in 1906), succeeds remarkably in remaining instructional and therefore in admitting little of the human complexity into which Brecht's imagination often led him willy-nilly. With almost the simplicity of a television educational program the episodes show how mother-love can become party-love and how maternal protectiveness can be transmuted into partisan activism in various educative and provocative exploits. The scenes might be translations into dialogue of a handbook telling party precinct workers how to deal with a series of basic situations in which workers, women, and peasants learn that they have misunderstood or mistakenly resisted the Communist truth of life. Pelagea Vlassova, having sublimated mother-love and hence discovered that, though illiterate, she is equipped with extraordinary instructional skills, always finds the right way to convert doubters and questioners to the true revolutionary course. As commentator and dramatist both point out,[7] she shows right reason and sound practice in combination, and embodies true womanhood in its political manifestation. Apparently naïve but wonderfully sly, she is a kind of Socratic cracker-box philosopher who always wins. Hence, despite lively and ingenious detail, the drama soon disappears for anyone for whom the irresistible triumph of her doctrine is not an adequate substitute for the revelation of character in action and in language. Lee Baxandall somewhat oddly defends agit-prop drama by relating it to the tradition of the medieval morality,[8] and one might carry this further by noting how agit-prop often speaks for secularized Christian values. But the original morality turned on profound conflicts in human nature and hence had dramatic possibilities not open to the stage of political dogma.

Roundheads and Peakheads has the enticements of a remarkable tour de force: it adapts both Swift and Shakespeare in a topical satire that presents the Nazi movement as a capitalist plot against the workers. This socio-political theme emerges gradually. At the start we are most aware of the satire of Nazi anti-Semitism. In this, the method derives from *Gulliver's Travels*, as we learn in the expository sentence that follows the list of characters: "The inhabitants of the land of Yahoo, in which the action takes place, consist of Czuchs and Czichs, two races, of which the first have round and the second peak heads." [9] Modeled on Swift's High Heels and Low Heels (and Big Endians and Little Endians), the roundheads and peakheads are Gentiles and Jews (in *Andorra* Frisch would have Nazis identify Jews by their feet). When the Hitler character is given power in Yahoo, he identifies all evil with the Czichs, and a series of very ingenious episodes reveals the blackmailing, racketeering, travesties of justice, and cruelty of the Czuchs and the evils sustained by the Czichs. But soon it appears that this simple conflict of asserted good and assigned evil is running into complications, for there are Czuch and Czich owners and Czuch and Czich workers: while most immediate responses on both sides are naïve, the drama turns skillfully on the ambiguity of behind-the-scenes power. The conflict of loyalties might make either a Czuch or a Czich landlord, for instance, into the tragic man that Brecht approaches once in *The Private Life of the Master Race*; but on the whole, Brecht's doctrine of evil, as well as his commitment to the identification of evil, does not encourage him to pursue the turmoil of inner life. He sees less dividedness than a dominant human motive, namely, an almost automatic pursuit of advantage, though the pursuit may be combined with a lack of clearheadedness that leads to disastrous results for the pursuer.

The Hitler figure is Angelo Iberin; he is the Angelo of *Measure for Measure*, which Brecht has bitterly parodied in applying its general plot outline to Nazi Germany. In Brecht's Yahoo, the kindly Duke who retires for a while to let Angelo, as deputy, restore moral order, turns out to be simply the *ancien régime* of landlords and rent-collectors. They are willing to let Angelo do the dirty work of restraining license—that is, putting down a revolution of "Sicklemen" or Communists—and are willing to tolerate, for the time being, his Czuch-Czich scheme of good and evil, at least as long as it does not get in the way of their keeping control. The sexual misdeeds which are central in *Measure for Measure* are skillfully paralleled but serve mainly as ironic commentary on other issues: sexual improprieties are evil in an evil class (the Czichs), or admissible if they can help someone achieve personal or political ends. So the new serenity at the end is not symbolized by a renewal of sexual order; rather it is the old economic order resuming formal power, having used Angelo-Hitler to quell the disorder of the tenants' revolution, and now making clear to him that some of his irrationalities will have to be held in check lest they interfere with keeping the workers in subjection.

Brecht is demonically skillful in translating episodes from Shakespeare into his own ideological terms. Claudio, for instance, becomes a rich Jewish landowner, and his sister is applying for admission to a nunnery: this enables Brecht to analyze her as sexually deficient and to satirize the Catholic order for expediency and graspingness. Brecht is clever in maintaining the tense air of an intrigue plot in which, despite the advantage of historical knowledge, we cannot foresee the details of action by which the complex interests and counterinterests will work out. Satirical melodrama is joined with the melodrama of struggle for power; this makes good theater. But the demands on us are finally rather slight, for there are no real puzzles of good and evil; we may not be sure who will win, but we are not involved in inner conflict. Brecht attacks the evil Hitlerian melodrama of anti-Semitism, but he substitutes for it the absolute melodrama of evil owners versus silly and good workers (the good ones join the Sicklemen). The human ambiguities of *Drums in the Night* and *Jungle of Cities* yield to the clear outlines of the political morality. The final saturnine melodrama of evil triumphing over good, it is intimated, will be turned upside down: the Sicklemen, singing at their execution, are sure of ultimate victory—the new breed of Christian martyrs, dying to assure an immanent political paradise.

The difference between *Roundheads and Peakheads* and *The Private Life of the Master Race* is the difference between the theoretical analysis of a coup by which an evil force gains power, and the concrete depiction of human life after that force is in power. The theatrical effectiveness of a fluid political situation, in which suspense is created by an unsettled struggle for power, is replaced by the dramatic effectiveness of a now finally clearcut situation, in which the evil power is only too well known, and human beings have to find their ways of going up or down or on. In this superior kind of melodrama we are not asked simply to pity a class which is good by definition; rather we are drawn directly into horrifying experiences in which ruthless power not only threatens our lives but tests our human quality. A variety of recognizable characters have to make choices, and so we are always on the edge of tragedy; but in the multiplicity structure which Brecht has chosen the relatively brief episodes do not permit the follow-through of individual consciousness and conscience (such as we get in Carl Zuckmayer's *The Devil's General* of the early 1940s) that characterizes the tragic mode. Instead there is a strong sense of humanity crumbling under pressure, and of irreparable destruction; the very situation all but eliminates the likelihood of what I have called the tragic continuity, and we have an image of ultimate disaster.[10]

III. Major Plays: Free Characters and Mouthpieces

While we have mainly used a chronological order, Brecht's achievements are not consistently a matter of before and after, of earlier and later. *The Life of Galileo* (1937–38, 1946) is a later play than *St. Joan of the Stockyards* (1929–30), but it is no more free of doctrinal exposition; on the contrary, the central character seems more of a mouthpiece for ideas than does the title character in the earlier play. In a number of Brecht's best-known plays there is almost a running battle between his imagination and his intellectual position. Brecht is able not only to invest characters with natures that elicit sympathy rather than produce detachment, but also to confer on them an inviting degree of freedom— that is, to equip them with inner divisions that imply choices and thus take them toward tragic existence. The problem is how far he lets them go before he reins them in and cuts back on the autonomy that would threaten the socio-political point, as free characters must always do. Though he rarely, if ever, lets them go entirely their own way, nevertheless a number of major characters do embody contradictions that draw us into their being rather than their meaning.

In *St. Joan of the Stockyards* Brecht actually uses a traditional tragic figure as model; the play, he says, "is meant to portray the contemporary stage in the development of Faustian man." [11] Pierpont Mauler, the chief meat king (not to mention the lesser meat kings, stockbreeders, packers, and so forth through whom he controls the American market), is only half a Faust, however; unaided by Mephistopheles he uses his knowledge to gamble for control of his universe, the American meat industry and symbolically the whole economy, and he wins. He pays no price; everyone else pays his. In his final triumph he gives lip service to spiritual values he never acts by; with an air of religious devotion he uses the ecclesiastical institution—the Black Straw Hats—as an instrument for keeping workers and general public in line. So the traditional figure of tragedy is here converted into an object of brilliant social satire. Though it has been stated that Mauler is made "convincingly human," [12] it appears to me that his emotional disturbances and cries of quasi conscience are introduced, not to suggest a real complication of being in him, but as deceptive or self-deceptive gestures that add ironic accents to an essentially undivided conquistador.

For the individual of tragic possibility—that periodic intruder, as it were, into Brecht's homiletic dialogues—we must turn to the title character, Joan "Dark," reminiscent of Shaw's Major Barbara as well as of the original Jeanne d'Arc. This Joan leads the "Black Straw Hats," ostensibly a charitable and spiritual uplift organization, in an endeavor to "re-introduce God" into "a world like a slaughter-house" when factories are closed, disastrously for workers, because of stock-market warfare engineered by the "Bloody Mauler" (ii). She does not want workers to lose their souls by using "brute force," and she has great hope that the humanity and religious feeling of the meat kings can be beneficently awakened. As she slowly learns a series of lessons about how things are in the world—she is even kicked out by the Black Straw Hats, since her following of her private voice interferes with their institutional well-being—her progress from naïveté to knowledge is the instrument for satirically revealing the nature of the big speculators' tyranny over the workers. But Brecht also wants her to embody the tragedy of the person of good intentions: she undertakes a mission for labor leaders—the delivery of a crucial letter in the effecting of a general strike—but, overwhelmed by cold, hunger, fear, and doubts about using force, fails in her mission; the strike fails, and the workers are the losers. Meanwhile she has won a great reputation as "St. Joan of the Stockyards," and in the final scene she is canonized. This scene (xi) opens, however, with her realization of her failure (in "the only service / demanded of me my whole life long!") and her bitter expressions of remorse ("I did not come; . . . I stayed on the sidelines"; "I did harm to the injured / and was useful to those who harmed them"). With this entrance of tragic feeling, there is a new magnitude, and it appears that the character is going to be allowed her freedom. But the perspective is held only briefly, and satirical Marxian melodrama quickly takes over. Joan is turned from self-understanding to indignation and blame, and as she dies, she delivers a sermon against religion and the exploiting classes, and in favor of changing the world and using force. The didactic is partly relieved by the irony of meat kings and Black Hats cooperating to drown out her voice as they join in canonizing her. But the irony itself serves the lesson, that finance and church are in collusion to save the status quo, and this has final place. We see Brecht's first use of the practice that he would come back to again—of letting a character almost develop into a tragic hero and then firmly pulling him back for his destined role as explicator or polemic orator.

The title character of *Mother Courage and Her Children* (1938–1939) is constantly pressing, through the variety of her motives, toward a human amplitude transcending a mere lesson in the evils of war. Along with cynicism, calculation, a business sense that at times seems to eliminate all other feelings, go a courage and ingenuity for survival under intolerable conditions, a maternal protectiveness too wise to be quite wise, and above all, even when it cuts off escape from desperate circumstances, a devotion to a grown daughter who cannot speak. She has elements of the picaresque hero, the stoic, the faithful but unsentimental parent; she can be gross or pitiable. Brecht characteristically uses the ironic to undercut the pathetic, with the effect less that of distancing than of involving the audience at a deeper rather than a shallower level. Thus when the wretched daughter Kattrin is killed by troops—after becoming much more than a flat victim by a brave, but deliberately suicidal, warning of an attack—Mother Courage is told by a peasant, "If you hadn't gone off to the town to get your cut, maybe it wouldn't have happened" (xii).[18]

Now at one point in the play such an irony definitely touches on the tragic. Mother Courage's son, Swiss Cheese, a regimental paymaster, has fled during a retreat and come to her trading wagon with the cashbox; he wants to go back and seek out his superiors, but she advises against this, saying, "I've brought you up to be honest because you're not very bright. But don't overdo it" (iii). Swiss Cheese is captured and is to be executed; he can be saved only by bribery, at which Mother Courage is an old hand; she is confident of rescuing him and on her own terms. During a bargaining scene that actually becomes quite tense as a go-between rushes back and forth, Mother Courage keeps holding out for a lower bribe than the asking price. At last she agrees, under great pressure, to the amount demanded. Then she says, as they wait, "I believe—I haggled too long," and we hear gunshots as her son is executed. Here, as inner conflict extends into crucial outer action and produces at least a moment of self-knowledge, the character takes on a largeness never to be reached again. Not that Mother Courage is called back to preach, as was Joan Dark, for the doctrinal element is much less overt in this play; her role is illustrative rather than hortatory. But while the play is exhibiting the grossness of war in both its causes and effects, at least at this point it goes beyond the presumptive plan. By the index of character it takes on a new dimension; the fullness of personality evokes not questions but participation.

Brecht specifically asserts that *The Life of Galileo* (1937-38, 1946) "shows the dawn of a new age," that it "is not a tragedy," and that the "characterization of Galileo should not aim at establishing the sympathetic identification and participation of the audience with him. . . ." What he says is consistent with the chief impression which the work gives—the impression of an expository dialogue somewhat like a Landor conversation. But Brecht also says, "one can scarcely wish only to praise or only to condemn Galileo"—words which suggest a tragic dividedness. Furthermore, despite his strong inclination to center evil in "Authority," here represented by the Catholic Church, Brecht does not treat Galileo as a victim, which is usual in a certain type of melodramatic thought, but calls his recantation a "crime [that] can be regarded as the 'original sin' of modern natural sciences," [14] by which he means, as he explains, that Galileo cut science off "from close contact with the people" and thus paved the way for such products of esoteric research as the atomic bomb. Whether or not this faith in a public, socialized science is naïve, Brecht's belief that Galileo committed a kind of original sin opens the way for a tragic treatment of character, and the drama moves in that direction.

Andrea Sarti, Galileo's pupil, who at first had repudiated his master because of the recantation, comes around and praises Galileo for having given up "a hopeless political squabble in order to be able to carry on with your real business of science" (xiv). Galileo bluntly rejects this favorable view of his recantation and says no, "the others" are "the victors"; "I recanted because I was afraid of physical pain." This is the most significant moment in the play, and its similarity to Joan Dark's moment of recognizing her own failure is evident. Yet Joan had been engaged in a long moral struggle, as Galileo has not been, and as he is not now, for he is almost entirely intellect. Though he uses some harsh words about himself, there is little of the emotional resonance achieved by the analogous episode in the earlier play. But whatever the difference, Galileo, like Joan, is called to another mission than coming to terms with himself. He does not sin so much by bringing science into specialists' secret laboratories as by giving up scientific freedom and becoming his master's voice—the fate that Brecht is always in danger of inflicting on even his most nearly free characters. The central Brechtian idea, however interesting it is as historical theory, is analytically rather than dramatically expressed. Galileo is pushed immediately into an essay of about five hundred words expounding his fidelity to Brecht's view that science exists not for the sake of knowledge but "to ease the hardships of human existence." A Galileo who is interestingly conceived is held away from the human fullness that is possible for him and used simply to drive home a point.

IV. Special Case

The Good Woman of Setzuan (1938–40) is the most ingenious of Brecht's "Parables for the Theater";[15] Brecht works out a convoluted set of relationships that fairly well conceals the mechanical responses (thoughts, feelings, and actions) of the human types that he uses. Hence the action dramatizes convincingly the moral puzzles that are the theme and draws us into these puzzles as experience rather than lessons us about them. Despite the absence of pointing, it does appear initially that we will have the familiar social melodrama in which the "haves" are the villains, and we are not reassured when the next standard step is taken and the gods turn out to be peddling platitudes instead of dispensing wisdom. But happily such old patterns are wrenched apart when the "have-nots" turn out to be as big rascals as the others. This might be grounds for Gulliverian disgust, but Brecht holds firmly to his cool analysis of a problem in values and in human nature. He shows a "good" woman, Shen Te (by a now overused irony, a prostitute)—generous to others because her heart is moved by their troubles—as a natural target for human knavery; indeed, the very knowledge that Shen Te is a "good" woman attracts spongers and brings out the predator in relatives and neighbors. In addition, these leeches have contempt for her easiness and yet blame her if she is not invariably an easy mark. What is more, her own generous instincts involve her in injury to others, for she has not the resources for all claimants, and has to rob one to pay another. Her new tobacco shop is soon in trouble.

In contrast with her is her "cousin" Shui Ta, a "man of principle" who, when he suddenly appears on the scene, sees through rackets and phonies, throws out spongers, cancels ruinous charities, takes over her business, sets handout-seekers to work, drives them without mercy, and makes a go of the business. Everyone complains that he is hard and brutal, everything that the now lamented Shen Te was not; but he is also respected, and he even seems, by applying discipline, to have made a man—or at least an efficient, if not amiable, factory manager—out of the vain and calculating rascal whom Shen Te had fallen in love with. In setting up this dilemma between alternative combinations of good and evil, Brecht achieves a sophisticated variation on the ordinary melodramatic structure. Then he takes it still further by having the alternatives represented, not by different allegorical figures, Shen Te and Shui Ta, but by one person: Shui Ta, it is gradually disclosed by excellent theatrical means, is simply a side of Shen Te which she can make operative only by disguising herself as her "cousin."

So Brecht has both saved Shen Te from the old role of the sentimentalized prostitute * and has worked his way into a conflict in personality which is potentially of tragic scale. For what Shen Te has is a dividedness of feelings which represents a sharp clash between incompatible imperatives. This could take her on into the tragic conflict of an Antigone or a Hamlet. However, the tone is kept on the comic side because the emphasis is on finding some accord with the way of the world rather than on facing truly destructive inner pressures. An adjustment like those of Euripidean romantic comedy seems in store when the gods, who have appeared to us occasionally in their quest for "good" people on

---

* One wonders whether Brecht, who was obviously not ignorant of eighteenth-century English literature, knew the original of the foolishly generous person, the title character of Oliver Goldsmith's *Good-Natured Man* (1768).

the earth, make one more visit. But again Brecht upsets a pattern by having the crucial action of the *dei ex machina* a going up rather than a coming down; they run away from a riddle instead of solving it. All they can do is praise goodness without facing the issue of what happens to the good person in the world. Shen Te cries that she needs her "cousin" "at least once a week," but they reply "Once a month! That's enough!" (x). It is left at that, not with a solution through character but with a Lady or the Tiger impasse in which character fades away before the conundrum.

This is doubtless what Brecht wanted. It may be perverse to regret that his intention succeeded, and, in a larger way, that a theorist who has become an epic figure precisely because of his theory, should seem to be imprisoned in that theory. For often, as we have tried to show, he instinctively escaped from it into dramatic freedom, into a fullness of character that invites our experiential knowing of a wide human reality. He had a feeling for character, and it is difficult not to think that he gave up the larger subject for a smaller one.

Friedrich Duerrenmatt has put the issue very well. He says that when Brecht "incorporates into his dramaturgy . . . the communist philosophy . . . he often cuts off his own nose. Sometimes his plays say the very opposite of what they claim they say, but this lack of agreement cannot always be blamed on the capitalistic audience. Often it is simply a case where Brecht, the poet, gets the better of Brecht, the dramatic theorist, a situation that is wholly legitimate and ominous only were it not to happen again." [16] At least the tragic poet kept trying to get the better of the pedagogical dramatist.

It is difficult not to think of Oliver Goldsmith on Edmund Burke: "And to party gave up what was meant for mankind." But mankind kept slipping by Brecht and getting back into his theater.

CHAPTER EIGHT

Max Frisch (1911——)

I N BRECHT's work there is, for the most part, an immediate air of "realism" which Duerrenmatt and Frisch, whatever their debt to him, have discarded more often than they have retained. They pursue reality by plunging us right into fantasy, nightmarish or farcical. They needle us with coloratura event or strange device; we are caught up in imaginative action while unconsciously transposing its extravagance into domestic idiom. Born only a dozen years after Brecht, Frisch has more surface similarities to him than Duerrenmatt does; for example, he uses a quasi-Chinese décor for one play, and draws on recent German history. Yet in the characters there is less of surface actuality, with significance somewhere beneath, than there is of symbolic existence in which surprise and sometimes enigma resist definition. They have the pressing vitality of tightly wound up toys. They excite, they get under our skin; at their best they call forth sympathy. Often they hover on a border line between being and meaning. Our present concern is with them as they slip over the line and become "anthropomorphic" rather than "ideomorphic" or "semamorphic." In the eight plays in English (six full length, two shorter) we can see characters taking on varying degrees of autonomous individuality in addition to carrying out their semantic function. Committed as Frisch is to the Brecht technique of "alienation," he keeps being drawn, like Brecht himself, into a characterization that provides an audience with an experience as well as a demonstration. It is in the two earliest plays, *The Chinese Wall* and *Count Oederland* (both first written in 1946 and then reworked over a considerable number of years),[1] that the characters stay closest to their assigned roles as demonstrators; one tends to remember what they communicate without clearly remembering who they are. The plays are fantasias, and Frisch calls *The Chinese Wall* a "farce." Frisch is always likely to draw on farcical effects, and *The Great Rage of Philip Hotz* (1958) is pure farce, though with the psychological implications that are important in every mode that Frisch uses.

While *Count Oederland* and *The Chinese Wall* are fantastic plays of public life—the major dramatis personae are public figures acting in public arenas—Frisch's three dramas that achieve greatest intensity of effect have in the foreground private persons and realistic or superficially realistic situations. These are *When the War Was Over* (1949), *The Firebugs* (1958), and *Andorra* (1961). Yet in the background there is always a theme of public life—of political disaster on a national or international scale; the plays come out of mid-twentieth-century troubles. The approach to such materials through the conflicts in personal life is a very effective one. In Frisch, of course, there is nearly always the tug of fantasy and symbol upon the realistic mode. *When the War Was Over* sticks closest to the private and realistic; one could almost imagine it as an Ibsen middle-period play. *The Firebugs* likewise employs a domestic mode with a quasi-realistic surface; hence the effectiveness of the emerging symbolic and fantastic, which we are almost forced to perceive as realistic. *Andorra* is like *The Firebugs* in these respects, but it also pushes more openly toward the arena of public life that Frisch used in the earlier 1940s plays. In this group of middle-career plays we are of course always aware of the characters as bearers of meaning; yet they also arouse the kind of interest that we feel in characters as such, and more than once Frisch injects a tragic sense of character.

Then in the 1960s Frisch turned from the public scene, actual or implied, to private lives in which the psychological action, insofar as it extends beyond itself, has metaphysical rather than socio-political implications—*Don Juan, or The Love of Geometry* (1953; revised, 1962) and *Biography: A Game* (1967). In *Don Juan* he returns to the mythic kind of theme he had used in the 1940s; in *Biography* he finds a new version of an early theme—the patterns in human life that are as persistent as the illusion of change. In characters, the movement is away from the individuation prerequisite to tragedy; yet something of tragic awareness at times enters into the style of the protagonists.

I. EARLY PLAYS

The dramas that had their first drafts in 1946, *Count Oederland* and *The Chinese Wall*, are both statements of eternal recurrence as a philosophy of history, but they go about demonstrating the concept somewhat differently. Of the two, *Count Oederland* stays closer to the symbolic use of character and event, from which, indeed, it hardly deviates. In making a stage allegory of recurrence, Frisch manages enough ambiguity to permit both socio-political and psychic readings, and a lively representation of the mechanisms by which societies and individuals respond to old situations and new stimuli. A Public Prosecutor understands only too well the boredom which leads an innocuous, hitherto well-balanced bank clerk to commit an ax-murder; the Prosecutor broods over this and as a result falls into a mental aberration (it appears) in which he uses an ax rather freely and lethally. So, in the popular mind, he is ironically identified with a folklore figure, Count Oederland (Wasteland), who according to an old song will be irresistible when he appears with an ax; as a result, under the symbol of the ax revolts break out everywhere, and the Prosecutor finds himself leading a revolution. It is the old business of liberty against order, joy * against duty, destruction against conscience, the lower recesses of the psyche against the upper, all this done with colorful and ingenious detail. Suddenly the Prosecutor recovers his ordinary mental state and believes he has had a nightmare. Then to his shock he finds that he has actually led a revolution and that the eighty-year-old President is now, in the middle of the night, insisting that the Prosecutor either "be executed as a murderer" or "form a government" (xii). The President voices the moral:

---

* "Joy," of course, is a reminder of the Nazis, whose deeds provide at least a starting-point for five of the Frisch dramas examined here. It is possible to regard the Prosecutor's "revolution" as simply a version of the Nazi movement. But it is always Frisch's tendency to widen the subject; and, as I read the play, the Oederland uprising is an ambiguous affair which is not to be dismissed as only an evil outbreak of violence but which embodies a half-truth able to harness energies because of weaknesses in the existent order. The characters who stand for order have nothing more to recommend them than do the revolutionaries; hence the drama does not compel us to be on their side.

"Whoever overthrows power, in order to be free, assumes the opposite of freedom, power. . . ." The pendulum swings, and all is the same, except that the public has apparently enjoyed a catharsis during the violence that accompanies a change in regime. Or, less cynically, the tension between freedom and power is rarely an ideal balance; the rival claimants that share in reality have empires that are now too great, now too small. Such meanings, however, are conveyed by the directed exercises rather than by the free interplay of personalities or the exploration of full individual personality.

In *Count Oederland* the thematic burden of the events is not clear until the end; until then, all attention is pre-empted by the singular actions and by dreamlike episodes and atmosphere that make one think of Franz Kafka. Perhaps this more stark and cryptic formulation was a result of long work, for the play did not achieve its final form until 1961. On the other hand, *The Chinese Wall* was revised in 1955.[2] Here Frisch's sense of *Plus ça change, plus c'est la même chose* is expressed in a less fantastic, though still a very fanciful, form. The surfaces are all more or less realistic, but the dramatis personae include historic and literary characters of different ages, a modern intellectual, and a Chinese emperor.* The way of the world at wall-building time might well be the realm of bitter comedy, but Frisch, always alert to the advantages of understatement, calls the play a "farce." Though this generic term may seem to trivialize the affair, it actually has a technical applicability, not to the stage romps which the term usually connotes, but to the substance of the play. Farce is the world of mechanical action—of mechanical men (puppets, toys, robots) all of whose responses are patterned and who inflict injury without hurting and endure blows without being hurt.† It

---

* The play has been compared with Thornton Wilder's *Skin of Our Teeth*, which has had a considerable vogue in Europe (Duerrenmatt praises it). In other respects it is reminiscent of Brecht's *Caucasian Chalk Circle* and *The Good Woman of Setzuan*, and even of Gilbert and Sullivan's *Mikado*. In the mingling as contemporaries of individuals who have a permanent status in the human imagination (Brutus, Columbus, Don Juan, Pontius Pilate, Romeo and Juliet) it has resemblances to Tennessee Williams' *Camino Real* (and hence to the *Inferno*, on which Williams drew). It is panoramic, diffuse rather than concentrated in effect, though not without moments of tension. Whereas *Camino Real* is concerned with psychic habits and their moral implications, *The Chinese Wall* has its eye mainly on the socio-political world and its historical habits.

† In *The Great Rage of Philip Hotz*, a one-act play of 1958, farce in large quantities is freshly combined with the irony of character, especially in a husband's self-deception and in his striving to force his wife into adopting a new image of him. Perhaps the best irony is that formal anticonventionalism can itself become a

is also the world of mechanical public action, in which events roll on in repetitive cycles that are indifferent to individual feelings and choices; acts of will are no more than small jets that minutely nudge orbiting societies driven by their own natures to go where they have been before. In *The Chinese Wall* the crooked, tyrannical, and egomaniac old Emperor is so bad (ever fighting, repressing, profiteering on the wall) that a revolution springs up; but it is ineffective until the Prince, always the chief warrior for the Emperor, resents the slowness and inadequacy of his rewards, and becomes a leader of the people. We see him going ahead to "liquidate . . . All of them" in the old order (xxi); Brutus says that the "angry mob" "hoist—they, throwers-down of tyranny— / Their newest leader and their next oppressor"; and "The Contemporary," the intellectual whose voice has most authority, announces that "the farce is going to start all over again; again we must repeat it" (xxii).

Yet this sense of the farcical in men's history is qualified in a number of ways. It is neither condescending nor dully despairing; rather it acts as a critique of a flabby utopianism. Victims can seize advantages: the mother of the Emperor's chief scapegoat refuses to exonerate her son, as she could, because she sees that the official accusation of guilt (that he is the subversive "Voice of the People") makes him important and may give him a big role in the revolution. Victors may lose: Cleopatra says, "I am the girl who offers consolation to the victors" (xii). Critical individuals persist, as they do not, for instance, in *Animal Farm*. Instead of *saeva indignatio* there is ironic, unillusioned, virtually urbane regret. The Contemporary keeps telling everybody that "the bomb" has altered the course of history by making it possible, for the first time ever, to end history, but in the end he has to acknowledge wryly that he has spoken in vain and that "Here we go again" is the rule. Indeed, when the Contemporary tells the Emperor that he is a tyrant and monster, the Emperor gives him a special decoration to show his regard for the truth-telling intelligentsia (a scene reminiscent of the canonizing of St. Joan in Brecht's *St. Joan of the Stockyards*). Besides such Shavian ironies that betoken the capacity of farce—of this farce—to ingest the suprafarcical,

convention, and that the reversals engaged in by quite self-conscious people can work out much the same as the reversals of characters who, by the rules of traditional farce, are conventional and wholly unselfconsicous. A quite self-conscious husband and wife engage in a contest of wills, fall into an unwilling separation, and joyfully come together again.

there is a strong infusion of epistemological drama. Pilate creates a leit-motif in the drama by continuing to ask, "What is truth?" The Emperor is "he who is always in the right"; so "no one comes forward and says what really is"; the Emperor believes in getting at "the truth" by torture. To him, the "Voice of the People" is "a liar"; if a prisoner does not speak, the court angrily feels that he is "thinking the truth." To Columbus, the "truth" is that he discovered India, not a place they called America. The Contemporary says first that the truth, when embraced, is "two-edged," then that the relativism of time and space means that there is no truth; finally the Princess Mee Lan, who has come to love him, says that "the truth we have learned" is that "we stand here in our time, and the world rolls forward over us" (xxiv).

This morality play, dramatizing the idea that history is farcical, implicitly talks about tragedy. What it shows is that men do not want to engage in tragic truth-facing; their aim is to live always in a melodrama of power. The heart of the Emperor's life is a paranoid sense of enemies. He conquers the great foreign enemies, "the barbarian dogs of the steppes"; he builds the wall against all possible others. On the one hand he realizes with rage and horror that "There are no more enemies left" (Cleopatra has to console him) (ix). But then he starts hunting down enemies at home; whoever disagrees with him is "obviously an enemy"; the "Voice of the People" is "our final adversary" (xiii). He learns to use words like "Terrorists" and "Agitators" that "nip truth in the bud" (xiv). Exactly like the Emperor is the Prince who eventually leads the people in revolt. Princess Mee Lan says to him, "Fighting the bloodiest battles is easier for you . . . than listening to the common, everyday truth . . . ," and "You believe in happiness through power" (xvii). Fairly close to the center of the drama is this critique of the melodramatic, the untragic habit of mind: the substitution of unending conflict for the looking at the self. Columbus speaks a key line when he tells Don Juan, "There still remains for you, young man, the continent of your own soul, the adventure of truth" (xvi). Columbus' words, which almost repeat a passage in Montherlant's *Master of Santiago* (1945), point out the human attitudes that lead to the generic forms of melodrama and tragedy. While calling his morality play a farce, Frisch reveals the tragic sensibility, which tends always to be at least a hidden component of the morality play.

II. Three Dramas of Private Life and Public Issues

In *The Chinese Wall* the Emperor is regularly greeted with a chorus of "Heil, heil, heil." The Third Reich is always active in Frisch's imagination; in one form or another, "The Nazis Are Coming" is a recurrent theme of his. Out of this might emerge a standard form of political melodrama, with a limited historical scope, but Frisch so develops the subject as to make it open out widely. He does this, paradoxically, by compressing it: that is, he presents the threats and the ominousness of public evil, not in the panoramic mode which is the easier way to claim universal resonance, but as forces that compete with other forces in private life. Through representative individuals what starts as a historic evil becomes the expression of nonhistoric human potentialities. This is the mode of *When the War Was Over, The Firebugs*, and *Andorra*, which are the central works of the period that extends from 1949 to 1961. Sometimes the historic and the socio-political are very evident dimensions of the play; sometimes they are only implicitly present, specific formulations of impulses that are not temporally limited.

When the War Was Over (1949) illustrates with great clarity the fact that tragedy and melodrama are forms of experience as well as theatrical modes. Here Frisch looks keenly at a basic melodrama of life, war: not the primary facts of battle, but the impact of war on people, its reliance upon and its furthering of melodramatic attitudes. The scene is Berlin, 1945. Horst Anders, minus one arm, has just escaped from prison camp, after five years in the army, and joins his wife Agnes in hiding in the cellar of their home. The upper stories are occupied by Russian officers, whose music, drinking, and indoor target practice imply the barbarism which, as it was put in *The Chinese Wall*, we always attribute to "the others." In the foreground there is the straightforward melodrama of the Germans' struggles to elude discovery, to escape, to survive. The Germans' words for the Russians are "Mongolians," "filth," and "swine," and we hear stories about Russian "atrocities" (I.i).[3] When Agnes, having been discovered by a Russian orderly seeking wine for the officers, resists going upstairs, the orderly says, "Madam believes me to be an animal . . . ?" and assures her that the men above, as officers, "are all fine men—all gentlemen" (I.i). However, when Agnes is forced to go up, the Russians, who are shooting at victrola records, grab her, lift her skirt, cry "German pig, German bitch," and thus sum up their view of the relationship: "Who won the war, you or me?" (I.ii). Both sides live in the old melodrama of attributing generic evil to the other, and of knowing the proper role for victors and victims. Frisch presents another phase of the melodrama of survival by making the Russian orderly, Jehuda Karp, a Warsaw Jew who was in the ghetto massacre of 1943 and who is on the lookout for Germans who took part in it. When Jehuda suspects the piano-tuner Halske (once a concert pianist), Halske promptly denies that he was in Warsaw but says that Horst Anders was (II.ii); when Jehuda confronts Horst with this, Horst claims first that he was in a different unit in Warsaw, and then that he was in the hospital (II.ii). But Agnes has said that since Warsaw he has been less communicative.

Frisch interprets people, then, as living (by outer necessity or inner need or choice) in melodramas of gross national judgments, of survival, triumph, and revenge, and to the extent that we inevitably empathize in these situations, we are also having a melodramatic experience, not through a mere stereotype but through the dramatic imitation of historical reality. Yet *When the War Was Over* also works at another level by essentially challenging the melodramatic attitudes and, while not entirely freeing us from their claim—the passion for survival is not easily put aside—still exacting a strongly divided response. There is some effort to put the audience into a detached position: when we see both sides call the other "pig," we are pushed toward an awareness of melodramatic habits in general, that is, our own.* But rather we are asked to sympathize with Agnes as she resists the simpler combat stance into which most characters fall easily (as Horst says, "In combat I was never helpless . . ."—[I.i]). She challenges Horst's phrase "Russian swine" by saying that it "reminds" her of " 'Jew swine' and all the other things our own swine have said" (I.i). Here, then, she is moving toward the kind of tragic consciousness that Sartre would develop further in *Altona* a decade later. Then she dramatically denies the validity of melodramatic nationalism by finding in Stepan Ivanov, the Russian commandant, a kindred soul: hoping to deal with him as the enemy of Horst and herself, she is drawn beyond the official categories of good and evil, and she

---

* Several times, also, Frisch uses the Brecht device of having Agnes leave the dialogue and make announcements or give quick historical summaries directly to the audience.

and Stepan discover each other as fellow human beings. Echoing Shylock, she says that "If a man cries out, if he bleeds," types disappear, and humanity emerges; the climax of Act I is her seeing that Stepan, who has been cleaning up broken bottles, is "bleeding" (I.ii).

The "love" between them could make Agnes the tragic character—an Antigone caught between a forbidden passion and devotion to the crippled husband imprisoned in the cellar. At one time, indeed, she is so troubled that she begs Horst to shoot her—a request, it appears to him, to save her from "dishonor," and a choice, it first appears to us, of punishment for and an ending of what she does not approve. But then she postpones choice by defining "shoot me" as she did not do at first: "Believe in me or shoot me!" (II.i). So she pursues a strategy and veers away from the tragic, which is not the playwright's interest here. Frisch apparently sees her as evading choice, also, by a kind of emotional casuistry: she praises Horst to Stepan and says, "Often, it almost seems to me that you two are one and the same man" (II.ii). Again, Frisch is interested in presenting an ambiguity in Horst: on the one hand, like Claudio in *Measure for Measure*, he seems willing to let Agnes' sex protect him from the enemy upstairs; on the other hand, he may be nursing an intention to risk all by coming up and finding the couple acting as he suspects. As the play moves to an end, the cryptic and ironic take over. What depth are we to see in the relationship by which Agnes and Stepan surmount the barriers of nation and war? They cannot understand each other's language: is this a comic garnish and guarantee of romance, as in Shakespeare, or an ironic undercutting of their apparent oneness? Agnes loves to be so "open and free," to tell Stepan "what I could never tell any other man," and yet delights that "it all remains a secret—my secret" (II.ii). What appears to be a communion of two souls, then, is perhaps only a catharsis for one.

From this ambiguous romance the play moves into a quick final melodrama that is also ambiguous: Horst does come up, is accused by Jehuda of helping shoot Jews in Warsaw, and pulls a gun. Then Agnes makes her choice by stepping in front of Stepan, and Stepan makes his choice—by going away. The drama evades the easier solution of violence and follows a subtler path that allows its audience no easy emotions. We have to assume that Stepan has given up a relationship, though it seems to have been valid for him, because it involves too many complications of feeling. Ironically, he has freed the German couple from the invader.

But the German husband and wife, despite the bonds of marriage and nationality, gaze at each other, as the concluding stage direction tells us, "as though across an unbridgeable abyss." Abysses everywhere, then, is the final note; the protest against melodramatic separation withdraws, as it were, before the crude facts of life. But the abyss is not the utterly lucid one between good and evil; instead of that easy satisfaction, the audience is forced to have a complex, divided response. The drama makes no quick profits on the melodrama of experience.

The Firebugs[4] (1958) manages an even greater intensity than *When the War Was Over*, in part because it makes a sharper demarcation between good and evil and at the same time has tragic potentialities. Though it carefully works up a realistic décor, it becomes essentially expressionistic, and in doing this it illustrates clearly what I have called the kinship between postrealist expressionism and prerealist allegory.[5] On the one hand the play uses characters as bizarre signposts to meanings and human habits, and insouciantly by-passes realistic probability to present reality in a disturbing new key. On the other hand *The Firebugs* has as subtitle "A Morality Without a Moral"; its main character is named Biedermann, a type name for "good man" or "honnête homme," suggesting Everyman; and at one point it refers to and makes dramatic use of Hugo von Hofmannsthal's *Everyman*. The phrase "Without a Moral" is a jest, for there is a Chorus which regularly pushes the point home; that there is a point becomes apparent in another way when Biedermann directly addresses the audience (v). Yet despite these conscious echoes of Brechtian style, the play draws the audience in; the basic situation is melodramatic, and it is developed in such a way as to provide an experience that borders on the tragic. Taken simply as melodrama, *The Firebugs* employs a novel treatment of the antagonistic forces, and it derives great monopathic power from an original use of a traditional structure. Frisch's basic tension is between destructive wielders of power and the victim of power, but he has completely reversed the modern convention by using, as victim, the well-to-do middle-class businessman with social and financial resources, and, as merciless persecutors, a pair of "outsiders," "underprivileged" men, whose only resources are brazenness, deftness, and an eye for vulnerable spots (as in Albee's *Zoo Story*). What is more, the presumably secure man is victimized in his own stronghold while he is perfectly conscious of what is happening. Schmitz and Eisenring simply move into Biedermann's house, gain a psychological upper hand over him and his wife, take over the attic, and openly set about installing drums of gasoline and firing devices, while Biedermann, hardly believing what he sees, or rather wishfully disbelieving it, curries favor with them in the vain hope of keeping them from the incendiarism which they openly jest about as they prepare for the big blaze that ends the play.

Schmitz and Eisenring, the worms who turn into fire dragons, are of course any antisocial evil that lives upon destruction; they could be German Nazis or American bomb-throwers; universal riffraff with a talent for moral blackmail, a total absence of scruple, and a sense of how to organize against an apparently stable order; like Iago they combine amiability, when it is useful, and ruthlessness. To place them aesthetically, we might say that they are picaresque heroes who live by their wits but whose clever gamesmanship is the tool of a tireless destructive malice. So in them Frisch adds a new twist to the sinister villain. The most effective twist is that the villains say outright what they are doing; Biedermann wonderfully fails to believe what is happening to him because he is "hoodwinked," as Eisenring puts it, by three methods which Eisenring jocosely explains to him: their telling him the truth, their jesting to him about it, and their using "sentimentality," that is, stories about a hard childhood which make it more difficult for Biedermann to take action against them (iv). Hence the melodrama is complicated by a satirical revelation of self-pity as strategy and of human vulnerability to this strategy.

On the face of it the drama plays for the terror created by an enemy's slowly taking over and cutting off all avenues of escape.* Yet Biedermann is not helpless. He could summon a watchful fire department, and Frisch uses a Chorus of firemen to push the moral explicitly. They are always waiting to be called, trying to alert Biedermann to his danger, pointing out his error in "Hoping that good will come / From good-natured actions" and commenting

---

* We can see how Frisch has modified the traditional melodramatic pattern if we compare the attitude of Schmitz and Eisenring to Biedermann with the attitude of Orlick to his prisoner Pip in *Great Expectations*. Orlick is direct and voluble in expressing envious hate; Schmitz and Eisenring maintain a grotesquely chuckling demeanor, a quasi-good-natured impersonality, as they prepare the holocaust. Orlick has trapped Pip in an out-of-the-way death house; the fire bugs, with calm assurance and compliments to the host's generosity, take over their victim's house. Pip is the conventional physical prisoner who can do nothing about it; Biedermann is a moral prisoner who still could do something about it.

He who fears change
More than disaster
What can he do to forestall
The threatening disaster? [6]
[iii]

When they speak to him directly, he rebuffs them, thinking that a report to authorities might make his unwanted guests angry. Though Biedermann is practicing what used to be called "appeasement," and though elsewhere a casual reference to "the Party" acknowledges a political orientation, still Frisch has so developed his materials as to go beyond political allegory.* At one point the Chorus says that Biedermann is blind to the facts because he is so busy being "indignant / Over some distant disaster" (iii)—that is, regularly enjoying a melodramatic posture. More important, however, is the opening Chorus, which is a vigorous attack on man's employment of the idea of "Fate" to cover his own stupidity, a method which is "unworthy of God, / Unworthy of man"; then there is a direct adjuration, "Bestow not the name of Fate / Upon man's mistakes" (i). In addition, then, to criticizing an addiction to melodramatic feeling (a legitimate emotion that has become a habit-forming drug), the Chorus is speaking for a tragic attitude: recognizing an error instead of blaming Fate. It inveighs against the untragic view that nothing can be done about threatening danger; it interprets, as tragic flaw, passivity and foolish hopefulness.

This introduction of the tragic sense might be no more than a choral annotation, but the fact is that a good deal of the tragic is embedded in the dramatic structure. Biedermann is not only a victim but a divided man: he wants to get rid of the intruders and get on with life and business as usual, but he also wants to avoid the unpleasantness, the possible damage and injury and suffering, that a forcible ejection of the scoundrels may entail. So he placates instead of fighting, and thus ironically he digs his own grave. He is split between a knowledge of the truth that is struggling to shape itself in his mind, and a simple inability to face that truth and its practical consequences. Again, the traditional formulation is originally handled: whereas the tragic hero is characteristically driven toward an evil violence or aggression and does not listen, until perhaps too late, to the disapproving voice of an

---

* Insofar as ruinous cooperation with "the Party" is the theme, the play is to be compared with Sartre's *Altona*. Cf. my *Tragedy and Melodrama*, pp. 256–59.

imperative or a counterimpulse, Biedermann is driven toward an evil peace and does not listen to the imperative to act violently in an attempt to save his own life. He is a little like the modern Zero character who cannot find a necessary oneness.

In accounting for Biedermann's being passive when he should be aggressive, using a bribe instead of a boot, Frisch makes considerable use of another element that we have not yet mentioned—Biedermann's guilt. Here again the tragic pattern is sharply altered, for whereas tragic guilt ordinarily is incurred in the main action, Biedermann is burdened with guilt before the main action starts, and the invaders are sure that his own guilt feelings will prevent his turning them in to the police (iii). The guilt theme gradually expands. Biedermann has fired a good employee named Knechtling, who is convinced that Biedermann has stolen an invention from him; Biedermann rudely refuses to see Knechtling at his house and says, "Let him put his head in the gas oven" (i); then a policeman reports that Knechtling has indeed put his head in the oven, and Biedermann is morally unable to use the officer's presence and turn the arsonists over to him (iii); when the widow Knechtling calls, the maid tells her that Biedermann "said he wouldn't have anything more to do with you" (iv), and later he dismisses her himself (v); at the big dinner party which is Biedermann's final placatory gesture to his destroyers (it is ironically called a "Last Supper"), Eisenring throws the tablecloth over Schmitz, who, in an outright parody of the banquet scene in *Macbeth*, pretends to be the ghost of Knechtling, while Eisenring ironically upbraids Schmitz for this unkindness to a man of such humanity as Biedermann (vi). Thus, working on his guilt, they hold Biedermann in line in a way that is a little reminiscent of the special efforts of Mephistophilis and other devils, in Marlowe's *Dr. Faustus*, to pull Faustus back whenever a move toward repentance threatens to remove him from their power. Biedermann's actions throughout are a kind of enlargement of those of Faustus in Marlowe's closing scene, in which Faustus, despite frenzied struggles toward salvation, cannot sufficiently overcome his sense of guilt to throw himself upon the divine mercy and trust to a saving grace.

The comparison with Faustus should go no further, however, for Biedermann has neither the Faustian stature nor the Faustian intelligence. Unlike Faustus' guilt, Biedermann's is a pre-existent illness; hence its inhibiting effect rather leads to a disaster of personality than inheres in a tragic action. As for intelligence, it is not that Biedermann is entirely stupid, but that he has so choked back his powers of perception that imperceptiveness has become a habit; and he continues to contribute to the disaster with an ironic blindness that, while it is a good allegory of the human capacity to miss the point up to the very end, prevents his coming to the tragic stature which seemed possible for him. *The Firebugs* has shifted back to a hortatory morality.* Yet out of an expressionistic allegory, with its strong satirical note, Frisch has made a dark melodrama of total disaster in the world. The melodrama, however, draws its strength from the tragic ingredient: evil succeeds only through the consent of its victim. Here the tragic possibility is in the central character.

In *Andorra* (1961), as we shall see, there is a tragic possibility in a lesser, though an important, character. It is perhaps remarkable that it enters at all in a play that, though many of the actions are private, has a public theme—anti-Semitism. Yet *Andorra* is much more than a treatise. Basically it is a melodrama of the victim; in a noticeable parallel to Duerrenmatt's slightly earlier *The Visit* we see the community's oppressive and inexorable closing in on its single victim, Andri, and then destroying him in a brilliantly imagined expressionistic scene that achieves extraordinary freshness and immediacy: wearing black masks, everyone in town marches barefoot past a "trained . . . Jew Detector" who by observing feet, laughs, hair, pocket contents, and the like can infallibly identify Jews and free others from suspicion ("No

---

* It undergoes another generic change in the "Afterpiece," which is not always produced along with the main drama. The scene is Hades, and Schmitz and Eisenring, whose destructive skills have already seemed demonic, turn out to be Beelzebub and a fellow leader. They have taken over the stage now, and they are quarreling with Heaven for making Hell a second-rate place by using pardons indiscriminately to grab all the more important souls. Hence Hell is going on a jurisdictional strike, and the play has moved into the realm of satirical farce. By now Biedermann and his wife have, if anything, decreased in intelligence. They think they should be in Heaven; they say they are "victims" and prate about "rights" and "restitution." They are now figures in a satirical melodrama. All this is very good fun, and it functions a little like traditional "comic relief": the terrifying destroyers are, *sub specie aeternitatis*, only underprivileged devils who can be done out of their due by unfair tactics from above, and the human pair who brought on a dreadful holocaust by an illusioned misconstruction of the obvious are now clamoring, with noisy clichés, for a better deal in court. The comic relief acts by letting us cut loose from disaster-inviting characters in whom we could only see ourselves; it frees us from the characters by trivializing them. The lesser the character, the smaller his power to cry out to us, "mon frère!" It is the large tragic figures whom we cannot deny.

Andorran has anything to fear") (xii).[7] This fierce satire of the gentile world has originality not only in its lurid details. For one thing, Frisch to some extent enlarges the theme: until the final scene, anti-Semitism appears not as a solitary phenomenon but as one instance of a parochial exclusivism of feeling that manifests itself in racism generally, community self-adulation, national defensiveness, and xenophobia, and is tightly linked to the instinctive quest for scapegoats. Frisch makes possible this thematic opening out, though it is not his principal business, by adding another dimension to the plot: not only are there the local tensions in the small state of Andorra, but Andorra is threatened by the people on the other side of the border, "the Blacks" (whitewashing is a symbolic activity in Andorra, whose people believe that the neighboring Blacks envy their whiteness; thus Frisch comments on the self-congratulatory melodrama of international feeling). Now the Blacks have been noted for their anti-Semitism, and Andorrans have felt very superior to the Blacks on this account; so Andorrans have not only the traditional imperatives against anti-Semitism, but also the powerful motive of maintaining national self-respect. It is not as though some evil possibility sneaks up in their midst without their ever recognizing it, for they are conscious of attitudes to and feelings about Jews. The point of the satire is that they are just as bad as the Blacks whom they despise. In the terms of this essay, Frisch is pointing to the untenability of the usual melodramatic posture in the world (the black-and-white view of reality) and demonstrating that guilt can quickly overtake the accuser himself.

Early in the play, indeed, we learn that for some time the Teacher has been saying that Andorrans are "no better than the Blacks across the border" (as in Duerrenmatt's *Visit* it is the teacher who sees the truth and who must drink to relieve the strain). In Andorra it is commonplace knowledge, or at least common rumor, that "When the Blacks come everyone who is a Jew will immediately be taken away" (i). In the closing scene the "Jew Inspection" is carried out by the invading Blacks, who declare Andri guilty of being a Jew and take him away; it is the agency of the Blacks that permits the Andorrans to separate themselves from the deed and maintain something of their illusions about themselves. But Frisch has carefully shown Andorrans drawing away from Andri long before the invasion, and now, when the enemy is at hand, only too glad to have Andri as a scapegoat. The greatest stroke of Frisch's satirical strategy, however, occurs earlier. A señora from the country of the Blacks visits Andorra and is taken for a "spyess," but at first she is saved from xenophobic mistreatment when someone says that Andorrans should not give provocation to the Blacks (viii). After she has seen several men beat up Andri, however, mob feelings break out; the Señora leaves the stage, and we suddenly learn both that she has been murdered and that Andri, who has never left the stage, has been accused of throwing the stone that killed her. Frisch thereby permits the inference that the Andorrans, while incidentally indulging xenophobia by killing the Señora, are instinctively performing a crime that they can blame on Andri, and thus getting ready a victim to hand over to the Blacks when the Blacks come. In one great emotional and political coup the Andorrans can indulge in anti-Semitism, placate the Blacks, and save themselves.

Frisch sticks carefully to the satirical mode; evidently he does not think that a tragic treatment of the Andorrans is possible. He does not see in them the power to know what they have done, much less to judge themselves. On the contrary, at the end of nearly every scene one or another of them addresses the audience directly to excuse himself and his fellows: "It wasn't my fault. . . . It wasn't my fault" (i). "It's not my fault . . ." (ii). ". . . it was partly his fault. . . . It wasn't my fault . . ." (iii). Soldier: "But I didn't kill him. I only did my duty" (vi). "I don't know what the soldiers did to him. . . . There must come a time when we are allowed to forget, I think" (ix). "What did I do? Nothing whatever. . . . I'm not in favour of atrocities. . . . It wasn't my fault . . ." (xi). The insistent disclaimers of responsibility by individuals who actively took part in commenting on and suspecting Andri's Jewishness exactly identify the satiric as opposed to the tragic mode. The regularity of the Andorrans' self-exculpations is punctuated only by the Priest's "I too was guilty at that time. . . . I too made a graven image of him, I too put fetters on him. I too bound him to the stake" (vii). Here is a brief tragic accent, but an accent rather than an experience because the Priest's moral feeling is less important than his expository function: "Graven image" means the supposed generic identity that prevails over the individual truth of human beings.

Andorra, like Frisch's other plays, can be interpreted simply as a fable about Nazi Germany, but the unlocalized, somewhat surrealistic scenes and the dreamlike blurring of identities have a universalizing effect.* We have already noted Frisch's expanding the theme of anti-Semitism and relating it to other phenomena of self-affirmation and self-magnification (somewhat as Miller would do in *Incident at Vichy*). Frisch amplifies the theme in another way by a great technical tour de force: as the scenes pass before us, we gradually become aware that Andri is not Jewish at all. He has been brought up by the Teacher, who long ago had introduced Andri as a Jewish orphan whom he had mercifully brought across the border when the Blacks were conducting pogroms. On the one hand, Andri's non-Jewishness makes possible a further sharpening of the satirical barbs against the Andorrans; when they express regret for, and dissociate themselves from, the treatment of Andri, they half-betray the feeling that the wrong done was less the torture and murder of a human being than getting the wrong victim. The line that tends to crop up, despite their self-watchfulness, is "We didn't know he wasn't one." The more profound point is that, acting on a mere word used by the Teacher, the Andorrans have made Andri into a Jew. They are so sure of what Jewish characteristics are, and so frequently detect these in Andri, that he actually begins to exhibit them or to believe that he is exhibiting them. The height of the irony is that Andri comes to accept himself as a Jew and to believe that his fate has to be the Jewish fate of the scapegoat or the sacrificial victim. The assurance that he is not Jewish is incredible to him, and meaningless. He tells the Priest, "one feels a thing like that. . . . Whether one is a Jew or not" (ix).

Here the drama, which in general is a sociological document rather than a tragedy, glides from the pure sociological to the epistemological: there is a pirandellesque elusiveness of reality in the unclear, shifting realms of idea, word, and objective being. "[S]uddenly you're what they say you are," Andri says (ii); and the Doctor, all but a Tartuffe in modern medical dress, insists, "his behaviour . . . became . . . more and more Jewish . . ." (xi). In a word, a Jew is not born but made. The drama of the scapegoat will become tragic when a dramatist can use the perspective of a representative member of the community, can dis-

---

* In historical terms, Andorra would be any small country overrun by the Nazis, failing to resist, and in effect finding safety by handing over its Jews to the invader. But Frisch's "Notes" for production (pp. 166–67) all stress a desire to go beyond the topical. "Costumes should not be traditional." The scene should be "typical of any southern country." The lady visiting from the land of the Blacks is a "Señora." Andorra is not the name of a specific place; it "is the name of a model." The suggestions of the south remind us that "andorra" is Spanish for "street-walker"—a satirical jest at the town's sense of its own virgin whiteness.

cover in him deep self-knowledge and through it the revulsion that leads not to despair but to conversion—the conversion, really, of a vast primitive energy to other than primitive uses. The model is the conversion, in Aeschylus, of the Erinyes into the Eumenides. Aeschylus, it may be, was ahead of our times. Until we have our own Aeschylus, this kind of drama has to be a painful record of disaster.

Frisch is on the edge of tragedy in his treatment of the Teacher. What made possible the judaization of Andri was the Teacher's identifying him as a Jewish child. We learn in time that Andri is the Teacher's own illegitimate child; the mother is the very Señora who crosses the border into Andorra, sees her once-lover and her son, and is killed by the xenophobic mob (an unexpected echo of the well-made plot). At the time of his affair with the Señora, the Teacher felt the pressure of Andorran mores, which would oppose loving a foreigner and having an illegitimate child; so he concealed his misdeeds by marrying a native woman and passing his natural son off as a rescued Jewish victim; this latter step not only covered up the truth but made an affirmative play for admiration by claiming a deed that gratified the community's belief in its generosity and humanity. So the Teacher is divided between spontaneity and self-protectiveness, between his own falseness and his commitment to truth, between the will to survive in the community and his prophetic insight into the dark depths of the community: his is a tragic split. But he tries to resolve it in drink; when the crisis comes, he can only protest ineffectively; after Andri has been "taken away," he can say to all, "Go home to your mirrors and feel sick"; and at the end we learn that he has hanged himself (xii). It is not his play; we do not see him looking into his mirror; his self-confrontation is not what Frisch is concerned with. He provides a tragic accent in a morality play on community self-love.

III. PRIVATE LIVES AND TIMELESS PROBLEMS

Tragic accents continue to appear in the major plays of private life that mainly occupied Frisch in the 1960s—*Don Juan, or the Love of Geometry* (original version, 1953, revised, 1962) and *Biography: A Game* (1967). Moving now from the historical realm into a realm of ideas and existence, Frisch is often at the door of tragedy; yet the tragic view is not finally the one that he chooses to espouse.

Don Juan moves for a while in a neutral zone which Frisch, with his manipulative skills, might have made dominantly comic or dominantly tragic. A traditional tale that ends with a descent into hell might well have had a Faustian tinge (such as is present in *The Firebugs*). And when on one occasion Don Juan kneels before Donna Anna "in my humility, in my guilt," declares that "Only mercy, not forgiveness can save me from the world I have made," and a little later speaks of having "knelt in repentance" (III),[8] the play seems intent on an inner action of tragic dimension. But then the statement, "Love is a tragedy!" is put into the mouth of a madam (Intermezzo after Act III), who has already complained with disgust that her girl Miranda, "the most famous whore in Seville . . . must fall in love!" * (Intermezzo after Act I). Then Miranda, having converted romantic passion into worldly good sense (after thirteen years), assures Juan, the man of many adulteries and murders, that marriage with her, now a wealthy duchess, would almost "wipe out your stupid guilt" (IV). Juan, plotting a magician's trick of descent into hell (he would actually escape into a life of anonymous scholarship), says that he will go down with "an appropriate scream— one which will, according to Aristotle's recipe, arouse pity and terror" (IV). Such passages show Frisch dealing playfully with the tragic rather than practicing it. And when, near the end, the plump Bishop, who at this time has the role of *raisonneur*, wittily declares, "God punishes man by creating him as he is, not as he ought to be" (V), his words underscore the evident fact that the world depicted is not that of Sophoclean tragedy but rather that of Euripidean melodrama and comedy.

Frisch's Don Juan, like Shaw's, is a victim,† but Shaw's domain is

---

* The same motif—the "mother's" grief for the whore fallen unprofessionally into feeling—would appear later in Duerrenmatt's *The Meteor* (see chapter 9). Incidentally, the paradoxes of prostitution, as imagined by different writers in flight from the cliché, can come out quite differently. Frisch has his madam, delightfully named Celestina, declare that "here for once the men get some respite from false emotions," and attributes to "Don Octavio, the wise judge," the ironic observation, "So long as we have our polite literature breeding its false emotions in the world, so long will a bordello be a necessary part of every self-respecting city" (Intermezzo after Act I). This kind of reversal of expectation is to be contrasted with that in Genet's *The Balcony*, in which the equally businesslike madam, Irma, defines her place as a House of Illusions and attributes its success to the nurturing of self-inflating fantasies in the customers. That is, here they can enjoy their "false emotions." The tie that binds the Frisch and Genet madams is the sense of the whorehouse as a refuge from the world that imposes on men either its limitations or their own.

† If someone offered a prize for a paradoxical Don Juan play in which Don Juan is a victim of women, Shaw and Frisch might tie for first place. There is even one major parallel in plot: the traditional seducer is reduced to marriage—in *Man and Superman*, Jack Tanner by Ann Whitefield (Juan and Donna Anna), and in

MAX FRISCH   [205]

socio-psycho-biological, while Frisch's is metaphysical. Shaw's Ann
Whitefield is an instrument of the Life Force that conquers Jack Tanner; Frisch's Miranda, the prostitute turned Shavian wise woman,
explains that "a wife—whoever she may be—" is "the only path, Juan, to
your masculine geometry" (IV). Juan's love for geometry, which Frisch
considered important enough to include in the title, is less a dramatic
fact of character than a symbolic instrument. At one time Juan equates
geometry with "God" (II); at another time he praises "the play of
knowledge" and "the calm delight of science"; he calls himself "in-
satiably curious about Nature" and professes to have seduced his best
friend's wife as a sort of scientific experiment; an ultimate phase of curiosity occurs "when we want to know *who* we are" and "something keeps
whispering in your ears that you no longer know where God lives" (III).
At times geometry appears to be the quest of the Platonic idea; individual women are of no account because they are poor imitations of the
idea. Hence the sameness of all nights with women and "the instability
of love," "because once again we have sought and failed to find the
impossible: permanence" (IV).

But instead of wholly accepting this novel analysis of obsessive promiscuity—as the male victim's perpetual rejection of the transitory—Frisch
endows it with ironic ambiguity (as he did the central emotions in
When the War Was Over). Miranda, who has made a living by knowing men, tells Juan, "You are a man—you have always simply loved yourself, Juan, and yet you have never found yourself. So you hate us
women. You have always thought of us as women, never as wives. . ."
(IV). The metaphysical quest of the idea as self-love, the intellectual
mastery of the permanent as self-love—this is the central paradox of the
play. (It is now that Miranda, with utmost shrewdness, presents marriage, not as duty to or gratification of the woman, but as man's best
route to the fulfillment that he has defined for himself.) And it is here

Frisch's play, Juan by the prostitute who fell in love with him, Miranda (the name,
one assumes, an ironic borrowing from *The Tempest*). Besides, Jack is the author
of a pamphlet on revolution, and Juan is a rebel against conventions, especially
the matrimonial ones. But there the resemblances end. Jack Tanner, in 1901–3,
could not be given the freedom of bedrooms available to a Don Juan re-created over
half a century later. Juan is all but kidnaped by wives eager to be seduced but
utilizing verbal morality as a cover for success or as a compensation for failure.
Juan's sexual charisma is related to that of the "rank misogynist" whom, as George
Meredith puts it, women "hunt down as far as he will go. Him they regard as the
noble stag of the forest, and to catch him they disencumber themselves of many
garments retained in a common chase" (*The Ordeal of Richard Feverel*, chap. i).

that once again the play borders on tragedy, for it interprets the quest of the absolute as the ultimate egotism, a Faustian will to be held within no limits. But Frisch does not grant his Don Juan that kind of magnitude. Weary of sexual exploits, he settles for marriage to Miranda in a big castle; thus he not only avoids his traditional fate, but is wholly free for geometry—for science, truth, ultimate ideas. Ironically, he sees this life as less an opportunity than a "prison" (V), perhaps a Sartrian "*huis clos*" (the dramatist invites jokes about marriage as hell by warning against them), and his energy goes less into free thought than into feeling hemmed in. A wise woman has reduced a supposedly Faustian intellect to a domesticity where the problem of adjustment elicits no more than complaint. Marlowe turned the Faust tradition into "the tragedy of knowledge"; [9] Frisch has turned the Don Juan tradition into the comedy of knowledge.

Biography: A Game (1967) is another drama that employs private life to meditate on a problem of man's psychic and moral nature. It happens to be reminiscent of several of Brecht's earlier dramas and of a number of plays in English,* though these reminiscences suggest interesting similarities rather than derivations. The ideas that inform the

---

* One might imagine *Biography* as J. M. Barrie's *Dear Brutus* (1917) filtered through T. S. Eliot's *Cocktail Party* (1949) and ever so slightly tinged by S. N. Behrman's *Biography* (1932). Behrman's female artist decides not to write "her biography," which would have some impact on other lives; Frisch's male scientist, given an opportunity to revise or even "change [his] biography," already "written" by his having lived it, finds that every choice may mean a radical change in the life of someone else. Barrie filtered through Eliot would have less "whimsy" and sentiment, but, in retaining a great deal of fantasy, would fall short of both the mystery and the immediate "realism" of Eliot. In both Eliot and Frisch there is a couple who after a few years of rather rocky marriage have come to a reckoning; both husbands get some help or direction from an initially ambiguous but seemingly prepotent man—Eliot's "Unidentified Guest" and Frisch's "Recorder." At one point the husbands respond alike to this figure: Eliot's Edward says, "But I don't know who you are" (I.i), and Frisch's Kürmann asks, "Who are you actually?" (I). The Recorder and the Unidentified Guest both have in them something of a director of consciousness and something of a director in a theater; Frisch indeed gives the Recorder "the authority of the theatre" but denies to him the "metaphysical authority" eventually revealed by Eliot's Unidentified Guest. The Recorder's kinship is more with Barrie's Lob, who can introduce characters to a "might have been" or "second chance" through imagination. Besides, Barrie's title, with its allusion to *Julius Caesar* ("the fault . . . is not in our stars but in ourselves"), would have some applicability to Frisch's play. But while Barrie's people are temporarily thrust into other lives closer to heart's desire, Kürmann reviews his life as if it were a written "biography" subject to alteration; while Barrie plays with ironic reversals that contribute, finally, to a greater adjustment to the way things are, Frisch has Kürmann wrestle with the problem of destiny and of the extent to which he would and could change the course of events.

action in *Biography* are at least related to the concept of eternal recurrence that appeared in *Count Oederland* and *The Chinese Wall*. There are various reminders of *The Firebugs*: the allegorical name of the central character—here, Kürmann, the man who chooses; the idea that the victim consents to what happens to him; the idea that "Fate" is a faulty term for what man has done. But while Biedermann of *The Firebugs* can choose to fight against a public disaster, Kürmann can choose to alter a life which he has already lived. The earlier play presents a failure of foresight; the later, the incomplete power of hindsight.

In *Biography* the symbolic action presents a life as the script of a play; the first living of it has been, as it were, a rehearsal; and on a rerun, which is likened to another rehearsal in the theater, man can change the script. This is a kind of "game," as the subtitle indicates; the word and its cognates appear frequently in the text. Thus the action is different from that of ordinary reality. What it objectifies is a dialogue between Kürmann and himself as he ponders the question, "Given a second choice in life, what would I do differently?" As Kürmann makes decisions, he gives directions to the "Recorder," who confirms or alters the existing script accordingly (while the other characters in Kürmann's life wait around to see whether their careers will be changed by his decisions). The play turns on the fact that Kürmann "chooses" to "change" very little. The central fact of his adult life was his marriage to the clever Antoinette, who was unfaithful to him; like Vershinin in Anton Chekhov's *Three Sisters*, quoted in Frisch's epigraph, he had supposed that on a second go-round he would avoid marriage. But Antoinette turns out to be no less irresistible than on the first time around. What we construe as mistakes have their own rewards, and we do not easily substitute new wisdom for them.

Nevertheless, as if profiting from one of the morals of *The Firebugs*, Kürmann has resisted the idea of "destiny," of unalterableness in the events as they have happened. What he learns, however, is that destiny is not a prior formula imposed on him from without but something that he has created in an interplay between action and character (George Eliot puts this idea very well: "Our deeds determine us as much as we determine our deeds"). A man's major choice is colored by previous choices; all his freedoms cumulatively frame a life that is not greatly alterable by an apparently free second choice. In fact, Frisch garnishes the central actions with kinds of images that suggest either inherent irreversibleness or eternal recurrence (here, of course, is the point of contact with *Count Oederland* and *The Chinese Wall*, though these deal with the ways of public institutions rather than with the mysteries of the individual psyche). The chess images imply a set of rules that do not allow unlimited options. The ballet school next door, and the accompanying piano that keeps playing "the same bars of music" (II),[10] imply continuing patterns of behavior. The point is even more strongly made by the references to Kürmann's musical clock, in which "the same figures always go through the same movements" (I, II); though Kürmann once orders, "Get rid of it" (I), it keeps coming into the picture, and it is present at the very end. Finally, whenever the Recorder, in quoting from the biographical script, turns to a new year, he always reads off a kind of headline summary of the political events of the year—the doings of Adolf Hitler, Fidel Castro, John F. Kennedy, and others. Though this old device may seem, on the face of it, only to help place the private doings in public times, the true effect is to suggest a massive structure of unalterable events that mock the personal game of making alterations and renovations of an old record.

But Kürmann is less the victim of a metaphysical joke than the embodiment of a human irony: that retrospective utopianism, despite all the benefits of foreknowledge in a reopened past, depends on quasi-rational choice and therefore denies the wholeness of the human being that is inevitably present in every choice. Man cannot be a Houyhnhnm because he cannot act as the fragmented human being who alone can evade the imperfections of life. The play asserts his full humanness, then, and at the same time it asserts his ability to understand, at least in part, the complexity of the motives in actions that in terms of their consequences had seemed hasty and over simple. More important, if he recognizes that some actions come out of impulses not subject to judgment, he can also make judgments of other impulsive actions. Speaking of his first wife Katrin, he says, "I misused her to forget Helen [his mulatto mistress in America], and she misused me to have a child" (I). Speaking of her suicide after he had said to her in an argument, "Then go and hang yourself" (an echo of Biedermann's words to Knechtling in *The Firebugs*), he says, "My guilt is unbearable" (I). He says of Antoinette, his second wife, and himself, "We diminished one another" (II). Two of these judgments of self, it is true, are combined with judgments of another, and none is a guide to restorative action; still, they are tinctured with the self-knowledge that helps complete the tragic rhythm. That Frisch can mingle a perception of man's illusions with a sense of man's ability to see himself in moral perspective indicates that *Biography* is at least partly in the realm of tragedy. That the drama has taken on this character, perhaps going beyond the author's original plans, is what is probably referred to in the sentence with which Frisch concludes his "Author's Note": "I intended the play to be a comedy." But the words might also allude to a final scene in which Kürmann is doomed by cancer, a way out that, though it has a symbolic dimension, returns us to the nontragic world of disastrous event.

IV. TRAGIC ELEMENTS IN FRISCH

To look at Frisch from the perspective of tragedy is to locate some central elements in his moral and aesthetic style. For him, a repeated source of wrongdoing is what we might call the simplified melodramatic consciousness—the sense of evil as the property of other individuals and other classes; it is a theme that often lies beneath farce and fantasy, jest and riddle. It is there in the panoramic allegory *The Chinese Wall.* It is the overt substance of *When the War Was Over* and *Andorra;* behind the nationalistic antagonisms of Germans and Russians in the one, and anti-Semitism in the other, Frisch discovers the self-congratulatory parochialism of all class feelings, be they those of country or of race. He observes different modes of melodramatic life: a healthy man may have to fight others to survive, and a sick man may express the absolutism of self by destroying others (as in *The Firebugs*). Most men drift into melodrama and find comfort in it. This observation, urbane or bitter in different plays, is central in Frisch.

He is always aware, then, of the tragic alternatives, though in his view man does not readily choose them. Frisch's own detachment inhibits the passionate imaging of tragic emotion which would give it preeminence in a drama; more than once we have to say that though a given plot could develop tragically it is not what he is after. However, the tragic possibility is rarely absent. Even in *The Chinese Wall* Columbus tells Don Juan that there is still "the continent of your own soul" to be explored—a major strand in the tragic theme. *The Firebugs* inveighs against applying the term "Fate" to one's "mistakes," that is, evading the tragic view. In *Biography* Kürmann's belief in "choice" gives him a tragic potential. Agnes in *When the War Was Over*, the Teacher in *Andorra,* and Don Juan all have something of the sense of guilt which belongs to the tragic rather than the melodramatic style. For the Teacher it is central; in the others, Frisch sees it as an emotional episode rather than an ultimate motive. It is as if he were observing their lack of range and thus anticipating disaster rather than moral discovery. His treatment of guilt is most ironic in *The Firebugs,* in which Biedermann's guilt is the door not to clear-sightedness but to a fatal vulnerability.

But Biedermann, like other Frisch characters, consents to disaster; in that sense the play, if not the character, partakes of the tragic view. The view enters even into *Don Juan* when one character, who appears to have authority, defines all of Juan's aspirations as a form of egotism. It enters most subtly into *Biography,* which says in effect that a man cannot choose to act with a part of himself instead of with his whole self. That is in essence a declaration against melodramatic living.

CHAPTER NINE

Friedrich Duerrenmatt (1921 ⸺)

WHEN Duerrenmatt told lecture audiences that the poet sometimes overcame the dramatic theorist in Brecht, he spoke as a dramatic poet who was rather less troubled by theoretic impulses. Not that he does not have theories, both dramatic and political, but that they are felt more in the realm of perspective than in that of program; in drama, he is the reflective man rather than the political activist. As a poet in the theater, he is an extraordinary "maker" of plots and of surrealistic figures to carry them ahead. Like Frisch, who is ten years his senior, he turns persistently to the ways in which men destroy others and themselves. In portraying the human destructiveness that operates both in individuals and in societies, however, he has a somewhat more opulent, phantasmagoric inventiveness than Frisch (not that Frisch is ever unoriginal), perhaps a wider diversity of theme and attack. Duerrenmatt is a creator of fairy tales who can do either the gay invention or the grim fantasia; indeed, he began with the former, in mid career executed the latter brilliantly, and more recently has employed a farcical, at times Shavian, medium for staging his sense of how the world goes. Of his first three dramas that we have in English, two are in a playfully ironic style; they are little affected by the study of obsessed personalities which, though it already attracts

Duerrenmatt, does not impinge strongly on the dramatic tone until a little later. These two are *Romulus the Great: An Historical Comedy Without Historic Basis* (1949) and *An Angel Comes to Babylon* (1954). Between them comes *The Marriage of Mr. Mississippi* (1952),[1] the first of the plays in the later manner, where the satirical-grotesque pushes on toward revenge melodrama with tragic overtones. The later mode is carried on by *The Visit* (1956) and *The Physicists* (1962). Yet in *The Physicists* the pace, the rush of surprises, and the diminution of human range in the characters mark the shift toward the farcical communication of ideas that is conspicuous in *The Meteor* (1966) and *King John* (1968).

I. Comic Fables

Romulus the Great shows Duerrenmatt speaking, as he would do more than once, through a witty man of totally heterodox views but not yet attempting a character with the inner contradictions that may lead to self-knowledge. The influential roles are held by remarkably well-integrated people who are sure of themselves and of their values; their problems are only with the pressure of circumstances. Romulus, the last Roman emperor in the West, has assumed the throne to help liquidate an empire which he considers vicious and which is going down hill fast. Other leading Romans come up with various clichés about "saving the Empire" from the advancing Teutons, but no one has enough resources, or energy, or ability to do more than talk; finally most of the Roman leaders are drowned while trying to escape to Sicily on a raft. Romulus' daughter Rea tries to impose on herself the romantic suffering of giving up her real love Emilian to marry Caesar Rupf, the rich Roman pants manufacturer, who can buy off the Teutons for ten million sesterces, but her father, the urbane and serene realist who wants the empire not to be saved, adopts a more romantic position than she, and emphatically asserts that love has priority over politics. Romulus is a brilliant and often epigrammatic moralist who, like a Shaw spokesman, turns every cliché upside down; his triumph will be not mastering a world physically or symbolically, but calmly and even amiably wrecking a world unfit to live. His ultimate reversal of the expected is "I sacrifice Rome through sacrificing myself" (III).[2] So he stays to be killed by Odoaker, the Teuton ruler, only to find that Odoaker not only is as civilized as himself (he spots a Praxiteles that

Romulus had thought was a fake) and like himself a chicken-fancier, but astonishingly wants to keep him in power so that a humane and just way of life may survive. The real enemy, Odoaker says, is his nephew Theodoric, a water-drinking, perpetually exercising Spartan type who dreams only of conquering the world—an archetypal figure of German militarism. Duerrenmatt delights not only by unseating the expected and by paradox but by using terms that suggest the contemporaneity of the affair: "total mobilization," "collaboration," "resistance," "catastrophic capitalism," "the ancient guilt of our history," "absurd," and even the rising value of "German primitives" that are bringing down the second-hand market in classical art. Duerrenmatt has written a sermon in the form of a grand jest—the comic parallel, in exotic expressionistic costume, of the morality. He foreshadows the didactic farce of his most recent plays.

An Angel Comes to Babylon (1954) is closer to *Romulus* than to the other plays, but the atmosphere is much more fabulous, and the fable is so spontaneously rich and elaborate that full justice to it would take more pages than my plan of operation permits. *An Angel* deals not only with relations between Heaven and Earth (two leading characters are an angel and Kurrubi, a maiden created especially by God to be given to "the lowliest of men") but with complex relations among numerous human beings—kings, a Prime Minister, a Senior Theologian, various kinds of citizens, workmen, a hangman, and beggars. These latter all belong to Babylon, which Duerrenmatt intends to suggest both New York and Paris, to be "the metropolis." [3] An angel's visit throws everything awry there; it undermines the power of the state, bringing on a spontaneous revolution that all but dethrones Nebuchadnezzar, the king. All these goings-on permit many satirical pictures of the opportunism of those in power and the fickleness of the population generally; the Senior Theologian, for instance, bargains for half the national revenue for the established church and guarantees in turn to have the Angel denounced from every pulpit as a phony. On the other hand the Angel is so smitten with all the beauties and perfections of earth—he is apparently a cousin of Dr. Pangloss—that his inevitable return to life amid the galaxies is a reluctant one.

There is much high comedy, and the language is often made poetic by an infusion of rhymes and images. In looking at human conduct in a crisis, Duerrenmatt notes the high incidence of standardized responses, of expediency and self-interest, of idealism without willingness to pay the price (as in *Romulus*). Kurrubi, who as the "grace of God" is intended only for the poorest, is so beautiful that nearly everybody wants her, but on his own terms. Once an applicant discovers that he must "give his all to transform himself into the beloved one" (that is, the poor and lowly man for whom she is destined—Act III), he not only loses interest but begins to resent her. The exceptions, in whom the dramatic interest centers, are Nebuchadnezzar the king and Akki the beggar.

At the beginning of the play Nebuchadnezzar is determined to get rid of beggars because, according to his dogma, they do not belong in the "New Order," the "faultless Empire," the "grand design," the "welfare state," as his kingdom is variously described with meaningful allusiveness. Only Akki refuses to be integrated into the new order; he insists on remaining what he is, a very successful beggar (he is the cousin of Bérenger in Ionesco's *Rhinoceros*). To persuade him Nebuchadnezzar disguises himself as a beggar; he is drawn into a begging competition with Akki, and loses every round; as a losing beggar he is considered the poorest of all mortals, and he is awarded Kurrubi. This largesse only makes him discontented and resentful; his view is that the grant should be made to him as a king, not as a beggar. First he beats Kurrubi; then he trades her to Akki; later he reveals himself to her and tries to secure for himself as king that love which she had felt for him as beggar. He argues that he was disguised then when he was a beggar; she argues that he is disguised now when he is a king—"a ghost who frightens me" (III). When he will not give up the throne to become the beggar who can be loved, she makes a crushing explication of him, climaxed by "Your love for me is self-love"—another of Duerrenmatt's keen analyses of emotional life (III). The king orders the hangman to take her away and execute her.

What distinguishes Nebuchadnezzar from the others who reject Kurrubi, and makes him especially interesting to us here, is that he almost becomes the tragic hero. He understands what he has done: "I strove after perfection. I created a New Order. I sought to extinguish poverty. I wanted to inaugurate the age of reason. Heaven has turned its face from my works. I am without grace" (III). In trying to make his kingdom into a forcing-house for doctrinaire utopianism, he is allied to Dorothy Sayers' Faustus. Nebuchadnezzar is virtually the modern do-gooder as tragic hero—the man who sees finally that his premises are inadequate, or, perhaps more accurately, that his socio-political radicalism is simply the current dressing for egoistic aggressiveness. He can add, "I betrayed the maiden for the sake of my power" (III). This is his high point as potential tragic hero; from it he slides back into a lesser man who will now, like Shakespeare's Claudius, play his old game in a new key. The millennialist whom Duerrenmatt shows defeated in other plays, he now turns from actual to symbolic combat, this time against Heaven. Nebuchadnezzar becomes the melodramatic, undivided antagonist. In literary terms, he turns, as does the title character of *The Marriage of Mr. Mississippi,* into the revenger. He says quite literally, "I will forge weapons to revenge my shame. . . . Is Heaven so high that my curses cannot reach it? . . . I will oppose to the Creation out of the void the creation of the spirit of man, and we shall see which is the better: my justice, or the injustice of God" (III). He plans a great conquering project: the Tower of Babel. He is a Luciferian Ozymandias who has become modern man.

If Duerrenmatt denies, in Nebuchadnezzar, the tragic continuity, he asserts it, or something like it, in Akki the beggar, who belongs with Romulus and Übelohe (in *The Marriage*) among the "men of courage" in whom the "lost world-order is restored." [4] Akki refuses to be incorporated into the new perfect state; he continues to beg with brilliant success and to throw all his gains into the Euphrates—"the only way to relieve the world of riches" (II). He becomes the hangman, and hangings cease. When Kurrubi is turned over to him to be executed, he and Kurrubi run away, and at the end we see them fleeing through a wilderness in a sandstorm. In a way this is an understated, inglorious version of the melodramatic rescue and escape; amid punitive difficulties they are drawn by hope of "a land that forgets the past." But here is the description of the new land that closes the play: ". . . full of new persecutions, but full, too, of new promises, and full of the songs of a new morning" (III). The "new persecutions" that go along with the "new promises" and the "new morning" keep the hope of salvation from being that of the romantic idyl, or of Nebuchadnezzar's New Order by fiat. Here the sense of progress is singularly joined with the sense of the recurrent, the vision of escape with the full sight of the inescapable.

In this duality there is the moral realism of tragedy, but no more than that. The moral realism is not dramatized in a protagonist who errs representatively, brings disaster on himself and others, and comes to understanding and humanly significant recovery. Nebuchadnezzar comes fascinatingly close to that experience, but his recovery after self-knowledge is that of a narrowing personality bent only upon new self-inflative exploits. The spiritually affirmative note is carried by Akki, the little man whose security seems a native gift rather than the painful recovery from division. He is the voice of comedy in the Northrop Frye sense—the herald of spring, of the new order, yet a new order with the ineradicable old one in its heart.

II. "The Marriage of Mr. Mississippi"

The Marriage of Mr. Mississippi (1952) has links with both earlier and later plays. It is the first of the later three in which appear Jacobean elements such as the revenge motif; in which, in the worlds depicted, power is used madly or is held by the mad; but in which, also, the melodramatic intensity can approach the border of tragedy. The revenge motif appears, of course, in *An Angel Comes to Babylon:* Nebuchadnezzar is related to Mr. Mississippi, just as Akki, the bearer of restorative values, is related to Count Übelohe of *The Marriage.* Finally, *The Marriage* belongs with the earlier group in that Duerrenmatt calls it, without qualification, a "comedy." [5]

Comedy, Duerrenmatt says, "supposes an unformed world," and in his view "the comical exists in forming what is formless, in creating order out of chaos"; [6] to comedy he assigns a very profound role indeed, one that takes him into, or makes his play a commentary upon, other genres as we have discussed them here. On the face of it we might say that in *The Marriage* Duerrenmatt is writing a drama of disaster: a symbolic room on whose importance he lays great stress—all the actions occur in it—is in ruins at the end of the play. In a symbolic drama of this sort exact meanings cannot be assigned, but there are many suggestions of modern civilization in this room, with its mixed inheritance of art and culture, and its eerie outlook upon flora of north and south, upon Greek ruins and a Gothic cathedral. "The room stinks to high heaven" (I). Not only is the room largely laid waste by mob action in a Communist-led uprising, but, in a Jacobean slaughter, three of the four major characters meet death in it—one shot by Communist party executioners, and a husband and wife poisoned by each other.

The only survivor exists peripherally, the alcoholic and disintegrating

Count Übelohe. Yet it is through him that the play is turned from a drama of disaster, in our terms, to a comedy in Duerrenmatt's terms. For the Count has tried in various ways to love mankind, both in the person of Anastasia (whom another lover calls "that whore of Babylon") and through charitable efforts in Europe and in Malaysian jungles. By ordinary standards he has always failed, been "vanquished—the only role in which man again and again appears." "Even my love for you," he tells Anastasia, "has become absurd. But it is our love. We must bear its absurdity" (I). His belief is in "truth" and "a miracle." He states the meaning of his love: "Nothing but the hope that the soul of my beloved is not lost so long as I love her; nothing but this faith!" He loves her, not "for her works," as her husband does, "but as a woman who is lost." Nevertheless Anastasia rejects him; for her, "Fear was greater than love," and she is at best capable only of transient fidelity to transient holders of power. The Count goes off to become a homeless, ruined, sodden wanderer, to "plant" his never-weakening love, "in whose name I am resurrected again and again," in "the countries through which I shall now roam"—a cousin, less well but somehow less fragile, of Eliot's Celia Coplestone and Harry Monchensey. He is "nailed upon the cross of my absurdity, . . . a last Christ" (II). The Count then disappears from the scene, which is dominated by the clashes between Anastasia and her lovers, men of other philosophical persuasions, until their deaths conclude the formal action. Though Duerrenmatt chooses to underplay, sidetrack, and unheroicize the role of what we may call his "comic hero," he shows how much importance he attaches to the Count by having him reappear in a brief dream epilogue and speak the closing twenty-five lines of verse: now he is Don Quixote,[7] who still "defies" the windmills "filling your belly with nations / hacked to pieces by your wing that is dripping with blood." Accepting his actions as an "eternal comedy," he concludes the play thus: "Let His glory blaze forth, / fed by our helpless futility."

If Duerrenmatt is, as the Count argues in an address to the audience in Part I, inquiring "whether . . . God's mercy is really infinite, our only hope," he is also paradoxically involving the Count, the sot who loses everything in the world, in "the adventure of love, that sublime enterprise which, whether he survives or perishes in it, endows man with his greatest dignity" (I). In that sense, an outcast and failure, the Count is an agent or witness of God's mercy. What is more, Duerrenmatt explains in "Problems of the Theatre," the Count belongs to a group of his characters (Romulus, Akki) who do not despair but are "men of courage"; he continues, "The lost world-order is restored within them. . . ." [8] It is through the Count, then, that *The Marriage of Mr. Mississippi* carries out the extraordinary role that Duerrenmatt assigns to comedy—the role of bearing a vision of order that, though it may not conquer chaos, will not yield to it.

Actually, Duerrenmatt claims for comedy certain characteristics that, in my view, have traditionally belonged to tragedy. In the Count, for instance, there is that combination of failure and triumph (his sturdy adherence to courage and love) that we find generally in tragic heroes. Or to shift to other terms, there is an ongoing of values, a spiritual continuity, that is independent of success or failure in the world: the adventure of love, as we have just seen, gives man, "whether he survives or perishes . . . his greatest dignity." Hence it is interesting to find Duerrenmatt insisting that tragedy and comedy are "dramatic attitudes, . . . which can embrace one and the same thing," that we "can achieve the tragic out of comedy," and that "Shakespeare tragedies" are often "really comedies out of which the tragic arises." His claims for the affinity or overlap between tragedy and comedy make it reasonable to interpret some of his remarks, though they are formally about comedy, as stressing ways of understanding and meeting reality that, in the terms used here, are tragic rather than melodramatic. He challenges the doctrine of despair, which he describes as only an individual answer, not one universally compelled by the state of the world; thus he rules out melodramas of surrender, the form to which O'Neill's efforts at tragedy are confined by his pervasive hopelessness. Again, he insists that "in everything and everywhere, . . . the rule is: No excuses, please!" The truth is the thing, and it is not to be avoided by the peculiarly untragic device of substituting genetic palliation for qualitative assessment. Most important: "The world . . . is for me something monstrous, a riddle of misfortunes which must be accepted but before which one must not capitulate." [9] If he rules out despair, he also rules out illusions and foolish hopes; an adequate sense of reality guards against the simpler rules of being either victor or victim; in the face of depravity one does not simply give up, rather one gives up utopianism. In literary terms, Duerrenmatt would eliminate not only the melodrama of despair but also its counterform, the melodrama of triumph. This is one way of describing the generic theory implied by *The Marriage of Mr. Mississippi.*

In *The Marriage,* indeed, he gives less space and centrality, though not finally less emphasis, to the affirmative Count Übelohe action than he does to two other actions that represent the failure of the melodramatic attitude to the world—the dream of saving it, perfecting it, possessing it which is begotten by two competing ideological systems. These are represented by Mr. Mississippi and St. Claude. Their relationship to the Count is summed up in the symbolic poem in which, after their death, their spirits antiphonally chant a series of lines ending thus:

> We sweep by above your cities
> Panting as we flap our mighty wings
> That turn the mills which crush you.
> [II]

These "mills" are the windmills, "wing . . . dripping with blood," that Count Übelohe (Don Quixote), though "jeered at" and "wretched," continually "defies." That is to say, his valor and his love keep confronting, not imaginary enemies, but oppressive systems that develop out of millennial ideas. He will never triumph, but, like the tragic hero, he will by his effort contribute to the world a quality in virtue of which its "soul . . . is not lost." If the Count is anything but a traditional hero (he is faintly reminiscent of dispossessed and alienated value-bearers such as the mad Lear, the Fool, and "mad Tom"), Mississippi and St. Claude are not given a conventional treatment as "villains." They do not triumph, as they would in a work of cynicism or despair or in a bitter satire (this work is far different from 1984), but neither are they disposed of, for they represent tendencies that keep on finding new expressions after every setback. As their spirits put it in the antiphon: "Again and again we return, as we have always returned / In ever new shapes, yearning for ever more distant paradises." That is the nature of millennialism, ever starting anew with a utopian idea that becomes rigid, imprisoning, and self-defeating, but never losing its own life of illusion in the failure of its successive manifestations.

Anastasia, as we have seen, denies her love for the Count; she has loved, or protested her love to, all the other men, and betrayed them. As St. Claude puts it, she "could be neither changed nor saved, because she loved nothing but the moment"; as her lover the Minister puts it,

"You are an animal, . . . You have no plan, you live only in the moment. . . . For you what is will always be stronger than what was, and what will be will always triumph over the present. No one can grasp you . . . " (I); as Anastasia herself puts it after her death, "A whore, who passes unchanged through death" (II). With her infidelities that participate in the endless flux of history, Anastasia is a new version of the fickle world; ironically she rejects the Count's generous love more easily than she does the domineering attentions of those who "really take them [certain ideas] seriously and strive with audacity and vigour, with insane fervour and an insatiable greed for perfection, to put them into effect" (I). This picture of the world has that profound irony which is the common ground of comedy and tragedy.

Of these fanatics of the idea, intent on imposing an intramundane salvation, St. Claude is a Communist (and as such, one of Duerrenmatt's replies to Brecht) operating on the international scene, and planning an ultimate revolution against both West and East; he describes Mississippi and himself as "the last two great moralists of our age," but differentiates between them thus: "You want to save an imaginary soul and I a real body" (I). Mr. Mississippi, the ideological opposite number of St. Claude, is interesting because he is not quite what one might expect as rival dogmatist of the Communist—except insofar as he insists, "There is no justice without God!" But for him the ultimate reality is rather the Law of Moses, which he slaves to revive after three thousand years; for him, "Justice cannot be changed!" since he speaks for "absolute morality" (I); above all, he is a Public Prosecutor whose greatest pride, indeed all of whose life, is in the world-record number of death sentences that he has wrenched out of courts and juries. He is a rigid, merciless Puritan, punitive, and, in Duerrenmatt's sharpest insight, given to quantitative standards of moral improvement. He is a flagellant too: since he has killed his wife, and Anastasia her husband (the murdered spouses were having an affair), he sentences Anastasia to marry him, and himself to marry her: their marriage will be an endless penance, a hell, a punishment for their sins, and it will be held "in the Calvinist church" (I). Married, they go his way: he striving ever for more executions, she watching them, working with prisoners, and becoming "the Angel of the Prisons"—thus by her "works" justifying "the Law." Mississippi's greatest fear is that she had once, as the Count confessed in the interest of truth, been Count Übelohe's mistress: if she had, so to speak, loved love, then the theory of regeneration by the punitive law would be washed up, and Mississippi would be only a killer. In a symbolically meaningful version of Jacobean stage contrivance, they poison each other.

Before this, Duerrenmatt manages another sharp irony by having St. Claude invite Mississippi to assume the leadership of the Communist movement—the final seal of the spiritual consanguinity of these two utopians. They had come up together out of the gutter, through thieving, male prostitution, and running a brothel, and were possessed by the Mosaic and Marxian visions that even at the moment of death they dream of carrying out through a fresh start elsewhere. There is a touch of the Jacobean in Duerrenmatt's treatment of them, not of course in tracing their doctrinal fervor to a detestation of the ugly actualities they once knew (they have even dreamed up romantic names and fancy genealogies for themselves), but in letting us sense the element of revenge behind the eschatological dreams—the sheer pleasure of punishing people while carrying out a mission of noble import. Cyril Tourneur might have done it this way. In a sense, then, Duerrenmatt treats Mississippi as a writer of brilliant and mature melodrama might do. But at the same time he complicates the treatment by interpreting Mississippi as a false tragic hero, who can ape the tragic style and believe he has achieved the essential experience. Mississippi's forcing the marriage between Anastasia and himself because it will be a penance, a disciplinary "hell," becomes a magnificent parody of tragic sensibility and action: with Mississippi, guilt and penance are conceived in cold, rational, rigid textbook terms; they are elements in a formula that one applies by rule and that works automatically, whatever one's spiritual state; by a loathsome calisthenics the soul is made more fit, though it unremittingly detests the whole process. As long as one is being antihedonistic, one is being saved; the more revolting the medicine, the more complete the cure. Penance that is hellish enough is assumed to be working a spiritual miracle; one cannot help being improved, though one's vices remain essentially untouched; in fact one is free to let one's old impulses have even fuller sway—Mississippi piles up an ever fatter record of death sentences—and believe that they are rehabilitating the world. Mississippi has none of the sensibility of the real tragic hero, but he imitates him in a mechanical, literalistic way that shows how "works" can travesty a spiritual experience. Penitence is twisted into flagellation, ascesis is the other face of sadism, reform masks revenge.

Duerrenmatt's play, then, casts an unusual light on the generic problem. On the one hand, Duerrenmatt rejects the basic melodramatic ways of formulating experience—that which despairs of the world and that which postulates a triumph in the world. Then with extraordinary insight he shows how the tragic alternative can be perverted—how the salvation to be approached through self-knowledge and reparation can be nothing but the continuation of old habits; one may be so obsessed with redemptive suffering as to convert the endurance of pain into a justification for doing what one is driven to. The apparently self-punitive is really self-indulgent. In contrast with this is the ridiculous comic figure who, in his accumulation of failures, becomes a personification of flaw, and who yet contributes to the world a quality of being which offers as much hope of redemption as there can be. Despite the paradox of failure and hope that he embodies, Count Übelohe does not have, at the level of personality, the range which would permit us to consider *The Marriage* a tragedy. It is rather a morality, throwing into juxtaposition a set of different attitudes that we find regularly in different generic types. The action is somewhat spasmodic, and there are a number of quite long expository speeches, in part addressed to the audience. Yet even in characters in whom meaning tends to shadow being, we sense considerable depth and immediacy; beyond them, the pattern of relationships embraces a range of reality that takes the play out of allegorical narrowness and into a wide imaginative domain.

III. Mixed Modes

Duerrenmatt's two best-known plays—*The Visit* (1956), which the Lunts introduced brilliantly in New York in 1958, and *The Physicists* (1962)—both have some links with their predecessors. In *The Physicists* the topicality indirectly conveyed by verbal allusions and details of action and décor is overt; physics is one of our big topics. In *The Visit* the revenge theme that had some part in *The Marriage* and *An Angel* becomes the very center of the drama. But Duerrenmatt may feel that he has changed the tone, for he calls *The Visit* a "tragicomedy," his first use of the word, and applies no generic term at all to *The Physicists*. In these dramas the sense of the world is darker than that in the three earlier plays.

The Visit is generically the most complex of Duerrenmatt's dramas; this means a range that may make it the most durable of the canon. It is a drama of disaster and a revenge melodrama and a satire, and in this unlikely field there is a vivid flowering of the tragic.[10] Though, like the earlier plays, *The Visit* has its own kind of contemporaneity—the habits, beliefs, attitudes, idioms of the people might have been culled from the popular press of any Western nation—essentially it is a timeless drama of certain springs of human action: the passion for revenge, the love of money (or simply the material need) that overpowers other motives, the need for absolution which can employ every possible device of self-deception. Claire Zachanassian's revenge against her home town and the lover who betrayed her—a "million" to the town to murder the betrayer, Alfred Ill—might well be all of the play. Yet Duerrenmatt chooses to make the betrayer of long ago a moral agent as well as a destined murderee, a mere victim of malice and of his town's need of the million. Hence out of the melodrama there comes a special, highly interesting development in Duerrenmatt's work. There is nothing casual in his use of "tragicomedy" in place of the "comedy" that had served for the preceding plays.

Alfred Ill, the victim of a community which is a victim of a now rich woman who had once been a victim of Ill's, at first wants only to escape the townspeople who are closing in on him to secure through his death the million which will relieve their distresses. But he comes slowly to accept his guilt. He rebukes the Schoolmaster for attempting to "unleash the voice of thunder" and to announce publicly that the town "is planning a monstrous deed." When Ill commands the Schoolmaster, "Hold your peace" and "Get down," we do not at first know whether this closing of a possible avenue of salvation is pure despair. But we come to the big turning point when Ill explains, "I've realized I haven't the least right on my side. . . . That's all my fault, really. . . . I made Clara what she is, and I made myself what I am, . . . What shall I do, Schoolmaster? Play innocent?" (III).[11] From that point until the end he refuses to play innocent; he escapes from the "innocence neurosis" that is a staple of melodrama; he reiterates that he will "accept" the "judgment" of the community and that his "meaningless life will end," and he acquires a dignity that lasts through the murder scene that closes the play. Thus Alfred Ill, one of the few characters to whom Duerrenmatt grants a full humanity, provides a complete experience of tragic self-recognition.*

Ill is not central; hence his role constitutes a "tragic accent." Yet, tragic though he is, he does not provide the note of continuity into the future which Duerrenmatt sees in Count Übelohe in *The Marriage of Mr. Mississippi*. He is simply the most emphatic illustration of the fact that the townspeople's ultimate value is economic and that they can do any self-righteous and self-deceptive case-making required by what they commit for money's sake. They look out for themselves at Ill's expense just as, years before, he had looked out for himself at Claire's expense. The difference is that whereas Ill's self-interest gave Claire a profitable life, the community's self-interest gives Ill death; Ill has run into nemesis, the community has achieved "success." † It would be possible to argue that here we have the rare case in which the usual substitution of modes is reversed, that is, in which a man is acting in a tragedy when he ought to be acting in a melodrama of survival. The contention would be that when a character, however guilty, is about to be victimized by

---

* There is an unusual variant of this in the actions of the Schoolmaster, who desperately tries to tell the town what it is really up to, and who can get no hearing. He endeavors to make Ill help save himself, but, as we have seen, gets nowhere. Then this just accuser makes a statement perhaps unique in drama. After telling Ill, "They will kill you. . . . The temptation is too great and our poverty is too wretched," he adds, "But I know something else. I shall take part in it. I can feel myself slowly becoming a murderer. My faith in humanity is powerless to stop it. And because I know all this, I have also become a sot" (III). (Cf. the drinking of the victim's father in Max Frisch's *Andorra*.) This remarkable insight into self is different from the tragic self-knowledge in that it is predictive rather than retrospective; instead of representing an opening-out of personality, it is the most spacious point before the eventual narrowing down and the surrender of potentiality. The Schoolmaster has an insight denied to the others, and because of this and his position, a special responsibility; but these are entirely overcome by his need to be at one with the herd. At the town meeting which sentences Ill to death, with very high-sounding justifications, the Schoolmaster actually provides the citizens with the logic and rhetoric they need to carry it off. So the Schoolmaster's dramatic role is not to provide a ray of light but is instead to increase the moral gloom in which the play ends.

† In his postscript Duerrenmatt, with much ironic ambiguity, speaks of the people's action as though it were inevitable. But he does not make the people use a style which is morally inevitable; in fact, quite the contrary. In murderers, unless they are pathological, the expectable style would be remorse. Disaster might reduce human beings to murder and cannibalism; as human beings, they might later look back with anguish and horror. But the people of Guellen turn the murder of Ill into a community fiesta in which, under the eyes of "media" people from all over the globe, they praise their own morality and herald a new era of well-being.

a perversion of justice, his first obligation is to save himself, and to search out the occasion on which he could confront himself in freedom and accept a justice untainted by the machinations of self-interested enemies. This would at least place far greater emphasis on the tragic side of the action. In a context in which self-judgment coincides with being victimized for others' profit, Ill's bowing to the yoke leaves us not wholly contented. It may be argued, of course, that he had no choice. Even under pressure the disavowal of innocence is preferable to a complete absence of self-recognition, which would be the final evidence that universal darkness covers all.

The Visit comes close to the traditional morality play in that the human urgency represented, a brutalizing mixture of need and greed, is timeless. *The Physicists* (1962) is more topical, and, for all of its present relevance, one would expect it to date more rapidly. It is primarily a meditation on "the bomb," and especially on the relation between it and the work of scientific geniuses ("the Physicists") that made it possible. There is also a regular thicket of other themes: the relation between the new science and national policy (two physicists, "non-geniuses," now secret agents from "east" and "west," are trying to kidnap or lure "the greatest physicist" to their side); the crushing of love by political missions and the scientific imperative (the secret agents and the great physicist all murder the women who love them); the disparity between the immensity of the new scientific discoveries and the unreadiness of the world for them and its incompetence to live with them except by using them for destruction (the great physicist suggests that the best way to serve knowledge is to keep it secret; he has faked madness to get into an asylum and develop his theories without fear of their being known and misused by the world); the moral responsibility of physicists; the relation between the new science and big business (the head of the asylum, a hunchbacked female psychoanalyst, steals the physicist's advanced theories and forms a cartel to exploit them; in fact, she virtually holds him a prisoner); and, of course, the theme that is tending to become rather a chestnut—the relative sanity of the world outside and the world within the sanitarium walls (where the entire action takes place). Besides all this, there is some satire of psychiatric insight and attitudes, of the moral façades of Eastern and Western political orders as both enslave science to policy, and of the justifications for murder.

With its unusual combination of ingenious plotting, an almost Shavian dialogue of ideas, originality of detail, and reminiscences of other dramas,* *The Physicists* might be a hodgepodge, but the themes triumph and make it essentially symbolic. Whereas the characters in *The Visit* act out their allegorical roles so thoroughly that they come into at least a firm one-dimensional reality, the leading characters in *The Physicists* remain tenuous as persons and have to use a great many words explaining directly what they are up to. The genius, Möbius, deserts his family, flees into an asylum, spends fifteen years on his studies, murders a devoted nurse; "Newton" and "Einstein," foreign secret agents, fake madness to pursue Möbius here, spend respectively two years and one year at it, and murder nurses devoted to them; Dr. Von Zahnd, the old hunchback virgin who runs the asylum on her ancestral estate, views the three murders only as instruments of her own policy and really imprisons the three men to make them serve her cartel. These persons represent forces at work in the world, and they have little if any human reality; they are all but automatons who enter into the most extraordinary actions without apparent emotional engagement. The nurses intent upon an ordinary human life, with personal intimacy and feeling, are all murdered.

Hence the three men and the doctor, with their virtually mechanical responses, belong essentially to the farcical mode that in the later plays Duerrenmatt finds an increasingly congenial medium for his didactic impulse. Yet what is interesting is that at times the men, especially Möbius, almost escape from their roles and become tragic characters. Möbius shows traces of being moved by his murder of Monika and tells the Inspector, "I must ask you to arrest me" (I); but the mood is tem-

* The relation between what the scientist does and what his work leads to in the world was treated earlier in Brecht's *Galileo*. The simulating or willing of "madness" for private ends appears also in Sartre's *Altona*; both writers also present the great cartel as a final holder of power over individuals. The name of the asylum in *The Physicists*, "Les Cerisiers," points to a number of ironic similarities with *The Cherry Orchard*: the decay of an old family line, and the taking over by a new entrepreneurial spirit. Peter Weiss's *Marat-Sade* also stages all the action in a sanitarium, but is at once more clinical and less imaginative. The assumption of alien identities, as well as the efforts of individuals to impose identities on others, leads to an ambiguity of identity mildly reminiscent of Pirandello's *Right You Are* of many years before, but Duerrenmatt engages in ironic jests while Pirandello, another instructional user of the stage, was somewhat heavily protracting an identity problem (in which a half-truth is given an excessive claim) to three-act length. Of course, pretending to be mad to get into a madhouse goes at least as far back as Middleton and Rowley's *The Changeling*.

porary, and we soon find that he has burnt all his manuscripts so that his protective pseudo-madness will not be exposed (II). Next he insists to his fellow physicists that they must stay in the madhouse to be free as scientists and thus, by keeping their knowledge from mankind, to save mankind from destruction; he argues that if they leave, they are simply murderers, whereas if they stay, the nurses' deaths were "sacrificial." So, both to do penance for murder done and to prevent mass murders, they decide to stay: "Let us be mad, but wise. Prisoners but free. Physicists but innocent" (II).

Obviously, however, the tragic is little more than a minor accompaniment of the satirical, and the satirical roars into full possession of the stage: the physicists' moral decision vanishes as we learn that they are really being held prisoners by Dr. Von Zahnd, who had made photocopies of Möbius' statements of discoveries and is exploiting them financially through her cartel. What is more, she has made them prisoners by making them murderers: "I drove those three nurses into your arms. I could count upon your reactions. You were as predictable as automata" (II). As always, satire forces out tragedy and produces melodrama: in the end, the physicists who made victims of their nurses and try to make victims of each other turn out to be victims of the economic villain. As the physicists, in the final step of this Gulliverian fantasy, go back into the roles elected in the instrumental madness which they had assumed, one line in their mechanical closing speeches carries the satire into an unexpectedly large dimension. Möbius, now "King Solomon," says, "But my wisdom destroyed the fear of God, and when I no longer feared God my wisdom destroyed my wealth." Here, if only for a brief moment of exposition, we are in a wider realm than satire usually embraces; indeed, there is an intimation of the tragic as the chief character is again lifted from victimhood and permitted to acknowledge, in a tardy flash of light, that ultimate act of hubris that overshadows economic and political misdeeds—an act against the ultimate symbolization of the authority that can restrain the private willfulness.

IV. FARCE AS MEDIUM

At times Duerrenmatt's conveyance of ideas through comic surprise makes us use *Shavian* as a descriptive adjective. But more often *farcical* appears to be the accurate term for his way of doing things; this is especially true in the later plays. In *The Physicists* we saw him thinking

of characters as mechanical, almost puppet-like. This is the mode of
farce: the automatic supersedes the sentient choice. In the plays of the
late 1960s Duerrenmatt is much attracted by the farcical as a medium
for intentions that have nothing to do with ordinary farcical entertainment.

Yet the method is never a simple or obvious one, and Duerrenmatt,
who always keeps his fine touch for the puzzling surface, can work it
from different directions. One way of describing the earlier plays is to
say that Duerrenmatt gives them the earmarks of comedy and then slips
in the note of disaster or even something of tragic life. But in *The
Meteor* (1966) he all but reverses this procedure. In this meditation on
modes of life and death he strews the stage with almost as many corpses
as Shakespeare does in *Hamlet*, and there are several kinds of sexual and
filial unhappiness.* Hence we are not surprised when Professor Schlatter,
a surgeon, uses the word *catastrophe* (II), and it does not seem improbable when the word *tragedy* also appears in the text. But this is
where the expected is turned upside down. Early in the play the central
character Schwitter, the dramatist who is between his first and second
"deaths," declares, "Dying is nothing tragic" (I).[12] The play proves it:
the deaths are, in fact, technically farcical, that is, mechanical, outside
the realm of feeling; they are ideogrammatic, modeling ideas ("He died
of excitement"—Act I) rather than being ultimate human experiences.
Indeed, Duerrenmatt might be playing games with the loose popular use
of the word *tragic*. A critic eulogizing the apparently dead Schwitter
says, "He who rejected tragedy, himself came to a tragic end" (II).

---

* One man dies when he is pushed downstairs, another is arrested for pushing
him downstairs; a wife commits suicide; one man dies of excitement, and a woman
of exhaustion and something like despair; one man "dies" twice of natural causes,
and his double recovery makes his doctor threaten suicide. A husband is deserted
by his wife, who has just gone to bed with a "dying" man; a son is in despair because he is cheated of an expected patrimony; a publisher is ruined; and a realtor
is in anguish because he thinks his late wife was unfaithful.

In "Friedrich Duerrenmatt at Temple," *Journal of Modern Literature* 1
(1970):88ff., Violet Ketels reports some brief comments on *The Meteor* by Duerrenmatt. "I struggle with a theological fact: the resurrection" (p. 91). The minister
is "not a comic, but rather a genuinely moving figure." "The comedy of the play
lies in the doctor; the tragic figure is Muheim" (here Duerrenmatt uses the term
as loosely as do his comic characters). Schwitter is "a tragic figure." He "is the
modern man." Duerrenmatt compares him to Hamlet (p. 105). He objects to a
London production which made the play "like Anouilh" (p. 107). Asked if *The
Meteor* is "autobiographical," Duerrenmatt turns it off with a jest (p. 108).

"Tragic end" here alludes to death after a long illness, precisely the sloppy journalistic idiom, its false grandeur exposed by the fact that Schwitter is not dead anyway. A jest of a still sharper kind occurs when Professor Schlatter says, "That's the tragedy," alluding to his heroic efforts to save a doomed Schwitter who cheated him doubly by "dying" inconsiderately and then, declared officially dead, by undergoing a resurrection.

The phoenix myth and the resurrection myth are exploited most ironically by reversals of expectation reminiscent of Shaw. On the one hand the supposed death of Nobel-Prize-winning Schwitter elicits eulogies, formal statements, wreaths, candles, reverence, no smoking near the deathbed. More subtly, the presumptive grief of the survivors ritualized in these solemnities turns to disappointment and even unhappiness when Schwitter pops back into life. For one thing, being dead has given Schwitter "insights" (I) and hence a flair for painful candor. He calls his unpublished manuscripts "worthless" (II) and thinks his millions of profit are needless, so he burns up papers and paper money (forty years before, he had burned his paintings and been reborn as a writer); if this is a phoenix rebirth for him, it ruins the material life of others—especially Schwitter's publisher and his son. Schwitter tells Nyffenschwander, the indefatigable painter of "life" (whose wife is a model for endless nudes), that he is no good, and, with his own "life"-out-of-death, seduces the painter's wife. He makes the real estate tycoon Muheim miserable by presenting himself as the long-ago seducer of Frau Muheim, now dead. Schwitter's survival makes his doctor despair, causes the pastor a fatal "excitement," and provides Schwitter's mother-in-law an opportunity to lament that her daughter, now dead of love, had ruined her career as a whore by marrying Schwitter and thus admitting a ruinous "feeling" into life (what the old businesswoman wanted was to keep life mechanical, essentially a farce in which profitable scheming is not disrupted by disorderly feeling).* Finally Schwitter himself despairs of his continuing life, hoping for eternal death while the Salvation Army sings hymns about "eternal life."

In sum, one man's death—and that man not a "bad man" but an unusually successful artist—comforts virtually everybody else, and his "resurrection" is a disaster for all. To dramatize this reversal of conven-

* This is one of a number of reminiscences of Frisch's *Don Juan* (1962).

tion is to deal a needed blow to cliché ideas of tragedy; and to undermine a cliché is to help revive the more complex reality for which the cliché is a too accessible stand-in.

King John (1968) is a farce about political life. In rewriting Shakespeare, Duerrenmatt cuts out nationalistic and patriotic feeling, and ironically traces the "power-struggle within a system." [13] He calls *King John* both "a parable: a comedy of politics" and "an angry play." The former is the more applicable of the two terms. Duerrenmatt's manner is more detached than polemic; when there is intensity of feeling in the play, it wells up in a context of personality and of personalities rather than as a projection of authorial animus playing for indignation. Often there is an epigrammatic quality that makes us respond as in comedy of manners.* Sometimes the words approach bitterness; more often they note the ironic incongruity in political conduct. But the subtlest irony lies in the fact that love and murder and war and a world's destiny are dealt with in an idiom that is essentially farcical. Though the blows that many characters suffer are solider than those of the slapstick—King John is poisoned, for instance—their actions are the mechanical ones of farce. They are animate beings, but they live a quick-moving stimulus-and-response life, nonmorally and with minimum feeling and thought. Duerrenmatt treats political life as the creation, not of evil men, but of automatons. Rules of survival and self-interest, not ideal or sinister quests, govern their actions in a realm where all turns on power. They know instantly what is called for by any turn of the wheel; they respond as by computer, and alliances, wars, stances, and platforms shift like new totals coming off an electronic calculator, resembling the actions in a cinematic "chase" sequence. In a split second rulers adjust new events to the rules of the game, and one is not surprised to find in the dialogue a considerable scattering of play and game images. We see political croquet, in which some dash through the wickets of history by "sending" the balls of others—not always agreeable or healthful for those sent, but quite in accord with the rules.

* The Bastard says to his mother, alluding to his legal father Sir Robert and his actual father Richard the Lionhearted: "He was a feeble tomcat, but you climbed into bed with a lion, and conceived me in pleasure instead of honor" (I.i). Austria calls names in a fine climactic series: "You bitch, you slut, you . . . atheist!" (II.i), and protests thus against negotiations for peace: "This is war! My princes, why do you return to peace over and over again? Why do you vacillate back and forth? Why count the dead, whom no one can bring back to life? Why not use the living to wage war, and by means of war, bring about peace?" (II.ii).

Things are bad when a player gets into a temper and starts tearing up wickets or hitting other players with his mallet. This is King John's trouble—whims, unreasonable moods, and fits of revengefulness. Repeatedly he is saved by the Bastard, a hopeful humanist and voice of "reason," who proposes not ideal ultimates but more prudent and enlightened use of the system; John adopts the proposed tactics and thus survives longer than he otherwise would. (The Bastard symbolizes, ironically, the fact that a sound self-serving good sense is not "legitimate" in the system.) But what Essex says of hate—"hate never obeys reason" (IV.ii)—is true also of other emotions, and at the end the Bastard disgustedly flees the court to "sleep with every milkmaid" and "make bastards like myself and infuse the power of the lion into the people" (V.iii). (The play ends before it can test this romantic doctrine.) For the Bastard, the most painful emotion has been caused, not so much by the unresponsive automation of the system and the irrationalities of its managers, as by the deliberate malice of Blanche. She is bitter because the Bastard has preferred improving the world to sharing her bed: "Take him out. Tie him to a stake and whip him like a dog. Then let him go" (V.ii). This faint echo of Claire Zachanassian pushes the play momentarily from political farce toward revenge melodrama.

Early in the play the Bastard decides, "I . . . want to remain true to myself," but resolves, "I'll wade through the filth, and climb with daring hero's deeds to the top of the noble chicken roost" (I.i). The dual sensibility is Macbethian, and when the Bastard acknowledges, "I lost my way among the snares and dangers of this world" and declares that he too is "guilty" of Arthur's death (IV.ii), the farce flirts with tragedy. It does so, too, when Eleanor, about to die, sees imminent execution as the natural end of hating, of being faithless, and of loving power more than men; and when John says, "I overthrew myself" (V.iii). But both allude to the ways of *weltpolitik* rather than identify their own moral beings, and Duerrenmatt is didactic rather than tragic. The Bastard is only disappointed, Eleanor cries "nada," and John turns to blaming the Bastard.

V. DUERRENMATT'S RANGE

Nevertheless, Duerrenmatt's characters occasionally voice literally the sentiment that would be implicit in a fully developed tragedy. Several of them reveal their own modes of the hubris that belongs to the tragic hero, or, on the other hand, the hero's rejection of an antitragic despair. Several experience the moment of self-knowledge that is the final phase of the tragic rhythm. Others express in different forms, even in actions comic in tone, the continuity of values to which tragic actions characteristically give testimony. Duerrenmatt can reveal the tragic sensibility by parodying the operation of it in the willful Mr. Mississippi or in the more trivial people in *The Meteor*. He can convey the world's need of the tragic spirit by showing the moral insufficiency of characters whose being is essentially melodramatic—of such a ruler as Nebuchadnezzar, who out of sheer vanity would reform the world at a blow, and of revengeful millennialists like Mississippi and St. Claude. Or, in demonstrating the farcical in men's conduct, he can reveal their lack of the moral range that tragedy discovers in human life.

In one way or another, then, the tragic view keeps infiltrating into dramas whose main lineaments are satirical or farcical or melodramatic. To say this is to say also, in effect, that the satirical impulse and jests in different tones do not exhaust Duerrenmatt's talents. There is a sense in which the satirical mode is an easy one to practice; yet Duerrenmatt does not do things the easy way. To look at his works from the point of view of tragic form is to use a perspective that brings into relief his range and depth as a dramatist.

Afterword

RECHT, Frisch, and Duerrenmatt do not present themselves as writers of tragedy; hence it would hardly do to conclude by observing in what ways they do not achieve tragedy. Nor has a complete assessment of their work as dramatists been my object. But since, whatever their intentions, they do enter at times into the realm of tragedy, it is possible both to mention the relevance of their work to tragedy and, in noting their tendencies to diverge or converge, to attempt some partial generalizations about them.

Both Brecht and Duerrenmatt, for instance, have written plays about scientists—*Galileo* and *The Physicists*—and both plays tend to talk points rather than let full characters act freely. Yet the twenty-five years that separate the two plays symbolize a divergence of thought that has implications for drama. Brecht's critique of Galileo is that he fathered the move of science into an esoteric existence away from the domain of public awareness and hence social usefulness. Duerrenmatt's Möbius, on the other hand, argues that physicists best advance knowledge by working in a sanitarium, segregated from a public which cannot accommodate new discoveries except by using them for destruction. Now, even acknowledging that Möbius may not speak with authority and trying to allow for all the reversals possible in a play bathed in irony, it is still difficult not to read *The Physicists* as something of a reply to *Galileo*. I do not find in *The Physicists* dramatic evidence to contradict the view that society is incapable of making choices and is bound to use knowledge badly. For Brecht, on the other hand, the social guardianship of knowledge is the only guarantee of beneficent use. Brecht has faith in society; it will find the right answers. For Duerrenmatt, the scene of critical decisions is the individual consciousness; not that it may not err, but that it has a full awareness of options.

Brecht's faith in societal wisdom marks him as instinctively a melo-dramatist: the concern is with right in the world, whether one discovers the mechanisms to bring it about (*The Mother, Galileo, The Caucasian Chalk Circle, The Good Woman of Setzuan*) or displays the present wrongs that await the new broom (*Master Race, St. Joan of the Stock-yards*). Duerrenmatt, on the other hand, is drawn toward the tragic structure; that is, he usually attributes the public situation to the strong personality who attracts his primary attention—Romulus (who wants to destroy his decadent empire), Nebuchadnezzar and Akki (who respectively try to convert a country and resist conversion), Mississippi and St. Claude (converters in the name of rival but possibly interchangeable faiths), Claire Zachanassian (a vengeful scourge of society), Möbius (the reflective physicist trying to reconcile responsibility to the profession with responsibility to the civil community), Schwitter (whose "death"-given "insights" disturb the lives of all survivors), the Bastard (whose ambition leads him to try to introduce rationality into the political system).

But the basic orientation does not predetermine the fulfillment. For all of his sense of disorder in society and of the need for a social remedy of a given kind, Brecht more than once centers his drama in personal life. He began his theatrical career with dramas of private emotional experience (*Drums in the Night* and *Jungle of Cities*), and only at times did he succeed in subduing the human reality to the instructional end (he came close in *The Mother* and in *Roundheads and Peakheads*). However we interpret Galileo's recantation, Galileo says the reason for it was his fear of physical pain; if the anguish of crisis has less dramatic reality than that of John Proctor in *The Crucible*, still it is there. Mother Courage struggles between maternal devotion and the high price for her son's life. Shen Te's life is a conflict between imperative justice and impulsive generosity. Duerrenmatt starts with the disordered soul, a theater where tragedy is always hovering in the wings, but tends toward satirical melodrama or the Jacobean melodrama of obsessed, maniacal aggressor or sadist. *The Visit,* for instance, is a potential *Oedipus Rex:* Alfred Ill, at the apex of his career in his town, runs afoul of a local plague whose origins lie in a sexual misdeed committed by him long ago, and he accepts his guilt and punishment. But all the dramatic emphasis is upon the avenging fury—the Erinyes reduced to a single sophisticated woman of the world—who financially corrupts the town and thus makes it execute her malice (grossly against Ill, but subtly against itself).

Duerrenmatt manages his satire not by burdening his willful attackers of the world with heavy caricature, didactic assignments, and his own disgust, but by revealing in them, with an objectivity that is almost sympathetic, a kind of representative madness. In Claire Zachanassian the retaliatory passion is overt, in Mississippi and St. Claude it is a hidden motive behind Puritan and Communist utopianizing. They exhibit, as does Nebuchadnezzar, the hubris of a compulsory reordering of the world, of the imposed public reform rather than the private conversion. Schwitter, with the wisdom of the grave, strikes out carelessly or maliciously in many directions. On the other hand, there is a touch of the Brechtian debunking of the system in *The Physicists* and *King John:* in the former, the psychiatrist is an economic exploiter of a genius, and in the latter the machinations within the system reveal that power is the only end of leaders, and the Bastard's efforts to give reason a political role end in frustration. Yet Duerrenmatt's drama more characteristically centers in the individual, not as a concretion of a social entity, but as the embodiment of motives that echo through the social organism; when this individual becomes complex enough to experience conflict and self-knowledge, tragedy begins to take over from the satiric and melodramatic. *The Meteor,* of course, laughs at the pseudotragic.

In all three dramatists the genesis of drama may be topical, and the problem then is, as always, the extent to which the artist transcends the documentary and editorial writer. All three, of course, use a mechanical device of generalization: placing the action in a kind of placeless "everywhere," as in *The Marriage of Mr. Mississippi,* or in a vaguely southern "Andorra" (a "model," as Frisch calls it), or in distant places and times —China, ancient Rome, Babylon. Since generalization means indirection, and indirection requires interpretation, there is always the danger of too particularized interpretation. It is possible to reduce Mr. Mississippi, the furious Puritan prosecutor-zealot, to America, and St. Claude, the vengeful Communist, to Russia, despite Duerrenmatt's effort to make them not simply contemporary forces, but demonically possessed pressure-men who recur in human history.

The more effective escape from the purely contemporary is depth in characterization. In Brecht the best moments are those in which, instead of saying simply, such-and-such a current state of affairs is evil and remedies should be sought, the drama reveals the human dilemmas that characteristically arise under the pressure of evil and hence grasps a human reality that we continue to find meaningful even when we must turn to footnotes to identify the original external evil. In *The Private Life of the Master Race* the conflicts in loyalties, in which the topical becomes the human, may not be amply enough worked out to realize the tragic potential, but through these conflicts the play goes beyond German political history. In *St. Joan of the Stockyards* the satirical insight into the devices of institutional self-serving may go deep enough to survive a phase of economic history; but what is eminently nontopical is the key experience of Joan Dark, whose "tragedy of good intentions" is timeless and placeless. Frisch has one recurrent topic, the Nazis, or, more specifically, the kinds of human responsiveness to the political and moral pressures created by an upsurge of barbarism. He does in full what Brecht only sketches. Frisch is less writing political history than exploring conduct, and his characters develop from rather allegorical conceptions toward fully realized individuals who have choices to make. He presents the human division between the perceptive and the self-congratulatory, between the recognitive and the placative, between the sense of evil and the desire to play it safe, appease, pay blackmail, and thus avoid disagreeable confrontations. This experience does not date; it is the material of tragedy.

In some ways Frisch is most consistently on the edge of the tragic realm. In *Andorra*, true, the dominant mood is satirical: most of the community appease the evil invader without turmoil, and only an isolated soul or two do not share in the general depravity; but one man does have the tragic sense of having acted wrongly. The types of citizenry in *Andorra* are compacted, in *The Firebugs*, into Biedermann, a representative individual: he is the tragic figure who falls short of tragic stature by never seeing himself plain. Frisch's characters are often lesser Gloucesters in that they err not by endeavoring to subdue the world in their terms but by accepting it wholly in its terms; only, unlike Gloucester, they are not literally blinded and hence rarely come into a better sight. The disaster of the world is their failure to complete the tragic rhythm. Yet what is distinctive in Frisch is an impulse to the tragic that expresses itself more than once in derogatory portrayal of melodramatic attitudes in the world, particularly the sense of vice in other classes and in other souls (in *The Chinese Wall, When the War Was Over,* and *Andorra*); and in his sense of characters who approach or at times show self-knowledge and self-criticism—Agnes, the Teacher, Don Juan, Kürmann.

Though the intellectual component of tragedy is implicit rather than formal, the kind of thought that goes on in a play tells us something of its artistic stance. When Brecht can say, after portraying a comic-romantic "Golden Age," that it was "brief" and "almost just," he reveals a detachment that protects him against doctrinaire political melodrama. When Frisch more than once, and Duerrenmatt at least once, reveal a sense of the recurrent in human affairs, they go beyond topical urgency. When Frisch alters anti-Semitism to what we might call "Semitism," that is, thinking of men as generic representatives rather than as individuals (making a "graven image," as it is called by the Priest in *Andorra*), he enlarges a specific vice into a general human flaw that prevents the easy indignation of right-minded melodrama (just as Miller does in *Incident at Vichy*). When Frisch reflects a man's inability to face truth, and Duerrenmatt specifically proscribes despair, they are commenting on obstacles to tragic experience. And finally when Duerrenmatt's physicist, speaking as "Solomon," says, "But my wisdom destroyed the fear of God, and when I no longer feared God my wisdom destroyed my wealth," he voices the kind of ultimate recognition possible to the tragic hero.

He says this; it is not realized in the plot. But what these characters say does often come out of character and not merely out of a philosophic or doctrinal intention. That is, there is a strong tendency to anthropomorphism in characters conceived ideomorphically or semamorphically. At least a few of these develop a full human range, even in contexts where a dominant satirical intention inhibits maturation of personality. Brecht's Joan Dark fails in an obligation to others and knows it. Frisch's Biedermann fails in an obligation to protect himself against evil. Duerrenmatt's Alfred Ill has done evil and knows it. In the end, there is really only one point to be made: the presence of an impulse toward tragedy in the works of the three Europeans who, unlike the three Americans we have examined, hardly talk about tragedy at all, and formally practice other modes.

PART IV

Time and Theme

CHAPTER TEN

Decades and Dramatic Modes

HE SHIFT from an approach through authorship to an approach through chronology—the next step in trying out the concepts of tragedy and melodrama—does not mean an absence of continuity. There are, in fact, several lines of continuity between the preceding chapters and this one. The progress through the works of individual dramatists has been mainly chronological; chronology, once subordinate, now becomes central. Sampling is still the basic procedure. The six dramatists already looked at, however eminent and productive, are only a few of those who have claims to full attention; likewise the score or so of plays that now engage us are only a fraction of those that would be relevant in this context. The complications already unearthed seem likely to continue: though there are relatively straightforward types of the tragic and the melodramatic, there is vast evidence of the crossing, mingling, and modifying of forms. The subject is not often illuminated by the comfortable reading light of simple categories.

But whatever continuities accompany the change to the chronological perspective, the problem now is different: not what a dramatist's body of work looks like, but what a sequence of works, regardless of authorship, looks like. Are there visible trends, fashions, peaks? First of all, "chronol-

ogy" and "sequence" need temporal bounds. As a hedge against shape-
lessness, I have chosen to deal with plays by decades. Though decades
are obviously a convenience, still it is possible to make a few tentative
statements about them. These statements, it need hardly be said, do
not constitute a history of forms. It is a little tempting to try for a history, to go on and make observations about other plays by the dramatists
glanced at here, and about plays by other writers such as W. H. Auden,
Samuel Beckett, James Joyce, and Harold Pinter, W. C. Williams and
E. E. Cummings, Jean Anouilh and Eugène Ionesco, Günter Grass and
Fernando Arrabal, the developing Black dramatists, the versions of the
Cenci theme by P. B. Shelley, Antonin Artaud, and Alberto Moravia.
But the magnitude needed for even a short history would be excessive in
what is striving to be a critical essay. History needs many summary judgments, but the latter are possible only when the business is general
description rather than formal analyses; the latter are not easily compressed into assertions, but rely on some demonstration of organic relationships. Literary talk habitually uses modal terms too easily; if these
are to have some utility, we need to inspect with care the evidence for
those which we use. Obviously the number of inspections that can be
accommodated in one book is limited.

Hence sampling is inevitable. The plays chosen are earlier ones that
have some claim upon our memory and later ones that have an air,
perhaps deceptive, of being memorable. Admittedly the selective process
cannot be wholly free of chance and of undefined interest or preference,
but several facts, I hope, preserve it against both whimsy and tendentiousness. The plays are ones to which all sorts of labels, including
comedy, are conventionally affixed; so my own views of genre should
receive an adequately varied testing. Most of the dramatists and plays
have become habitués of the anthology circuit; to that extent they
should be representative. To use one play, or at most two, by each
dramatist means that more dramatists can be included: an additional
reaching for representativeness. If to the implications of plays noted in
the present chapter we add the implications of those noted in the preceding chapters, we should have at least a few clues to general historical
patterns. If we do, that is all to the good. But history is still a by-product:
the main business continues to be the application of the modal perspective to individual plays. The end in view is a sense of what each play is.

I. Before World War I

Two plays by Georg Büchner (1813–37) and one by Hugo von Hofmannsthal (1874–1929) that were produced in the decade before 1914 reveal again that modernity is not always modern. Each of the three plays does a kind of thing that would be much done after World War II: one reinterprets a historical subject, one speaks through fantasy, and one reinterprets a Greek myth. All use an exceptionally strong and free language. In their different ways, all exhibit a sense of reality which we are prone to think belongs to our day rather than theirs. Still, they have formal qualities that connect them with traditional modes.

Büchner came to theatrical life and critical esteem only after 1900. His first play, *Danton's Death* (1835; produced 1902), is remarkable as first work and as the product of a twenty-two-year-old. It springs from a varied, urgent, and strangely mature imagination. It does more than it apparently sets out to do. Presumably Danton speaks for the author when he asks, "What is it in us that whores, lies, steals, and murders?" and answers, "We're puppets drawn by unknown powers on wire; nothing, nothing in ourselves—the swords with which spirits fight—only one doesn't see the hands, as in fairy tales" (II.v).[1] In Büchner, we are told, "free will . . . is denied," and "plays are peopled with victims"; the dramatist "creates *passive* heroes, who are not authors of their own fates."[2] Since Danton at various times talks fatalistically, it may be possible to argue from the text that *Danton's Death* is a history of passive victims; still, the drama hardly comes across as a lesson in determinism— a composition of mechanical ironies, saturating pathos, and tedious impotence. The ironies are subtle, the characters have a remarkable vitality which all but excludes pathos, and in their maneuverings, choices, and pungent assessments of things and men they are anything but a monotonous register of implacable outer forces. In other words, a melodrama of history that might have only a humdrum predictability has a diversity of texture and impact that makes for distinction in melodrama and contains, besides, a latent thrust toward tragedy.

The action covers a short period in the spring of 1794 in which Danton and moderates who wish to humanize the revolution are denounced by Robespierre and the Terror faction, jailed, condemned in a managed trial, and executed. Nevertheless there is not a simple pattern of monsters and victims. The moderates are not weak or inactive: they are incredulous (Robespierre "won't dare"—I.v; II.i,iv), they debate with spirit at the Jacobin Club (I.iii) and in the convention (II.vii), they plan action (I.v). Danton confronts Robespierre and plans to go to the people (I.vi), Desmoulins plans to approach Robespierre (II.iii). They understand the tactics of the Committee on Public Safety and its position vis-à-vis the public: "The people is a Minotaur that must be fed with corpses every week if it is not to eat the Committee alive" (I.iv). That is, the moderates have an intellectual grasp of the situation which implies power rather than impotence. The public, though governed by credulity and habit, is shown as having something like a choice.* The Terror people do not take the outcome for granted but engage in the plotting and manipulation characteristic of all melodrama in which the outcome is in doubt: they discuss workable strategy (I.vi), pack the jury (III.ii), utilize a betrayer (III.v,vi,vii). In club and convention the attacks on Danton and his associates are not formalistic disposals of someone already considered finished, but ingenious and calculated diatribes, vigorous polemics that imply the strength of those whom the Terrorists seek to destroy (I.iii; II.vii). Above all, Robespierre is inwardly troubled, aware that his public stance may conceal private motives; he almost draws back from turning the Terror on Danton. In effect, he makes a decision (I.vi).

In other words, we sense an open world in which all is in doubt. Whatever Büchner believed, he so wrote as to get out from under the burden of an ideational system in which participants can only act out the predetermined courses of victor and victim. Instead he creates a genuine melodrama of forces competing for power in the world, and he does it with much originality. He lets Robespierre claim the role of Virtue and impute Vice to the moderate opposition—in part a jest at the view of life in popular melodrama. But Robespierre is rigid and self-righteous rather than hypocritical, and he is permitted to make at least a possible case against the moderates: they want to undermine the Terror because in their own vice they feel vulnerable to it (I.iii). Against

---

* Danton defends himself vigorously before the Revolutionary Tribunal, wins "applause" (III.iv), and arouses the public (III.vi); a crowd even cries, "Down with the Committee" (III.ix). Then charges of profiteering, luxury, and adultery against Danton bring them around to "Down with Danton" (III.x), though one citizen condemns the trial (IV.ii). The vacillation of the public is antideterministic in effect.

the severe revolutionary morality of Robespierre (Terror as Virtue) we have the humanistic code of the moderates—rights, happiness, protection (I.i). But closely interwoven with this is Desmoulins' demand for a "constitution" which reflects the world of physical delight, of "wicked, limb-loosening Love," and for "Epicurus and Venus with the lovely buttocks" as "doorkeepers of the Republic" (I.i). Lacroix says that Danton is "trying to discover the Venus de Medici piecemeal in all the tarts in the Palais Royal" (I.iv); in one scene Danton makes at least verbal love to several whores, and Lacroix says, "A girl's legs will be your guillotine" (I.v). Danton denies both Virtue and Vice and insists, "All men are hedonists" (I.vi). Büchner has yoked together traditional virtues and traditional vices and, by this ambiguity as well as that in Robespierre, has demanded a very complex response, just as he does by having each side rely on part-truths—Robespierre in his claim to Virtue, Lacroix in his analysis, "we are vicious; that is, we enjoy ourselves. The People are virtuous, that is, they do not enjoy themselves. . ." (I.v).

The characters simply do not have the simplicity that elicits mono-pathic responses. Robespierre does not have the total singleness that would free him from anguish. Danton is very complex. He is the aggressive defender who can sway the crowd, the ironic analyst (of the role of honest men [I.i]; of the people, "a child who smashes everything to see what's inside" [I.v]; of himself, "I am a relic" [II.i]), the bored and tired man who seems to Lacroix to be lazy (II.i), "sick of these vexations," and able to say that "to die with courage" is "easier than living" (II.iii); seeking "rest . . . in nothingness," wishing for "annihilation," since death "is only a simpler form of laziness" (III.vii); ready to "steal away from life," which "is a whore" (IV.iii). Danton is less the victim of fate than the lover of death; he seems rather to choose it than to be chosen by it.

Besides, he seems to triumph over death by stylistic mastery. Büchner controls a stylistic cornucopia that rarely gives way to ordinary prose; the pages flow with epigrams, images, paradoxes, neoclassical antitheses, and metaphysical conceits. All characters share in this, but it is especially the moderates who have stylistic virtuosity. Danton, who plays many verbal games with death, on one occasion presents being guillotined as a theatrical success, preferable to death "from fever or from old age" (II.i). Often he jests in sexual metaphor, "It's better to lie down in the earth than to walk on it with corns. I'd rather have her as a cushion

than as a footstool," and Hérault picks it up, "At least we won't have
warts on our fingers when we stroke the cheeks of the pretty lady putre-
faction." Philippeau shifts to an ecclesiastical figure, "We are priests
who have prayed with the dying. We have been infected and die of the
same epidemic" (III.i). Danton can use ecclesiastical figures, images
from social life, cosmic and archaeological images; he can use the rhetoric of public address and that of the special observer of actuality.*

The life of words gives a paradoxical sense of mastery in men about to
die; the stylistic vitality transcends the doom.† Men who speak thus
are not sociological pushovers, but special beings who are imaginatively
giving form to history. Their form of life in death creates mature melodrama. Besides, the triumph over death by unflagging poetic energy is
analogous to the transcendence of death in tragedy. Büchner not only
parallels tragedy[3] in this way; he constantly verges on a tragic concept
of character—of the dividedness in which man may sickly destroy himself or find a recovery in self-understanding. Danton takes a step toward
tragedy when he says, "I'd rather be guillotined than guillotine" (II.i).
He takes another step when he quotes, "It must needs be that offences

* Danton uses a church image for death: ". . . the void will soon be my sanctuary" (II.iv). He can rouse the public with a less esoteric irony: "How long
will the footprints of liberty be graves? You need bread, and you are thrown heads"
(III.ix). In one speech he can see death in two perspectives. One is that of the
physical actuality, with an overt sexual comparison: "Only work for the grave-
diggers! I feel as if I stank already. My dear body, I will hold my nose and pretend you're a woman sweating and stinking after a dance and pay you compliments." Büchner does not want to keep Danton in too narrow a range, however
brilliant; a few lines later Danton shifts to a stellar perspective that implies a cosmic order of saving percipience: "Like glimmering tears the stars are sprinkled
through the night; there must be some great sorrow in the eyes from which they
fall" (IV.iii). If this be pathetic fallacy, it is not sentimental; it is an effective
variation in a tough-fibered texture of irony. The texture can contain simultaneously
a cynical glance at actual disorder and a glimpse of ultimate order: "Liberty and
whores are the most cosmopolitan things under the sun. Liberty will now prostitute herself decently in the marriage bed of the lawyer from Arras [Robespierre].
But I think she will be a Clytemnestra to him; I don't give him more than six
months' respite. I drag him with me." He enlarges the point in an archaeological
figure: after the "deluge of the Revolution . . . with our fossilized bones men
can always break the heads of all kings" (IV.v).
Despite its virtues as a literary text, the drama may not be stageworthy. At
least the National Theatre production in London in 1971 was static and tedious.
† It is not only that they grasp the larger meaning of their death or can predict
its emotional consequences. Hérault can even jeer at their "phrases for posterity"
(IV.v)—an astringent critique of the martyr's posture that always threatens. It is
rather that they grasp life through words. In several scenes they engage in a sort
of poetry contest on the world about them and especially on death (III.vii; IV.v
—"making verses," as Danton says).

come; but woe to that man by whom the offence cometh" (II.v), which is a good definition of the tragic hero who in heeding one imperative violates another. But Danton wants to challenge this: "Who will curse the hand on which the curse of 'must' has fallen?" and he then enunciates his puppet theory of conduct. The theory is almost an escape from a sense of guilt. Then Danton, acknowledging a specific error, speaks most like a tragic hero, "It's exactly a year since I established the Revolutionary Tribunal. I pray forgiveness of God and humanity for it . . ." (III.iii). Hérault generalizes, "We stank quite sufficiently in our lifetime." Desmoulins picks it up in what is virtually a theory of tragic character: ". . . we are all villains and angels, fools and geniuses, and indeed all of them in one; the four find plenty of room in one body, they are not so large as people pretend. . . . We have all eaten ourselves sick at the same table and have now got the gripes; why do you hold your napkins before your faces?" (IV.v).

The impulse toward the tragic [4] is also present, though to a smaller degree, in Büchner's *Woyzeck* (written 1836-37, produced 1913). As with *Danton's Death* we hardly take the play to be a demonstration of the "fatalism of History." [5] We are more likely to see the Woyzeck of the first half of the play as a partly Chaplinesque figure, corrected, censured, and pushed around by the men for whom he works (the Captain and the Doctor) and even beaten by a rival lover (a Drum Major in the *miles gloriosus* tradition), and yet as a simple outsider providing a satirical contrast to the assured, moralizing, rule-bound possessors of status (i, vii, ix, xv, xvi, xviii).[6] We see him shakily occupying the slender strip between a special sensitivity to mysterious realities that ordinary people do not perceive, and nervous disorder. He hears sounds and movements in the earth, and detects ominous sights and sounds in the sky (ii, xiv, xxvi), and so on.* Such episodes prepare for the scene in an open field when Woyzeck, now made jealous by his girl, hears "someone talking down there" and is told to "stab the goat-wolf dead! . . . Stab her! Dead! Dead!" (xiii). The Chaplinesque special individual

---

* He feels "something that drives us mad" and thus makes his girl think "He'll go crazy" (iii). He proclaims, "Every man's a chasm. It makes you dizzy when you look down in" (x). Here, as in other details, we recognize the man of special gifts, the wise fool. Yet in the mysterious sounds and movements that he is aware of, he suspects the activities of toadstools and Freemasons (ii, vii), reports, "It followed me" (iii), tells the Doctor of a "terrible voice saying things to me," is diagnosed by the Doctor as having an *"aberratio,"* and replies, "It's in the toadstools" (vii).

shrinks into the lover who, undergoing a familiar psychic disturbance, becomes the murderer.

We have a sense of contraction as Büchner moves into the final steps of his intention to "discover and depict the determinism behind Woyzeck's actions," [7] in his use, that is, of characters to prove the non-existence of character. Though Büchner may question Woyzeck's freedom, he seems not to question his own, which is very great: in structure, technique, and style he innovates so strikingly that he seems a hundred years ahead of his times. The paradox is that something of the creator's freedom escapes into his creature, who seems to struggle against his imposed role as demonstrator of historical compulsion, as automatic victim and then revenger. As with Brecht, whom Büchner is supposed to prefigure, the characters may heed the imagination as well as the didactic intention of the artist; thus the contraction that we feel is accompanied also by a sense of continuing if unwilled openness. Woyzeck gains our interest not as an embodiment of dogma but as a sentient, fanciful, and quirky man who, reflective and aware of conflicting impulses, moves at least faintly toward a tragic role. On the one hand he is the faithful lover of Marie, on the other hand the man of strange visions; the family man at the fair, and the suspicious challenger of his woman; the hard-working youth, and the man of an *idée fixe*, as the Doctor puts it; the cryptic philosopher, and the passionate sufferer who has "got to see" the lovers; the man of ordinary speech, and the symbolic poet in whom such an intensely imagined line as "All I hear is: Stab! Stab! And it cuts at my eyes like a knife" (xiv) declares a free imagination and strong will rather than a passive register of outer forces. And this diversity of being, an implicit denial of determining circumstances, is formed into tragic division in two scenes. In one, foreseeing his own action, Woyzeck defines himself in the form of an attack on Man: ". . . he beats, shoots, stabs his own kind" (xvi). In the second, Woyzeck, having bought a knife, can bury it and urge himself, "Thou shalt not kill" (xxi).[8] But the potential dies there, and Woyzeck falls back into the obsessive punisher of infidelity, regaining some spontaneous life in the hysteria after the murder (xxvi), but then again, either as drowned man or as prisoner (the versions differ), contracting into the victim.

Marie too is accorded a kind of moral sentience that, if allowed to develop, could bring her toward tragic stature. "Why am I so bad! I

could run myself through with a knife!" (vi). She is fascinated by the
Drum Major, but on one occasion fiercely holds him off (viii); she can
be fiery with Woyzeck (x). She can read the Bible, hope for salvation
like the woman taken in adultery, can beg, "Lord God, give me only so
much strength that I can pray. . . . Savior! If only I could anoint your
feet!" (xx). Thence on, however, she is only the doomed woman.

Even as an ideologue Büchner lets fly with a free-swinging imagination that preserves him from the drabness of naturalists who come later
but seem to belong to an earlier generation. In verbal and actional imagery he is regularly vivid and fresh, often farcical and grotesque. "Nature"
is another name for the forces that determine us. At the fair the trained
horse, "still in a state of nature," "conducts itself indecently" (v). Woyzeck, constrained by "Nature," "pissed on the street" instead of using
his "will" and saving his urine for the Doctor's experiments (vii). If
Büchner finds the world oppressive, he still manages to express anguish
and disillusionment with an almost conquering vigor.* It is the language of superior melodrama, and at times it is that of Shakespearean
tragedy. Oddly enough, Woyzeck manages to sound at different times
like Othello (Marie "looks like innocence itself"—scene x), like Lear
("Man and woman and man and beast! They'll do it in the light of the
sun! They'll do it in the palm of your hand like flies!"—scene xii), and
like Macbeth ("Why can't you die?"—scene xxiv; "Am I still bloody?
I've got to wash myself. There, there's a spot, and there's another . . ."
—scene xxvi). Such reminiscences [9] suggest the attractions of another
world than that in which man is puppet only.

In both plays Büchner reveals not only a grasp of the complications of
melodrama but, on occasion, the tragic sensibility. The verbal and actional outpourings from his imagination imply the freedom of the
doomed (and dooming) as much as they present the inevitability of

---

* A tearfully drunken apprentice preaches a mock sermon on the theme that
"the world . . . is an evil place." How would the soldier live, he asks, "had not
God endowed Man with the need to slaughter himself?" (xii). A grandmother
tells "little crabapples" (children coaxing for a story) a parable of forlornness:
when everyone is dead, a "poor little girl" tries all the planets for companionship
but finds them only dull earthly objects. And when she gets back to earth, the
earth is "an upside down pot," and so she sits there crying, "all alone" (xxiii).
Woyzeck, in a paradoxical outburst against the way of things, exclaims, "What a
beautiful place the world is! Friend! My friend! The world! . . . Look! The sun
coming through the clouds—like God emptying His bedpan on the world" (xvi).
One understands the interest in Büchner that is attributed to Beckett.

doom. One wonders how fully his doctrine possessed his imagination.* To dramatize his theory, it is worth noting, he did not pick situations in which he could declare an accepted freedom illusory, but chose rather a private story and a public story in which the case for determinism seems tightest. Each situation is psychotic: that of an individual who hears voices, and that of a transitional society in which what is finally released is a pathological destructiveness. But even in tracing illnesses that must, so to speak, run their course, Büchner in various subtle ways slides out from under the constraining doctrine and into a world of ambiguity and even choice.

In *Electra* (1904) Hugo von Hofmannsthal foreshadows the "modern" in a quite different way. To reconstructing imaginations Electra is a figure of quite different potentialities: she can seek retaliation for the murdered Agamemnon and yet be aware of conflicting imperatives, as in Aeschylus and even in Euripides, or she can be a monomaniac revenger, as in Sophocles. Sophocles provides the model for Hofmannsthal, whose Electra, on stage from beginning to end, is tense, strident, bitter, hysterical, and even frenzied or possessed. She has the pressing egotism of one in whom all life has yielded to the suffering caused by others' viciousness. In the wild general outburst after Orestes' double murder, she is sure that "they all, / all, wait upon me to lead the dance"; she orders all who are "happy: / to be silent and dance"; as the stage direction tells us, she is "like a Maenad" as she does "an indescribable dance." [10] The "most tense dance of triumph" completes her emotional exhaustion, and she "collapses."

This victory celebration is possible because no interfering motive enters consciousness. After going offstage for the murders (seventy-five lines from the end), Orestes does not reappear; hence in this play the Erinyes do not exist. The end, then, simply completes the portrait of an undivided revengeful woman living wholly in her passion and incarnating the view that "the inner core of man is a fire consuming itself, a fire of agony, a glass furnace in which the viscous liquid matter of life re-

---

* It is tempting to theorize that because of his very luxuriant and kaleidoscopic imagination Büchner had a psychological need for a doctrine of fatalism or necessity as a security belt, a sort of imaginary controlling center of so many episodes, characters, ideas, and images which might otherwise seem to him to be running away centrifugally. This implies that he leaned on his theory more than he was possessed by it. In practice he finds unity in literary rather than doctrinal ways, aided perhaps by the sense of having a principle of order.

ceives its forms. . . ." * This is the stuff of the pure melodramatic personality, which Hofmannsthal, using an imagistic language of great original force, exploits wholly, uncapping all the wild pressure that can burst forth from a center of total obsession. His business here is the ultimate single human drive, not the pressure of alternatives that always tends to disturb Büchner's characters.

This monopathic appeal, for all its intensity, could be monotonous. But Hofmannsthal guards against this by adjusting Electra's style to different occasions and by contrasting her with other personalities. He verges on the tragic in his effective portrayal of the misery of Clytemnestra, who has terrible dreams and is scorned by Aegisthus. She says, "It's a terrible thing / to sink, alive and breathing, into chaos!"

> a something creeps
> across my body . . .
> and it is nothing, no, not even a nightmare,
> and yet it is so dreadful that my soul
> longs to be hanged.
>
> [pp. 174–75]

Elecrta is at different times scornful, cryptic, savage, sullen, maniacal; †
she is brutally rude to the Messenger (actually Orestes), and then, when
she knows Orestes, she bursts into a tirade of self-pity, self-justification,
and bitter psychic history, often in brilliant images:

---

* Hofmannsthal attributes this picture of man, presumably with approval, to Balzac in "On Characters in Novels and Plays," an "imaginary conversation." Balzac is also made to say that "any man, . . . in the true moments of his life," is "just as mad as Lear" and to accept the idea that his own concern is "The atmosphere of existences consuming themselves pathologically," "obsessed by their fixed ideas," "incapable of seeing anything in the world which they themselves do not project into it with their feverish eyes." This passage, which appears in Corrigan, *The Modern Theatre*, p. 163, might apply to Electra.

† In soliloquy she foretells a bloody nemesis for Agamemnon's death (pp. 167–68). She has scornful reproof for her sister Chrysothemis, who wants to "forget" and to have a woman's life of bearing children (pp. 168–171). To Clytemnestra she at first speaks cryptically of rites to be performed, relishing what is really a prediction of the murder of Clytemnestra, and then bursts out into a savage, sadistic picturing of her being killed by an ax (pp. 173–79). After this "wildest intoxication" Electra is reduced to sullen denial by the report that Orestes is dead, but then senses a new opportunity: she and Chrysothemis will "do it" in place of Orestes. Then, with urgings, threats, wooings, beseechings she subjects Chrysothemis to a mad pressure that terrifies her and makes her scream repeatedly, "Let me go" (pp. 181–84). To Orestes disguised as the Messenger she says, "O could I stop your mouth with curses! Get out of my sight" (p. 185), and he replies, "Where have they made you sleep your terrible nights! / Your eyes are dreadful" (p. 186).

For the dead are jealous:
and he has sent me hatred, hollow-eyed hatred,
as a bridegroom. And so to my sleepless bed
I took this horror that breathed like a viper,
and let him crawl on top of me and force me
to know all that happens between man and woman.

[p. 187]

What Hofmannsthal has perceived in the murdered man's daughter, dutiful in revenge, is less the sexual passion that would become central for O'Neill than her falling in love with hate and cherishing the illness of soul that can make extraordinary melodrama of undividedness. Here, as elsewhere, the modern imaging of a sick integrity reminds us of the Jacobean.

II. The Twenties and Thirties

Between the wars the one dramatist who resembles Büchner in having an ideological position to which his imagination is not altogether obedient is Brecht, whom we looked at earlier. Pirandello, true, has a theory, but his ingenuity in riddles and his artistic inventiveness go hand in hand. In totally different ways he and Sean O'Casey and Michel de Ghelderode have a sense of ironies and contradictions that permits us to think of their plays as complex in the way that *Danton's Death* is complex. Federico García Lorca, however, is on the Hofmannsthal side of the fence: he traces the passions that drive relatively simple men and women. But Giraudoux, though he reinterprets Electra, just as Hofmannsthal did, is a theatrical voluptuary: he puts almost every kind of theatrical dish upon the groaning boards simultaneously.

What is striking about these dramatists of the 1920s and 1930s is their use of the word "tragedy," which is also used by Camus early in the 1940s and then seems almost to disappear from the vocabulary of dramatists.[11] Beckett and Duerrenmatt both do use "tragicomedy" on one occasion, and Grass "A German Tragedy" ironically, but later dramatists are likely to insist on "comedy" and "farce" if they use generic terms at all (and there is, of course, Brecht's *Lehrstück*). The recurrence of the term may be a coincidence, but perhaps in these decades there was less of self-consciousness and of the fear of being portentous. At any rate, the occurrence of tragedy as generic fact is not much different from that of other decades.

Ghelderode calls *The Death of Doctor Faust* (1925) "A Tragedy for the Music Hall"—an ironic collocation of terms. But the play is, for all its jests and fantasy and mixture of tones, a serious one, and since it works with a traditional tragic subject, it is a good introduction to the subject of genre in the 1920s. In a prologue reminiscent of both Marlowe and Goethe, Faust has elements of a tragic style: "You end up by coming across yourself! And it is frightening! . . . Dying is not a solution. And living is going on betraying myself, . . . I am immeasurably ridiculous, petty, mean. And, fundamentally, I do not suffer in a proper manner! . . . I have counted the visible stars. They have wonderful names; but it is incorrect that our fate is written in them. . . . I am neither a poet nor a lover nor the distinguished doctor that everybody sees in me! I am nothing, and I am not able to become anything else! . . . Learned man! I am not a learned man. Science! I have remembered everything and I have a thorough knowledge of nothing." [12] But the self-recognition, with its strong note of ennui and *nausée*, dissolves into technical questions of identity: "Do I, after all, exist? . . . Me, a senile phantom! Who invented me? I am incomplete, unfinished!" Then, taking off into Carnival in Flanders, 1925, Faust initiates an epistemological fantasy that develops through highly ingenious detail and continues to his eventual death. His affair with Marguerite is carried on as a shabby intrigue, with occasional advice from the devil-figure, Diamotoruscant. At the same time an Actor Faust, an Actress Marguerite, and an Actor Devil play "The Tragedy of Faust" on the stage at the Tavern of the Four Seasons (with its obvious suggestion of the old mythical merry-go-round). The life-art counterpoint, with confusion of identity, is skillfully developed; the closing action is inaugurated when the "real" Marguerite screams "violation," a righteously enraged public vengefully pursue the actors, and these take refuge in the "real" Faust's house. The two Fausts confront each other, and the problem of reality is pursued further in a rather Pirandellian way (*Six Characters* appeared in 1921).

Meanwhile we see public, newspapers, and courts developing the story independently as if it were some contemporary scandal evoking stereotyped attitudes. The Actor Faust, maddened by the confusion, leaps into the crowd claiming that he killed Marguerite, and is killed by them; the "real" Faust, who is "real and false at the same time" (III), shoots himself. The Faust of myth has sunk into a petty figure of mass media and the hackneyed imagination of what Diamotoruscant calls "the century of democracy" (I); that is the sense in which he is destroyed. The play, in other words, records a particular kind of disaster: the loss of tragic stature in a major mythic character. The Wagner-figure, significantly named Cretinus, gleefully prepares to take over as successor to Faust. As it notes the truth of imagination surrendering to cinematic clichés, the drama of disaster becomes satirical.

Ghelderode manages another sharp twist by having the Mephistopheles character not triumphant at the end, but ironic and bitter about the turn things have taken. Diamotoruscant is given not only a critical mind but a highly interesting personality. He implicitly laments the passing of a more heroic day. When a movie barker tells him, "there's nothing infernal about you," he replies, "It's a manner one mustn't have any more" (II). He describes himself as alienated, hopeless, "misunderstood" (II). As if developing a brief hint of Marlowe's, Ghelderode makes Diamotoruscant grieve, at first in a self-consciously theatrical way, for his past: ". . . I have too many memories, such ancient memories! If you knew what I remember! I was a creature of love!" (II). And then for a moment he is "furious": "I too have an eternal soul that I would willingly swap, and for less . . ." (II). The devil actually takes on some of the marks of the tragic hero. This is an original tragic accent in a drama of disaster that is essentially satirical.

Pirandello, O'Casey, Lorca

Though Ghelderode's drama may anticipate Duerrenmatt's argument that the tragic, at least of traditional theme and form, is dead, other European dramatists of his day use the term and at times approach the tragic spirit. Likewise they show skill in the development of melodramatic forms. With one exception, the other dramatists of the 1920s and 1930s who enter this discussion have also the complication of plot and tone that appears in Ghelderode. In these respects they are reminiscent of Renaissance drama.

To *Henry IV* (1922) Luigi Pirandello gives a subtitle, "A Tragedy in Three Acts." Henry IV of Germany, whose identity is taken over for many years by a disturbed twentieth-century Italian gentleman, is called, in the text of the play, "the great and tragic Emperor" (I).[13] When it is announced that a group of relatives and erstwhile intimates are to visit "Henry IV" in the villa, in effect a sanitarium, in which he enacts his role, one of the attendants prophesies, "We'll have a real tragedy . . ." (I). After the visit, a psychiatrist who was among the visitors says of "Henry IV's" make-believe that it "seemed all the more tragic to us" because of the degree of perceptiveness shown by the sick man (II). At an allusion to the passage of twenty years since the originating accident (a blow on the head made an apparently permanent case of the gentleman who was masquerading as Henry IV), Donna Matilda, the object of his affections at the time, exclaims, "A disaster! A tragedy!" (II).* And near the end "Henry IV," now well and commenting on his role, says, "One walks about as a tragic character, just as if it were nothing" (III).

The language of the play suggests, then, that the action occurs within the realm of tragedy.[14] With Pirandello, of course, one had better play it safe and keep in mind that he may be using "tragic" and "tragedy" in a riddling way, for the play as a whole is a skillful exploitation of enigmas—the ambiguity of madness and sanity, of being and role, of identity, of time and history (who's mad? who's who? what's when?). When the social group depicted in the play decided on a masquerade (twenty years before the present visit to "Henry IV"), people hit upon roles in some way significant: Donna Matilda Spina that of Marchioness Matilda of Tuscany, and hence her coolly received wooer that of Henry IV (eleventh century). Between the historical characters there had been political enmity plus overtones of personal intimacy. During the masquerade the man fell off his horse, was deranged by a head injury, and was psychologically locked into his role as king. But we also learn that he was high-strung, easily acted roles, and experienced a sense of dislocation because of the discrepancy between acted and real feelings. When we see him as "Henry IV"—coherent, imperious, ironic, and apparently given to double meanings—we are not sure whether we have occasional partial lucidity cohabiting with madness, a kind of reason in madness, or a sound but flamboyant mind masked in madness. Matilda and her present lover Baron Belcredi (both of whom had been in the masquerade long ago), the psychiatrist, and two younger visitors interpret Henry differently, and their disagreements are a source of tension. But their own motives are not without ambiguity. Nominally they are participating in a renewed masquerade meant as situational

---

* Donna Matilda thus equates the two terms which, in my view, need to be sharply distinguished. Bentley simply translates "a catastrophe," employing a word that can be used of either the disastrous or the tragic.

shock therapy for Henry, but we also see in Matilda a kind of involvement that goes beyond therapeutic neutrality, in Belcredi much skepticism and at least occasional antagonism, and in the psychiatrist a pedantry often comic. The intertwining of past and present, of role and
actuality, of apparent normality and apparent abnormality, successfully
creates an elusive, enigmatic air; the main dish of psychological mystery
has a garnish of metaphysical puzzles. But while many lines, and principally Henry's gnomic observations and quasi-philosophic inquiries,*
suggest a drama of ideas, the ideas are not at the center, as they are,
for instance, in Sartre's *Flies*. The dramatic reality that finally comes
through is the intensity, the animus, and even the bitterness with which
Henry speaks, and his powerful feeling finally creates a drama of traditional form.

Henry IV is an original and extremely effective revenge melodrama,
and Henry might be a Jacobean revenger. Near the end he charges
that his horse threw him because it was deliberately pricked by someone's spurs; whether or not this is true, we have a traditional melodramatic pattern—either a malicious act, or paranoid suspicion. Henry
appears to have been a rather suspicious and resentful person, to have
felt mistreated by Matilda's unresponsiveness to his wooing. Unlike the
divided tragic character, he moves toward a monopathic singleness and
achieves it in his madness. Then within his singleness he moves into a
demonic duplicity: for twelve years he has been well. But "I preferred
to remain mad. . . . I would live it—this madness of mine—with the
most lucid consciousness; and thus revenge myself on the brutality of
a stone which had dented my head" (III). A stage direction defines

---

* Henry alludes to "that obscure and fatal power which sets limits to our will."
He insists, "We're all fixed in good faith in a certain concept of ourselves," and he
asks Matilda, "Has it never happened to you, my Lady, to find a different self in
yourself?" We masquerade for ourselves, he says in effect—for instance, when we
dye our hair. "But woe to him who doesn't know how to wear his mask . . ." (I).
"And one's dress is like a phantom that hovers always near one . . . phantoms . . .
are nothing more than trifling disorders of the spirit. . . ." "All our life is crushed
by the weight of words: the weight of the dead." "It's convenient for everybody
to insist that certain people are mad, so they can be shut up." "I don't say that
it's true—nothing is true. . . ." "Because it's a terrible thing if you don't hold on
to that which seems true to you today—to that which will seem true to you tomorrow, even if it is the opposite of that which seemed true to you yesterday" (II).
". . . we mask ourselves with that which we appear to be"—an explanation of
"that other continuous, everlasting masquerade, of which we are the involuntary
puppets" (III).

him as "meditating a revenge" against all of them for reproaching him, as he feels they are doing, for always having played mad.

What is original in this revenge melodrama—a form likely to become banal—is the implicit definition of revenge, of which Pirandello grasps the spirit with new subtlety: it is a mode of power. For the short-sighted, revenge may be a quick getting even, a violent leap from the role of victim to that of victor; but for the true practitioner, revenge is a system of domination. In his portrayal of Henry's madness, Pirandello adds a modern ingredient: the sense of illness as an instrument of power. In real and pretended madness Henry has been an absolute monarch, tyrannizing over paid attendants and now over his visitors. He makes the latter communicate through historical charades; he can change the script at any minute and force them into bumbling ad libs; he can sneer at them as "buffoons" and "frightened clowns" (II). He can indulge his bitterness at Matilda and Belcredi, befuddle the psychiatrist, terrify everyone with simulated returns of madness, and bully them by long tirades full of proud histrionic mastery and philosophic adventurism (in both nihilism and idealism). But then, ironically, he deserts his role of power through ambiguity and intellectual audacity and shrinks into the ordinary straightforward revenger: he stabs Belcredi. Thus he condemns himself to permanent life in the villa: by one commonplace theatrical act he has undermined his career on a special and brilliant stage.*

In Jacobean drama the subtitle might have been "The Revenger Over-Reached." The over-reacher, of course, embodies a hubris that is potentially tragic; but it becomes so only in a world where a sense of moral equilibrium is fundamental. That is not the issue here; there is only shock and perhaps a touch of pathos in Henry's fatal change of role. Henry undergoes no self-recognition; he knows only circumstantial consequences. So Pirandello may always be using "tragic" and "tragedy" in quotation marks. Be that as it may, his achievement is to practice an old melodramatic form with a uniqueness that virtually disguises the tradition.

When we turn to Sean O'Casey's *Juno and the Paycock* (1925), we

* One can imagine Pirandello regarding Henry IV as a Pirandellian playwright. If so, Henry's fate might be construed as Pirandello's warning to himself not to desert his proper theater for the more ordinary one in which the power of enigma yields to the power of straightforward impact.

find a somewhat comparable situation: the dramatist and his biographer Gabriel Fallon both call the play "a tragedy," but its excellence is of another kind. It is a melodrama of disaster that gains a special character from a large infusion of Falstaffian and satiric comedy. We look at the action entirely from the point of view of the Boyle family, who are the victims of a series of misfortunes that O'Casey has brought together almost too neatly. He uses the traditional method of first placing the Boyles on the heights of a new hope of prosperity and then plunging them into much lower depths than before. An unanticipated legacy leads the Boyles into buying various articles on credit and changing their style somewhat: neighbors even hint that they are pretentious. Then the legacy fails to materialize, because the will has been carelessly drawn by Charlie Bentham, a schoolteacher now becoming a lawyer, and the Boyles suffer both from creditors and from neighbors who hardly conceal a pleasure in their bad luck. Meanwhile Mary Boyle, twenty-two, a worker of "principle" (we remember the labor leader in Galsworthy's *Strife*), has fallen in love with Bentham, and she is broken-hearted when he lights out to England. What is more, he has left her pregnant. Bentham, in other words, comes fairly close to an old type of melodrama villain. But in portraying the agents of the Boyle disasters, O'Casey makes his sharpest attack on Jerry Devine, a young labor leader, Mary's sweetheart before she fell for Bentham. When Bentham and the legacy both disappear, Jerry comes back in hope of regaining Mary—until he finds that she is pregnant. Mary reads him the lesson: "—your humanity is just as narrow as the humanity of the others" (III).[15] The climax of the disasters is the death of young Johnny Boyle at the hands of the Irregulars, to whom he belonged: they are meting out justice for his betrayal of Tancred, who was killed a short time before. At the end Juno Boyle, the ever-enduring mother, is praying for strength to bear up under the series of blows.

This is characteristic modern drama of pathos; it is on the brink of patness, but it improves on the type because of O'Casey's ironic sense. The betrayer Johnny appears first as crippled by wounds received in Irish uprisings, but the potential hero-martyr is whining and self-pitying; he is frightened and superstitious, and once he has a Macbethian vision of the dead Tancred; this not only prepares for his being taken away to rough justice but is in nice contrast with the firmer character of his mother and sister. There is another kind of irony at the end when Juno thinks, on hearing of Johnny's death, "Maybe I didn't feel sorry enough for Mrs. Tancred when her poor son was found as Johnny's been found now—" (III). She is not guilty, of course, but this willingness to blame herself, when everybody else is blaming someone else, is a fine moment of tragic relief. The most continuous irony is created by the father, "Captain" Jack Boyle, a boaster, liar, loafer, and good-for-nothing, and his free-loading, sneaky, pub-crawling mate Joxer Daly. Their lines of pretense, irresponsibility, brazenness, and mutual disloyalty go on with little change, whatever happens. Jack's only response to the pile-up of disasters is tirades of injured dignity followed by a drunken stupor. The general effect is that of a pathetic drama of wretchedness sharing the stage equally with Falstaffian farce. The joining of diverse elements is O'Casey's great talent. But the irony is not that of tragedy.

Again in the 1930s the term *tragedy* has some life while the tragic mode tends to be only peripherally present. In Federico García Lorca's *Three Tragedies* the dramas have one main theme, deprivation—the sexual deprivation that makes two sisters compete for the professed lover of a third sister; a wife's barrenness; a mother's loss of a son who is killed on his wedding day when his new bride elopes with a former lover (who is also killed). The world is not unlike O'Casey's, except that O'Casey sees rather mild or even passive people in a mingling of pathetic and comic life. On the other hand Lorca, invoking special poetic resources, dramatizes exceptionally well the force of the wants, the longings, the griefs, the sexual and maternal passions, the resultant bitterness and hatred, that afflict and hound people implacably. "Blood" scourges them into reckless ventures in which a moment's triumph, if that, is followed by defeat and despair or death. Technically, they may have choices; against the urgent craving may be set a convention or loyalty or tradition. But these characters do not choose; they are filled by a need or a madness that takes over all of life, that by its sheer force has total authority and negates all other claims. Lorca creates brilliantly the seizures, the monomania, the tyrannical impulses that drive human beings—women more often than men—to plunge into disaster, not only for themselves but for others. They have unity of being, they are defeated, they die or are overwhelmed by grief. Understanding is scarcely relevant.

Of these moving dramas of disaster, the later two, *Yerma* (1934) and *The House of Bernarda Alba* (1936), offer less material for our purposes. *The House of Bernarda Alba* portrays a strong matriarch trying to control, with rigid rules of decorum, a household of five sex-hungry daughters (aged thirty-nine to twenty); she drives away the one lover that three of them have been competing for, and thus causes the suicide of her youngest. The daughters appeal mainly to our pity, but their competitive fury invites a more complex response than that for simple victims.[16] *Yerma*, subtitled "A Tragic Poem in Three Acts and Six Scenes," is actually a pathetic drama of a wife who despite a passionate desire to have children never becomes pregnant (*yerma* means barren). Her husband wants tangible property such as sheep instead of a family; the wife attributes her barrenness to the fact that her husband never brings to intercourse the warmth and intensity that she believes would end her sterility. When she finally realizes fully his antagonism to children, she kills him; she turns suddenly from victim to revenger. This classic type of melodrama is then varied by the addition of a poignant irony: in her speech which immediately follows her husband's death and closes the play, Yerma realizes that she is now barren forever. "I myself have killed my son!" (III.ii). She feels, not guilt, but a more bitter distress. The irony is the opposite of that of Clytemnestra, who, after killing Agamemnon, believes that she has ended a round of crimes and brought peace to Argos.

In *Yerma* and *The House of Bernarda Alba* Lorca was apparently intent on reducing the lyric element [17] that is especially conspicuous in *Blood Wedding* (1933), subtitled "Tragedy in Three Acts and Seven Scenes." *Blood Wedding* is dramatically the most interesting of the three, though on the surface it might seem only a more complicated variation on John Millington Synge's *Riders to the Sea* (1904). In Lorca, the irresistible source of misery is not the sea but blood—the uncontrollable passions that have led to murders in the past and lead to a fatal love affair in the present. In the past the Mother has lost a husband and son by the knives of a certain family; now her other son's new bride elopes on her wedding day with another member of the same family, and both men are killed (there are two kinds of "blood wedding"). Just as Synge's Maurya said, "They've all gone now," so the Mother here says, "They're all dead now . . ." (III.ii). In essence, then, *Blood Wedding* is another drama of disaster; as in the Irish play, the sufferers are victims of a natural force. Yet Lorca's drama is a much less simple affair, in part because there is an elaborate poetry of both language and scene, and in part because the overhanging destiny operates through human personalities rather than through a nonhuman destructive power; and personalities choose. Leonardo turns his back on his wife to elope with the Bridegroom's new bride, and the Bride consents to their desperate and doomed flight on horseback. Leonardo's "blood," however, gives him a hardly challenged oneness; a richer character is the Bride, who is mastered by "blood," too, but who is divided rather than univocally reckless. It is she who gives the play a dramatic fullness not present in the later two "tragedies." After both her "husbands" are dead, she cries "with anguish" to the Mother of the Bridegroom: "I didn't want to. Your son was my destiny and I have not betrayed him, but the other one's arm dragged me along like the pull of the sea, like the head toss of a mule . . ." (III.ii). Now she knows what has happened; she is prepared to accept vengeance, to suffer. She has the makings of a tragic character. But the play is not hers, for it is centered in the Mother's sense of loss that becomes total at the end. So again, in the Bride, we have a tragic accent that amplifies a drama of disaster.

Another Electra: Giraudoux's Modern-Dress Version

By coincidence an Electra play again comes up at the end of a section. Giraudoux's *Electra* (1937) is rich in contrasts and continuities. Hofmannsthal's Electra was an intense, frenzied being who was a world in herself; Giraudoux's is a stern reformer who is only part of a world in which various forces are at work. Hofmannsthal and Lorca both show drama moving toward the sustained dramatic lyric, the instrument of a single central passion; Giraudoux's métier is the social drama struggling to include all of a many-sided world. Again, there are two ways of modernizing a classical theme—devising modern characters and situations that covertly re-create those of the prototype (as in T. S. Eliot), and retaining the original characters but seeing them in modern terms, the way of Giraudoux (as well as of Cocteau, Gide, Sartre, and Camus). Giraudoux's modern Electra plot reintroduces the kind of variegated societal panorama that we saw in *Danton's Death*; since it can go in many directions, it anticipates the mixed modes of Frisch and Duerrenmatt a decade or two later.

Giraudoux's theatrical stew—or ragout, perhaps—contains the traditional ingredient plus a medley of others in a pinch-of-this-and-dash-of-that manner. For instance, there is more than a touch of detective melodrama: Agamemnon is supposed to have died an accidental death, Clytemnestra and Aegisthus have covered up, and Electra, whose hostility they feel, does not know "Why I hate both of them with a special hatred" (I.viii) [18] but is on "the trail." * There is something of bedroom farce in the carryings on of Aegisthus, as well as of intrigue comedy; there is political melodrama in Aegisthus' and Clytemnestra's effort to dispose of Electra; there is an incest motif; Electra talks at one moment like a woman's liberation spokesman, at another like a worldling in Restoration comedy, at another like a speaker in a metaphysical poem; another character resembles the traditional fool. † One of the cleverest workings of Giraudoux's fantasy is the transformation of the Furies into human beings: they first appear as mysterious "little

* Electra shocks Orestes by telling him that she has learned that Agamemnon was murdered and that Clytemnestra has a lover; their problem, she says, is to identify murderer and lover (II.iii). She puts great pressure on Clytemnestra until the truths do out (II.iv,v). The hatred between Clytemnestra and Electra is purportedly rooted in, or symbolized in, a long-distant episode which is also made mysterious: Clytemnestra had dropped the infant Orestes from her arms to the "marble floor," Electra accuses Clytemnestra of having "pushed" him, Clytemnestra accuses Electra of having "pulled" him, and much is made of the conflicting stories (I.iv,viii,ix,xiii).

† Bedroom farce and intrigue comedy: Aegisthus, who is regent, has been carrying on both with Clytemnestra (albeit lackadaisically) and with Agatha Theocathocles, the quite young wife of the sententious President of the Council (the ancient January-May theme), and also develops a passion for Electra (II.vi,ix). One whole scene is given to Agatha's warding off the suspicions of a jealous "young man" about another lover of hers (II.ii). Intrigue comedy and political melodrama are combined in the efforts of Clytemnestra and Aegisthus to marry off the troublesome Electra to a Gardener who is a minor member of the Theocathocles family; not only is there a comedy of cross-purposes in this (I.ii,iii), but Clytemnestra spoils everything by exercising woman's privilege of changing her mind about it (I.iv). The Gardener not only talks at some length about the virtues of his garden (I.iv) but, after he is rejected as suitor, is permitted a long monologue on love, truth, tragedy, and the gods (Interlude). After Orestes shows up, he and Electra are treated as lovers, indeed as husband and wife; in addition, Electra presents herself as her "father's widow" (I.iv) and as the mother of Orestes—an exploitation of incest in all dimensions. Electra calls "chastity" her mother's "worst enemy," and Clytemnestra retorts by accusing Electra of having been sexy at age two (I.ix). In succeeding parallel scenes Electra gives her mother the third degree on the identity of her lover, and old Theocathocles does the same to his young wife. Electra gives a woman's liberation speech on the unhappy lot of wives, and works out an elaborate metaphor on the symbolic modes of adultery; she uses the manner of Restoration comedy and that of the metaphysical poem, which Giraudoux calls on several times (I.viii; Interlude; II.viii). The invented characters include a Beggar who is taken for a god and functions like a traditional chorus and a traditional wise fool.

girls" who frighten people with their knowing ways, rude tongues, and "sick humor" (I.i), and finally, after several different manifestations, they become simulacra of Electra.*

Surprisingly, the continuous ingenuities of conception, of combination (murder and comedy of manners), of imaged detail, of verbal play all but pall after a while; the novel becomes overfamiliar, the variety monotonous, the surprises *déjà vu*; the problem is that unexpectednesses roll out as if from an assembly line, or as if the dramatist's imagination were a sort of computer "programmed" for shocks, upsets, reversals, for foreseeing the unforeseen. Automatism in originality is like a perverse banality. Yet Giraudoux piles on another novelty: the Corinthians are attacking Argos, riots have broken out inside Argos, destruction is imminent, and only Aegisthus, the amorous regent who is now "revealed" as a king in spirit, can save the city. There is a sharp clash between Aegisthus and Electra. Her line is justice before safety; the crime in the past must be punished, and "no pardon is possible." Aegisthus insists, "I must save the city and Greece"; Electra retorts, "I'm saving their soul" (II.viii), thus turning her revenge into a purification rite. Paradoxically, this last fanciful invention creates the most interesting conflict in the play; Giraudoux fashions a valid melodrama of priorities —survival versus reform. A patient of doubtful moral quality is in critical condition: one member of the family calls for extreme unction, another for new medical expertise.

Giraudoux skillfully exploits the ambiguity in the situation, and thus the rich theatricalism gives way to superior melodrama. Opposing monopathic sentiments drive the antagonists, but each makes a dual impact. Electra, the voice of justice, is, as Clytemnestra puts it, "heartless, joyless"; Aegisthus, the co-villain of tradition, is by no means contemptible when he tells her, "your country is dying," and convinces us that he can still save it. Now, if Clytemnestra were capable of doubt or guilt, or Electra of self-scrutiny, we might have the inner action from which tragedy would come; but Giraudoux does not choose to

---

* A few scenes after their first appearance, the Furies, now "about twelve or thirteen years old," act out a play-within-the-play in which Clytemnestra tries to persuade Orestes to kill Electra (I.xii). Next, aged fifteen, they warn Orestes that Electra is going to get him into trouble (II.iii). Finally, "of exactly the same height and figure as Electra," they set off to pursue Orestes, maliciously assuring Electra, "You'll never see Orestes again. . . . We'll not leave him until he's been driven to madness or suicide, cursing his sister" (II.x).

make them human beings of that kind. Both want control of the world
—the realm of melodrama—and both want life in the world to be
drama of a certain kind. Electra wants Argive life to be a melodrama of
revenge: she hates because she discovers blamable facts, and the justice
that she calls for takes an ultimate form—destruction. Clytemnestra
and Aegisthus want to live in the comedy of adjustment to the world
as it is: survival implies winking at many things. Their effort at a therapeutic marriage for Electra * is in one sense a crude effort to evade
nemesis, but the drama sketches a possible case for them. Aegisthus
argues that "dissension" and "moral crises" are caused by people "who
signal to the gods" (such as Electra) and that when the gods get into
the act, the results are irrational: good and evil people are treated alike,
and "humanity suffers" (I.iii). Aegisthus would practice any amount
of the expediency which always has some share in comic life. The President of the Council takes the same line; he fears "women who make
trouble," for it is they who ruin cities, "not . . . egoism and easygoing
ways." There is safety in "humanity's conscience, which always tends
toward compromise and forgetfulness. . . . A happy family makes a
surrender. A happy epoch demands unanimous capitulation." Giraudoux lets the President push to an extreme the comic resolution of life
and thus open a frightening abyss before us. But Electra's revenge melodrama has also opened a frightening abyss. The President acknowledges
her "justice, generosity, duty," but paradoxically blames these for ruining states and individuals. Why? Because "those three virtues have in
common the one element fatal to humanity—implacability" (I.ii).
Electra is indeed implacable, that is, self-righteous and unyielding. In
her, Giraudoux has spotted the ailing woman who has got hold of a
cause, the half-sick doctrinaire reformer who wants to punish vice rather
than see virtue take over—a familiar modern type.

Giraudoux has hyperbolized into their ultimate forms two positions,
those, so to speak, of justice and adjustment; one becomes the spirit of
the unforgiving feud, the other, total adaptability to the way of the
world. In one, man imposes his pride on the world, come what may;
in the other, come what may, he comes to terms with it. One remembers relentlessly, the other forgets casually. The comedy of accommoda-

* They argue that the marriage will be good for the state and for her. Her power
to "harm" will be "only local and in the middle class" (I.iii). The Gardener says
that, wedded to him, "she'll escape from anxiety, torture, and perhaps tragedy"
(I.iv).

tion may embrace cynicism; the melodrama of righteousness rampant, destruction. We are not given the easy choice of simplistic drama.

Electra wins. Queen and regent die; Orestes goes mad; the attacking Corinthians carry out a "massacre"; riots, pillage, and fires mark a "dying" city. Electra relies on "justice" and her "conscience." The Furies accuse her of "pride" and charge, "Now you're the guilty one." The Beggar closes the play with a choral irony, "it is called the dawn" (II.x).

If the final irony is heavy, nevertheless it sums up the ambiguities that are the meat of the play. At the end we have, succeeding the kaleidoscopic glitter that tires the eye, a centralized doubleness that holds the eye and mind, and nurtures insight into the contradictions, not of the self, the realm of tragedy, but of the world. This is one of the ways in which melodrama achieves the stature of which it is capable.

III. THE FORTIES

Giraudoux affords a fitting introduction to the brilliance of the 1940s. In our plays of the next decade, however, there is much less of prestidigitation, showmanship, and theatrical virtuosity; rather there is an extraordinary talent for the fresh dramatic formulation of the difficulties and contradictions of existence, whether these find their locus in private or public life. Repeatedly the drama seems to be less a playwright's contrivance that also incorporates intellectual issues than the outward form spontaneously molded by the pressure of intensely felt thought. There is much of reversal and paradox, and there is a constant pressing toward, or even into, the realm of tragedy. In all of the six plays, indeed, there is either an exemplary development of melodramatic potentialities, at times with what I have been calling a tragic accent, or an actual use of the tragic structure of experience. At least one, Camus's *Caligula*, is very rich in ideas; several present driving, almost obsessed characters such as we saw in the Electra plays and in Henry IV; three happen to deal with crises of private life, and three with political turmoil (so that they can be seen as a bridge from Brecht to Frisch). Since all the plays come within a six-year period, I will do little damage to chronology by taking them in an order that utilizes certain similarities and contrasts.

Betti's Political Drama

Ugo Betti's *The Queen and the Rebels* (1949) is perhaps the least complex of the group, but it so manages a political topic that a heroine of melodrama takes on a tragic coloring. Rather like Brecht in *The Caucasian Chalk Circle*, Betti uses the devices of melodrama of adventure (disguises, surprising identifications, mystery, life-and-death confrontations) as the machinery of a political melodrama (in a crisis a new revolutionary regime tracks down the "Queen" who has been in hiding for five years and who has been made a scapegoat for all difficulties) which focuses finally on the moral quality of the human beings involved in it, and therefore develops the best possibilities of the form. There is a certain amount of pity for the old Queen, who has lived a wretched incognito life of flight, and whose only triumph is, when caught, to be able to take poison before there is time for her captors to inflict torture, of which she has long been terrified. There is unremitting satire of the new "Unitary Government," which is demagogic, unscrupulous, terroristic. The sharpest satire of all is directed at the calculating young man Raim, who says he believes only in money, who cynically latches on to the new rulers to feather his own nest, and who in the process kicks out and is willing to betray his former mistress, Argia. Shrewd satire is directed at the way in which rulers and people unite in blaming everything on the old Queen: Betti is ridiculing the scapegoat mentality, the sense of grievance which is real or which can easily be ignited by demagogues. In our terms, he is satirizing a representative melodramatic habit of mind. It is one of the subtler achievements in a political melodrama.

The revolutionary party has things under control, and the only room for choice is in the mode of response to unchecked power—terror and flight, unobtrusive knuckling under, willing subservience, collaboration for profit, or opposition. (The situation is like that in Brecht's *Roundheads and Peakheads*, in Frisch's *Andorra*,* and in Miller's *Incident at Vichy*.) The individual has not the freedom to be tragic, though he can be honorable and take the consequences. This is the course followed by Argia the prostitute, who is partly mistaken for the Queen and partly

---

* The inspection of hands as a clue to guilt is like the inspection of feet as a clue to Jewishness by the anti-Semitic invaders in *Andorra*. Likewise the scene is unlocalized.

forced into the role because the regime needs a symbolic victim, and who then accepts the role and enacts it with distinction. Betti manages a great irony here by having the actual Queen, pitiable as she is, assume some of the traditional coloring of the prostitute: she has given herself to men, had a child, deserted it because of an overriding concern for her own safety, and finally in effect betrayed her friends. On the other hand the prostitute, catapulted into the queenship by a flamboyant independence of manner, tells harsh truths instead of letting fear govern all things, responds affectionately to the child said to be the Queen's, refuses to give up the names of the Queen's friends that, intent upon blackmail, she had got from the Queen; refuses, that is, to buy the safety which, dishonestly or not, Commissar Amos holds out to her. She has become a queen in spirit, and, en route to execution, she speaks these final words: "Unquestionably, this is a seat for kings, and in it we must try to live regally." [19] Thus she refutes the spiritual leveling close to the heart of Commissar Amos' cynicism. Like John Proctor in Miller's *Crucible*, she exhibits the kind of affirmation that is possible in the melodrama of the victim.

Betti even takes her a step further by having her rise above the sense of an imminent unjust death to the level of tragic recognition: "I have made sad and improvident use of my person, my words, my thoughts, and for the most part, of the whole of my life. I laid the blame for this upon others, when the blame was all my own. This I understand too late. I have often told lies, and even now . . . I am sinning still, since of what I have done tonight I am a little proud . . ." (IV). To imagine the victim not only transcending victimhood by refusing to pay a dishonorable price for safety, but also being capable of the tragic spirit, is an interesting modification of melodrama. It does not create tragedy, for Argia's flaws were not the source of the principal crisis, but it does introduce a forceful tragic accent. (Her situation would become central in Duerrenmatt's *Visit*.) When Argia blames herself for falling into the common man's blaming of others—such as the blaming of the Queen by which the whole nation made itself feel good—she signifies the persistence, in unlikely human conditions, of a saving tragic sense.

Camus and Montherlant

Two plays by Albert Camus and one by Henry de Montherlant, bunched at mid-decade, have in common a strong fusion of feeling and thought, of passion and intellectual subtlety; the major characters in two of them, and a major character in the third, are people of driving will encountering frustrations of thought or experience. In one way they are plays from the study, and yet a study that is more a furnace than a cold room or dusty library. Montherlant's foreground theme is religious, Camus's are political and familial; but the real issues are kinds of personality, with different degrees of tragic possibility.

Betti's political play is focused on victims; Camus's political play, *Caligula* (1945)[20] on the victimizer. In *Electra* Giraudoux asks what may be said for Aegisthus, the corrupt ruler; Camus asks what may be said for Caligula, the crazy emperor, and makes him into a philosopher who finds answers that compel despair. Though it is impossible to ignore the philosophical dimension in the play,* we need not follow the practice of treating a Camus play as simply a restatement of ideas set forth in his philosophic writing; *Caligula* is a "taut and compelling play" in its own right, and something may be said for seeing how it looks from the perspective of genre.[21] One would expect a play about Caligula to be a *Richard III* kind of melodrama of evil, a portrayal of a sadistic monomaniac and his victims, a history of malice and suffering and eventual salvation by regicide. That is there, of course, but it is Camus's genius to invest this simple plot with a doubleness that exacts an uncomfortably complex response.

On the one hand Camus makes Caligula into an evil force beyond clichés; on the other hand he makes Caligula in many ways look better than his victims. He has "rare insight into the secret places of the heart"; as he terrorizes men, he shows how fear makes them pusillanimous, servile, hypocritical, how they lack "the spunk for an heroic act" (II).[22] He is a scourge of human frailties who often sounds like Gulliver on the Yahoos.† When Caligula, like Volpone, has it reported that he is dying, two patricians fall into the usual hypocrisies: one would give two hundred thousand sesterces, the other his life, to save the emperor; Caligula, eavesdropping, pops out and accepts both offers. He has a competition among poets on the subject of death and throws out the

---

* One's attention is inevitably caught by the periodic appearance of the word *absurd* in the dialogue, particularly in Acts II and III.

† Likewise, a "projector" in Part III of *Gulliver's Travels* might have hatched Caligula's scheme to increase the earnings of the National Brothel by awarding a Badge of Civic Merit for assiduous attendance at the brothel and requiring all men to earn the badge in twelve months on pain of exile or death (II).

first six because of their clichés (IV). The brilliant satirist is also a brilliant casuist—witness his argument that he is not a tyrant. He is "no coward"; he "appreciates courage" in others; he has "always loathed baseness" and confounds a betrayer of the hostile patricians.* He takes a great deal of candid criticism from Scipio the poet, and of open opposition from Cherea the man of letters (II, III), and it pleases him to destroy the only written evidence that Cherea is engaged in the conspiracy against him (III).

Not only is the evil tyrant capable of dazzling intellectual and moral tours de force, but he has a kind of magnanimity that enables Scipio and Cherea, who finally lead the assassination, to speak with him candidly. A key line is Cherea's "[I don't like you] because I understand you far too well. One cannot like an aspect of oneself which one always tries to keep concealed" (III). Scipio later says to Cherea: "And yet something inside me is akin to him. The same fire burns in both our hearts" (the "lunatic" and the "poet," as it were). Since Scipio and Cherea are "sympathetic" characters with whom the reader empathizes, the reader is really asked to see his own affinity with Caligula; this demand on the reader is emphasized by numerous lines that call for the "understanding" of Caligula; † and it is most subtly expressed in Cherea's "He forces one to think. . . . That, of course, is why he's so much hated" (IV). Being forced to think is objectionable, of course, only when it makes one question the comfortable assumptions about oneself. Camus's brilliant innovation, then, is to demand that the reader, instead of simply hating and being horrified by the villain, see his own relationship to the villain. This is as far as melodrama can go.

---

* A tyrant, says Caligula, is "a man who sacrifices a whole nation to his ideal or his ambition," whereas he himself has "refused to embark" on three wars, the smallest of which would have cost far more lives than "all my vagaries" (III). He shows his appreciation for courage by rewarding a slave who, "though he was tortured nearly to death, wouldn't confess to a theft he had committed" (IV). He makes the betrayer of the patricians' conspiracy retract his betrayal to avoid being "put to death" (III).

† "*Try to understand him,*" Caesonia, Caligula's mistress, intensely urges Scipio (II). Scipio is troubled: "I understand all—that is my trouble" (IV). Near the end he tells Caligula, "I think I've come to understand you. There's no way out left to us, neither to you nor to me—who am like you in so many ways. I shall go away, far away, and try to discover the meaning of it all" (IV). If here there is something of *tout comprendre, c'est tuot pardonner,* nevertheless amnesty for Caligula is not the final note. To Scipio's last urging, "Try to understand," Cherea replies, "No, Scipio" (III), and Scipio himself, rather than going "far away," joins Cherea in leading the regicides.

Here it comes very close to tragedy, but the difference is that an identification is demonstrated rather than made imaginatively irresistible. Caligula does not draw one in; he functions more like a figure in a Brecht *Lehrstück*.

Finally, we are asked to see in Caligula an ultimate development of ways of thought and desire that, far from being aberrations, are thoroughly recognizable in human terms, and come close to home. Caligula is defined by several terms that have favorable connotations for us. He insists on himself as a man of "logic," and we are made to see logic as an agency of one's own preconceptions; * Cherea tells the patricians that they must wait until Caligula's "logic founders in sheer lunacy" (II). "Lunacy" is used more than once, in punning definition of human aspirations. Caligula announces that he seeks "the moon" (Act I; the motif occurs also in Acts III and IV), that is, "the impossible," "or happiness, or eternal life": basic human dreams are presented as "lunatic." Through Caligula, also, we see some of the implications of other value terms. He is the one true exemplar of freedom, which he argues he can prove only by arbitrary injuries to others: "One is always free at someone else's expense. Absurd perhaps, but so it is" (II)—in effect a prediction of a libertarian phenomenon of the late 1960s. With love of freedom goes love of truth: Caligula cannot "bear lies," and he announces a program, "I wish men to live by the light of truth. And I've the power to make them do so" (I)—a vision of compulsory truth which also became familiar in the 1960s. Power—that human craving that transcends the devotion to logic and freedom and truth—is the final object of Caligula's love, and he carries it to its ultimate implications even more than he does the others. Repeatedly he speaks of envying the gods, of wanting to surpass them.† In such statements he is per-

---

* Caligula uses "logic" to justify taking the money and lives of the patricians (I). His brain-truster Helicon develops an ironic syllogism to prove that all men are guilty and must die (II). Cherea argues that life and happiness are not possible "if one pushes the absurd to its logical conclusions" (III). Cf. Eugène Ionesco's *Rhinoceros*, in which logic is farcically treated as a mechanical exercise that proves its own irrelevance in a crisis.

† He wants, not "to be a god on earth," but to be "far above the gods" (I). He finds "the rivalry of the gods . . . rather irksome." He uses power, he insists, "to compensate. . . . For the hatred and stupidity of the gods." When he destroys the evidence of Cherea's complicity in the plot against him, he commands, "Admire my power. Even the gods cannot restore innocence without first punishing the culprit" (III).

haps always a little the ironic actor, but witty detachment does not disguise the obsessive super-Faustian longing carried to a logical end: ". . . follow where logic leads," he says to himself. "Power to the uttermost; willfulness without end" (III). Camus interprets unlimited willfulness, which we naturally take to be madness, as an extension of impulses familiar to the human heart.

Camus traces the course of power to its final stage: the annihilation of all outside it. "This world has no importance. . . ." ". . . the truth about love; it's nothing, nothing" (I). In Cherea's words, Caligula "counts mankind, and the world we know, for nothing" (II). Caligula makes the patricians repeat a litany containing this line: "Make known to us the truth about this world—which is that it has none . . ." (III). Finally, freedom, power, and nihilism appear in an ultimate trinity. Caligula is "freer than I have been for years. . . . I know now that nothing, *nothing* lasts." * With "this freedom . . . I have won the godlike enlightenment of the solitary. . . . I live, I kill, I exercise the rapturous power of a destroyer, compared with which the power of a creator is merest child's play." So he wins "glorious isolation," "the utter loneliness that is my heart's desire" (IV). Solitude is the fanatic annihilator's own nihility—the end of a nihilism which begins by showing up everyone else's illusions and continues by showing up everything as illusion, by killing people or declaring their nothingness. Caligula is a version of Goethe's Mephistopheles: "I am the spirit that denies," but combined, by a brilliant imagination, with a Faustian striving for infinity.†

Camus's feat is to analyze Caligula's madness, which we might take

---

* However, he has to kill Caesonia because of a "shameful tenderness," with its implication that love does last. The murder that destroys love lest it interfere with principles or pursuits anticipates the murders by the scientists in Duerrenmatt's *Physicists.* Cf. the grief felt by madams when whores fall in love in Frisch's *Don Juan* and Duerrenmatt's *Meteor.*

† I have not discussed other complicating elements in Caligula and in the play: a theatrical sense which leads Caligula to act various roles; the suggested sources of his actions in the period represented by the play; his reduction of other people to puppets; the conflicting views of him held by others; his self-pity; his suicidal impulse; his strange resemblance to a gangster with very loyal followers, including a mistress; the union of the charismatic and the terrifying in one character.

The Caligula in John Mortimer's stage version of Robert Graves's *I, Claudius* (1972), although much less complicated than Camus's Caligula, almost steals the stage from the title character.

to be simply a clinical disorder, as the extreme possibility of virtues (logic, freedom) and impulses (love of power) close to everyman's heart. He tries to entice everyman into seeing himself in Caligula by preventing the usual withdrawal from the evil tyrant; this he does by giving the tyrant some qualities which make him, apparently, superior to many men. So we are not permitted to flee or fear him but are compelled to study him (to "understand" him), and thus through Scipio and Cherea to find what we have in common with him.

Had he humanity as well as representativeness of meaning, he would be the tragic protagonist. At one point, indeed, his style appears tragic. Shortly before his death he looks at himself in the mirror, as he has done twice previously, and cries out in anger and despair at the difference between the "impossible" he had sought and the actual self: ". . . I've come to hate you. I have chosen a wrong path, a path that leads to nothing. My freedom isn't the right one . . . we shall be forever guilty" (IV). It sounds like the tragic anagnorisis, but it is less an acknowledgment of guilt than an admission of a technical mistake. It means he did not finish in first place. But he tries one more course. Almost his last desperate words (he is "screaming") are "To history, Caligula! Go down to history!" Maybe he is inconsistent, or maybe history lasts, the one not-nothing refuting the nihilist in his grave, a consolation "impossible." Yet it ministers to no godlike solitariness: it has to be shared with others. The irony in this last mad snatch beyond nothing is an ingenious final stroke in the strangely compelling portrait of a melodramatic figure who, like other such figures of our day, fuses the recognizable and the monstrous and thus communicates in that unexpected way that we think of as Jacobean.

Camus had already caught the subtle link between aspirations and destructiveness, either in impulses or in objective action, in his drama of private life, *The Misunderstanding* (1944) (also translated under the title *Cross Purposes*). In speaking of both plays he himself significantly uses such terms as *tragic* and *tragedy*,[23] as we might expect of a dramatist who believes that modern life provides the conditions of tragedy.[24] In my view he comes closer in *The Misunderstanding*, which he specifically calls "an attempt to create a modern tragedy." Though his source is modern, his plot is the very old one of the son who returns home incognito and is murdered by his family,[25] and what is more he invests it with so many suggestions of biblical myth that "modern" might seem to connote chiefly the present meaningfulness of ancient traditions.* Other myths are also implicitly present † in a drama that

---

* Jan, the returning son, "expected a welcome like the prodigal son's" (Act I; quotations are from *Caligula and Three Other Plays*), and just before he is killed, he reflects ironically on this (II). In her dissatisfaction with him, his sister Martha is a little like the prodigal's stay-at-home brother. But when, after the murder of Jan, Martha exclaims, "What concern of mine was it to look after my brother?" (III) and continues to pour forth bitterness against him, the echo is of the Cain-and-Abel situation. Again, Martha is enormously "practical" after the murder; Jan's devoted wife is named "Maria"; hence these "sisters" remind us of the sisters of Lazarus. It is only a step from Lazarus to Christ, and it dawns on us that Jan has come from another country, a very lovely one, to bring "happiness" (I); he wants to "atone for" neglecting mother and sister, but it is difficult to find words which "reconcile" (II) (later his sister is willing to "leave this world without being reconciled"—III). Such language is much like that which alerts us to secondary meanings in T. S. Eliot. Now the beautiful sunny land from which Jan comes is where Martha and her mother have wanted to go. But the Mother, thinking also of retaining "the hope of sleep," suggests postponing the murder: "And perhaps it's through him we shall save ourselves" (I). But Martha is for murder now: "I swear it is in our hands to work out our salvation" (Act I; we think of the puritanism of the Governess in James's *Turn of the Screw*). So they kill Jan, whose "innocence" is constantly stressed (the lamb), and next morning Martha says, "I feel as if I'd been born again, to a new life; at last I am going to a country where I shall be happy" (III). It falls little short of a parody of the crucifixion of the Savior; indeed, Jan "redeems" the world of victims of evil because his death leads to the suicide of the doers of evil. These different biblical echoes, in which a not immediately apparent consistency might be discovered by typological criticism, are related at least by parodistic irony.

† In Jan's leaving his home to return to that of his parents, insisting on going to the family inn alone and having his wife stay at another, and deciding to appear incognito instead of identifying himself, his wife Maria sees the inevitably wandering male, "dreaming dreams, building up new duties, going to new countries and new homes." Men, she says, "can't prevent themselves from leaving what they value most." Her last words to him are, "You—you're going forward to adventure" (I). So the trip home takes on something of the Quest; "dream" and "duty" in combination might apply to Aeneas. But this adventure is also going back to his family home: the return of the native. The prodigal son is the dutiful son. He is specifically returning to Europe, like the successful immigrant son coming back from America. The country from which he comes is not named: sea-bordered and sunny, it is contrasted with the Central Europe to which Jan returns—cold, dark, gloomy. The climatic contrast symbolizes another—that between an unhappy, laborious, harsh life, and one of gaiety and joy: the ascetic and the hedonistic, or the old North-South contrast again. Jan has had a happy life with Maria, in contrast with his sister Martha, who says bitterly to her mother, "No one has ever kissed my mouth and no one, not even you, has seen me naked" (III). But at the same time she talks to her mother as if they were lovers; this odd hint of lesbian incest is repeated by the jealous way in which Martha speaks of her brother and mother when they are dead: "I shall leave them to their new-found love, to their dark embraces" (III). The imaginative tentacles extend in various directions; Camus seems to be connecting us simultaneously with several fables. One more

commingles several kinds of action and appeal. At the simplest level *The Misunderstanding* is a drama of crime, with a traditional suspense: the son may be killed, or he may leave in time, or he may bring about a change of plan or heart in the prospective murderers. The straightforward melodrama of danger is enhanced by a peculiar ominousness that Camus creates, through the foreboding felt by Maria, the wife of the returning son, then by Jan, the son, and finally by the Mother and the sister Martha, the murderers. All of them mysteriously sense more than the facts warrant, as if meaning were trying to break through (the identity of the son, the plans of mother and sister), and they were just barely failing to grasp at a saving knowledge (a motif already exploited by Cocteau in his *Infernal Machine* of 1934). Further, there is an original drama of the double entendre: each side (guest and hosts) has a special knowledge which he feels impelled to introduce covertly into speech after speech, savoring his secret like a hidden power, unconsciously wanting to betray it, and yet betraying himself by not betraying what he knows. The cryptic leads us into the symbolic. Family life —jealousies, tensions, self-withholdings, nonidentifications, forgettings, latent destructiveness—is symbolized in the filicide, as it is in the key event in Kafka's *Metamorphosis*. Cruelty begins at home; death is in every bedroom. Though the drama of ideas is less conspicuous than in *Caligula*, it is there, as in the recognition theme. Maria opposes her husband's return incognito; she urges the "normal way of acting . . . telling one's name" (I). But Martha asserts to Maria, as a general law of life, "that in the normal order of things no one is ever recognized" (III), that is, made immune by identity. Partly this view flows from Martha's profound envy and resentment, but it gains authority from her domination of Act III.*

example: Martha and her mother, who have killed several inn-visitors for their money, speak of their victims in such terms as these: ". . . you said that ours suffered least, and life was crueler than we," and "I'm always glad to think they never suffered" (I). Such lines might have been spoken by the mad sisters in Joseph O. Kesselring's *Arsenic and Old Lace* of three years earlier (1941).

* As a whole the play justifies Martha more than it does Camus when he claims for it "a relative optimism as to man." Jan's self-identification would have saved him; hence, "in an unjust or indifferent world man can save himself, and save others, by practicing the most basic sincerity and pronouncing the most appropriate word" (author's preface, p. 7). It is difficult not to think that Camus is speaking ironically here. Maybe Jan's "basic sincerity" would have saved him, but this is to forget that he is only one in a series of murder victims; we have no evidence that each of the others had available a "most appropriate word" with protective properties.

The basic melodrama of killers and victims is greatly transformed by these other elements. Indeed Camus instinctively moves away from the concept of victims. Even Maria, widowed and left desolate, and brutally lashed at by sadistic Martha, can partly blame herself: "I knew this play acting was bound to end in tragedy and we'd be punished, he and I, for having lent ourselves to it" (III). Jan, of course, contributes to disaster by insisting on anonymity, but he suffers more from coincidence than nemesis, and dies before he knows the facts and can reflect on his course.

More important, the two murderers, who dominate Act III, do not elicit the simple responses possible in a melodrama of crime. There are tensions between them, and the two women are sharply differentiated. Martha is a driving but less vulnerable Lady Macbeth: she leads, supplies the moral force, keeps her mother in line, articulates the dream (a happier life on sunny shores) and attends to the practical problems of poisoning and drowning the guest, rebuffs her brother when his talk tends to create a personality and relationship that would make murdering him more difficult. After his death she rejects both guilt and atonement; she is passionately jealous of her brother; in her isolation and defeat she can only try to injure or destroy Maria. In Martha there is the fearful intensity of a character monopathically conceived (as in the Electras that we have seen).

The Mother has the greater range and depth of the tragically divided character. On this occasion she is rather unenthusiastic about the end (sunny shores) and reluctant about the means (murder); she resists in various ways; * she does not actually attribute qualms of conscience to herself but repeatedly speaks of being "old" and "tired"—metaphorical understatements for a growing moral awareness, as if she suspected the rhetoric of self-judgment, and Camus feared she might sound facile or sentimental. Yet when she finds that the dead man is her son, she speaks straightforwardly: ". . . when a mother is no longer capable of

---

* She urges, "Not tonight" (I). She makes an involuntary gesture toward keeping Jan away from the medicated tea; she objects to Martha, "I don't like your way of riding roughshod over my reluctance," and she says that "it's not too late yet" (II). Once, when Martha urges her to "be *sensible*," she retorts, "when you tell me to be sensible, it's only to quench the little spark of goodness that was kindling in my heart." When Martha snaps back, "What you call a spark of goodness is merely sleepiness" (I), she is wrong, but she uses a kind of language that Camus ordinarily attributes to the Mother, who once says, "I can't manage to feel guilty . . . only . . . to feel tired" (I).

recognizing her own son, it's clear her role on earth is ended . . . for all murderers a time comes when . . . they are dried up within, sterile, with nothing left to live for. . . . But it's true that by one act I have ruined everything. I have lost my freedom and my hell has begun" (III). She rejects her old nihilism, of which Martha reminds her: "It only proves that in a world where everything can be denied, there are forces undeniable. . . ." "Forces undeniable" is another name for what I have called imperatives. The mother has the tragic sense of an imperative, but she prefers to speak only of her "grief" and "that intolerable love which I must now kill—together with myself" (III).

But the tragically conceived mother leaves, and more than half of Act III belongs to grieving Maria and to Martha, unrepentant, almost frenzied in defeat, consumed with jealousy of brother and mother, self-pitying, driven to virulence by an innocence neurosis fed by her great strength. For such a person the only way out is revenge, and Maria is the only possible victim. Playing out her frantic melodrama of revenge, Martha tells Maria the truth about this murder and others, sardonically rubs it in, denies any meaning to Maria's "love," pictures the dead bodies in the river, tells Maria, "You revolt me," pushes her away with "a fury of disgust" at anything "resembling the foul love of men," trying to "drive [her] to despair" by insisting that "what has happened" belongs to "the normal order of things." Passionately striving to make her own pain destroy Maria, she explodes into a crescendo of strident screaming against metaphysical injustice ("We're cheated, I tell you"), against the grave where we all "feed blind animals," against a God as hard as stone. Camus's "modern tragedy" finally becomes the maniac melodrama of untempered willfulness blazing out in a death-paroxysm of symbolic aggression against a guilty universe. Martha's punitive excessiveness in the curtain scene again reveals the Jacobean genius for the perverse.

Like *The Misunderstanding*, which it follows by only one year, Henry de Montherlant's *Master of Santiago* (1945) is a drama of private life that has great power in a special melodramatic mode and in some aspects is very close to the tragic. Interestingly Camus, who in the main admires this play, calls it a "dramatic work in which the style, if not the situation, is already perceptibly tragic." [26] Montherlant's feat is to create what we may call a melodrama of the spirit. Don Alvaro Dabo, resisting all the claims and blandishments of the world—specifically an assignment in the West Indies (in 1519) designed by friends to recoup his fortunes and provide a dowry for his daughter Mariana—successfully takes Mariana along with him into a climactic religious ecstasy, with visions of salvation in oneness with God and a "sublime nothingness" (III.v).[27] In utterly rejecting the world, Don Alvaro voices some sentiments that sound like cries for the tragic life. "Expeditions overseas" are for the young, who, he says, have not daring, respect, or understanding; but "high adventures are for the men of our age, and the high adventures are within" (I.vi). Still more markedly: to "alter" things in the colonies instead of at home is "like wanting to alter something in the outside world when everything needs altering in oneself" (I.iv). It is a call for the tragic in place of the melodramatic view. Yet the irony of it is that as far as Don Alvaro is aware, very little in himself needs altering. For a moment he is almost drawn to the Indies by a skillful ploy which Mariana herself has designed but which at the moment of decision she remorsefully betrays to her father. Otherwise he is a monolithically unified man, a god-seeker sure of his course and unfailingly dextrous in refuting all counterclaims, even, by sheer force of conviction and being, those of his daughter's love for a young man. In contrast with the disasters of personality so frequent in O'Neill and Williams, here is a triumph of personality—a firm walking into and welcoming of the annihilation which means a transcendent spiritual victory.

This spiritual melodrama may sound like a too simple affair. Yet Montherlant has not made it any such thing; rather he secures a duality of response that can be evoked only by the skillful treatment of an apparently unified being. It is not so much that Don Alvaro's achievement runs strongly counter to the predilections of a modern audience, or that the joint ecstasy of father and daughter is, if one wants to do it that way, translatable into sexual terms of which the participants are not aware. It is rather the subtle doubleness of Don Alvaro: the successful dramatic mingling in him of a quixotic idealism and honorableness and steadfastness of purpose with pride and hardness and an all-but-insolent self-assurance ("I only tolerate perfection"—II.i). He is an extraordinary man who exacts admiration from an audience which he renders critical and even repels. Part of his strength is a mastery of logical toughness and paradox in demolishing all the claims of country, friendship, and family. Yet Montherlant not only lets these claims be forcefully put but gives to Don Alvaro's antagonists every reductive interpretation that can be made of Don Alvaro's attitudes. Montherlant's imagination nearly always puts Don Alvaro a step ahead. In the longest scene in the play (II.i), an intense debate between Don Alvaro and Bernal (the father of Mariana's young man), both men are skillful combatants; as each comes up with fresh arguments that go to the heart of things, incisively and often epigrammatically, one is reminded of stichomythic Compton-Burnett dialogue, though in the play the moral urgency admits no indirection. No holds are barred, as the man of the world tries to undermine a fanatic, and the fanatic, of whose vulnerability we are always aware, still never quite loses the upper hand. In such scenes Montherlant, as Camus puts it,[28] is "slightly rhetorical" but does secure "authentic tension." At the heart of this extraordinary melodrama he creates a subtle Tamburlaine of the spirit who sounds, as Tamburlaine never does, like a potential tragic hero.

Sartre and Zuckmayer

Reminders of Marlowe continue in two other plays in that remarkable group packed into the war decade—Jean Paul Sartre's *No Exit* (1944) and Carl Zuckmayer's *The Devil's General* (1942–45). Here the likenesses or analogies are with *Doctor Faustus:* Sartre pictures hell, and Zuckmayer implies that his protagonist has gone there. In Sartre the situation is "posttragic"; in Zuckmayer, the tragic gradually assumes the center in a great melodrama of politics and war.

In one detail we can derive Garcin, one of the three occupants of hell in *No Exit*, from the Marlowe Mephistophilis, who says:

> Why, this is hell, nor am I out of it:
> Think'st thou that I, who saw the face of God,
> And tasted the eternal joys of heaven,
> Am not tormented with ten thousand hells,
> In being deprived of everlasting bliss?
> [I.iii. 76–80]

Garcin says—in a vulgarly ornate drawing room which no one can leave —"I understand that I'm in hell" and goes on to speak the most famous words in the play: "Hell is—other people!"[29] No Sartre character, naturally, is going to lament his separation from God and heaven. But for both Mephistophilis and Garcin, hell is the ineluctable conditions of where you inescapably are. For one, no everlasting bliss; for the other, the loss of the quasi bliss of self-ignorance. Garcin's "other people" is the new element that apparently resists comparison—and yet? It may not be too fanciful to read the compulsory presence of other people—at least of these "other people"—as a secular definition of the absence of God. No divine love or grace; only hostility and a relentless spirit of accounting, in ways reminiscent of Dante's Hell. The others hate and despise; they never let one off the hook. They are mirrors in a literally mirrorless room—relentless mirrors as in bitterness each helps destroy the self-images, the self-love, of the others.

Three are slowly and agonizingly forced into self-knowledge: Garcin, the journalist, who suspects himself of cowardice; Estelle, the young wife and sexpot indifferent to all imperatives but those of the flesh; Inez, the lesbian postal worker equally destructive of others and herself: "I can't get on without making people suffer. Like a live coal. . . . When I'm alone I flicker out." The other two cross-examine Estelle, who makes a game of innocence, until she confesses that she and her lover killed their baby, and that the lover then committed suicide. She ignores her truth while trying to make Garcin her lover. Garcin is a poor lover because he is painfully trying to define his truth, while Inez flaunts hers.

Garcin undergoes a long painful struggle in which the others force him through several layers of self-deception to a harsh self-knowledge. At first he tries to get by as a bad husband: "I'm here because I treated my wife abominably," and he spells out the guilty husband's hatred of his long-suffering wife (as in O'Neill's *Iceman Cometh* and Camus's *The Fall*). But he slowly comes around to facing the fact that while he had always striven to be a brave man, he had actually been a coward. Inez cries out that he is a "coward, . . . because I wish it, I wish it . . . I wish it." Their quarrel seems at first to pose an epistemological crux, but it turns out rather to objectify Garcin's inner doubts: the accusations from without, giving life to those from within, are the essence of hell.

Though the coming to self-knowledge is a key action in tragedy, *No Exit* is not tragic in tone or effect. Tragic self-knowledge is a product of dividedness, a proof, as it were, of the duality of available moral directions. But Estelle has always been fixed in a role of lusts covered by proprieties, and Inez in one of intelligent destructive malice; for the most part, what they must acknowledge comes close to total corruption.* Only in Garcin is the fixed singleness partially modified by the need to probe integrity; only he could be thought to have been choosing as well as driven. But whatever choices might be imagined in the past, there are none now; the trio are on a treadmill; as the title suggests, there is none of the tragic openness in which the changing tone of a life can symbolically modify the tone of life. Sartre simply presents a lively post mortem (somewhat as Frisch would do in *Biography*, though with the added illusion of the ability to choose differently). *No Exit* is "posttragic" in the same way in which *Murder in the Cathedral* is "pretragic": Eliot's martyr both feels the pull of the abyss and draws safely back, whereas Sartre's trio are irrevocably in it. Tragedy holds both damnation and salvation in solution; that is its wholeness.† To look at Hell alone is to produce a drama of disaster, indeed the ultimate drama of disaster; nothing can be changed; the flagellation is like that of an unbreakable neurosis, or a never-ending star chamber; nemesis is too much and too late. This is a nontragic world of stasis in misery: self-knowledge is not the avenue to regeneration but the rack of torture.

In *The Cocktail Party* (1949—another of the brilliant productions of the decade), Eliot chose to present the quest for salvation in a comedy-of-manners milieu, thus complementing Sartre's innovation in *No Exit*: presenting damnation in a comedy-of-manners milieu.‡ Eliot has some touches of the farce that comedy of manners ordinarily admits, but Sartre lets farce take over at the end. His trio fall into prolonged belly laughs. Garcin has the curtain line: "Well, well, let's get on with it"—that is, the torture business. This is the essence of farce: action is mechanical, and the actors are like automatons, with sensibilities reduced or eliminated. Estelle stabs Inez: Inez, unhurt, laughs and says, "I'm dead." In a sense all farcical characters are "dead": they are

---

* Estelle: "I'm just a hollow dummy, all that's left of me is the outside. . . ." Inez: "Human feeling. That's beyond my range. I'm rotten to the core." Even Garcin can add, "I'm dried up, too."

† Or, in Aristotelian terms, the downfall of the bad man is not a tragic action. To the Inferno, Dante added a Purgatorio and a Paradiso: thus he incorporated the restorative that is implicit in tragic experience (though, because the outcome was "fair," he called his work a "comedy").

‡ We can describe the three figures in terms of their individual generic potential. Estelle, with her simple itch under a surface of good form, would be a figure in satire; Inez, with her perversity and demonic intensity, a Jacobean villain-hero; Garcin, with a greater range, a possible tragic hero. These differences in part explain why they are good torturers of each other.

safe from ordinary human vulnerabilities. Sartre's trio do remain vulnerable; they have not the total immunity of death. Still, the process of punishment is mechanical; their required attacks on each other resemble the eternal "chase" of cinematic farce.

I am not laboring the issue of generic placing but calling attention to an unexpectedness that might be read in different ways. In an older tradition of criticism, the laugh-producing incongruity of the final episode—the nonhuman grafted onto a human experience of pain—might be treated as necessary "comic relief" (compare the epilogue in hell which Frisch appended to *The Firebugs*). By a later critical perspective the outbreak of farce might free us from our previous engagement (since we instinctively respond from our humanity and deny our inhumanity) and thus transform us into disengaged observers better equipped to get the "message": in a word, Brechtian distancing. My own concern is with the information about genres to which the unexpectedness alerts us: the subterranean connection between two affectively unlike modes—drama of disaster and farce. The closer disaster comes to totality, the closer the characters approach total mechanization, that is, the puppetlike quasi life of farce. Granted, if we feel the mechanization as a loss of the human, the effect may be that of horror. The point is that the transition from the human to the belly-laughable is not arbitrary but reflects concealed formal likenesses between two perspectives on experience. Our sense of these likenesses, though it remain unspoken, is evidenced by emergence of a new critical term that in the 1960s seemed well on the way to becoming fashionable— the grotesque.

Back to Garcin and Mephistophilis: their partial resemblance underlines the difference between two dramatic worlds—one where choices are made, and one where they are impossible. Marlowe, however, might have written a posttragic epilogue in the Sartre manner: Faustus in hell, plagued not by demons but by contemporaries jeering at his motives on earth.

At first glance what we sense in Carl Zuckmayer's *The Devil's General* is an encyclopedist's virtuosity: Zuckmayer tries to force a comprehensive survey of Nazi Germany into a unified three-act play. Yet in this novelistic mass of the documentary and the editorial we find an unexpected and unlikely domination of the tragic perspective. This is the more unlikely when the historical materials would seem, like those of *Richard III* and Camus's *Caligula*, to permit only a melodrama of evil and its victims. Zuckmayer develops an enormous panorama of types in wartime Germany, from sinister and treacherous Nazis through the industrial collaborator von Mohrungen, who helped finance the Nazis to create "a weapon against Bolshevism, a weapon we could control" (I),[30] through General Harras and other air-force officers loyal to Germany but somewhat separated from the regime, to mysterious saboteurs risking torture and death to help defeat their country because its rulers are evil.*

There is a fine melodrama of conflict in the world, and tragedy would seem impossible: the calculating and inhuman rulers are evil, and their opponents and victims are good by definition, so that they can have no inner life. Yet between the two extremes are middle characters with a diversity of positions from incomplete assent to the regime to doubt of it, or to contempt for it conjoined with loyalty to the war. The more aware they are of choices to be made, the more they are in the realm of tragedy. The key figure is General Harras, hero of two wars, air administrator, patriot, philosopher, lover, drinker, even singer; knowing how the war goes, knowing the truth about Germany, and commenting with grim jests; forceful, charismatic, contemptuous of Hitler and the Nazi elite, gay, ribald, free spoken, for a while secure in his sense of being indispensable. He is in many ways the "good man"—understanding injustice and acting against it, seeing through slogans, resisting the diabolic Pootsie.† Furthermore, he has something of tragic rashness: he fails to follow up when he senses that a room is "bugged" by the Nazis (I), and he talks recklessly about the state of the world, perhaps unconsciously doing penance for his collaboration. His is the tragic dividedness, for he serves a regime that his best self repudiates.‡ Yet

---

* Zuckmayer also presents several versions of love—the romantic married love of von Mohrungen's daughter and the air hero Captain Eilers, who is killed during the play (in a plane made defective by sabotage); the naïve and hard sexiness of von Mohrungen's other daughter Pootsie, a product of the Nazi youth who dumps her quiet air-force fiancé and propositions General Harras because he is "born to rule" and can "get to the top" (II); and the romantic new love between Harras and the opera-singer Diddo Geiss, half his age.

† He calls the Spanish war "slightly sickening," tries to help Jewish victims escape (I), says, "The shit is up to our chins and seems to be in the process of rising"; "We're guilty of what's happening to thousands of people. . . . Guilty and damned for all eternity"; "I'm sick of . . . the insane delusion of grandeur." Pootsie, pursuing him, uses the New Testament metaphor, "I'll show you the world" (II).

‡ The tragic situation is echoed briefly, though not developed, in two minor characters: Schlick, the artist, who says, "I'm also a bastard," for he had agreed to

he likes to believe that as a patriot he has "no choice"—the old ploy of the hero wanting to keep things in the easier melodramatic or mono-pathic mood.

But the key action turns on the fact that he does have a choice: he is given ten days to deal with the sabotage of fighting planes. We follow, not a conventional melodrama of success or failure in this task, but his inner struggle as he endeavors to avoid choice: God, he says, "would have made me face decisions that I would rather avoid" (III).* He has to make a choice when he discovers that his utterly reliable investigator of sabotage, Oderbruch, is chief saboteur—one of the effective situational ironies in the play. He reveals much about himself when he chooses not to turn in Oderbruch, who tells him, "Your soul is at stake" (III).

His ultimate choice is externalized in a physical option that has been carefully prepared. Since Act I we have known that Harras has a little sports plane and since Act II that he has been "thinking of clearing out" by means of it. We also know that on the runway stands a fight-ing plane which may or may not have been secretly damaged by sabo-teurs. Oderbruch wants Harras to fly the sports plane to Switzerland and help Germany from there. Harras talks of an "experiment" with "divine judgment": "I've been the Devil's General on earth too long. I'm going to fly an advance mission for him in hell too—in preparation for his imminent arrival." As Harras walks out to the runway we do not know what choice he will make. He takes off in the fighting plane; the engine dies, and the plane falls.

After long and heavy movements in reportorial and didactic direc-tions, Zuckmayer brings the play to a concentrated and subtle finale, where the only issue is tragic self-knowledge. Yet Harras' final choice is ambiguous. In choosing a probably damaged plane he may, as a man who knows himself, be choosing the punishment that fits the crime. But this plane might not be damaged, and if not, what then? Escape? Or is he simply despairing, as some of his words to Oderbruch suggest:

divorce his Jewish wife because he "believed a German could only paint in Ger-many" (II); and Hartman, the idealistic pilot, who on learning that the atrocity stories are true, asks, "Could I get to be like that? Is there no defense against it?" (III)—a sketch for the character of Franz von Gerlach in Sartre's *Altona*.

* In the same scene Harras is attacked by Anne, widow of the dead pilot Eilers, as Eilers' "murderer," because Harras let Eilers die for what Harras does not believe in. Her long denunciation of Harras, which is not very plausible, is Zuckmayer's device for bringing home to Harras the evils of collaboration.

"Too late. . . . But mercy? Naw, can't use it." Oderbruch urges him
to escape: "You could be of more use alive. . . ." In rejecting this
course, Harras may be rejecting a more appropriate and more exacting
penance—the penance of really fighting against a regime that he has
despised but served.

In that case his courting of death in the probably damaged plane is
the easier way out, the rejection of an obligation implied by his own
understanding. He has seemed to accept punishment but in fact has
evaded the full denial of the regime that would be open to him through
escape. The play makes clear, in fact, that in dying he has done a final
service to the regime: it is to be announced that he was killed "in the
performance of his duties to the Fuehrer and the Third Reich," and
that he is to have a state funeral. This is what Zuckmayer means: his
subtitle for Act III is "Damnation."

So we come back to Faustus once again. Like Faustus, Harras rejects
suicide when a pistol is offered him. Yet his commitment to the evil
power—he has served "too long" as "Devil's general"—is too strong
to break. Faustus cannot open himself to God's grace, Harras cannot
receive the grace inherent in going abroad and turning his back on a
lifetime's commitment. Both retain the loyalty of their fellows; both
despair, both reject an obvious physical suicide, both in effect commit
spiritual suicide. The parallel simply emphasizes the remarkable tragic
turn that Zuckmayer has given to a human situation where the melodrama of survival is the expectable form.

IV. THE FIFTIES AND SIXTIES

In approaching the plays of more recent decades, one runs the risk
of being dazzled by the new or having the new clouded by the exceptional brilliance of the 1940s. So he can only hope that the plays that
seem to justify criticism have a middle-ground position with something
of both representativeness and durability. The remaining plays are all
written in English—a balance against the European plays, many of
them from the 1950s and 1960s, that were the exclusive concern of
Part III and that dominate the preceding sections of chapter 10. Three
plays of the 1950s manage the melodramatic structure with different
kinds of excellence. Ray Lawler's *Summer of the Seventeenth Doll*,
which has been called Australia's best play, transcends the obviousness
latent in the theme—the aging that ends triumphs possible only to

youth. Two plays by John Arden treat social conflicts with a detachment that challenges conventional expectations without losing the intensity inherent in the situations. Edward Albee's rise to eminence in the theater justifies looking at two plays of his, especially since they represent different modes—the traditional domestic drama and the cryptic-symbolic that has flourished in our day.

Lawler and Arden

In *Summer of the Seventeenth Doll* (1957) Ray Lawler does not exploit pathos or push self-pitying middle-aged men into polemics against time. We think of "Golden lads and girls all must" when one character, Roo Webber, trying to face the decline of strength and of superiority in his work, pounds the floor with his hand and cries, "This is the dust we're in and we're gunna walk through it like everyone else for the rest of our lives!" (III).[31] We think of the myth of autumn when Emma, the cynically observant mother of Olive, the romantic heroine, tells Roo, "and reapin' is what you're doin' now" (III). We think of Michael Henchard, the mayor of Casterbridge, and Donald Farfrae when Roo, a Herculean sugar-cane-cutter who for years has been master of a stellar gang of cutters, is surpassed and replaced by young Johnnie Dowd and is made bitter by thoughts of the "new champion" (II.ii). Such associations come up because Lawler has enriched what might be only a sad record of the passage of time: he has infused it with a human love of illusion that adds a moral dimension to the routine events of superannuation. Roo and his pal, Barney—respectively the epic hero and Don Juan—take the glories of youth as inalienable endowments; when the two men start slipping they do not just fade away pitiably but fight back—against new heroes, against each other, against friends, against anybody who in some way symbolizes destiny—with a violence almost like that of a tragic hero trying to snatch the world. Though they are not men trying to be gods, they are men who have accepted themselves as gods.

In this they have help, and the meaningful irony is doubled. The cutters work for seven months in the fields; for sixteen years they have spent the other five months in a glamorous idyll with two women in Melbourne. One, Nancy, has just been married; in the seventeenth year she is replaced by a substitute, Pearl. Through Roo's girl, Olive, we learn what apparently imperishable glory these annual five-month holidays have taken on. For Olive they still incorporate a Platonic idea of golden existence which all other lives only poorly and distantly imitate. Olive has romantically glorified a life by exalting the two men at the center of it. They were "men," not husbands, "a coupla kings"; they brought "five months of heaven every year" (I.i). They were "two birds of paradise [32] flyin' down out of the sun" (II.i). The two couples created a myth of paradise that even circulated in the North and that made all outsiders feel as if they belonged to a lesser breed. "But," says Roo in the same passage in which he acknowledges the "dust" as his long fate, "there's no more flyin' down out of the sun—no more birds of paradise" (III). He and Barney have come to some sort of terms with the truth and, as best they may, must trudge uncrowned in the dust. But Olive cannot be reconciled; she calls frantically for the restoration of Eden; at the end she staggers away in shattering grief for a lost dream.

All this borders on the tragic, in which illusions are always dissolved. Yet the trio's illusion is not really of tragic largeness; a thoughtless complacency about the permanence of one's talents is not hubris; and crying for the moon is not tragic. On the other hand, Olive's vision of Arcadia is not trivial either. It is an imaginative transformation of life rather than a vapid flight from reality; Olive's anguish is that of the imaginative person who sees imagination grossly betrayed by the facts. It is not that the imagination is repudiated, but that an enduring imaginative transformation has to be continuous, sensing the movement of life and the never identical graces that the facts may bear. Olive's imagination once transformed life, and she tried to fix that transformation forever. She had the invaluable symbol-making faculty, but she clung to the same symbols and meanings when both had withered. The main objects that she had made symbolic were dolls. So she remains, as Roo calls her near the end, a "little girl," in whom the pathos of ended childhood does not grow into the tragedy of misused maturity.

John Arden's skill in playing variations on melodramatic patterns appears in two plays in which he sets up a conflict between two sides; the conflicts are in the world, and the problem is what kind of person or force will prevail at a given hour or in a given sector. But the plays do not really take sides; there is at least something to be said on both sides. Both sides are immensely energetic, and the combative spirit produces vivid theatrical situations. The audience hardly becomes partisan; it has the mixed feelings of a spectator drawn now this way, now that, his emotional habits having to yield to the ambiguity in the situation.

A drama of the victim, as we have observed more than once, is ordinarily monopathic because the victim is by definition exempt from moral inspection. Nevertheless in *The Waters of Babylon* (1957) Arden takes a Polish refugee in London and treats him in a novel fashion. Though in our day a refugee is inevitably a victim, Arden presents Krank as slum landlord, brothel-keeper, and pimp, who in a climactic action is trying to rig a lottery. This virtually transmutes the victim into the villain, but Arden pulls off still another confounding of expectation: the villain falls very little short of becoming the picaresque hero whose racketeering is more delightful than odious. Indeed, what with an assortment of characters on the make, a welter of accidents and coincidences, much funny detail, and a parody of the plotting and counterplotting of intrigue literature, we have rather a musical-comedy version of crime and punishment. Insofar as this shapes up into more than a potpourri of original episodes, a meaningful form is suggested when Krank, the crooked "hero," is shot and killed by a fellow Pole, the fanatic Paul, who has unsuccessfully sought Krank's assistance in blowing up Bulganin and Khrushchev on their 1956 visit to London. The realist has been done in by the idealist, the businessman by the patriot, the opportunist by the hysteric. Krank calls Paul's (and also the Englishman Ginger's) "national pride and honour" "lunacy," and declares himself "a man of time, place, society, and accident"; they, he says, pursue the "world . . . running mad in every direction," while he himself follows "Only such fragments as I can easily catch" (III).[33] The reasonable, nonpolitical man is a petty scoundrel trying to be a big one; the man of pride and honor seems hardly balanced. Arden has eliminated automatic responses, and thus he has used a melodramatic pattern with great originality. When Krank is killed, we are not asked to rejoice; if anything, he has had rather the better of it.

Live Like Pigs (1958) uses much less fantasy and much more of immediate reality, and gains much more intensity. A low-class "family" (three generations of improvident, larcenous, drinking, rude, noisy, dirty, easy-to-bed types) are moved during an urban-renewal campaign into a government housing project and so befoul the place, disturb and frighten the more orderly neighbors, and inferentially challenge all their mores that the older residents physically attack the unwilling invaders, ready to drive them out or even kill them. So we have a class war, a majority against a minority; and a public accustomed to seeing the theater satirize the bourgeoisie and the entrenched will probably expect to be on the side of the besieged handful. But the "gypsies," as the old order calls them, have little going for them except spurts of energy and agility, a limited resourcefulness, and an expedient but incomplete group loyalty. They are a threat to order, and in the end they cannot be tolerated. On the other hand, the majority suffer from the disabilities customarily imputed to them—complacency, condescension, rigidity, and finally group hysteria, that is, the expectable defects of those on the side of order. Arden has caught the inevitable embarrassment of an imperfect society in dealing with deviants and delinquents; he has a sort of modern, grubby community version of Henry rejecting Falstaff. His subtlest stroke is to show, through two quick sexual episodes, a certain insidious appeal of the low life to the established residents; order's violent (and disorderly) reaction to disorder is in part a suppression of an impulse within. Such insights make for unhackneyed melodrama.[34]

Edward Albee

Two 1960s plays have had a great imaginative impact, and so we may use them as final samples of more recent generic tendencies. Here, of course, the risks due to failure of perspective in time are doubled, and one can only hope that he will not be blinded by the closeness of the object.* There are other obstacles in that Edward Albee's *Who's*

---

* Of still more recent plays, Peter Luke's *Hadrian VII* (1968) would be interesting to analyze as an exploitation of simple emotions beneath a surface of apparent complexity. The audience enjoys a fantasy of triumph and then is restored to reality, the harshness of reality muted, however, by the pathos of the returnee. The imaginatively experienced triumph is the old one of the gifted outsider over the institution, as in Brecht's *Caucasian Chalk Circle*. The idealistic outsider priest can take everyone in the audience with him because his fantasy is on the archetypal track of triumph by fantasy: he has the true central virtue between the corrupt Catholic institution to the right and the dreadfully vulgar Protestant leader on the left. Underneath, in other words, it is straightforward melodrama, with no challenging of standard theatrical attitudes. Mart Crowley's *Boys in the Band* (1968) purports to be little more than a documentary on homosexual life, but the divisions in the central character, Michael, make it approach the realm of tragedy. But Jerome Lawrence and Robert E. Lee's *The Night Thoreau Spent in Jail* (1970) is only a quasi documentary that exploits popular sentiments of the late 1960s without becoming a drama at all.

Afraid of Virginia Woolf? (1962) looks more like a bitter comedy than anything else, and that *Tiny Alice* (1964) moves into the expressionist idiom in which concept of character is rarely a distinctive feature. Still the Albee plays are not irrelevant.

A reviewer of *Virginia Woolf* found it his most "shattering" theatrical experience since *Long Day's Journey*. If O'Neill shattered him, it is surprising that he survived Albee at all; not that Albee challenges endurance, but that, whereas O'Neill gets mired in a rather nagging recital of troubles, Albee advances sharply (though at equal length) through the ever-changing but always merciless moves by which troubled people keep revealing more of themselves. O'Neill says that everybody is what he seems, and all remains the same; Albee, that appearances have to be peeled off relentlessly before we know the score, and that the score was not fixed forever in the first inning. Nevertheless, even if the reviewer was not looking through the shatter-proof glasses of cool criticism, he was not wrong in seeing some resemblances between *Long Day's Journey* and *Virginia Woolf*. In both, the conflict is within families, recrimination and fighting for position and the infliction of pain are the major actions, there are other bonds than those of antagonism itself, and the *in vino veritas* principle is given a workout. Yet there the similarity ends. For one thing, the chief characters in *Virginia Woolf*—the husband and wife George and Martha—have a sharper intelligence than the Tyrones, they have more sheer energy, and above all they have extraordinary imaginations; though they can go at each other in a very ordinary language of abuse or threat, what predominates is the spontaneous wit and artistry in the fierce "games" that ritualize a complex interchange between them—of competitiveness, defensiveness, punitiveness, disappointment, grief, the need to hurt, hatred, and yet understanding and a strong affinity. So they are rarely tiresome. Above all, however, Albee might almost be replying to a basic O'Neill tenet—denying, if not the despair that hangs over more than one O'Neill drama, at least the most conspicuous ground for it. What most frequently devastates the O'Neill character is the inrush of truth; what saves him is the protective wall of illusion. *Virginia Woolf*, on the other hand, shows the husband, in the climactic action of the play, destroying a fantasy that for a long time has somehow served the pair. After George has "killed" an imaginary son that they have used in their complex "games"—he "had to," he says—he tells Martha, "It will be better" (III).³⁵ They do not delude themselves that living without the fantasy will be easy; there is only George's faith that "it will be better."

The renunciation of a dream is an act in the tragic mode; in that sense *Virginia Woolf* helps maintain a climate in which tragedy is possible. When a journalist says that the play "goes soft" at the end, he not only fails to see that the ending is in character, but he also exhibits a familiar kind of aversion to tragedy—to an "all passion spent" quietude in which the truth is to be lived with. The play "goes soft" only if one believes that evil spirits cannot be cast out (Act III has a special title, "The Exorcism") but must go on forever inciting destructive rampages (Act II is called "Walpurgisnacht"), that is, if one sees unending melodramatic conflict as the only possibility. The play has a good deal of that conflict, and it is managed with great originality. George and Martha plunge madly into symbolic revenge and homicide, mainly against each other, but incidentally also against their all-night guests, Nick and Honey, who are now victims, now foils, now minor echoes of the main pair (even, perhaps, in going through shock treatment for fantasies). Through George and Martha the play affords a wild catharsis of aggressive malice; by giving the reader a sense of being on a fearful emotional binge, this version of academic life achieves a universalizing force that dramas of faculty life almost invariably lack.*

The devilish ingenuity of George and Martha in sadistic schemes reminds one a little of the madder Jacobean revengers. Yet what is especially interesting about them is a consciousness of what they are doing, a watching of themselves at work. If Miller in *After the Fall* did an "essay about" tragedy, *Virginia Woolf* is a comment on or an exposition of melodrama. It shows people craving, enjoying, and in the end making an art of melodramatic combat; there is a subtle suggestion of art itself as melodrama (the "games," their rival stories, George's "novel," and the fantasies both within it and around it)—as a mode

---

* I do not attempt to deal with the rather elaborate symbolic ramifications, which center in the different modes of flight from the difficult present: antiquarianism (George as history professor), utopianism (the eugenic future that George foists on Nick), fantasy (in George and Martha). In all of these, as well as in other matters, there is a note of sterility, the George-Martha literal fact that has psychological parallels in Nick and Honey. Albee invests the subject with great emotional energy. Too, *Virginia Woolf* very interestingly reverses *Taming of the Shrew*. It does contain something like a taming, but the method is antithetical: Kate finds salvation in being able to share Petruchio's imaginative transformation of reality, Martha in accepting the death of a fantasy in which George had joined her.

of revenge on others. Yet this is the means by which the play becomes something special, for Albee imagines the couple as more than deadly antagonists. They know what they are doing, and in the end they can forswear the misuse of art for getting around or one up on reality. The action is analogous to the final tragic enlightenment, and its presence renders the play a sophisticated extension of melodramatic possibilities.

As a "pulpit conundrum"—one, too, that glances steadily at ecclesiastical matters—*Tiny Alice* rather teases us about its meaning than invites our participation in characters in action. It touches on the relationship between faith and the material well-being of the church as an institution, between destiny and choice, and, above all, on the relationship between faith and actuality, with some Freudian *obiter dicta* on the ambiguity of religious ecstasy. The credistic problem hinges on metaphysical issues, introduced by constant phrases such as "concept of reality" (II.i); "representative of a thing" and "the thing itself" (I.ii); "symbol" and "substance" (II.ii), "model" and "replica" (II.i), "reality" and "appearance" (III), "THE ABSTRACT? . . . REAL? THE REST? . . . FALSE?" (III).[36] Platonic idealism is most strongly suggested by the treatment of the title character: there is a flesh-and-blood (apparently) "Miss Alice," a "surrogate" for "Alice," and "Miss Alice" tells the man who has married her, "you have married *her* . . . through me" (III). Long before this we have been told that the man may be "pushed . . . to the Truth" (II.ii); the Lawyer refers, if ironically, to "the true world. The ceremony of Alice" (III). Since *Alice* is derived from Greek *aletheia*, truth, we are apparently meant at least to meditate whether what lies behind the full-scale flesh-and-blood "surrogate" is a valid entity or a hoax acceptable only to a mind easily "intimidated."

For "Alice" is made stage-worthy as a figure in an outsized scale model of the outsized castle in which most of the action takes place; the model is the magnetic, attention-seizing stage property, and the correspondence between it and the castle itself, even at the level of action (a fire in the castle is signalized—or vice versa?—by a fire in the model), is among the mysteries that contribute to the theatrical effectiveness of the play. "Miss Alice's" husband, Julian, resists (Tiny) "Alice." He does not want "wonders" scaled down to the tangible and the visible. "I have . . . fought against the symbol." "There is no one *there!*" "I HAVE DONE WITH HALLUCINATION." But "Miss Alice" argues: ". . . accept what's real. I am the . . . illusion." Julian, shot because of his recalcitrance, has a long dying, and a long struggle on the nature of truth. His dying words, as he leans in a crucified position against the model, end the play: "I accept thee, Alice, for thou art come to me. God, Alice . . . I accept thy will" (III). A humble man, accepting what is given, however little it accords with his desires and preconceptions? Or an innocent victim of the world forcing him into a martyrdom founded on an illusion? Or something of both?

By Julian's carrying out his "mission," the Church wins a huge grant of money for twenty years; insofar as the play says that martyrs are good business for ecclesiastical institutions ("Miss Alice" observes that "half its saints were . . . martyred either for the Church, or by it"—II.iii), it is a satirical melodrama. The Cardinal, to whom Julian, a lay brother, had been private secretary, is eager to have Julian "accept" the "mysteries," the "act of faith," and he is paid off before the eyes of the dying Julian. But *Tiny Alice* appears to aim at more than either simple anti-Establishmentarianism or philosophy-course problems. Julian is seduced by "Miss Alice" with the aid of her butler (whose name is Butler) and her lawyer; the three constitute a team who act not on their own volition but as "surrogates" or "instruments." They are mysterious beings with an unexplained mandate and unusual powers. They have engaged in such activities "For ages" and will continue "Until we are replaced" (III). So we are in the realm not only of mysteries but of eternal recurrences, of myth. Yet Albee has nearly all the characters slide back and forth between symbolic activity and various kinds of human responsiveness. Miss Alice is to attract Julian to her, but is in danger of "error," of being too "human," of "enjoying her work a little" (II.ii). Hence the Lawyer, her collaborator but also her lover (she says), is "human" too and suffers from severe jealousy. They are a little bit like an international intrigue group, inhumanly "dedicated" to an objective, but internally subject to everyday naturalistic strains and tensions. The mutual detestation of the Cardinal and the Lawyer is so well concretized that their exchanges effect a catharsis of malice as do the "games" between George and Martha in *Virginia Woolf*. In other words, the spectator is hardly ever permitted to rest in some simple stance such as elementary melodrama invites; this is a complex business in which one is strongly but often puzzlingly moved, and in which every tentative partisanship is undercut by another.

In one sense the play is a melodrama of the victim. Julian, the rather innocent soul who confesses the attractions of sacrifice, is in various ways used by the others, in the language of the play "diddled" (either literally gulled or ironically seduced to a nobler destiny than he would have elected). As sacrificial lamb he could be merely pathetic or even exasperating, but Albee makes him intrinsically interesting through his wrestling with the problem of faith. Once when he lost his faith he had himself committed to an asylum, since loss of faith implied loss of balance (here, as elsewhere, the play raises the old problem of the relative sanity of sanitarium inmates and of the presumably well world outside). He could not, he says, "reconcile myself to the chasm between the nature of God and the use to which men put . . . God," and he adds, "Men create a false God in their own image, it is easier for them!" (I.ii). Julian is criticizing men for what we have here called the flight from tragedy, that is, from the kind of imperative which makes self-judgment inescapable. He makes a severe criticism of his own "self-importance" and "pride" in his early passion for "service" and "humility" and "obedience" (II.iii). Later, a bit smug in his marriage to Miss Alice, Julian can speak of "our guile and pride" that "betray us." But when he cannot face or "accept" "Alice" and the "model" as his "priesthood," as his "service," the Lawyer accusingly challenges the Cardinal, "Don't you teach your people anything? Do you let them improvise? *Make* their Gods? *Make* them as they *see* them?" (III). There is an ironic recoil upon Julian of his own criticism of the world. In his searching, in his insight, in his wish to choose, in his error—if it be that—Julian has affiliations with the tragic hero. Granted, there are ambiguities; at least on the surface he is under the gun of others' wills, like Alfred Ill in Duerrenmatt's Visit,* and this interferes with

---

* There are other resemblances to *The Visit*: an immense sum is being paid to an institution (town, church) by a wealthy woman, and the sacrifice of an individual is involved. As in Genet's *Maids*, two characters enact a scene in which the first portrays a third person, and the second acts as the first (II.iii). "Miss Alice" responds to Julian somewhat as the Sphinx responds to Oedipus in Cocteau's *Infernal Machine*: with a personal warmth that represents only one part of her nature and apparently may conflict with her mission (Anubis and the Lawyer are the respective voices of duty). After noticing this, one is struck by the Lawyer's language: "If the great machinery threatens . . . to come to a halt . . ." (III). However, Albee does a better job than Cocteau of creating a sense that a mysterious machine is operating. At the climax of the "seduction" scene, Miss Alice has her back to the audience: ". . . she takes her gown and, spreading her arms slowly, opens the gown wide: it is the unfurling of great wings" (II.iii). In Lorca's *Blood Wedding* the Beggar Woman (death) also "stands with her back to the audience. She opens her cape and stands in the center of the stage like a great bird with immense

our sense of him as free agent. On the other hand, in his long dying (in a solitude that would be a modern cliché but for the freshness of the detail) the action has become entirely his; his is the quest, and his the decision—between, unless we misread, despair and an acquiescence in what is given. The riddles hang over, but the personality belongs in the tragic realm.[37]

In the energy, in the omnipresence of the symbolic which is often cryptic, in the tense drama of personalities that alternate between being and meaning, in the sliding relationship between engagement and detachment, and hence in the mingling (or wavering) of generic modes— in these ways our final drama appropriately concludes a survey that, whether we look primarily at dramatists or decades, has repeatedly raised the kind of issues that come up in *Tiny Alice*. If it has less of the immediate surface realism [38] that is also the mode of a large number of plays, it nonetheless strives, like its fellows in either style, to penetrate reality, and in an unhackneyed way.

wings" (III.i). But the most striking reminiscences are those of T. S. Eliot—especially in the agitating of problems of faith and spirit that in *Tiny Alice* are at least as pervasive as the satire. Like Eliot's Thomas à Becket on the road to martyrdom, Julian has his own difficulties, and he specifically records his "temptations," even using a paradoxical style not unlike Eliot's (II.iii). Still more marked are some resemblances to *The Cocktail Party*—the combination of the realistic and the mysterious, especially in Miss Alice, the Butler, and the Lawyer, whose apparent dual status is analogous to that of Harcourt-Reilly and his assistants. Though they proceed with outward certainty, they seem privately to have some doubts and hesitations, and a sense of possible "error." Their acting on Julian is somewhat like Harcourt-Reilly and his cohorts' steering Celia to her destiny. The references to Julian's problem of being "reconciled" recall Harry Monchensey's problem in *Family Reunion*, which uses the same word. And *Family Reunion* makes use of Alice in Wonderland, which Albee's title, *Tiny Alice*, cannot help suggesting. Finally, in a play which makes use of various mythic or generally representative figures, the name Julian is bound to call to mind Julian the Apostate, and the reader is left to meditate in what, if anything, this Julian's apostasy consists.

CHAPTER ELEVEN

Dramas of Money: Some Variations Since 1875

T HE FINAL trying-out of generic theory—an examination of a number of plays that deal with the money theme—means not so much a new approach as a formal emphasis upon an aspect of drama that has at least been implicitly present in the preceding discussions. The chapters organized by authorship and chronology have repeatedly noted, if not specifically commented upon, the thematic substance of the plays considered. It would be possible to proceed now by a reassessment of these plays in thematic terms. There would be the theme of politics in Brecht, Frisch, and Betti, of familial rivalry in Miller, Camus, and Albee, of the religious personality in Albee and Montherlant, of kinds of public leadership in Camus, Giraudoux, and Zuckmayer, of sick and obsessed souls in Williams, Pirandello, Lorca, and Hofmannsthal, of protective illusion in O'Neill. It is better, however, to avoid repetition and to make a thematic approach to generic form by using both plays and a theme that have so far had only a minor role, if any at all, in this volume.

Insofar as they allude to theme, earlier chapters observe how a single imagination transforms different themes; the present chapter inquires how a single theme is transformed by different imaginations. Though there are some themes that have life only in a given historical context, it is the nature of themes to live on with little regard for the passage of time. Hence a thematic approach to a given period is likely to have the advantage of counteracting the artificial isolation of the period and of providing at least a peripheral reminder that no age is an island. Our age needs to remember that for all its technology it is not unique; it may even find some advantage in knowing that materialism is not only a contemporary heresy. Dry and limited as it seems at first glance, the money theme is ancient and is rarely dormant in the theater; it provides one lively demonstration of the connection between modern times and other times. Since this continuity makes it quite natural to look also at earlier practices, the money theme makes the account of the modern open out into a glimpse of a larger world. Likewise the money theme incites treatment in various modes; the account of it opens out, then, into a survey of most of the generic forms of drama. This double opening out seems a fitting way to end an essay mainly operating within limits that are chosen rather than obligatory.

I. GENERIC PATTERNS

In the last century the money theme has excited the imaginations of dramatists sufficiently diverse in their practices to furnish interesting evidence on generic forms. Many of them, however, tend to adhere to a traditional theatrical style that depends on the illusion of reality (whether we call it "illusionistic" or "realistic"). We will look first at plays in this mode and then move on to those in which expressionistic and didactic methods modify or supplant dependence on verisimilitude.

Older plays about money reveal that the subject offers several options. The author of *Everyman* works in what may be called the realm of tragedy: by that I mean that the essential drama lies in Everyman's inner dividedness between the charms of the world and the claims of religion. He has drifted into a life of social and material gratification; Fellowship and Goods define his working values. For him the crisis that in all tragedy tests values is the summons of Death: though Everyman would cling to the world, he returns gradually to the spiritual values that he has neglected. The charms of the world have not taken him too far, however; in the absence of nonreversible catastrophe we have "realm of tragedy" rather than achieved tragedy (we might also use the term "pretragic" that I have applied to Eliot's *Murder in the*

Cathedral). George Barnwell, on the other hand, does not pull back soon enough, and George Lillo's *London Merchant* (1731) then becomes technically tragic; here, of course, the initial evil is theft rather than materialism, and a poorly controlled would-be Shakespearean style makes both crime and repentance unconvincing.

To jump to the opposite extreme: in William Congreve's *Way of the World* (1700) money is treated in the style of high comedy of manners. As in *Everyman*, however, money is not the sole value that influences conduct; Mirabell and Millamant very much desire money, but they also seek a mode of life in which passion, personal dignity, and good sense have a major part. While the tragic turns on a sense of irreconcilable values, the comic theme is reconcilability, and reconciliation is effected through compromise. One accepts the world but is not uncritical of it; one pays various prices to be of it, but not the price that diminishes personality. Money is not despised, but it is not worshiped either; there is a tension between money-mindedness and devotion to other values; money is a means, not an end. Once this tension is broken and love of money dominates the personality, the balance on which comedy of manners is founded is replaced by an imbalance which is the ground of satire, as in Ben Jonson's *Volpone* (1606) and Molière's *L'Avare* (1668). In satire we are asked to be contemptuous of, or perhaps horrified by, the excesses or deficiencies that mark an individual's deviation from normal balance: to both Jonson and Molière there is something monstrous in the money-mad. Satire and comedy are both related to melodrama: comedy in the broad sense that its arena is also the divisions in the world rather than in the personality, satire much more intimately in that it tends to use a dualism of villains and victims and thus to push toward the more strenuous emotional impact of vice working injury in the world. And yet both Jonson and Molière qualify the satirical tone by giving original turns to the generic form. In Jonson, to a considerable extent, the victims of greedy people are other greedy people, so that the satirical partly gives way to the picaresque: we are asked not only to detest greed but also to be delighted by the game of wits in which a clever trickster's triumph over others is more important than the getting of goods and money. In *L'Avare* there lurks behind the surface ridicule a sense of disorder and even suffering in the ridiculed person; insofar as it is illness that troubles him, he is closer to the victim of nonsatirical melodrama than of satire, and insofar as he picks up any sense of alternatives, he may even have a touch of the tragic. Harpagon looks forward to Silas Marner, in whom the literal relation between *misery* and *miser* is explored.

The money theme, then, is amenable to various perspectives and generic interpretations; the older examples disclose some of the possibilities open to more recent dramatists. On the face of it, Jonson's satirical imagination seems to have hit on central symbols of recurrent appeal. He writes *The Fox*; Lillian Hellman, *The Little Foxes*. Jonson has characters named Corbaccio and Voltore; Henry Becque's play, to which we now come, is entitled *Les Corbeaux*, and this is translated *The Vultures*. Both Jonson and *Everyman* make early use of the connection between money and death that we will see repeatedly: in *Everyman* the action turns on the approach of death, in *Volpone* on the simulated approach of death.

II. Standard Idiom and Variations

I want first to look at a group of plays in which theatrical conventionalities are dominant. I make this rough initial definition only for convenience; it implies nothing about whether conventions are well used or poorly used, and likewise it does not imply that innovation is admirable or successful in itself. Let us simply say that in all these plays an ordinary theatergoer would not find anything immediately unfamiliar or enigmatic. This is not to say, however, that he would be gratified by stereotypes; familiar patterns, such as those of realism, do not guarantee easy gratifications. In Section III our business will be with plays that either are less conventional at the surface level or proceed from a familiar surface into depths that might not be expected.

Henry Becque's "The Vultures"

In Becque's famous naturalistic drama, *The Vultures* (written 1877, produced 1882), we see the relationship between satire and melodrama: Becque is satirizing the greedy—here, strong people who prey upon the weak and are untroubled by any inner dividedness. The principal tension is that between money-centered, predatory worldlings and their victims, who have negligible resources for maneuver and combat. As so often in dramas of money, death is a disaster for some and an opportunity for others: Vigneron, a *nouveau riche* manufacturer, dies before putting all his affairs in order. His widow and three daughters are then defrauded and reduced to poverty by his former associates Teissier, Bourdon, and Lefort; Mme. de Saint Genis snatches back her son George, the lover of daughter Blanche Vigneron; and the music teacher Merckens, who had praised the musical talents of daughter Judith, runs away. Teissier, Bourdon, and Lefort, satirized for their brutal money-minded self-interest, are the single-motive figures of melodrama; they have total unity of theory and practice. Bourdon says of marriage: ". . . the question which is really the most important [is] the question of money. . . . You ought to know there is no such thing as love. . . . Marriage is a business . . ." (IV).[1] Becque's satire, as I have indicated, works by portraying not only these greedy men, but also their pathetic victims, the Vigneron women. Significantly, the latter are not complicated by any responsibility for their fall or by any power of retaliation. Hence they too are figures of melodrama.

Becque is earnest, almost plodding; he has a documentary tenacity; and we soon settle down for the dismal procession of predictable indecencies. The effect is monopathic in an exemplary way; the tone is that of "naturalistic tragedy," a version of melodrama. The monetary monists grind ahead mechanically; Becque tends toward plot clichés, and up to the final scene he is markedly without irony.* In *Volpone* the same unillusioned view of money-love comes across in ingenious and vivacious ironies: a pretended fatal illness in one vulture fools the others,[2] and they cheat each other, betray themselves, and by hubris assist their own downfalls. In Jonson's satiric melodrama, ironic overreachings ironically sustain justice; in Becque's, there is plain disaster.

Surprisingly, however, Becque manages a final ironic turn and something of a dividedness of appeal that cuts into the prevailing expectedness. Marie Vigneron, the daughter who has shown most sense of reality, marries Teissier, the head vulture, aged sixty. In "popular melodrama" this could be a horrible fate, the ultimate disaster, or, in a romantic twist, a happy outcome after all. Here, it is neither. Marie chooses—one of the few choices possible in this world of moral auto-

---

* The cliché note appears in the Ophelia motif, not plausibly managed, in Blanche; the faithful servant; the aesthetic ignorance of the *nouveau riche* family; the spoiled son; the watchful creditors who need watching. However, a few details are ironic: when predators give warnings against each other, or recommend virtues to their victims, or support conventional morality.

mation—"a little shame and regret" in preference to "a host of terrors of all kinds that might end in a terrible misfortune" (IV). She saves her family, and the play does not insist that the price is unbearable. Indeed, in dealing with sex and marriage generally, Becque comes closest to the ambiguity possible to melodrama. He does not turn Mme. de Saint Genis, who gets her son away from Blanche, into a mere maternal bitch. Instead, he lets her speak plausible lines about the bitterness of the poverty-stricken marriage: against Blanche's *amor vincit omnia* she develops an *omnia vincunt amorem* that is at least a part truth (III). Rather than taking sides, Becque offers alternative perspectives; grays replace simple blacks and whites. Becque stresses, not the shortcomings of Marie's marriage, but one appreciable advantage: the play closes with Teissier's running a crooked creditor out of the Vigneron apartment. Here Becque's social Darwinism turns toward the wryly ironic rather than the banally oppressive. Out of the melodrama of disaster emerges an accommodation to the world that belongs to comedy. Insofar as the price paid is high and authentic needs remain unsatisfied—this is left ambiguous—the mode approaches that of "black comedy." * (To combine "black" and "comedy" is to point to one kind of dividedness of appeal.)

Three plays of the 1930s—Clifford Odets' *Awake and Sing* (1935) and *Golden Boy* (1937) and Lillian Hellman's *Little Foxes* (1939)— reflect a strong sense of a competitive materialistic world, one in which Becque's Teissier would be very much at home. The competitive world is a natural field for melodrama, for its rivalries are a ready-made form of conflict. In one play Odets attempts some variations upon the expected, but Miss Hellman sticks, for the most part, to a straightforward melodramatic pattern. Her pattern differs from Becque's, however, in that the potential victims show some will and ability to resist; so we have combat and intrigue instead of cumulative disaster.

---

* Becque works in the same direction in *La Parisienne* (1885). In this comedy everybody enjoys satisfactory arrangements in the world and pays the price, whether willingly or unknowingly: manipulation in place of spontaneity, deceit instead of straightforwardness, amenability to management rather than sharpness in challenge or self-assertion. Clotilde keeps happy a husband whom she helps secure an appointment, a lover whom she uses to help get the appointment for her husband, and a jealous lover who loves her. Clotilde has the good sense of Eliante in Molière's *Misanthrope* (1666), the dual capacity of Shaw's Candida, and the wifely sagacity of Maggie in *What Every Woman Knows* (1908).

Lillian Hellman's "The Little Foxes"

As melodrama, *The Little Foxes* teeters between the slick and the substantial. By the slick I mean a skill in theatrical manipulations which make our responses too easy; Miss Hellman puts together a smooth succession of clichés and gimmicks to which we are vulnerable if we let slip that vigilance which is the price of freedom in the theater. By the substantial I mean a sense of reality which has some continuing power to gain assent. The slick predominates. Of the dramatic versions of "The love of money is the root of all evil" *The Little Foxes* has the most clear-cut division between bad guys (the brothers Ben and Oscar Hubbard, their sister Regina Giddens, and Oscar's son Leo) and good guys (Oscar's wife Birdie, Regina's husband Horace and her daughter Alexandra, and their black servants Addie and Cal). The Hubbards have got rich in business, and they have no scruples about getting richer; they scorn their less money-minded spouses. Their plots and counterplots, including robbing Horace and outsmarting each other, move ahead briskly, the over-all expectedness combined with entertaining unexpectedness of detail.* There are no surprises of character in the calculating Hubbards or in the nicer people, who are sensitive, musical, socially conscious, not very happy, and rather the worse for wear because of the Hubbards. There is pathos: Birdie drinks alone; Horace is at death's door because of a bad heart; Alexandra is pushed around by her scheming mother. Obviously we can do nothing but side with decent underdog Davids against tough-skinned Goliaths.[3] Characters get new light on what others are up to, but none on themselves. Instead of the drama of divided personality we have the theater of duplicity in action; the clever deployment of single-track personalities invites numerous alternating responses rather than complex ones. The execution is strictly monopathic.

What is substantial is Miss Hellman's sense of the intensity of monetary self-seeking, of love of power, of how it works and what it leads to.

---

* Surprise: Horace plans, by writing a new will, to turn their robbery of him into a punishment of his wife. Surprise: he dies (with help) before the will is written. Surprise: Regina uses her knowledge of the robbery to make her brothers toe the financial mark and cut her in for more profits than they intended. Surprise: Alexandra revolts against Regina, and brother Ben hints that he may still get the upper hand of Regina by learning a little more about Horace's death.

She tries for the general validity that lies beyond stereotypes. Ben tells Regina that "the world is open . . . for people like you and me. . . . There are hundreds of Hubbards sitting in rooms like this throughout the country" (III).[4] Insofar as this applies to the twentieth century or to the "new South," the realm is that of social documentation. A truth more general than historical appears in a common element in *The Little Foxes* and Jonson's *The Fox*: in both there is the foxiness of the acquisitive operating against each other—the persuasive irony of dishonor among thieves. This complexity crops up effectively in the final situation: as the Hubbards look ahead to a fatter world, they also face each other, and that means no final peace or certainty about advantages gained. This is a touch of the black comedy that we saw in Becque. But the dividedness of appeal achieved by Becque is not produced by the final confrontation of the Hubbards; they simply make us wonder which of them will be cleverer in the next round.

Death appears, almost inevitably. In *Everyman*, death was an opportunity for spiritual reassessment, and in *The Vultures*, for the predators to move in on the vulnerable; in *The Little Foxes*, death is a made opportunity: Regina assists an ailing husband out of a troubled life. The action stays on the melodramatic level: Regina is untroubled by restraining imperatives.

Odets' "Awake and Sing"

Dramas of money can take off from greed or need; the former is the province of *The Little Foxes*, the latter of *Awake and Sing*. But in dealing with those who have much and want more, and those who have little and want some, there is the same risk of a stock appeal to sympathy or condemnation. It is easy to damn the acquisitive and unscrupulous and to arouse pity for victims, to settle for a thin melodramatic texture. Both Hellman and Odets have a theatrical expertise that can trick the dramatist into a facile gratifying of monopathic expectations. Both do opt for a relatively easy aesthetic solution in which the proffered reassurance understates the rigor of the actualities that have been evoked.

Odets' choices stand out clearly in contrast with those of Arthur Miller in *Death of a Salesman* (1949), which has some remarkable similarities with *Awake and Sing* (like Hellman and Odets, Miller is a knowing theatrical craftsman). In each play we see a four-member lower-middle-class urban family just squeezing by economically, undergoing the strains brought on by big worldly dreams and small incomes from routine jobs. In each, the struggling family is contrasted with a materially successful uncle (present literally in Odets, in others' imaginations in the more inventive Miller). In each, finally, the end turns on a suicide intended to produce, for survivors, a nest egg from insurance (yet another version of the death-as-an-opportunity that is almost a fixture in money dramas).

These are the materials of melodrama of disaster. Miller is more faithful to the disaster inherent in the situation.[5] His emphasis is all on the pathos of failure; Willy Loman clings to a fantasy of monetary triumph long after it is too late. The false dream has hung over the family, corrupting the sons and arousing passions that give great vigor to the melodrama. Willy's resentfulness and quarrelsomeness complicate the pathos of failure. On the other hand his son Biff, who between filial disillusionment and get-rich-quick dreams has become a bum, actually reaches a degree of self-knowledge. The ironies in Willy's life, especially his resistance to any knowledge that would alter the singleness of his vision, and the tragic accent of Biff's painful coming to insight—the first such accent that we have seen in the money plays—give strength and maturity to *Death of a Salesman*. Odets is less faithful to the difficulties in the lives he has pictured; he lets people off the hook and injects a hopefulness not grounded in character.

In *Awake and Sing* the suicide is not that of the despairing protagonist, but that of grandfather Jacob, an intellectual. He is the father of Morty, successful in the clothing business, and Bessie Berger, who tries to manage the lives of her husband Myron and her children Ralph, aged twenty-two, and Hennie, aged twenty-six. Jacob, a Marxist and idealist, constantly holds forth on contemporary evils: ". . . in a society like this today people don't love. Hate!" (II.ii).[6] He urges hopeful Ralph, "Go out and fight so life shouldn't be printed on dollar bills" (I), and favors a "revolution" at least in terms of "Awake and sing, ye that dwell in dust, and the earth shall cast out the dead" (II.ii). Jacob commits suicide, his death somehow invigorates Ralph ("I saw he was dead and I was born"), and the play ends with Ralph's ringing decision, in the spirit of "Awake and sing," to work for a better future (III). Since this affirmation does not come out of a hard-earned insight by the character, Odets might treat it ironically as at once admirable, immature, and illusive; but it is evidently meant to be taken straight, a rainbow amid the materialistic flood, and is therefore sentimental.

Indeed, the play ducks away from its real game. Ralph unhesitatingly forgives his mother [7] for trying to cheat him out of the insurance money of which he is the stated beneficiary. We assume that he forgives her for indecent meddling in his romantic affair with an orphan girl named Blanche. He seems to have forgot the nasty behavior by which she at least contributed to the suicide of her father Jacob (in a fit of temper she smashed all his gramophone records). Ralph cheers on his married sister Hennie as she is about to elope to a new world of good things and good sex with her lover, Moe Axelrod, a hatchet-tongued, tough-nut, heart-of-gold type who has made his pile in some undefined racket. Hennie goes out of her way to treat her rather gentle husband with harshness and contempt. People rush through hard decisions, their expectable feelings are ignored, and their indecencies are hurried over. What is called for is either sharp satire or the tragic facing of issues; instead we have a brave new world proclaimed with musical-comedy naïveté. Never was there an easier victory over the money orientation that dealt so harshly with people in *Death of a Salesman*.

Oddly enough, the lightweight melodrama of good cheer runs counter to the expectations created by one real strength in *Awake and Sing* —the language. The characters regularly use a racy, colloquial urban idiom, in which offhand ironies and blunt images and vigorous man-in-the-street rhythm combine effectively with everyday speech and clichés. It is the language of an unsentimental, unillusioned, and undefeated adjustment to the world, and it is a pity that it does not have more impact on the tone. But a good ear for verbal patterns does not guarantee a good eye for moral realities.

Odets' "Golden Boy"

In *Golden Boy* (1937) Odets turns an epigram that might have been spoken by one of Becque's money-men. Eddie Fuseli, the gunman, reminds Joe Bonaparte, the boxer who has the title role, of his worldly gains. Joe says, "There are other things," and Eddie replies, "There's no other things!" (III.i).[8] But other things also have dramatic strength, so that money-love is not the solitary norm as in *The Vultures*. Too, money is conceived less as a metaphysical essence than as a means of "success." In *Awake and Sing* Odets moves from the sympathetic portrayal of worldly failure to an affirmation of moral success; in *Golden Boy* his theme is the moral failure of worldly success. Here the lesson, which is standard equipment in Odets, is less conducive to a glossing-over of actuality. Odets remains the agile entertainer, and he gives some rein to his documentary side, uncovering rackets in prizefighting. Still, there are no surprises in depth; reportage, reversals, and shifting camera angles create a lively realistic surface for a rather allegorical demonstration[9] that public triumph may be private destruction. It is not a new point, and the play has an air of the *déjà vu*.

Golden Boy is more disappointing, however, because it does not do well with Odets' chosen point of view. His basic conflict—the Hellman opposition of the crass and the decent, the profit-seekers (the boxing crowd) and relaxed, *gemütlich* people (the Bonaparte family)—is concentrated in Joe Bonaparte: he is a divided character. Hence the money theme is interpreted tragically rather than melodramatically. Joe can be boxer or violinist, but since boxing means hand injuries, he cannot be both, and he must choose. He suffers from a representative modern dividedness between impulses, and even between an impulse and an imperative: the musical career comes to symbolize a harmonious and creative life,* and boxing an aggressive and destructive life.

Odets arouses great hopes, but he simply fails to bring the thing off: *Golden Boy* shows us that having a tragic structure and achieving tragic excellence are different things. One can set up a potentially profound conflict and yet fall into the truistic and mechanical. Though Joe has moments of strong passion, the conflict itself is more schematic than passionate. From the start we see Joe only as a coming boxer, cocky and eager to "have wonderful things from life" (I.ii); there is no dramatic evidence that he has musical talent or even likes music. (We have to ignore the more superficial implausibility that he has spent two years becoming a boxer without his family's having any idea what is going on.) Hence we do not really feel, in Joe, the asserted conflict between the "fighter" and the "boxer" (who can protect his hands). Under needling Joe decides to become a fighter; the motive, which we

---

* Music easily becomes a cliché symbol of nonmonetary values: it has this role both in *Awake and Sing* and in *The Little Foxes*.

learn about only belatedly, is that he has always been unhappy, has had hurt feelings, and has not sensed a compensating triumph in music; we also find that he has a passion for fast driving as a means of "looking down at the world" (I.iv). These characteristics are not convincing; they are added because there has to be a reason for Joe's choosing to become a fighter. Odets contrives disaster by insisting on other murky depths in Joe: in his biggest fight he puts what he calls "the fury of a lifetime" into his knockout blow and feels ready to "beat up the whole damn world" (III.ii). The revengeful killer in him is no more plausible than the musician, for he has come out of a Bonaparte family life which we have seen as affectionate, devoted, noncompetitive.

Joe kills his opponent; he tries to face the fact that he "murdered a man"; he acknowledges, "I murdered myself, too." This is in the tragic manner, but Odets does not hold to it. Joe is claimed by his girl friend Lorna, a tough worldling with unworldly dreams; they dash off romantically for an all-night ride to be "on top of the world" and are killed. The catastrophe seems as willed as the rainbow at the end of *Awake and Sing*. In sum, the tragic potential is not realized because neither side of Joe's divided personality is dramatically established, only one side really leads to action, the critical self-recognition is hurried over, and the automobile wreck is theatrical rather than intrinsic. The moralizing by the survivors underlines Odets' strong didactic bent.*

In these four plays, which have in common only the assumptions of the realistic theater, the money theme takes on a variety of dramatic forms: we have found a tragic structure that is unsuccessful, a melodrama in which the better values triumph too easily, a melodrama in which better values at least survive while the money-value people dominate the scene but still have to face each other, and a melodrama in which the money-value people are ruthlessly self-serving but in which their victims also achieve an ambiguous *modus vivendi*. This last is of course Becque's *Vultures*, perhaps the most interesting of the group in the dividedness of appeal which breaks in at the end. Oddly enough, it is the earliest of the group, antedating by half a century the 1930s plays and achieving an effect often thought of as "modern." In this it has some affiliations with our next group of plays.

---

* Odets is really in the tradition of old writers of domestic tragedy such as Heywood and Lillo: they sketch out a tragic structure, but, attuned to lessons rather than passions, they fall into a mechanical development that makes the point but asserts human conflicts rather than catches their fullness and depth.

III. OLDER PLAYS AND DIFFERENT IDIOMS

The next plays either use traditional structures very capably or else gain freshness by modal innovation and alteration. They regularly give us a sense of effective management of the chosen form. Yet these plays were all written before World War I: the early modern period, if we may so call it, was capable of dramaturgic performances that continue to hold up. They have intrinsic interest rather than simple historic significance. For convenience I will take them in chronological order. This will have the incidental advantage of juxtaposing Odets' *Golden Boy*, which uses a tragic perspective unsatisfactorily, and Leo Tolstoi's *Power of Darkness* (1886), which convincingly traces the protagonist in the archetypal slow transformation from melodramatic to tragic consciousness.

Tolstoi's "The Power of Darkness"

Tolstoi's drama is enough like a nineteenth-century naturalistic novel to surprise us when it develops nonnaturalistic qualities. It is novelistic in its inclusiveness; it has little of the concentration that Ibsen had already made known.[10] It is naturalistic in its portrayal of a scheming, money-centered, gross, even murderous life in a peasant village; it takes Becque's theme much further. Though everyone talks the language of Christianity, it is largely habitual and unfelt; "sin," an often used word, becomes a neutral term like "accident." In a style that would saturate Gorki's *Lower Depths*,[11] people call each other "mad dog," "cur," "beast" (I), "worse than a snake," "bitch," "prison rat" (III).*

Yet this world of unredeemed nature is not finally a *Lower Depths* world. Gorki's theme is the disaster of personality, the decay of will;

---

* Characters compare themselves and others to animals in appearance or role, or explain and justify conduct by reference to animals: "like a work horse," "like a jackass," "Even calves have their fun," "Horses don't run away from oats," "Stick his orders under a dog's tail." Powders meant to relieve a wife of her husband are "good for cockroaches too" (I). A husband feels "deserted . . . like a dog"; his wife is to look for his hidden money "like a dog looks for fleas" (II). Her husband makes Anisya "feel like a wet hen"; fat will make a man lazy since it "makes a dog go mad"; Nikita is reported "drunk as a fish," and justifies himself: "Even a hen drinks" (III). People at a party are "like a dog in the manger"; of Nikita, reluctant to conceal his adultery by murdering his bastard, "Does he want to feed lice in prison?" (IV). But he does it, and his mother thus advises him how to handle the situation: "But if you run away from a wolf, you run into a bear" (V).

in *The Power of Darkness* Tolstoi paints rather an urgent will, little inhibited by imperatives in the quest for money (or sex). Encouraged by his mother Matrena, Nikita hastily turns out his old mistress Marina so that he can hang onto his married mistress Anisya, whose husband Petr is well off but not well. Petr is helped to his grave by the administration of powders (in *The Little Foxes*, Horace is helped to his grave by the nonadministration of medicine): mother Matrena, ambitious only for cash, is the driving Lady Macbeth who masterminds the operation. Widow Anisya and Nikita marry, Nikita controls Petr's money, drinks, is prodigal, and becomes the lover of Akulina, Petr's daughter by his first marriage (and now, of course, Nikita's stepdaughter). The birth of Akulina's baby, just when Akulina is about to be betrothed, produces the second crisis: Anisya, an embittered wife, joins with Matrena in the relentless pressure under which Nikita kills and buries the infant. Akulina gets married, and in the last act Matrena and Anisya once again join forces to make Nikita do their will, this time blessing the new couple.

Through such actions "the power of darkness" is reminiscent of "this gloomy world" in *The Duchess of Malfi*: a genuine human evil goes on its sinister course, apparently unresisted. But Tolstoi makes little use of the Jacobean pathos of the victim, nor does he derive evil from perverse passions, reckless revenges, or sadistic delights (true, the murder of the baby is recorded in macabre detail: we are to hear the crushing of the skull). Rather we watch scheming * for small profits and social security in a tiny local world. Further, Tolstoi uses a tape-recorder kind of speech that, at least in translation, is tediously full of the colloquial and the ungrammatical; this prosaism † looks like the final turning away from great Jacobean melodrama and toward a narrow-gauge realism. The one potentially large-scale melodramatic figure, ironically, is Ma-

---

* Nikita's mother Matrena is the chief hatcher and executive director of schemes: her son Nikita must be saved from his girl friend Marina to marry Anisya, because Anisya will have money; Anisya's husband Petr must therefore be got out of the way; his hidden money must be found and put under Nikita's control. When Akulina, made pregnant by Nikita, gives birth, the baby must be done away with so that life can go on as usual. Matrena sums up afterward: "All's covered up clean" (V.i).

† However, there are occasional symbolic overtones, as in the fact that Akim, the man of Christian feeling, is a cesspool cleaner; his influence helps bring to light the hidden cesspool in the family. But as a literal object, the cesspool is used for irony: when Akim came home from work one day, his evil wife Matrena "puked and puked" (I).

trena, the cool schemer for rubles and respectability: she has a tremendous will and coerces others like an evil spirit. Yet her ends are petty, so that if the play remained a melodrama of evil, there would be a threat of anticlimax. But in an arid life from which we would expect only dreary naturalism or conventional social satire, Tolstoi remarkably imagines the appearance of a tragic consciousness.

The dividedness in Nikita which dominates after mid-play is prepared for by the division between his parents, the unscrupulous Matrena who first influences Nikita, and his father Akim, the man of moral insight.* Though Akim may be merely the voice of Tolstoi after his conversion, Nikita's repentance is not superimposed, is not a moral illustration rather than a convincing outcome of personality. Nikita is imagined, not used. He comes across as a genuine man of dual capabilities. Under stress he at first seems inconsistent, but in retrospect we see in apparent inconsistency the evidence of deep inner division (such as never becomes real in Odets' Joe Bonaparte). Initially he is the sexual charmer: three women fall for him, and he seems only the high-spirited amoral accepter of favors. "And if women love me, I'm not to blame"; he is as delighted by this as by being able to say, "I think that everybody likes me" (I). Challenged by his father Akim about his relations with Marina, he jests, evades, then lies, swearing an oath and crossing himself. "If I married 'em all," he soliloquizes, "I'd have a lot of wives." He prefers the unmarried life: ". . . people envy me." He sneers at his oath: "They say it's scary to swear to what ain't true. That's all bosh. Nothing but words anyhow" (I). Thus to the naïve egotism of the gay rake-despite-himself is added a tougher skepticism like that of Edmund in *King Lear*. Tolstoi brings out the harder side of Nikita's self-interest, but then reveals, for the first time, a different kind of responsiveness in him. Ailing Petr, the husband of Nikita's mistress Anisya, mildly reprimands Nikita about his work, but then quickly apologizes, "Forgive

---

* Akim names his son's vices ("an injury to the girl"—I; "He's just lazy," "A drunkard's not a man," "Your life is bad," "Your wealth . . . has caught you in a net"—III); defines spiritual shortcomings ("Oh, they've forgotten God! . . . We've forgotten God, forgotten God!"; "Ah, Nikita, you need a soul"—III); is the voice of nemesis ("the tear of an injured girl don't flow in vain, y'see; it drops on a man's head"—I). He is made "ecstatic" by Nikita's confession (V.ii). He shows his own integrity by rejecting a needed ten rubles from Nikita after he sees how Nikita lives. Still Akim is a little too much like the Doctor in the morality play (he and Mitrich talk at length about the evils of banking), though his verbal mannerisms ("y'see" and "you know"), tedious as they are in their excessiveness, have a humanizing touch that modifies his allegorical tendency.

me for Christ's sake if I've sinned against you," and "weeps." Nikita replies, "You forgive me; maybe I've sinned more against you," and he too "weeps" (II). At this point we take him to be only rather emotional, and see a contrast between the hysterical man and the calculating women. For he does not oppose the women's plans to hurry Petr to his dying and get his money, and he marries Anisya. But he wants to think of himself as their victim: "These women are crafty. They make a man dizzy," he says (II).

As husband, Nikita becomes a bully, a spendthrift, a drinker, and the lover of his stepdaughter Akulina, whom he tells, "I don't love her [Anisya] any more; I love you" (III). This looks like the usual rake's progress, but when his father Akim censures him for his vices, Nikita is seriously disturbed; he complains, "Oh, life is hard for me, awful hard!" and again "weeps" (III). By now it is clear that he is seriously troubled by inner conflict, but also that he wants to be blameless rather than face the issue; "life is hard" implies not a choice, but a disaster visited upon him from without. Nikita's inner turmoil, hinted at in the earlier acts, is the meat of Act IV: Nikita is at the center, wanting his and Akulina's baby to be got rid of, wanting the women to do it, resisting both plaintively and angrily when they press him to dig a hole for the body and then to do the actual killing. His conscience at last emerges as a full reality, but still in conflict with the longing to conceal guilt. Again there is the human love of innocence, the favorite emotion of the tragic hero not yet ready to be tragic: "What a life! Oh, those women! . . . Again I'm not to blame for it a bit! . . . Oh, what a lot you women are! . . . I've ruined my life, ruined it. What have they done to me?" But rejected guilt forces itself to the surface almost as it does in Macbeth: Nikita thinks he hears the murdered child still crying and screams, "Don't bury it; it's alive!"

Nikita is still sharply divided in the first scene of Act V. He would like to escape into a renewed affair with the once rejected Marina, now married, but she refuses. Tolstoi wonderfully imagines Nikita's effort to blame her: "I loathe myself. Ah, Marina, you could not hold me fast, and so you ruined me and yourself too! Well, is this a life worth living?" He talks of suicide. Then comes the key scene which derives some of its effectiveness from the fact that it excellently parallels an earlier one. In Act IV, Matrena and Anisya pressured Nikita to get rid of Akulina's baby; now they pressure him to offer the final blessing—everybody is waiting for it—at Akulina's wedding party. Earlier, he did away with new life; now he is to sponsor it. Again Nikita resists; again there is the intensity of struggle between him and the women. Again he complains, "Oh, what have you women done to me?" Then he takes three steps which bring his own life and the action to a resolution: he becomes mature and tragic. He refuses to come and give the blessing—his first true resistance to pressure. He rejects suicide—that final form of the escape which he has repeatedly sought. He then goes to the wedding party and takes responsibility for his actions, confessing what he has done—the seduction of Marina, the death of Petr, the seduction of Akulina, murder of the baby. He performs the most difficult act of contrition: he asks forgiveness, "for Christ's sake," of Marina, of Akulina, and then of his father Akim.

I have gone into so much detail to show how excellently Tolstoi has traced the emotions of profound dividedness. Tolstoi's sense of tragic life is penetrating, and he images it compellingly. Yet *The Power of Darkness* is not quite tragedy in the grand manner. Though we can see its excellence by comparing it with *The London Merchant*, to which it has a number of detailed resemblances,* it has its own kind of limitation. Let us put it this way. Nikita, the promiscuous young lover, commits technical incest with Akulina, and he marries the widow, older than he, of the man whom he had at least helped murder. Hence we could describe him in mythic terms: Don Juan as Oedipus. These names attest to Tolstoi's originality, but they also tell us what the play is not: Nikita does not have a mythic largeness and dynamism, and the play does not really open out. There is not a philosophic dimension; there are no cosmic echoes. I do not mean that Akim's Christianity is not strong and deep, but it is ethical and regulative rather than imaginative and resonant. At the end Akim asserts, as tragedy characteris-

---

* Though Tolstoi disapproves of banking while Lillo approves of commerce, both deal with common life, locate evil in a money-sex-murder triad, show protagonists who accept responsibility, and evaluate conduct in specifically Christian terms. The contrast with Lillo simply shows how much more talented Tolstoi is: he avoids tasteless homilies, rarely gets into the patly allegorical, and has a real feeling for the depths of character and for conflict in character. Lillo's George Barnwell seems to be seduced, to rob, and to murder, not because he has real passions, but because his actions have to illustrate various evils and their consequences. But Nikita is full of spontaneous life and is complex enough to prevent our foreseeing how he will develop; Tolstoi skillfully turns the irresponsible, self-pleased sexual athlete into the tragic hero who moves ahead plausibly from freedom of the flesh to freedom of conscience.

tically does, the preeminence of the spiritual ("repentance") over the legal (the policeman's "document"); but we are not quite carried out of the parochial scene into the conviction that imperatives are being reaffirmed for mankind.

Frank Wedekind's "The Marquis of Keith"

While *The Power of Darkness* derives its surface method from contemporary naturalism and its individuality from the traditional tragic form that gradually takes over the play, Wedekind's *The Marquis of Keith* (1900) is often praised as innovative and ahead of its times. In it we do indeed find the shifting of tone, the cryptic in character or dialogue, and the priority of brilliant scene over structural cohesiveness that sometimes characterize more recent drama. Yet *The Marquis of Keith* contains various familiar things. When Scholz, the conscience-ridden man of wealth, theorizes that his wealth may have been "the only reason for my misfortune," the title character, a financial adventurer, exclaims, "That's blasphemy!" (I),[12] and thus asserts a belief already articulated in Becque's *Vultures* and later to be repeated in Odets' *Golden Boy*. One conflict in the play is between the old friends Scholz and Keith: it is a conflict between two views of the world, the standard material of intellectual melodrama. Scholz is potentially tragic. Keith echoes Goethe's Faust in saying of Scholz that "there are two souls in his breast" (II), a good metaphor for tragic dividedness; Keith also refers to Scholz's "spiritual conflict," and Scholz to his "pangs of conscience" (III). But in an amusing ironic reversal of the tragic course of events, Scholz hopes to find a cure for his addiction to duty, and by reform to become a sensualist or hedonist. He fails to advance from the quasi tragic to melodramatic single-mindedness; he falls back, not so much into a sense of imperatives, as into Ibsen's "sickly conscience." When he finally urges Keith to join him in a retreat from the world, he makes no real dent in Keith's unagonized worldliness. Keith resists a similar pressure from the other side: Molly, a combination of mistress and drudge to Keith, passionately urges him to give up his worldly schemes and associates. She is drowned, apparently a suicide, and the melodrama of ideas shifts briefly into a melodrama of physical danger: the people who pull Molly's body out of the water threaten Keith. When Keith, shaken for once, replies, "I—I am not responsible—for this disaster" (V), his denial of responsibility is in the spirit of melodrama, and, if he is not responsible, *disaster* is indeed the correct word.

Keith never loses his singleness. But as a man on the gold standard, he is different from the money-creed people in other plays that we have seen. Wedekind treats the money theme originally, just as Tolstoi does: both unexpectedly fall into a traditional form. Tolstoi's is tragedy, Wedekind's is the picaresque. Wedekind unites this with more serious matters than we expect (Scholz's conscience, Molly's concern and death): hence a certain dividedness of appeal. Like all clever rogues, Keith has to travel from place to place, at each stop playing a game of wits until ordinary reality catches up with him. He has been in America, North and South, and he is now in Munich, where by energy, imagination, and charisma he almost pulls off a "financial deal" in which local men of wealth would provide the cash and Keith would have a fine controlling position. But despite his hypnotically attractive style he is finally in a jam. At the end he has a gun in one hand and ten thousand marks in the other. For the third time he rejects withdrawal from the world; he keeps life and money, and only withdraws from town as all picaresque heroes must do, saying, "with a grin," "Life is a slippery business" (V).

The picaro's game is the melodramatic life of competition in the world. Keith's near-success in Munich is founded on a knowledge of what the world believes in—business and profits—and a proposal to sell men of money what they want to buy. When the trickster becomes the huckster, the drama of adventure also involves social satire. The picaro leading affluent men into self-betrayal is very much the situation in Jonson's *Volpone*. To say this is to say that *The Marquis of Keith* is finally on the comic side, but Wedekind is ingenious in introducing melodramatic and tragic perspectives that contribute an unexpected soberness.

John Galsworthy's "Strife"

Strife (1909) is the conventional well-plotted realistic play. It is better held together than *The Marquis of Keith*: there are no surprising juxtapositions of contrasting tones; there is little of the symbolic and none of the enigmatic. Since it deals with money by means of a topical subject in which there have been many changes in six decades, capital versus labor, we might expect *Strife* to be only a historical exhibit. But it retains great vitality. Galsworthy has converted his subject into durable melodrama by securing a marked dividedness of appeal instead of inviting a monopathic partisanship. He presents a worker-owner dispute that calls for compromise: in literary terms, the solution of comedy, the distribution of reasonably edible half loaves. This does occur at the end but only, ironically, after bitter months of struggle of melodramatic intensity. Anticomic emotional pressures are generated by an irreconcilable board chairman and an irreconcilable labor leader. What takes place is the process that we described in theoretical terms in chapter 2: personalities are distilled from the ferment of issues, and from the conflict of principles there emerges a personal feud with overtones of a revenge melodrama.

Galsworthy might have produced a quite simple melodrama by weighting the play on one side or the other. Though the atmosphere is generally prolabor, the drama is much more complex than a confrontation of a more deserving and a less deserving side. Galsworthy sees a a relentless clash of wills between John Anthony, the board chairman, and David Roberts, the workers' leader, two unyielding men of "principle" who are the source of ironic effects not always available in melodrama. Each wants total victory; each risks ruining his side to get it; each reserves his ultimate respect for his chief antagonist. Each is finally "broken" by rebellion in his own ranks as men of expediency declare it against "nature" (the principle invoked against "principle") to continue the strike until the workers are starved and the company broke. The battling warriors are not a white knight and a scoundrel, but utterly convinced antagonists for both of whom Galsworthy makes the best case he can. On both sides the strength and integrity are heroic and yet—this is the final irony—mad: either can be satisfied, as in a feud, only by the destruction of the other.

Galsworthy complicates this fine melodrama further by presenting the conflicts within each side. Emotions are not fixed from the beginning, but change: although Anthony's daughter is initially prolabor, she is shaken when labor women do not share her crisp views, and defends her father to the hilt. But her brother Edgar becomes increasingly outspoken in his view that the company is "responsible" for the suffering of the workers; he even uses the word "criminal." Here, then, is a note of the tragic, but it leads into an irony of an almost comic sort: Edgar's line makes his fellow board members more uncomfortable and resentful than anything the strikers do or say.

Strife is a less "sophisticated" drama than Brecht's *St. Joan of the Stockyards*, at least in that Brecht focuses on the devious, the hypocritical, and the sinister in economic struggles, and often replaces the literal with a daring cartoonist symbolism. Galsworthy shows a more forthright, all-cards-on-the-table, no-quarter duel, and he sticks to a realistic manner. Yet he actually has more detachment than Brecht; he does not let a prior decision about the right push him toward an easy-love and easy-hate characterization. About all his major characters he has the "divided mind" that, if it does not produce tragedy, still keeps him a long way from the stock responses that are the risk of partisan melodrama.

Georg Kaiser's "From Morn to Midnight"

Strife and *From Morn to Midnight* (1912; produced 1916) have, amid many differences, one likeness. For both of them money is a starting point rather than a major theme: either money loses its primacy, or it is initially a means to nonmaterial ends. In *Strife* one side wants to get more money, and the other side does not want to give it, but the chief antagonists find that they would rather lose money than lose the fight. In *From Morn to Midnight* a man steals money and then spends it profligately, hoping to buy passional satisfactions; the root of evil is not the love of money but the belief that money can buy love and other excitements.

The difference between the two plays is that between the theater of verisimilitude and the expressionist theater. While Kaiser's expressionism has been seen as influencing new forms in O'Neill and Elmer Rice, Kaiser also registers the influence of an older form: in him we see again the link between postrealist expressionism and prerealist allegory. Not only does *From Morn to Midnight* have much in common with the moralities of Hofmannsthal;[13] it has more than usual of the oblique reminiscences of *Everyman* that hover about various money melodramas. The unnamed characters are identified only by type or role—Cashier (the lead), Lady, Bank Manager, Lady's Son, Salvation Lass, Penitents. The actions do not so much develop individual character in the Cashier as constitute instructional episodes for him: the robbery, the attempted sexual adventure,[14] the search for other "goods that are worth the whole sum" (iii),[15] the rejection of death, the trial visit to home and family (mother, wife, daughter), repentance at the

Salvation Army Hall, acceptance of death. Everyman wants to ease death, the Cashier to escape deadly routine. Neither gets much help from others, who have their own kinds of self-interest.

Insofar as the Cashier runs into money-lust, the play has the infusion of satire that we often find in melodramas of money. The Cashier, of course, is not grabbing but throwing away, seeking a *vita nuova* in which passion will burst out and disturb or destroy habit and custom. He becomes "a thief and a criminal" (ii), impulsively stealing sixty thousand marks in the hope of running away with a woman he mistakes for an adventuress; he prefers "complications" to death (iii); having terrified his family with his "wild . . . look" and cryptic images, he rejects "The magic of familiar things," decides that home "doesn't stand the final test" (iv), tears out, and at racetrack, cabaret, and Salvation Army Hall tries unsuccessfully to find or incite a passionate escape from daily ritual and order.* At the hall the Cashier is moved, as Everyman was in time, to "confession and repentance." Here Kaiser achieves a satirical master stroke: when the Cashier "scatters . . . broadcast" the last of his stolen money, convinced that by these salvation-seekers it will be "torn and stamped underfoot," the penitents get into a free-for-all fight over it. What is more, the Salvation Lass, who has dogged the Cashier for three scenes, encouraged his confession, and promised him, as Knowledge did Everyman, to stay "at your side," now turns him in to the police to get the reward. The Cashier shoots himself in the heart.

Beneath the satirical surface, however, the essential life of *From Morn to Midnight* verges on the tragic, as it characteristically does in moralities when they shift from preachment to presenting the tension

* At the race track he offers unusually large prizes, and this stimulates such competition among bicycle racers that crowds are driven to a frenzy. He exclaims in delight: "Differences melt away, veils are torn away; passion rules! The trumpets blare, and the walls come tumbling down. No restraint, no modesty, no motherhood, no childhood—nothing but passion! There's the real thing. That's worth the search. That justifies the price!" But he withdraws his "generous patronage" when the arrival of the king in the royal box quiets things down: "The fire that was raging a moment ago has been put out by the boot of his Highness" (v). The routines that hold at bank, home, and race track also dominate a cabaret; the Cashier cannot command spontaneity or passion, and when he looks beneath the masks or costumes of the entertainers, he finds hostility or ugliness (vi). Routine is dramatized with greatest effectiveness at the Salvation Army Hall, where confessions are ground out mechanically and almost identically as a series of moral exhibitionists describe careers in sin and salvation (vii). Their pseudo-spiritual case histories ironically sum up the events of the Cashier's own day.

of man's dividedness. Kaiser neither preaches nor sets things up patly. The Cashier does not stray from an obviously good life to practice an obviously bad one; in fact, most of what he is trying to get away from is dull and petty. He is Everyman as romantic: he thinks that one can leave the ordinary behind and plunge into the great exploit, the grand gesture, the passionate gamble; a petit-bourgeois Faustus, he wants to banish ennui, to light fires, to jump magically into a heaven where all delights and excites. He has not so much chosen a bad end as he has misconceived the nature of reality. He yearns and errs understandably, and throughout he is a suffering man, driven, seeing, hoping (and even having an Edenic dream near the end), but always doomed to disappointment.

He has much of the tragic, but not all. Though understandable, he never really understands; he does not have a Faustian grasp of truth; the ultimate quality of his failure is never articulated; his hopelessness is pathetic rather than tragic. He has less the tragic dividedness out of which self-knowledge comes than the dividedness of appeal that marks superior melodrama. We sympathize but remain detached and judging. He lacks magnitude: he is still the "little man" of the modern stage, and we are not so much participants as spectators at a marionette show. If we peer behind this carnival mask, we see Willy Loman. Hence the Cashier cannot sustain the identity implied by the words "Ecce homo" that seem to be formed by the "gasp" and "sigh" of the dying man. There is nothing sacrificial in the death which he prefers to jail; nothing is affirmed.

Whether or not it works, the hinting of a Christ in the Cashier is an effort to discover a secret stature in the "little man." Thus the effort implies, rather early in the game, a subconscious measure of dissatisfaction with the little man as such. To declare that he is larger than he is risks sentimentality, but perhaps it is a lesser risk than simply being content with him as he is.

IV. Convergence of Idioms: Duerrenmatt's "Visit"

One play, and significantly the most recent of those examined in this chapter, brings together the various styles and modes that we have noted in a half-score of plays in which the money theme figures. Duerrenmatt's *The Visit* (1956) has a good deal of realistic theater: the town Guellen is an individual place, not a generalized no-man's-land or everyman's-land; we have a sense of participating in actual lives; there is a tight over-all plot rather than a set of illustrative scenes as in *From Morn to Midnight*. Yet there is also a strong air of the morality play; most of the characters are simply identified by position (Mayor, Priest, Schoolmaster, Claire's "Husbands VII–IX"), and they are different manifestations of Everyman. Finally, Duerrenmatt makes striking use of expressionistic devices to give a new edge to moral reality: a rich woman arrives in Guellen with a fancy black coffin amid mountains of baggage, two gangsters who speak in unison and carry her in a sedan chair, two fat little blind eunuchs who echo each other's words, an eighty-year-old ex-judge as butler, a black panther as a lap dog, and an offer of a "million" to the town if they will kill a popular citizen about to become mayor. They say no, but they act yes.

Even more striking than the technical diversity is the modal range. At the beginning we see Guellen in a desperate economic plight: we are in a melodrama of disaster. But a former resident, now the very rich Claire Zachanassian, is due for a visit, and all expect a bonanza. It appears that a *dea ex machina* may produce a happy-ending melodrama. Then we find that it is Claire herself who has brought about the economic doldrums: we are in a revenge melodrama with a revenger who in her thoroughness and ingenuity reminds us, as do other obsessed modern characters, of the Jacobean. Having wrecked the town, she will now save it handsomely: she will pay a great price and charge a great price. To get the "million" the town must kill popular Alfred Ill because years ago he had got her pregnant, charged her with promiscuity to save his skin, and thus driven her out of town and into prostitution. They turn her down, but Act I closes with her words, "I'll wait." In all this there is a Tourneur brilliance.

Though vastly intensified by malice and made sinister by an offhand ironic manner, Claire is like Volpone: both succeed in proving that people will do anything for money. Insofar as this is the burden, each play is a melodrama of the worst kind of disaster, the moral. But in *Volpone* the pay-any-price characters are actuated by greed; in *The Visit*, by need. In theory at least, greed is getting too much icing on the cake: one chooses to gobble, and can choose not to. Need does not allow a choice; one cannot do without bread. Hence the *Volpone* plot can have a gamesomeness that brings to mind the picaresque. In *The*

Visit there is no hit-and-run roguery; in revenge or starvation there is an all-out intensity, close to desperation. Hence there enters another dimension that one would never look for in *Volpone*, the tragic.

What Claire has done is put the people into the position of the tragic hero divided between impulse and imperative—the impulse to regain average good health in the community (work and pride as well as food), and the imperative not to kill, not to violate friendship, not to violate honor. The play examines the ability of the town to be tragic, and Duerrenmatt uses two methods of showing that it half tends to be so: it would like to adhere to the imperative and live with the consequences. His first method is to show the town initially rejecting the role of murder, incorporated. The second is to condense this mood in one sentient person, the Schoolmaster, and have him seek to by-pass the bitter choice: he tries to warn Alfred Ill, the designated victim, about the town's turning against him, and he tries to persuade Claire to take another tack. But humanistic reason is ineffectual in the face of the passion for revenge and the passion to survive. The Schoolmaster desperately feels himself being sucked in by the community spirit, a final ironic comment on the impact of the humanities on humanity.

In rejecting what we might call death with honor, the town, like all tragic heroes, lets an impulse rule. It goes further and invents a phony imperative: with a pretentious ritual of executing justice it murders Ill and gets the million (it is as if Thebes had done away with Oedipus for a bonus). It even plays its own game a step further and honors Ill after the event (a parallel to the strategic canonization of Joan Dark in *St. Joan of the Stockyards*). Yet it could still be tragic; it could still be divided in feeling; it could recognize what it has done; and it could keep in mind the cost of the town's life. But the town has forced division out of its soul; it has got rid of the conscience which it showed when the offer was first made; it seems to have secured the comfort of an undivided embracing of the profits it has chosen. In other words, it has decided to live permanently in a melodrama instead of a tragedy. Claire's revenge against Ill, whom she has caused to be murdered, is much less subtle than her revenge against the town, which she has bribed to commit murder and to translate the payoff into the just reward of civic virtue. We can view Duerrenmatt as a ferocious Gulliverian satirist of human crassness, or as a detached observer noting that people will do anything to survive and to substitute the relative comfort of melodrama for the tragic suffering that could lead to spiritual renewal. In either role we could detect a wholly antitragic cynicism.

Yet, for all of his cool skepticism, Duerrenmatt does not deny the possibility of tragic life. Alfred Ill, who Oedipus-like precipitated the community disaster by casual wrong conduct years before, is presented tragically. He is reduced from leading citizen to enemy of the people; public disgrace is a painful punishment. He might be able to run away; the scene of his abortive departure from Guellen is done with such skillful ambiguity that we are not sure whether an apparent moral preventiveness in the townspeople is an objective reality or an objectification of his own sense of guilt. If he could not actually avoid the penalty, he could at least resist it by self-exculpation, blame, and indignation: minimize the past, insist on present virtue, charge Claire with mad malice, whine at and vituperate his faithless friends. The point is that he does none of these things but accepts his own guilt. He even accepts the humiliation of a judgment by tainted judges. Yet he maintains his dignity: he will not run out by a suicide that would take his neighbors off the hook.

So we have a significant strand of tragic action in a fabric dominantly melodramatic. We can regard it as an ironically inadequate counterbalance to a despairing view of the whole human scene. But tragic heroes are always a minority of the population. At least there is a tragic accent to affirm the persistence of the tragic consciousness.

V. MONEY AND MODES

The money theme, then, can be treated in different modal styles. Expectably there is a good deal of satire, which is really a melodrama of the dramatist as good man against the bad conduct of some men. Or the drama can interpret money-seeking less as a correctable folly open to ridicule than as an almost nonhuman force, like an epidemic: hence the naturalism in Becque and Tolstoi, who write basically the melodrama of the victim. Another dramatist may see the money game as a rather charming adventure, less a matter of unbalanced values than of skillful gamesmanship, as in a perverse knighthood: hence the picaresque. Beside the doomed quest for triumph by the charismatic rogue is the equally doomed quest of a romantic everyman, hoping by monetary extravagance to capture emotional extravagance: the Kaiser morality play that, verging on a tragic inner conflict of values, secures at least a dividedness of appeal. There are other ways of altering the basic monopathic character of melodrama. Miss Hellman sees the successful worldlings in a final uneasy stasis in which their own rivalries render triumph ambiguous; Becque modifies the naturalistic gloom with a final glimpse of an ambiguous survival of victims. Galsworthy manages a completely polypathic treatment of melodramatic conflict: the possible conflict of good versus evil does not materialize as each side goes into battle with a complex mixture of principle, will to triumph, and internal disharmony. In contrast, Odets' *Awake and Sing*, asserting hope by ignoring the human frailties that have been dramatized, exemplifies melodrama on the sentimental side.

A third of the plays aspire to the tragic: they center on the man with the flaw, the man who tries to beat one game or another, who is the victim not of others but of himself, and who understands or comes to understand his actions. Odets' *Golden Boy* is the least successful of these: the tragic concept is betrayed by an inadequate sense of character, the design by a thinness of flesh and blood. Tolstoi and Duerrenmatt portray convincingly the coming to self-knowledge of men who can break away from the crassness of their own communities: the tragic possibility of salvation—the rejection of ignorance, of self-justification, of blame of others, of indifference—is maintained, if not literally for the community as a whole, at least symbolically within the community. Tolstoi's community is too narrow to give his drama full tragic resonance. Duerrenmatt's community is more of a microcosm, but, in contrast with Sophocles' Thebes, the plague goes on in a counterdimension, sickness yielding to the illusion of health. The closing note is sardonic rather than tragic. Still, the tragic individual remains imaginable.

Epilogue

To go back to chapter 1: there we saw Camus and Duerrenmatt giving or implying definitions of tragedy and talking about the possibilities of tragedy in the twentieth century. Addressing an audience in 1955, Camus ascribed to our era the cultural conditions—the rival authorities of conflicting beliefs and values in a transitional age—which might nourish great tragedy. Talking to an interviewer in 1969, Duerrenmatt put a finger on another aspect of our times—the vastness and impersonality of power (and by extension the smallness and insignificance of man)—and declared it hostile to tragedy.

After looking in some detail at a few score of plays, we may have done enough sampling to declare in favor of one or the other. Yet the evidence does not wholly justify one or the other. Camus was making a prediction, and a great deal more of the future will have to become the past before we can look back with assurance and credit him with foresight. It will be a long time before we know whether we have produced the quantity of tragic writing which is a precondition of quality; and if we were to profess a complete conviction of quality in our contemporaries, history might smile at our naïveté. Duerrenmatt was mentioning only one aspect of the modern situation, not picturing it completely; he did not name conditions that are favorable to tragedy, or acknowledge that dramatists of talent may surmount unfavorable conditions.

Let us transpose the statements of both men from the predictive idiom into the descriptive: then Camus is saying that tragedy is expectable in our day, and Duerrenmatt is saying that it is not. Still there is the problem of "our day," which we cannot reduce to a decade or two. We cannot see the present in its future extension; hence we may legitimately treat "our day" as including some of its roots in the immediate past. Since the nineteenth century has not been thought of as an age of tragedy, to give it some share of our survey may seem only to increase the odds in favor of Duerrenmatt. Yet in a period of about one hundred years we find a reasonably steady activity of the tragic sense. We mention it repeatedly in discussing the three Americans; we speak of the "presence of an impulse toward tragedy in the works of three Europeans who . . . formally practice other modes"; of an apparently representative protagonist in the plays surveyed by decades we can say that the "personality belongs in the tragic realm." If our plays do not often elicit the word *great*, still there is much of the authentic. Granted, the appearance of the words *tragedy* and *tragic* on title pages, in prefaces, or in texts does not itself guarantee the authentic. When Camus writes a work that makes him willing to use the term *tragedy*, he comes very close, but when it is used by, or applied to, Lorca and O'Casey, we find that the literary object is actually a drama of disaster. Ghelderode's *Death of Doctor Faustus* may be a kind of farewell to the tragic possibilities of the myth; on the other hand, Tolstoi takes the unlikely nonmythic theme of money-lust in a tough little village and turns the material of naturalism into true tragic form. Even of the field of money dramas, which we might expect to be infertile, we say that the "tragic individual remains imaginable."

By "the tragic sense" I allude not to an essence from which flows formal perfection, but to the imagination that, with greater or less skill, takes hold of reality in tragic terms. ("Tragic impulse" conveys the same meaning.) The dramatist with the tragic sense sees individual choice as the origin of significant action and situation, the strength of the tensions within man, his dividedness, his capacity both for error and for ultimate understanding, his moral substance that rebels against blindness and despair. It is interesting to find touches of this even in a dramatist philosophically committed to a societal view of reality, such as Brecht; he perceives dividedness in the title characters in *St. Joan of the Stockyards* and *Mother Courage,* and to an extent in *Galileo.* In other words, the tragic sense may be present in a dramatist without leading him into an encompassing use of tragic form. Hence I have repeatedly used such terms as "realm of tragedy" and "tragic accent" to describe either the general tendency of a play or the presence of certain elements in it.

We can say of O'Neill that he worked dominantly in the realm of tragedy. His characters are nearly always inwardly troubled, often clearly divided, men. Sometimes, however, O'Neill drifts toward the panoramic or the allegorical; once or twice he credits people with a salvation that seems to come about rather quickly; more often his divided characters tend to be ailing and weak and unable to find their way out of an emotional or psychic morass. Thus, though he works in the realm of tragedy, his most characteristic inner form is the disaster of personality, that is, the melodrama of failure, with the pathetic note gaining ascendancy. O'Neill is virtually obsessed by man's inability to bear self-knowledge, his weakness before fact, his need of illusion: in this sense he all but says that tragedy cannot be written. Yet the integrity of his sense of disaster, and the passionate assertions of human failure, give his work a singular massiveness.

Tennessee Williams likewise works mainly in the realm of tragedy: he has O'Neill's sense of inner discords as the genesis of significant action. He also has O'Neill's sense of human liability to disaster, but in place of O'Neill's almost cosmic despair Williams has a sense of clinical disability in individuals—Blanche, Brick, Alma, Sebastian. His characters may veer toward total illness or strive for self-knowledge, which for them is not the catastrophe that it is for many O'Neill characters. With Williams, the problem is to find in potentially tragic beings the kind of strength that appears, for instance, in Hannah Jelkes and that could create full tragic character.

Arthur Miller deliberately made a turn away from victims, who, like Willy Loman, can never be tragic, to the strong self-injuring personality in *A View from the Bridge.* If Eddie Carbone resists self-knowledge to the end, he at least does not suffer from passivity and debility; in his aggressive vigor he is potentially tragic. Miller likewise presents such strong characters in *The Crucible,* in which several dramatis personae are capable of self-criticism, and John Proctor at least contributes to his own disaster. Above all, the Reverend John Hale discovers that his effort to cure an abomination has created another abomination. He could be the tragic hero, but his role is minor: through him, then, the play has a "tragic accent." Hale has the hubris of the savior; the protagonist of Lawler's *Summer of the Seventeenth Doll* has the hubris of the young champion who believes he will be a young champion forever. He, however, stops short of doing the irreversible injury of the full tragic cycle. The aggressive antagonists in Albee's *Who's Afraid of Virginia Woolf?* also stop short of an irremediable evildoing, but not of the self-understanding and rejection of illusion that conclude the tragic rhythm. Julian in *Tiny Alice* is partly the victim but also partly the man capable of choice and self-examination, that is, the tragic figure.

Of numerous plays we can say that, like those just mentioned, they border on tragedy or have a tragic accent. This may happen even in ideological plays, like those of Brecht as we have seen; Büchner sets out to prove determinism, but more than once his characters have the air of being free and of choosing and indeed of sensing an ambiguity in their own rectitude. There are infusions of the tragic even in a picaresque drama like Wedekind's *Marquis of Keith* and in a morality play of the little man such as Kaiser's *From Morn to Midnight*. There are touches of self-judgment in the romantic heroine of Betti's *The Queen and the Rebels*. At one point Frisch's Don Juan threatens to escape his imposed role of philosophic aspirant and to become the self-judging flawed man. In satirical melodrama we repeatedly find the self-critical man who knows his own responsibility—the schoolteacher in Duerrenmatt's *Visit* and in Frisch's *Andorra*. Though Duerrenmatt denies that tragedy is possible and proposes to transfer tragic functions to comedy, he has given the strongest possible tragic accent to *The Visit*—in Alfred Ill, the original wrongdoer who has brought disaster to his town but who, when everyone else develops moral callousness in the struggle to survive, decides to flee his innocence and to embrace his guilt. The tragic character has a still larger share of the stage in Camus's *Misunderstanding*, in which the son-murdering mother accepts her guilt and rejects the survival in the world that is possible to her. In three dramas of modern politics in which one might reasonably expect only the melodrama of survival, center stage is held by a tragic figure whose self-judgment in his climactic action: Sartre's *Altona*, Kingsley's *Darkness at Noon*, and Zuckmayer's *The Devil's General*.

The tragic sense is also maintained in indirect ways. In *The Marriage of Mr. Mississippi* Duerrenmatt dramatizes a strange paradox, the perversion of the tragic by the figure of Puritanism: Mr. Mississippi's self-judgment becomes a self-flagellation which is finally self-indulgent and coexists with a punitiveness toward the rest of the world. Frisch's *Biography* and Sartre's *No Exit*, which I have called posttragic, show man, after it is all over, coming to see the relationship between his choices and his personality, and gradually acknowledging a truth that he has spent an adult life in concealing from himself.

The tragic sense persists tenaciously, then, despite the old saw that our day does not nourish it, and despite many elements in the culture that are clearly not hospitable to it. Whether it survives more tenuously than in previous ages it is impossible to tell; if we seem not to match the ages of great tragedy, we can remember that they do not occur frequently and that some ages have no tragedy. Wherever we come in comparatively, the tragic perspective on reality is not dead, and this is fortunate. Our problem has been that we talk a good deal about the tragic, and that *tragedy* and *tragic* are clichés; unhappily they have become vulgarisms too, that is, so inaccurate and gross in meaning that we have been in danger of losing all perception of what the tragic is. In popular usage—ordinary conversation, press, television, and even much of education—tragedy is used to mean nothing more than undifferentiated unpleasantness and misfortune. This usage shuts out all distinctions between the disaster in which we are not implicated and the more meaningful troubles that come, in one way or another, out of our own choices. This failure to make distinctions can let us think that we are innocent and that suffering comes only from bad luck and bad people, that is, other people. This state of mind is inferior equipment for facing reality.

Since tragedy is a fact of life as well as a form of literature, it is well for us if we can distinguish the tragic, in which we are implicated, from the disastrous, in which we are victims. Hence the importance of our having an authentic literature: it should serve as one counterinfluence against the popular view of catastrophe in which essential distinctions are not made. There is always the older tragedy, which we cannot do without. But because we are especially attuned to drama in recent idiom, there is great importance in what our theater has been doing and is doing. Life does imitate art. The modes of intuiting reality which govern the stage do make an impress on the imagination; hence, in however subtle forms, they influence our sense of what is and of what is possible. And that sense can hardly help being reflected, if only at a distant remove, in action. Réné Wellek regards it as possible that "important historical changes have come about through the insidious influence of books, slowly, deviously, in inextricable combinations with other factors." [1] If drama steadily maintains an image of tragic life, there is less likelihood that a culture will slip into an inadequate one-sided view of the evil—or for that matter the good—in the world. In view of the antitragic elements in our culture (which we reviewed in chapter 1), we might say that the steady persistence of the tragic form implies a transcendence of the times by art.* But it is probably more

---

* That art does transcend its times is a truth, but the truth is not without its problems. For one thing, it can become a truism, a loose, unanalyzed rendering of tribute. For another, the idea of art as transcendent is easily diminished into the idea of artist as rebel, an idea of vocation that may reduce the holder of it to a pamphleteer. The artist's only sound "rebellion" is actually the affirmation of validities not esteemed at the moment, but this may lie underneath and be sensed as rebellion only in retrospect. The self-conscious rebel is not likely to achieve any kind of transcendence, for as rebel he is committed to obvious targets: in our day, for instance, "The Establishment," that all-purpose whipping boy against which a few blows are generally taken as the mark of an independent thinker. Not that establishments never deserve whipping, but that their errors stand out in plain view and make rebellion an easy form of conventional anticonventionality. It is more difficult to rebel against injurious habits of mind when they are subtle than when they are conspicuous. We see little rebellion against the idea that tragedy embraces all kinds of rebuff and misery, though the persistence of the idea will be fatal to a great dramatic form; the idea rather charms us by democratically ennobling every man's pursuit of unhappiness. If there is no serious rebellion against such a majority cliché, how much less likely is rebellion against what we might call minority clichés—those that appear in the book-review section rather than on the front page. No one rebels against *indictment* or *compassion* as primary terms of praise for literary accomplishment, though these qualities may appear in third-rate art, and though the frequency of the terms strengthens the evildoers-and-victims way of looking at the world and weakens the tragic way. It is hard to rebel against self-exonerating clichés, especially when they are of elite provenience and currency: the stress on the genesis of conduct, which tends to undermine the idea of answerableness (an elite cliché which has actually been democratized); the idea that the modern world is more formidable to its human constituents than were earlier worlds to theirs, and hence renders individuals less capable of bearing it and of engaging in significant action; the idea that existence is in all parts an irrational muddle that must evoke despair, that the "human lot" is too grim for tears.

It should be obvious that this is not a bland, unqualified attack on such views and habits of thought; I am not saying that there is no degree of truth in them,

accurate to say that art is reflecting the less conspicuous elements in modern consciousness.

We live both melodramas and tragedies as well as write them; so it is a good thing for our sense of life if both are written well. If I devote more time and attention to the achievements in tragedy, it is only that it is the more easily threatened form, that its demise has been predicted, and, above all, that the melodramatic is a much more readily adopted mode of feeling and thought. We instinctively fall into a posture of confrontation with the world; it is much harder for us to confront ourselves. It is this latter, indispensable confrontation that tragedy subtly serves through the impact that imaginative life has upon moral life. Hence the meaningfulness of the persisting tragic tone in drama, be it in full-scale tragedies or in the frequent presence of the tragic realm and of tragic accents.

We should remember that tragedy as well as melodrama can fall short of its best possibilities. This happens when the course from dividedness to self-knowledge is too short, the moral recovery too easy, the penance too welcome, the guilt almost gay. The historic examples are Thomas Heywood's *Woman Killed with Kindness* and George Lillo's *London Merchant*. There is something of the too-quick coming around in O'Neill's *Days Without End* and *A Touch of the Poet*, and Odets' *Golden Boy* suffers because the dividedness is not plausibly dramatized. Since we tend to use *melodrama* as a pejorative term, we are the more aware of its characteristic failing—the simplifications that offer us a too easy pattern of life. They are expectable; in confrontations with the world or some part of it, we naturally see ourselves as unmixed figures—victims, winners, always competitors on the right side, against others who are at best doubtful. This is the situation in Odets' *Awake and Sing* and Hellman's *Little Foxes*. The pro-virtue, anti-evil stance is hard to resist; it produces, and in turn gains strength from, a flood of popular plays and novels.

There are two alternatives to this stance: to see the dividedness in oneself, and to see the dividedness in the situation. The former is the way of superior tragedy, the latter the way of superior melodrama. In two plays, neither very effective as drama, Arthur Miller speaks for

and that there is no area of relevance for them. The point is rather that in our day they have a peculiar appeal that it is not easy to challenge, and that they are all inimical to the tragic perspective.

these two ways of escaping from an inadequate sense of reality. In both *After the Fall* and *Incident at Vichy* he attacks man's assumption of innocence and his denial of guilt; that is, he tells man to be aware of his own tragic complexities. Further, in both these dramas Miller attacks the idea that people, individuals and classes, are easily divisible into good and evil—that is, the basic concept of "popular" melodrama. In *After the Fall* Quentin refers to the time "when there were good people and bad people" and to "how easy it was to tell." Both Miller's *Incident at Vichy* and Frisch's *Andorra* start with a clear-cut evil, anti-Semitism, and try, while not mitigating its horrors, to carry it into its universal dimension, to interpret it as one symbol of all parochialism and particularism of feeling—the melodramatic simplification of all emotion by reducing it to class feeling, complacency and vanity on one's own account, and scorn and hatred of "the other." In *When the War Was Over* Frisch takes up the same problem at the level of nationalistic feeling.

To oppose the stuff of easy-to-take melodramatic life is to speak for good melodrama, that is, for a sense of the dividedness in the situation which calls for dividedness of response. With courage Miller makes Quentin sum it up this way: "The worst son of a bitch, if he loved Jews and hated Hitler, he was a buddy." That is, when melodrama works from the way things are and not from the way we like to see them, it offers no painless loyalties and choices, for it catches the doubleness in men and in situations. Modern drama is often excellent in this melodramatic mode. In *Jungle of Cities* Brecht gets hold of an ambivalent relationship that conjoins love and hate. Galsworthy's *Strife* transmutes a capital-and-labor dispute into a struggle for power between two opposed leaders who have the same virtues, strength and integrity, and the same vice, ruinous relentlessness. In the pursuit of spiritual perfection Montherlant's *Master of Santiago* manages to be as arrogant as he is dedicated. In Miller's *The Price* Victor Franz may be the faithful son of a failed father, or a resentful man who has used self-sacrifice as a weapon against his brother, or both. Giraudoux's Electra has a cause and stands for virtue but is inflexible and even destructive; Aegisthus, always a sinner in myth, convinces us that he can save the city in a desperate crisis. Traditional victims, in Arden, become people difficult to put up with, and, in Frisch's *Firebugs*, destroyers; in the latter, the traditional oppressor is victimized and destroyed, but he is also guilty and foolish. One of the finest of modern melodramas is Camus's *Caligula:* the title character is a ruthless sadist, but he is also ruthless in intelligence and in his own kind of morality; and finally, indeed, he is the embodiment of certain everyman virtues and motives carried to an extreme.

Caligula is in part a revenger, a type rendered brilliantly in other modern characters—in Camus's Martha in *The Misunderstanding,* in Duerrenmatt's Claire Zachanassian in *The Visit,* in Pirandello's Henry IV, and in Hofmannsthal's Electra. Here the melodrama proceeds by the complete grasp of an overwhelming passion, a passion that starts in justice and goes on to become something monstrous and diabolic, embracing a doubleness that we have long thought of as Jacobean.

By grasping the dividedness in persons and situations, such plays forbid hackneyed responses. They are committed against the cliché. Whether they are expressionistic or realistic, mythic or topical, they are avoiding the expectable. They forgo indictment and compassion, the modes of editorializing that so easily draw us in; they do not damn what oft is damned, or praise what is patently praiseworthy; they use no common trademarks of good and evil. Instead they proceed freshly, often fantastically, to set forth the ageless lineaments of human conduct in crises, the contradictions inevitably present because motives are mingled and situations ambiguous. The masters of melodrama do not capitalize on the never dormant readiness to damn, pity, or applaud. On the contrary, in prodding us by strange devices and fantastic parables to "see ourselves for what we are," they help prepare the climate for the tragedy in which the individual creates catastrophe and moves through it to self-knowledge. Their imagining of the disorder in the world opens the door to knowing the disorder in the soul.

Good melodrama makes dividedness in the world visible to us in the audience. When we are accustomed to seeing this dividedness, we are at least prepared for imaginative entering into dividedness through the consciousness of the hero, that is, for the tragic mode, for the experience of knowing incompatible motives, of making choices, of being responsible. In life we do not always welcome this experience; we find reasons why we cannot be responsible. Rolf Hochhuth points to one consequence: ". . . it would be the end of the drama if one were to take the position that man cannot be held responsible for his fate." [2] It would certainly be the end of great melodrama and of tragic drama. But if the plays at which I have looked in this essay are representative, we have not come to that unhappy end. Something in the climate helps keep the major forms alive, and they in turn help maintain the climate. Melo-drama contributes to a perception of doubleness, especially the double-ness of a singleness that has become excessive or even oppressive. The role of tragedy is to imagine man in strength as well as weakness, a strength that is not created by sheer undividedness of being but per-sists despite dividedness; that manifests itself in evil action but does not commit man unalterably to evil; that enables him to come to self-recognition rather than leads him to flee from it, and to live with what in time he knows.

Notes

Chapter One

1. *Lichtenberg: Aphorisms and Letters,* ed. and trans. Franz Mautner and Henry Hatfield (London: Jonathan Cape, 1969), p. 54.
2. Violet Ketels, "Friedrich Duerrenmatt at Temple University," *Journal of Modern Literature* 1 (1970):95.
3. Ibid., pp. 94, 105.
4. The quotations in this paragraph are all from p. 94.
5. Albert Camus, "On the Future of Tragedy," *Lyrical and Critical Essays,* ed. Philip Thody, trans. Ellen Conroy Kennedy (New York: Alfred A. Knopf, 1968), pp. 297, 298.
6. Ibid., pp. 301, 302, 304, 305.
7. Ibid., pp. 306, 308, 309.
8. Marguerite Yourcenar, *Memoirs of Hadrian* (1951), trans. Grace Frick (New York: Farrar, Straus and Young, Anchor Books, 1955), p. 288.
9. Camus, "On the Future of Tragedy," pp. 305, 307.
10. Eugene Goodheart, "Lawrence and Christ," *Partisan Review* 31 (1964):44.
11. Pauline Kael, "Movie Chronicle: Little Men," *Partisan Review* 29 (1962):564.
12. Harold Rosenberg, "Literary Form and Social Hallucination," *Partisan Review* 27 (1960): 647.
13. Louis-Ferdinand Céline, *Journey to the End of the Night,* trans. John H. Marks (New York: New Directions, 1960), p. 416.
14. Mary Renault, *The Mask of Apollo* (New York: Random House, 1966), p. 64.

15. Ruby Cohn, *Currents in Contemporary Drama* (Bloomington and London: Indiana University Press, 1969), p. 86. Cf. her remark on the paucity of "heroic plays" in America (p. 151).

16. John N. Morris, *Versions of the Self* (New York and London: Basic Books, 1966), pp. 102–3.

17. Carlo Levi, *Christ Stopped at Eboli*, trans. Frances Frenaye (New York: Farrar, Straus, 1947), p. 155.

18. Ruby Cohn notes that Peter Weiss "seeks to encourage indignation through the theater" (*Currents in Contemporary Drama*, p. 52). John Russell Taylor entitles a book *The Angry Theatre* (New York: Hill and Wang, 1962; rev. ed., 1969).

19. F. R. Leavis, *The Common Pursuit* (New York: G. W. Stewart, 1952), p. 86.

20. Reinhold Niebuhr, *The Nature and Destiny of Man* (New York: Charles Scribner's Sons, 1946), I:100–101.

21. Eugene Goodheart, *The Cult of the Ego: The Self in Modern Literature* (Chicago: University of Chicago Press, 1968), p. 75.

22. Ziolkowski, *Dimensions of the Modern Novel*, p. 46.

23. Ibid., pp. 144–45.

24. Mary Renault, *The Bull from the Sea* (New York: Random House, Pantheon Books, 1962), pp. 323–24. Another novelist, Janice Warnke, has a similar perception: ". . . those crippled souls who struck out against their fellow men in a vain attempt to murder the universe. . . ." This is in *A Pursuit of Furies* (New York: Random House, 1966), p. 309. Camus comes at this situation from the opposite direction: "For there is only misfortune in not being loved; there is misery in not loving. All of us, today, are dying of this misery" ("Return to Tipasa," *Lyrical and Critical Essays*, p. 168). Cf. Rainer Maria Rilke's theory of love (Ziolkowski, *Dimensions of the Modern Novel*, pp. 35–36).

25. James Baldwin, *Notes of a Native Son* (New York: Dial Press, 1963), p. 91.

26. An analogous thought is expressed in Arthur Miller's *Incident at Vichy* (New York: Viking Press, 1965), p. 66: "Jew is only the name we give to that stranger, that agony we cannot feel, that death we look at like a cold abstraction. Each man has his Jew; it is the other. And the Jews have their Jews." One of the first strong treatments of "the other" is Emily Brontë's portrayal of Heathcliff in *Wuthering Heights*.

27. Ketels, "Duerrenmatt at Temple," p. 103.

28. Henri Peyre, *French Novelists of Today* (New York: Oxford University Press, 1967), p. 369.

29. Cf. Cohn, *Currents in Contemporary Drama*, p. 24.

30. Ketels, "Duerrenmatt at Temple," p. 98.

31. Saul Bellow, *Herzog* (New York: Viking Press, 1964), p. 290. Cf. the previous quotations from *Memoirs of Hadrian* (p. 9) and from Goodheart on Lawrence (p. 11).

32. Ziolkowski, *Dimensions of the Modern Novel*, pp. 44–45.

33. Renault, *Mask of Apollo*, p. 64.

34. Diana Trilling, "After the Profumo Case," *Partisan Review* 31 (1964):62.

35. Quoted from *The Tangled Bank* (1962) by Griffin Taylor, "The Province of the Poem Is Not Dark," *Sewanee Review* 72 (1964):701–2.

36. Cf. Hugh Dickinson, *Myth on the Modern Stage* (Urbana, Chicago, and London: University of Illinois Press, 1969), and Cohn, *Currents in Contemporary Drama*, pp. 86–103. Thomas E. Porter's *Myth and Modern American Drama* (Detroit: Wayne State University Press, 1969) has some usefulness here, though its main concern is the dramatic use of more modern "myths."

37. Robert Penn Warren, *All the King's Men* (1946), and T. Harry Williams, *Huey Long* (1969). Long, of course, contains only the seeds of Warren's Willie Stark. Williams does not press the point, but more than once he identifies, or implies, specifically tragic features in Long.

38. Ruby Cohn says that tragedy, which needs heroes, "virtually disappears from the contemporary stage" (*Currents in Contemporary Drama*, p. 154).

Chapter Two

1. Albert Camus, "On the Future of Tragedy," *Lyrical and Critical Essays*, ed. Philip Thody, trans. Ellen Conroy Kennedy (New York: Alfred A. Knopf, 1968), p. 301.

2. For a longer justification of the term see my *Tragedy and Melodrama* (Seattle and London: University of Washington Press, 1968), pp. 74–87. We might designate the form by such a term as "paratragic," which would have the advantage of acknowledging certain affinities with the tragic, i.e., the presence or threat of catastrophe. But *paratragic* implies not only resemblance but deficiency or falseness, whereas *melodrama* implies, I hope, a formal entity with its own kind of achievement.

3. Herbert Greenberg, *Quest for the Necessary: W. H. Auden and the Dilemma of Divided Consciousness* (Cambridge, Mass.: Harvard University Press, 1968), p. 202.

4. Ibid., p. 85.

5. Gene Baro, "Montherlant and the Morals of Adjustment," *Sewanee Review* 69 (1961):704–5.

6. The first quotation is from a letter to Edmund Gosse. See Linette F. Brugmans, ed., *The Correspondence of André Gide and Edmund Gosse 1904–1928* (London: Peter Owen, 1960), p. 158. The second quotation is from the editor's note on the passage, p. 159.

7. M. A. Ruff, *Baudelaire*, trans. Agnes Kertesz (New York: New York University Press, 1966), pp. 89–90.

8. Oscar Wilde, *The Picture of Dorian Gray* (New York: Random House, n.d.), p. 145. Dorian speaks to the painter of the portrait, Basil Hallward, who carries on: "The prayer of your pride has been answered. The prayer of your repentance will be answered also" (p. 175). *Pride* and *repentance* name not only moral opposites such as those noted by Montherlant and Gide, but those often associated with tragedy.

9. Camus, "On the Future of Tragedy," p. 304.

10. J. A. Bryant, Jr., *Hippolyta's View* (Lexington: University of Kentucky Press, 1961), p. 112.

11. Greenberg, *Quest for the Necessary*, p. 116.

12. Mary Renault, *The Mask of Apollo* (New York: Pantheon Books, 1966), p. 189.

13. Mary Renault, *The Bull from the Sea* (New York: Pantheon Books, 1962), p. 93.

14. Martin Esslin rarely speaks banally. But he surely did so in saying that Oedipus' guilt was "senselessly imposed on him by a blind, implacable fate." This was in a syndicated theater piece several years ago.

15. Clifford Leech, *Tragedy* (London: Methuen, 1969), p. 39. This is interesting, for on the whole Leech's view of tragedy differs considerably from the one advanced in this volume; for Leech, the tragic situation is a certain inexorableness of things of which the ultimate model is death.

16. John Holloway, *The Story of the Night* (Lincoln: University of Nebraska Press, 1963), p. 124.

17. Tom F. Driver, *The Sense of History in Greek and Shakespearean Drama* (New York: Columbia University Press, 1960), p. 200. Driver here quotes the Niebuhr passage from *The Self and the Dramas of History* (New York: Charles Scribner's Sons, 1955), p. 78. Driver believes that what is true of the Greeks is not true of the Elizabethans; here I disagree with him and do agree with Camus.

18. Ruff, *Baudelaire*, p. 131. Ruff also points out that in his "Poëme du Haschisch" Baudelaire "was denouncing the sin of disembodiment" (p. 130)—i.e., a superinduced "angelism." Ruff's following statement should be unusually meaningful after the developments of the 1960s: the drug "brought on the paroxysm: 'I have become God!' "

19. Renault, *Mask of Apollo*, pp. 193, 196. A similar view of Pentheus appears in a brilliant longer analysis by William Arrowsmith in the introduction to his translation of the *Bacchae* in *The Complete Greek Tragedies*, ed. David Grene and Richmond Lattimore (Chicago: University of Chicago Press, 1956–59), 4:534ff.

20. Camus, "On the Future of Tragedy," p. 302.

21. Ibid., pp. 301–2.

22. John N. Morris attributes to William James the view "that only the sick soul,' the 'divided self' who has 'in his own person become the prey of a pathological melancholy,' can know the world for what it is" (*Versions of the Self* [New York and London: Basic Books, 1966], p. 20). Though this is a different matter, it is related to the experience of the tragic hero. It applies almost literally to Lear.

23. Camus, "Return to Tipasa," *Lyrical and Critical Essays*, p. 169.

24. Marguerite Yourcenar, *Memoirs of Hadrian*, trans. Grace Frick (New York: Farrar, Straus and Young, 1954), p. 33. There is some relevance in the title of a recent book by Honor Matthews—*The Hard Journey: The Myth of Man's Rebirth* (New York: Barnes and Noble, 1968). Though she does not use the word *tragedy*, Miss Matthews writes of the achieving of self-knowledge as a central human experience. She examines the spatial imagery frequently used in imaginative accounts of this experience—journey, descent, return, etc.

25. Greenberg, *Quest for the Necessary*, p. 57. Auden also offers, as the best means for achieving the good life on earth, "Self-understanding" (p.

72). But this has to do with a moral regimen rather than with the disturbing anagnorisis of tragic life.

26. William Willeford, *The Fool and His Scepter: A Study in Clowns and Jesters and Their Audience* (Evanston, Ill.: Northwestern University Press, 1969), p. 165.

27. Violet Ketels, "Friedrich Duerrenmatt at Temple University," *Journal of Modern Literature* 1 (1970):101.

28. "The Almond Trees," *Lyrical and Critical Essays*, p. 136. In another essay Camus offers a very "healthy and immediately applicable thought": "What, in fact, does 'literature of despair' mean? Despair is silent. . . . Literature of despair is a contradiction in terms" ("The Enigma," p. 160).

29. Albert Camus, *The Fall*, trans. Justin O'Brien (Harmondsworth, Eng.: Penguin, 1965), p. 84.

30. *The Letters of Oscar Wilde*, ed. Rupert Hart-Davis (New York: Harcourt, Brace and World, 1962), p. 502.

31. In Anthony Shafton's novel *The Apostate Heriger* (New York: Grove Press, 1962), p. 48, the sinner says to his confessor, "But perhaps the wish to express myself, to detail my perversion to you, Father, is no more than vanity and pride— . . ."

32. Cf. Janice Warnke, *A Pursuit of Furies* (New York: Random House, 1966), p. 309: ". . . despair or guilt, the familiar low-burning diseases of the times."

33. Dorothy Richardson, *Pilgrimage* (New York: Alfred A. Knopf, 1967), 4:607.

34. Joyce Cary, *Herself Surprised* (New York: Harper and Brothers, 1941), p. 37. In using her words literally because they are appropriate in this context, I am taking them out of an ironic context; the injunction "Know thyself" is really inapplicable to Cary's urban child of nature. Self-knowledge becomes the material of pathetic comedy in Murray Schisgal's *The Typists* (1963).

35. J. Percy Smith, *The Unrepentant Pilgrim: A Study of the Development of Bernard Shaw* (Boston: Houghton Mifflin, 1965), p. 256. He is speaking of the self-understanding that is reached in comedy.

36. C. P. Snow, *The Masters* (New York: Charles Scribner's Sons, 1951), p. 52. In seeking self-knowledge, of course, one can be pat, hasty, or premature. Well-intended as his quest may be, a youth cannot find out "who I am" because he isn't yet. Being is not discoverable in becoming.

37. Quoted by Smith, *The Unrepentant Pilgrim*, p. 250.

38. Leech, *Tragedy*, p. 54.

39. Cf. Giraudoux's view, set forth in his "Discourse" of 1931, that drama "communicates through feeling rather than through understanding; without knowing it, the spectators, through their participation in an act of communal ritual, absorb the prophecy and vision of dramatic art at its highest reach." This summary is made by Haskell M. Block and Robert G. Shedd, eds., *Masters of Modern Drama* (New York: Random House, 1962), p. 700. Cf. also Morris Freedman, *The Moral Impulse: Modern Drama from Ibsen to the Present* (Carbondale and Edwardsville: Southern Illinois University Press, 1967), pp. 111–12.

40. Leech, *Tragedy*, p. 51. Again, this is not central in Leech's thought,

but his obiter dictum is valuable. Cf. also Cleanth Brooks, *The Hidden God* (New Haven, Conn., and London: Yale University Press, 1963), p. 132.

41. I have quoted from the Hofmannsthal version, which does condense somewhat. Cf. H. A. Hammelmann, *Hugo von Hofmannsthal* (New Haven, Conn.: Yale University Press, 1957), p. 35. For the literal translation from the Greek, see *Lucian*, Loeb Classical Library (London: Heinemann, 1936), 5:283.

42. Henry James, *The Art of the Novel: Critical Prefaces*, ed. Richard P. Blackmur (New York: Scribner, 1934), p. 62.

43. Ruby Cohn's *Currents in Contemporary Drama* (Bloomington and London: Indiana University Press, 1969) refers many times to the influence of Brechtian theory and practice on plays and playwrights.

44. Brooks, *The Hidden God*, p. 4.

45. Edward Alexander, review of Albert J. LaValley, *Carlyle and the Idea of the Modern*, in *Journal of English and Germanic Philology* 68 (1969):298.

46. See Eric Bentley, *The Playwright as Thinker* (New York: Reynal and Hitchcock, 1946), pp. 45ff.

47. Quoted from the "Apology" to *Mrs. Warren's Profession* by Smith, *Unrepentant Pilgrim*, p. 211.

48. Both Giraudoux quotations are Winifred Smith's translation in *Masters of Modern Drama*, ed. Block and Shedd.

49. Several years ago Sidney R. Homan and I independently reached similar conclusions about this structure and hit upon almost identical terms for it. See Homan's perceptive "Chapman and Marlowe: The Paradoxical Hero and the Divided Response," *Journal of English and Germanic Philology* 68 (1969), 391–406. My original terms were "dividedness of appeal" and "duality of response" (*Tragedy and Melodrama*, pp. 226, 289). I here adopt Homan's "dividedness of response" but stick to my original "dividedness of appeal," since I allude less to self-contradictions in characters than to the copresence of elements to which we do not respond identically. Incidentally, Homan and I used one example in common: George Chapman's *Bussy D'Ambois*. However, Homan does not make my distinction between tragedy and melodrama; he uses only the generic term *tragedy*. A somewhat different aspect of "dividedness of appeal" is discussed in "The Mixed Mood," chap. iv of Ruby Cohn's *Currents in Contemporary Drama*, pp. 154ff.

50. In Giraudoux's *Electra* Clytemnestra, who is on the defensive, puts it this way to Orestes and Electra, who are accusing her: "All the evil in the world is caused by the so-called pure people trying to dig up secrets and bring them to light" (II.iv in Winifred Smith's translation).

51. Ruby Cohn says the term would "describe any Sartre play" (*Currents in Contemporary Drama*, p. 60). Cf. Bentley, *Playwright as Thinker*, p. 237.

52. Apropos of this there is an interesting line in Carl Zuckmayer's *The Devil's General* (1942–45). General Harras is joking about a specially constructed bar in his apartment: "Everybody is born with a certain amount of bad taste. You have to fight against it to raise your general level, a kind of aesthetic self-analysis" (Act II, in the translation by Ingrid G. and William F. Gilbert in *Masters of Modern Drama*, ed. Block and Shedd).

53. Except in neoclassical France, modal purity has not been strongly marked in Western drama. Cf. Cohn, *Currents in Contemporary Drama*, pp. 53, 58.

54. Leech, *Tragedy*, p. 29.

Chapter Four

1. Eugene O'Neill, *The Iceman Cometh* (New York: Random House, 1946). This and the following quotation are in Act IV. The present comments on *Iceman* are relatively brief; there is a fuller analysis in *Tragedy and Melodrama*, pp. 49–55. Throughout I arbitrarily use upper-case roman numerals for "acts," lower-case romans for "scenes" and "episodes."

2. Jean Genet, *The Balcony*, trans. Bernard Frechtman (rev. version; New York: Grove Press, 1966), p. 35 (v). This is a translation of Genet's revised edition of 1962.

3. The phrase is used of him in the opening stage direction in I.i. Quotations are from the text in volume 3 of the three-volume edition of *The Plays of Eugene O'Neill* (New York: Random House, [1941]). Several characters in much later plays also have a "touch of the poet."

4. Most of the action of *The Straw* (1921), another pathetic drama, takes place in a tuberculosis sanitarium.

5. References are to the text in volume 2 of the three-volume edition.

6. References are to the text in volume 3 of the three-volume edition.

7. References are to the text in volume 3 of the three-volume edition.

8. Bible-reading and God-seeking (I.i), praying "like a Saint in the desert" (I.i), reading à Kempis (II.ii).

9. Arthur Miller, *After the Fall* (New York: Viking, 1964), Act I.

10. O'Neill also does this with the guilt and self-pity of Nina Leeds in *Strange Interlude*. Tennessee Williams was to do it repeatedly.

11. Citations are from the text in volume 3 of the three-volume edition.

12. The idea of "God the Mother" instead of "God the Father" is toyed with, inconclusively, by Nina Leeds in *Strange Interlude*.

13. References are to the text in volume 3 of the three-volume edition.

14. John H. Raleigh, *The Plays of Eugene O'Neill* (Carbondale: Southern Illinois University Press, 1965), p. 62; John Gassner, *Eugene O'Neill* (Minneapolis: University of Minnesota Press, 1965), p. 41.

15. Citations are from the text in volume 1 of the three-volume edition.

16. Christine says, "you forced him into your horrible war—!" and Ezra replies, a little later, "I've made a man of him" (Part I, Act III; in volume 2 of the three-volume edition, p. 48).

17. Maud Bodkin, *The Quest for Salvation in an Ancient and a Modern Play* (London and New York: Oxford University Press, 1941).

18. O'Neill presents the same theme with comic irony in *Hughie* (1959).

19. Of the surviving work, the latest, *A Moon for the Misbegotten*, was written in 1941–42. This date is given by Donald Gallup, curator of the O'Neill collection at Yale, in the prefatory note to his edition of *More Stately Mansions* (New Haven, Conn., and London: Yale University Press, 1964), p. vii. Raleigh gives 1943 (*The Plays of Eugene O'Neill*, p. 35); Gassner says it was completed in 1943 (*Eugene O'Neill*, p. 36). Gallup

gives the following dates of composition for the later work: A *Touch of the Poet*, 1936; *The Iceman Cometh*, 1939; *Long Day's Journey*, 1940; *More Stately Mansions*, 1938–41 (prefatory note, pp. vii–viii). I use these dates.

20. *A Touch of the Poet* (New Haven, Conn.: Yale University Press, 1957), Act IV.

21. Gallup, prefatory note to *More Stately Mansions*, p. vii.

22. This heavy use of the Irish theme in O'Neill's final productive period is very interesting. A *Touch of the Poet* (1936) was his first play in fifteen years to find its cast of characters largely in an Irish family; the predecessor was *The Straw* (1921).

23. The exception is *The Iceman Cometh* (1939). Earlier exceptions to his centering the drama in the family (as if he were working from Aristotle) are *The Emperor Jones* and *Lazarus Laughed*. It would not be straining the evidence, however, to think of Harry Hope's entourage in *Iceman* as the family writ large.

24. See the discussion of A *Moon for the Misbegotten* a little later in the text. James's "hates life" appears in *Mourning Becomes Electra*; it is an old O'Neill stand-by.

25. The critical problems presented by the play are unrelated, naturally, to the autobiographical significance. Yet O'Neill's well-known use of family materials makes an unfavorable judgment seem a little like the desecration of a grave.

26. The production by the Greek National Theater in Athens in 1965 managed some of this to comic effect. The National Theatre production in London in 1972 maintained a remarkable level of melodramatic intensity.

27. The word is used in the descriptive stage direction at James's first appearance (A *Moon for the Misbegotten* [New York: Random House, 1952], Act I).

28. The confession and its beneficent effect are slightly reminiscent of Stephen Dedalus' confession in James Joyce's *Portrait of the Artist as a Young Man*.

29. Excluding, of course, the final decade, since O'Neill destroyed the work of those years.

30. See Gallup, prefatory note to *More Stately Mansions*, pp. vii ff.

31. His father-in-law, Con Melody, in A *Touch of the Poet*, attached his fantasies to Wellington.

32. Raleigh and Gassner both emphasize it.

33. "Eugene O'Neill" (1958), trans. Barbara Melchiori Arnett, *Sewanee Review* 68 (1960):494–95.

Chapter Five

1. *A Streetcar Named Desire* (New York: New Directions, 1947).

2. *Summer and Smoke* (New York: New Directions, 1948).

3. Compare the interpretation in Ian Watt, *The Rise of the Novel* (London: Chatto and Windus, 1957), pp. 228–38.

4. *Camino Real* (New York: New Directions, 1953).

5. *Cat on a Hot Tin Roof* (New York: New Directions, 1955).

6. Printed editions usually contain both versions of Act III, and, after the first one, Williams' two-page "Note of Explanation" of the circumstances of his writing the second version.

7. *Sweet Bird of Youth* (New York: New Directions, 1959).

8. For a detailed analysis of the mythic content of the play, as well as of its earlier form, *Battle of Angels*, see Hugh Dickinson, *Myth on the Modern Stage* (Urbana and London: University of Illinois Press, 1969), pp. 278–309. Dickinson attributes a "tragic choice with tragic consequences" to Val Xavier (p. 308). As his chapter subtitle, "Orpheus as Savior," suggests, Dickinson also points out Williams' desire to inject Christian values into the myth, and he cites various other critics who note the appearance of Christ figures and of the idea of Christian redemption in later Williams plays. Yet this development does not entirely cut Williams off from the D. H. Lawrence myth of nature, as several plays in his 1970 volume, *Dragon Country*, indicate.

9. Quotations from *Suddenly Last Summer* are from *Garden District* (London: Secker and Warburg, 1959).

10. Quotations are from *Period of Adjustment: High Point Over a Cavern: A Serious Comedy* (New York: New Directions, 1960).

11. In Author's Notes (London: Secker and Warburg, 1964), p. 5. The phrase "sophisticated fairy-tale" is used in a stage direction in scene iii. Williams has reworked this play several times. The quotations are from the 1964 edition.

12. Cf. chapter 11, "Dramas of Money."

13. *Dragon Country* (New York: New Directions, 1970) contains four very short plays that I do not deal with here and four others that might be thought of as long one-act plays or short two-act plays. Three of them have been produced: "The Mutilated" and "The Gnädiges Fräulein" in 1966, and "In the Bar of a Tokyo Hotel" in 1969. "Confessional" was copyrighted in 1970.

14. One short play is entitled "The Frosted Glass Coffin."

15. Such a pair obviously has a strong hold on Williams' imagination. It appears in two other plays in this collection, "Confessional" and "A Perfect Analysis Given by a Parrot" (1958).

16. Cf. a different expressionistic treatment of the same theme (the artist and society) in Pinter's *The Birthday Party* (produced 1958).

Chapter Six

1. Introduction to *A View from the Bridge* (New York: Bantam Books, 1961), p. vi. Subsequent quotations of Miller's critical opinions are from this introduction, and citations of the text are from this edition.

2. *The Crucible* (New York: Bantam Books, 1959), pp. 1–6, 12–13, 30–33, 37–38. All are in Act I. Citations of the text are from this edition.

3. Ibid., introduction by Richard Watts, Jr., pp. xiii, xiv.

4. Ibid., p. xiv.

5. *After the Fall* (New York: Bantam Books, 1965), p. 1. The quoted words are the first sentence of the first stage direction. All references are to this edition.

6. Edward H. Rosenberry, "The Problem of *Billy Budd*," *PMLA* 80 (1965):490.

7. Robert Penn Warren, *World Enough and Time* (New York: Random House, 1950), p. 506.

8. Quotations are from *The Price* (New York: Bantam Books, 1969).

Chapter Seven

1. "Bertolt Brecht and His Work," reprinted with Eric Bentley's translation of *The Private Life of the Master Race* (New York: New Directions, 1944), p. 131.

2. From the translation by James and Tania Stern, with W. H. Auden, in Bertolt Brecht, *Plays* (London: Methuen, 1960), 1:3ff.

3. Brecht did much reworking of texts, so that dating is approximate. Ordinarily I use the translator's date for the text he is using or the date of the first production, unless either of these is considerably removed from the period of actual composition.

4. From Act II of Frank Jones's translation in *Jungle of Cities and Other Plays* (New York: Grove Press, 1966).

5. See the translator's note, ibid., pp. 93–95.

6. In translator's note to *Jungle of Cities*, ibid., p. 10. Scene numbers are taken from Hollo's translation in this volume.

7. See Lee Baxandall's introduction and Brecht's notes in the Baxandall translation (New York: Grove Press, 1965), pp. 9–32, 133–58.

8. Cf. Robert B. Heilman, *Tragedy and Melodrama: Versions of Experience* (Seattle and London: University of Washington Press, 1968), pp. 238–39.

9. Quotations are from the translation by N. Goold-Verschoyle in *Jungle of Cities and Other Plays*.

10. These aspects of the play are discussed more fully in my *Tragedy and Melodrama*, pp. 278–79.

11. Quoted, from the author's note in the first edition (1932), by Eric Bentley, ed., *From the Modern Repertoire*, Series 3 (Bloomington: Indiana University Press, 1956), p. 513. If it was Marlowe who stirred Brecht's imagination on the Faust theme, then this is the second time that Marlowe was a starting-point for Brecht; in 1922 he had done a version of Marlowe's *Edward II*.

12. By Frank Jones, the translator, in the Bentley edition, p. 523. Citations are from the Jones translation.

13. I have used Eric Bentley's adaptation in the acting edition (New York: S. French, 1955ff.). Quoted passages are literal translations from the German.

14. From the "Notes on 'The Life of Galileo,'" as printed in Bertolt Brecht, *Plays* (London: Methuen, 1960), 1:335ff. Quotations are from Desmond I. Vesey's translation of the play in this volume.

15. The fitting title under which Eric and Maja Bentley published their translations of *The Good Woman of Setzuan* and *The Caucasian Chalk Circle* (Minneapolis and London: University of Minnesota Press, 1948). Quotations are from this edition.

16. Duerrenmatt said this in a lecture, "Problems of the Theatre," which he delivered a number of times in 1954 and 1955. Translated by Gerhard Nellhaus, it is included in the volume *Four Plays 1957–1962* (London: Jonathan Cape, 1964), pp. 9–41. The quoted passage is on p. 13.

Chapter Eight

1. According to Michael Bullock, Frisch did a first draft of *Count Oederland* in 1946; this was produced in 1951. There was a second stage version in 1956, and then a definitive version in 1961. See translator's note, p. 91, in Max Frisch, *Three Plays* (London: Methuen, 1962). Quotations are from Bullock's translation in this edition.

2. "Max Frisch," a prefatory note to *The Chinese Wall: A Farce*, trans. James L. Rosenberg (New York: Hill and Wang, 1961), p. 5. Quotations are from this translation.

3. Quotations are from the text in Max Frisch, *Three Plays*, trans. James L. Rosenberg (New York: Hill and Wang, 1967), pp. 105ff.

4. The German title is *Biedermann und die Brandstifter*. In the English translation by Michael Bullock the title is *The Fire Raisers*; in the American translation by Mordecai Gorelik, the title is *The Firebugs*. I use the latter for convenience, since it is probably a more widely known term for arsonist.

5. In my *Tragedy and Melodrama*, p. 47.

6. Quotations are from the text in Bullock's *Three Plays*.

7. Quotations are from the text in Bullock's *Three Plays*.

8. Quotations are from the text in Rosenberg's *Three Plays*.

9. Cf. R. B. Heilman, "The Tragedy of Knowledge: Marlowe's Treatment of Faustus," *Quarterly Review of Literature* 2 (1946):316–32.

10. Quotations are from *Biography: A Game*, trans. Michael Bullock (New York: Hill and Wang, 1967).

Chapter Nine

1. These dates are from Bruno Berger's one-volume edition of Wilhelm Kosch's *Deutsches Literatur-Lexikon* (Bern: Francke Verlag, 1963). Dates provided in the volume of translations are sometimes based on later editions.

2. For all the plays except *The Visit* the references are to a single volume, Friedrich Duerrenmatt, *Four Plays 1957–62* (London: Jonathan Cape, 1964). The translators are as follows: *Romulus the Great*, Gerhard Nellhaus; *The Marriage of Mr. Mississippi*, Michael Bullock; *An Angel Comes to Babylon*, William McElwee; *The Physicists*, James Kirkup.

3. "Problems of the Theatre," *Four Plays*, p. 21.

4. Ibid., p. 34.

5. Ibid., p. 19.

6. Ibid., p. 32.

7. It is interesting that Quixote, as an exponent of durable values, is also used in Tennessee Williams' *Camino Real*. Williams makes him speak against self-pity.

8. "Problems of the Theatre," p. 34.

9. Ibid., pp. 33, 34, 36.

10. These generic aspects of the play are discussed at greater length in my *Tragedy and Melodrama*, pp. 44–47, 60–61, and in the present volume, chapter 11.

11. The quotations are from the translation by Patrick Bowles (London: Jonathan Cape, 1962).

12. Quotations are from the manuscript translation by Arthur O. Ketels, who has generously permitted me to use his work.

13. He uses the phrase in "The Principles of the Adaptation," an afterword. Quotations are from the manuscript translation by Arthur O. Ketels and Ann Laeuchli, to whose kindness I am indebted.

Chapter Ten

1. Quotations are from the translation by Stephen Spender and Goronwy Rees as it appears in Eric Bentley, ed., *From the Modern Repertoire: Series One* (Denver, Colo.: University of Denver Press, 1949), pp. 29–86.

2. Lee Baxandall, in his introduction to Büchner's *Woyzeck and Leonce and Lena*, trans. Carl Richard Mueller (San Francisco: Chandler, 1962), pp. xiii, xiv. Cf. Bentley, *From the Modern Repertoire: Series One*, p. 382.

3. Eric Bentley notes the tragic elements, though he uses a different concept of tragedy (*From the Modern Repertoire: Series One*, p. 382).

4. Clifford Leech says that in both plays Büchner "made it evident that tragedy was coming to a new birth." This is in *Tragedy* (London: Methuen, 1969), p. 21.

5. The phrase is Büchner's. See his letters reprinted in Robert W. Corrigan, ed., *The Modern Theatre* (New York: Macmillan, 1964), pp. 5–6. For a discussion of the determinism of the play, see Lee Baxandall's introduction to Carl Mueller's translation of *Woyzeck and Leonce and Lena*, pp. xv–xvi, and the translator's note, pp. xxi–xxii.

6. The Mueller translation is used in the Chandler edition and in Corrigan's *Modern Theatre*, both cited in previous notes. The scene numbers are identical from i to xv but then vary slightly in the two editions. For references after scene xv, I use the scene numbers in Corrigan, since this version includes some materials excluded from the other. Büchner never decided on a final text, and editors and translators have made different arrangements. For the Chandler edition of 1962 Mueller had a twenty-four-scene arrangement and made a strong defense of it, but by 1964 he presented a twenty-nine-scene arrangement that runs counter to some of his earlier arguments. Fortunately the additions amount to only a small number of lines, they come in the latter part of the play, and their principal effect would be a difference in immediate theatrical impact.

7. Baxandall, introduction to *Woyzeck*, p. xv.

8. Mueller includes these two scenes in the 1964 edition, having excluded them in 1962. The omission of the scenes brings Woyzeck closer to the role of pure victim of history.

9. Bentley notes the Shakespearean characteristics of Büchner (*From the Modern Repertoire: Series One*, p. 383).

10. Quotations are from the translation by Carl Richard Mueller in

Corrigan's *Modern Theatre*, pp. 165ff. Since there are no act or scene divisions, I use page numbers for the quoted lines.

11. One exception is William Alfred's *Agamemnon* (New York: Alfred A. Knopf, 1954). Alfred calls the play "a tragedy," which he defines as made up of "wrath" and "justice" (p. viii). They are equivalents of what I have called "impulse" and "imperative." However, the major actions are not traced to a dramatic dividedness within the major characters, least of all in the title character. Cassandra is half the mistress to whom Agamemnon is devoted, half the unstable person finally unbalanced by doubts of him. Aegisthus has an attachment to queen and palace, but also to an idyll with a girl in the country (cf. Giraudoux's earlier version of this). Cassandra's and Aegisthus' roles, however, are secondary. Clytemnestra comes closest to being the moral center of the play, and she faces a final tragic issue of truth and illusion. But even she is more acted upon than acting; only at the moment of Agamemnon's return home does she learn how Iphigenia died, which had been incredibly concealed from her for ten years. So her murder of husband and rival is rather an off-the-cuff affair, after which Clytemnestra is in a state of collapse and much is left unresolved. There are other technical problems that prevent *Agamemnon* from being an achieved tragedy. There is a heavy burden of plotting, and the language shifts from colloquial cliché to complex metaphor. Nevertheless the poetic language has a good deal of life; it constitutes a dramatic poem on a theme with tragic elements.

12. Michel de Ghelderode, *Seven Plays*, trans. George Hauger (New York: Hill and Wang, 1964), 2:99–150. All quotations are from this edition.

13. Quotations are from the translation by Edward Storer as it appears in *Masters of Modern Drama*, ed. Haskell M. Block and Robert G. Shedd (New York: Random House, 1962), pp. 510–31. I have compared key passages with the translation by Eric Bentley, which makes a number of adaptations for benefit of pace and audience.

14. A view accepted by Frederick Lumley, *New Trends in 20th Century Drama* (3rd ed.; New York: Oxford University Press, 1967), pp. 32–34. But the following quotations show that Lumley uses terms rather vaguely: ". . . the outstanding tragedy in the modern theatre—indeed, critics have called *Enrico IV* 'a twentieth-century *Hamlet*' " (p. 32). "*Enrico IV* is not, however, a tragedy in the classical sense, for as Giraudoux notes, tragedy and comedy are interwoven in the modern drama. The tragic vision, however, is that of a soul who relinquished the real world twenty years previously when he became mad" (p. 32). "In the character of Enrico IV . . . we have a genuinely tragic creation, for whom 'the time is out of joint,' as it was for Hamlet, and whose tragedy also becomes 'a tragedy of reflection' " (p. 32). "But here lies the tragedy: how could he take up his former life again?" (p. 33). Tragedy seems to mean little more than "unhappiness" or "difficulty." Block and Shedd are more precise as they seek a reason for Pirandello's use of the word: ". . . Henry IV enjoys the freedom of his masquerade. It is his by choice, not by necessity" (p. 509). This implies a sound sense of one ingredient in tragedy.

15. Quotations are from the version in Thomas H. Dickinson, ed., *Chief*

Contemporary Dramatists, Third Series (Boston: Houghton Mifflin, 1930), pp. 161–94.

16. Lorca felt successful if he could make an audience uncertain whether to laugh or cry. See Francisco García Lorca's introduction to *Three Trage-dies*, trans. James Graham-Luján and Richard L. O'Connell (New York: New Directions, 1947), p. 16. All quotations are from this volume.

17. Ibid., pp. 15, 18, 22.

18. Quotations are from the translation by Winifred Smith as it appears in Block and Shedd, *Masters of Modern Drama*, pp. 701–29.

19. The closing speech of the play as it appears in *Three Plays by Ugo Betti*, trans. Henry Reed (New York: Grove Press, 1958), pp. 11–99. Quotations are from this edition.

20. Camus preferred this version, expanded from the original 1938 form, and also altered as late as 1958. See Block and Shedd, *Masters of Modern Drama*, p. 817.

21. The phrase is from Block and Shedd (*Masters of Modern Drama*, p. 817), who also take pains to deny that the play is a "cold and abstract intellectual dialogue." For a treatment of Camus's drama in terms of ideas, see Jacques Guicharnaud, in collaboration with June Beckelman, *Modern French Theatre from Giraudoux to Beckett*, Yale Romanic Studies, Second Series 7 (New Haven, Conn.: Yale University Press, 1961), pp. 131–52. In the author's preface, trans. Justin O'Brien, to *Caligula and Three Other Plays*, trans. Stuart Gilbert (New York: Random House, 1958), Camus expresses surprise, perhaps with tongue in cheek, that *Caligula* should be called a "philosophical play" (p. v).

22. Quotations are from the translation by Stuart Gilbert in *Caligula and Three Other Plays*.

23. In the author's preface to *Caligula and Three Other Plays*, pp. v–vii.

24. See chapter 1 of this volume.

25. The widespread story of filicide is, in modern times, of Jacobean provenience. It appears in an English crime pamphlet of 1618 and in several seventeenth-century histories; one of these was the source of George Lillo's *Fatal Curiosity* (produced, 1736). Lillo's play influenced German "fate drama"; the plot appears in plays by Karl Philipp Moritz (1781), Zacharias Werner (1810), A. G. A. Müllner (1812), and in Franz Grillparzer's *An-cestress* (1817). See the introduction to William H. McBurney's edition of *Fatal Curiosity*, Regents Restoration Drama Series (Lincoln: University of Nebraska Press, 1966), pp. xii, xviii, and notes, and Appendix B, pp. 55–58. McBurney refers to an article of 1882 which lists various continental and oriental analogues (p. xii, n. 15). An American version of the story appears in Robert Penn Warren's "The Ballad of Billie Potts" (1944). Warren records that as a child he "heard this story from an old lady who was a relative of mine"; the scene of the action was "in the land between the rivers" in Kentucky. See *Selected Poems: New and Old 1923–1966* (New York: Random House, 1966), p. 223. For a look at Camus's play in the light of analogues, see Reino Virtanen, "Camus' *Le Malentendu* and Some Analogues," *Comparative Literature* 10 (1958):232–40. Camus ap-pears to have used a contemporary story: "When Camus chooses a news item (*le Malentendu*), he chooses an exceptional one . . ." (Guicharnaud,

Modern French Theatre, p. 144). Art anticipates life, as it were. For further notes on the provenience of Camus's drama and for some comparisons between Camus's work and Warren's, see Curtis Whittington, Jr., "The Earned Vision: Robert Penn Warren's 'The Ballad of Billie Potts' and Albert Camus' *Le Malentendu*," *Four Quarters* 21 (1972):79–90.

26. Albert Camus, *Lyrical and Critical Essays*, ed. Philip Thody, trans. Ellen Conroy Kennedy (New York: Alfred A. Knopf, 1968), p. 308.

27. Henry de Montherlant, *The Master of Santiago and Four Other Plays*, trans. Jonathan Griffin (New York: Alfred A. Knopf, 1951). All quotations are from this text.

28. Camus, *Lyrical and Critical Essays*, p. 308.

29. Quotations are from the translation by Stuart Gilbert as it appears in Jean-Paul Sartre, *No Exit and Three Other Plays* (New York: Random House, 1955), pp. 3–47. *No Exit* is a long one-acter without scene divisions.

30. Quotations are from the translation by Ingrid G. Gilbert and William F. Gilbert as it appears in Block and Shedd, *Masters of Modern Drama*, pp. 911–58. Cf. the plot of Brecht's *Roundheads and Peakheads*.

31. Quotations are from Ray Lawler, *Summer of the Seventeenth Doll* (New York: Random House, 1957).

32. The English edition has "eagles" instead of "birds of paradise."

33. Quotations are from the text in John Arden, *Three Plays* (Baltimore: Penguin Books, 1964).

34. Ann Messenger, indeed, speaks of Arden's "tragic vision." This is in a paper read at the 1970 meeting of the Philological Association of the Pacific Coast.

35. Quotations are from Edward Albee, *Who's Afraid of Virginia Woolf?* (New York: Atheneum, 1962).

36. Quotations are from Edward Albee, *Tiny Alice* (New York: Pocket Books, 1966).

37. William Willeford makes a much fuller interpretation of the play in "The Mouse in the Model: Edward Albee's Tiny Alice," *Modern Drama* 12 (1969):135–45.

38. The realistic manner entirely controls *All Over* (1972), an effective melodrama of family infighting around a deathbed. Albee takes up a frequent theme of O'Neill, Williams, and Miller.

Chapter Eleven

1. Quotations are from the translation by Freeman Tilden in *Treasury of the Theatre* (*Ibsen to Ionesco*), ed. John Gassner (3rd College Edition; New York: Simon and Schuster, 1960), pp. 98–131.

2. In another kind of melodrama, death, instead of attracting carrion birds, puts men to flight. This latter is most subtly treated in Ivan Bunin's "The Gentleman from San Francisco" (1916).

3. In the 1969 production by the Seattle Repertory Theatre the actors playing Regina and Ben tried very hard to complicate the characters by suggesting sympathetic elements in them; the method was to reduce hardness in Regina wherever possible, and to invest Ben's competitiveness with a certain urbane irony.

4. Quotation is from the text as it appears in *The Modern Theatre*, ed. Robert W. Corrigan (New York: Macmillan, 1964), pp. 1113ff.

5. Here I introduce Miller's play only briefly for purposes of comparison. There is a detailed discussion of *Death of a Salesman* in my *Tragedy and Melodrama*, pp. 233–37.

6. Quotations are from the text printed in *Masters of Modern Drama*, ed. Haskell M. Block and Robert G. Shedd (New York: Random House, 1962), pp. 647–68.

7. On Bessie as the real source of trouble in the play see Morris Freedman, *The Moral Impulse: Modern Drama from Ibsen to the Present* (Carbondale and Edwardsville: Southern Illinois University Press, 1967), pp. 105–6.

8. Quotations are from the text in Gassner's *Treasury of the Theatre*, pp. 952–82.

9. Cf. ibid., p. 951.

10. Cf. ibid., p. 174. Gassner points out that Tolstoi did not particularly approve of Ibsen. Quotations are from the translation by George R. Noyes and George Z. Patrick as it appears in Gassner, *Treasury of the Theatre*, pp. 175–204.

11. In *The Playwright as Thinker* (New York: Reynal and Hitchcock, 1946), Eric Bentley mentions *The Power of Darkness*, Becque's *Les Corbeaux*, and *The Lower Depths* together as the "Naturalistic masterpieces of the New Theater movement" (p. 218).

12. The quotations are from the translation by Beatrice Gottlieb in Block and Shedd's *Masters of Modern Drama*, pp. 272–98. In this edition, many lines are different from those in Miss Gottlieb's translation as it appeared earlier in *From the Modern Repertoire: Series Two*, ed. Eric Bentley (Denver, Colo.: University of Denver Press, 1952), pp. 125–76. The text used in this 1951 translation is also used in the translation by Carl R. Mueller in Corrigan's *The Modern Theatre*, pp. 126–59.

13. On these see Ronald Peacock, *The Poet in the Theatre* (New York: Harcourt, Brace, 1946), pp. 135, 137, 142ff.

14. The movement from business to sex and robbery to disaster is another of the strangely recurring echoes of the moralistic George Barnwell plot.

15. Quotations are from the translation by Ashley Dukes in Block and Shedd's *Masters of Modern Drama*, pp. 489–507.

Epilogue

1. Réné Wellek, "Closing Statement," in *Style in Language*, ed. Thomas A. Sebeok (Cambridge, Mass., and New York: Technology Press of Massachusetts Institute of Technology and John Wiley and Sons, 1960), p. 415.

2. Patricia Marx, "An Interview with Rolf Hochhuth," *Partisan Review* 31 (1964):367.

Index

Aeneas, 273n

Aeschylus: *Eumenides*, 30, 36, 93, 102-3; Aegisthus, 50; Agamemnon, 30, 50, 99, 250, 260; Clytemnestra, 260; Electra, 250; Erinyes, 103; Eumenides, 203, Iphigenia, 30; Orestes, 30, 33, 36; Prometheus, 30

Agit-prop drama: as morality play, 177

Albee, Edward, 288; characters, 21; family conflict as theme, 295; religion as theme, 295

—Works
All Over, 347
Tiny Alice, 40, 134, 289, 291-94, 325
Who's Afraid of Virginia Woolf?, 38, 289-91, 292, 325
Zoo Story, 12, 195

Alexander, Edward, 46

Alfred, William: *Agamemnon*, 345

American theater, 70

Anderson, Maxwell: *Winterset*, 146

Anouilh, Jean, 242

Arden, John, 285, 286, 329; *Live Like Pigs*, 287-88; *The Waters of Babylon*, 287

Aristotle, 42, 157

Arnold, Matthew, 15

Arrabal, Fernando, 242

Arrowsmith, William: on Euripides' Pentheus, 336

Artaud, Antonin, 242

Atreus, 50

Auden, W. H., 25, 28, 33n, 34, 242

Baldwin, James, 17

Balzac, Honoré de, 251n

Barrie, J. M.: *Dear Brutus*, 206n; *What Every Woman Knows*, 300n

Baudelaire, Charles, 26, 31, 32

Baxandall, Lee, 176-77; on Büchner, 243, 344; on *Woyzeck*, 248, 344

Beckett, Samuel, 18, 50, 242, 252

Becque, Henry, 320, 321; *La Parisienne*, 98n, 300n; *The Vultures*, 47, 298-300, 302, 304, 306, 312

Behrman, S. N.: *Biography*, 206n; *The Second Man*, 91n

Bellow, Saul: *Herzog*, 18

Bentley, Eric, 57, 255n, 344; on Brecht, 171-72; *The Playwright as Thinker*, 338, 348

Betti, Ugo: *The Queen and the Rebels*, 266-67, 268, 325; the political theme, 295

Biblical myths: as subject, 273n

Black comedy, 300

[349]

ROBERT BECHTOLD HEILMAN has been professor of English at the University of Washington since 1948 and was chairman of the department until 1971. He has held elective offices in various professional organizations and has lectured widely and contributed to numerous journals and critical volumes in both America and England. His work has been recognized by honorary degrees from Lafayette College and Grinnell College, and his *Magic in the Web: Action and Language in Othello* won the Explicator Prize as the best work of critical explication in 1956. He held a Guggenheim Fellowship in 1964-65 and was a Senior Fellow of the National Endowment for the Humanities in 1971-72. Both years were spent mostly in London, studying at the British Museum and going to the theater.